ABOUT THE ANNOTATED
INSTRUCTOR'S EDITION FOR

Public Speaking

Thank you for considering this book for your cou[rse.] This
Instructor's Edition is part of a complete teaching [...] to
help you successfully teach public speaking from a cultural perspective.
This AIE (as well as the student edition of the book) integrates public
speaking and culture from the outset in natural, meaningful, and practical ways—always with the goal of helping students become skilled,
confident speakers.

This Annotated Instructor's Edition includes notes, teaching suggestions, and references written by the author to make this book
an even more effective teaching tool. To find out more about
Public Speaking: A Cultural Perspective, and to answer some of
your questions about implementing it in your classes, please
take a few moments to read the preface. It elaborates on
the book's approach and the specific ways it promotes
skillful, culturally informed public speaking.

The following is further information on the ancillary
resources that enhance the teaching and learning of
public speaking from a cultural perspective. Should
you have further questions about this book and
its ancillaries, please contact your local ITP
Higher Education representative or Wadsworth
Publishing Company.

Teaching and Learning Resources to Accompany
Public Speaking: A Cultural Perspective

Annotated Instructor's Edition

Annotated by author Clella Jaffe, this special version of the text includes:

Teaching Ideas Culled from class-testing of this book, these suggestions for teaching approaches and class activities appear in the margins at topic-specific points.

Notes These notes in the margins provide Jaffe's insights on specific sections in the text and related resources in the ancillary materials.

Cross References These references point out connections to related material elsewhere in the text or ancillaries.

For Further Reading Further readings are referenced in the text margins next to the related topic, point, or example.

Speech Assignments Additional speech assignments are suggested at appropriate points throughout the text.

Culture Icons (also included in student edition)
These icons indicate points, examples, and comparisons that illustrate the diversity of ways in which culture influences public speaking, and speaking affects culture.

Instructor's Manual with Test Items

Written by Clella Jaffe, the Instructor's Manual contains:

- research summaries
- supplementary lessons and activities
- transparency masters
- test items for each chapter in the text
- definitions of key terms

Transparency Acetates

Transparency acetates feature selected figures from the text as well as charts and presentation materials suitable for lectures.

Videocassette

Developed for *Public Speaking: A Cultural Perspective*, this videotape features original speeches delivered by a diversity of speakers. Whether viewed in class in or a lab, this videotape gives your students additional opportunities to view and analyze speech performances.

Student Resource Workbook

The Student Resource Workbook provides your students with additional speech outlines, assignment guides, and opportunities for self-analysis and study reinforcement. The Workbook is available for student purchase.

Custom Publishing with Adaptable Courseware

You can custom publish any combination of chapters and modules from *Public Speaking: A Cultural Perspective* through our Adaptable Courseware program. You can also personalize your textbook with your own lecture notes, syllabi, handouts, and activities. For more information about Adaptable Courseware, please call 1-800-223-0300. (Please use this number for Adaptable Courseware questions only. For other questions, please fax your query to Wadsworth at 1-800-522-4923 or contact your local ITP Higher Education representative.)

W Wadsworth Publishing Company
An International Thomson Publishing Company
10 Davis Drive, Belmont, CA 94002-3098

Public Speaking

Library
Western Wyoming Community College

Public Speaking

A Cultural Perspective

Clella Iles Jaffe

St. John's University

DISCARDED

Wadsworth Publishing Company

I(T)P™ An International Thomson Publishing Company

Belmont • Albany • Bonn • Boston • Cincinnati • Detroit • London • Madrid
Melbourne • Mexico City • New York • Paris • San Francisco • Singapore
Tokyo • Toronto • Washington

Communications Editor: *Todd R. Armstrong*
Editorial Assistants: *Joshua King and Laura Murray*
Production Editors: *Angela Mann and Cathy Linberg*
Designer: *Carolyn Deacy*
Print Buyer: *Barbara Britton*
Art Editor: *Nancy Spellman*
Permissions Editor: *Robert Kauser*
Copy Editor: *Robert Fiske*
Illustrator: *Seventeenth Street Studios*
Cover: *Superstock/Diane Ong*
Signing Representatives: *Tamy Stenquist and Gerry Levine*
Compositor: *Jonathan Peck Typographers*
Printer: *R. R. Donnelley & Sons*

*This book is printed on
acid-free recycled paper.*

COPYRIGHT © 1995 by Wadsworth Publishing Company
A Division of International Thomson Publishing Inc.
I(T)P The ITP logo is a trademark under license.

Printed in the United States of America

For more information, contact: Wadsworth Publishing Company

Wadsworth Publishing Company
10 Davis Drive
Belmont, California 94002
USA

International Thomson Publishing Europe
Berkshire House 168-173
High Holborn
London, WC1V 7AA
England

Thomas Nelson Australia
102 Dodds Street
South Melbourne 3205
Victoria, Australia

Nelson Canada
1120 Birchmount Road
Scarborough, Ontario
Canada M1K 5G4

International Thomson Editores
Campos Eliseos 385, Piso 7
Col. Polanco
11560 México D. F. México

International Thomson Publishing GmbH
Königswinterer Strasse 418
53227 Bonn
Germany

International Thomson Publishing Asia
221 Henderson Road
#05-10 Henderson Building
Singapore 0315

International Thomson Publishing Japan
Hirakawacho Kyowa Building, 3F
2-2-1 Hirakawacho
Chiyoda-ku, 1Tokyo 02
Japan

All rights reserved. No part of this work covered by the copyright hereon may be reproduced or used in any form or by any means—graphic, electronic, or mechanical, including photocopying, recording, taping, or information storage and retrieval systems—without the written permission of the publisher.

1 2 3 4 5 6 7 8 9 10—01 00 99 98 97 96 95

Library of Congress Cataloging-in-Publication Data

Jaffe, Clella Iles, 1944–
        Public speaking: a cultural perspective/Clella Iles Jaffe.
                p.   cm.
        Includes bibliographical references and index.
        ISBN: 0-534-23064-4
        1. Public speaking. 2. Multiculturalism. I. Title.
PN41212.J25   1995   94-29028
808.5'1—dc20

Brief Contents

Contents

1

Introduction to Public Speaking

2

Overview of the Speechmaking Process

3

Public Speaking and Culture

4

Communicative Competence

5

Speakers and Pluralistic Audiences

6

Listening

7

Researching the Speech

8

Supporting Materials

9

Organizing the Speech

10

Audiovisual Resources

((

Language

12

Delivery

13

Narrative

14

Informative Speaking

15

Reasoning

16

Persuasive Speaking

17

Public Speaking in Organizations

Preface

The civilization of the dialogue is the only civilization worth having and the only civilization in which the whole world can unite. It is, therefore, the only civilization we can hope for, because the world must unite or be blown to bits.

Robert Hutchins, 1967

I decided to write this book while at a communication conference a few years ago. The instructor beside me at a publisher's booth picked up an introductory public speaking book, skimmed the index, and scowled. "Nothing on culture," she muttered as she set the book back down. Curious, I checked through a few intro books myself. She was right: In book after book, culture had either a token presence or no presence.

Whatever the reasons for that shortcoming, I felt a personal challenge to rectify it. My academic background is in communication, education, and anthropology, and my doctoral work was on aspects of intercultural communication. My personal background includes having lived in a predominately African-American speech community, having lifelong family-like relationships with Navajos, and having moved from New Mexico to Oregon to New York City. Being a public speaking instructor has enabled me to tie all these threads together in the classroom; the experience at the book booth convinced me to tie them together in print.

Culture and Public Speaking

I wrote this book because I believe that public speaking and culture are not two separate subjects; they are intertwined. Culture shapes public speaking, which in turn shapes culture. Public speaking is a way we express, reinforce, transmit, change, and blend cultures. In fact, the very things public speaking has always aimed to influence—beliefs, values, attitudes, and actions—are precisely the things that make up cultures. In the classroom, cultural backgrounds influence students' perceptions of the role of public speaking, their perceptions of themselves as speakers, their perceptions of their audience, and their perceptions of other speakers. Culture also influences their topic selection, research methods and resources, and reasoning styles.

More than ever before, today's students need to understand other cultures, because the world now features unprecedented interaction between cultures.

Public speaking is often the interface between cultures. People from one cultural background increasingly find themselves speaking to audiences from other cultural backgrounds. As media and transportation technologies become ever more sophisticated, the pace of cross-cultural interaction will only quicken. Our students need to tune in to the different ways in which people from different cultures speak and listen. In addition, students need an increasing awareness of global issues, which they can develop as they select international topics and consult resources of ethnic and international origin during their research.

In short, I believe that a book that teaches public speaking without strongly emphasizing its cultural component gives today's students an incomplete education.

Culture and This Text

This is therefore not a traditional public speaking book with a dollop of cultural awareness added on the side. Nor is it two books—one about public speaking, one about culture—bound uneasily together. Rather, it is a culturally informed book that never loses sight of its fundamental purpose: to train students to be effective public speakers. In fact, it aims to make them even more effective by sensitizing them to the crucial cultural aspects of public speaking. It applies 2,500-year-old principles to the requirements of a rapidly changing pluralistic society. Its discussions of classic public speaking topics are all grounded in an awareness of the impact of cultural nuances—ranging from male/female differences to subcultures within the United States to the traditions of other nations. This provides students with a key element in being an effective public speaker: a heightened awareness of and sensitivity to the audience.

The cultural component does not detract from building basic public speaking skills; it actually broadens the repertoire of skills taught. This book was conceived and written from the ground up with cultural awareness integral to the teaching, not tacked on as an afterthought. That sensibility suffuses the text. Examples are drawn from a wide variety of cultures from within the United States and from around the world. I recognize, however, that most readers of this book will do most of their speaking within patterns that are common in the United States, such as lectures, introductions, demonstration speeches, and sales speeches. So this book coves such forms carefully. It also gives guidelines to help students from various cultures and subcultures succeed within the cultural tradition they are likely to encounter in U.S. classrooms.

Distinctive Features

Besides cultural awareness, there are several other distinctive ways this book goes about teaching public speaking:

- *Communication as dialogue* This book is based on Helmut Geissner's theory of communication as dialogue.

- *Narrative* It devotes a separate chapter to narrative and includes narrative as a form of reasoning.

- *Communication anxiety* Because communication anxiety is such a problem with so many students, this book gives it considerable coverage. Specific examples help reduce the anxiety by making the principles of public speaking clear and giving students a wide variety of styles and topics as models for their own speeches. Humor sprinkled throughout the text helps lighten the tone and make the subject less daunting.

- *Women's organizational patterns* It includes Cheryl Jorgensen-Earp's groundbreaking research on women's organizational patterns (which had not yet even been published as this book went into production).

- *Beliefs, values, attitudes* While my texts deal with beliefs, values, and attitudes in the persuasion chapter, I have added a chapter that discusses core cultural belief-value-attitude and action systems that need to be reinforced and maintained—or produced and changed—as the culture evolves.

- *Special occasion speaking* While many texts discuss special occasion speaking, this book covers that topic in the chapter on speaking in organizations and does so from the perspective of organizations as cultures.

- *Reasoning* It emphasizes throughout that there are other forms of reasoning and proving ideas. Generally, material that contrasts with the dominant U.S. forms is included in boxes.

- *Selecting a topic* This book gives particular attention to selecting a speech topic, narrowing its focus, and doing the research. It offers many examples of topics and describes a step-by-step process for developing a topic.

- *Dialogical ethic* I want students to become ethical communicators, so I use the dialogical ethic throughout, emphasizing co-creation of meaning in several chapters.

- *Comparisons* This book compares and contrasts public speaking traditions within the United States and other parts of the world.

- *ESL* Where appropriate, it specifically addresses students whose first language is not English.

- *Translators* It covers how to speak through a translator.

- *Technology* It covers recent technological developments that affect the way we prepare for and deliver speeches, including electronic research resources and computer-generated visual aids.

Organization

The text is organized into three sections. The first section (Chapters 1–6) sets up basic principles of speaking and listening. The second (Chapters 7–12) develops the principles found in the five canons of rhetoric. The third section (Chapters 13–17) discusses the applied contexts in which we speak publicly.

I won't describe every chapter here, but let me highlight two. Since students usually need to start speaking early in the semester, Chapter 2 equips them to prepare and give their first speech. It provides an overview of the entire speech-making process and introduces ideas that will be fully developed later in the text. It guides them to select their speech topics and purposes early—something that often concerns students. Chapter 3 elaborates the basic theme of the text that public speaking affects and is affected by culture.

Each chapter begins with a preview of the chapter's goals, then pauses every few pages to review the preceding section's key concepts. Each chapter concludes with a summary of the entire chapter's line of thought, a review of key terms, and questions and exercises. Many chapters include case studies. A number of sample student speeches and outlines are located throughout the text and in the Student Resource Workbook.

A pluralistic attitude is a way of thinking. While students live and study and work within the U.S. culture, they can have a less ethnocentric, more global orientation. I intend this book to help them develop one as they develop basic public speaking skills.

Acknowledgments

Every book is in some ways a co-created product in which an author relies on the insights and encouragement of others. Victoria O'Donnell of Montana State University, Sean Patrick O'Rourke of Vanderbilt University, and Anne Zach Ferguson of Linn-Benton Community College initially encouraged me to undertake this project. In addition, several reviewers across the country provided insightful comments at various stages of the manuscript—some of which I incorporated into the text. These included Martha Ann Atkins, Iowa State University; Dennis Beaver, Bakersfield College; Carol Berteotti, University of Wisconsin, LaCrosse; Carole Blair, University of California, Davis; Bruce G. Bryski, Buffalo State College; Jacquelyn Bukrop, Ball State University; Norma Flores, Golden West College; Charles Griffin, Kansas State University; Susan Hellweg, San Diego State University; Mark Hickson, University of Alabama, Birmingham; Janet Hoffman, Southern Illinois University at Carbondale; Susan Huxman, Wichita State University; Karla Jensen, The University of Kansas; Shelley D. Lane, Collin County Community College; Jo Ann Lawlor, West Valley College; Steven March, Pima County Community College; Patricia Palm McGillen, Mankato State University; Mark Morman, Johnson County Community College; Teresa Nance, Villanova University; Mary Pelias, Southern Illinois University; Mark Stoner, California State University, Sacramento; Patricia Sullivan, State University of New York at New Paltz; Marsha Vanderford, University of South Florida; Donald E. Williams, University of Florida; Lee Winet, State University of New York, Oswego.

Finally, my daughter, Sara Jaffe Reamy, provided a student's perspective on early drafts; my nephew, Mark Iles, contributed several pieces of art. In addition, the editors and designers at Wadsworth paid necessary attention to details at each stage of the project. My valued colleagues and students at Oregon State University and St. John's University (Queens) also contributed examples, outlines, and other important suggestions throughout the project.

You can help make the second edition of this book even more useful. Please send your comments on the book, suggestions for improvement, corrections, and other thoughts to

Dr. Clella Jaffe
c/o Communications Editor
Wadsworth Publishing Company
10 Davis Drive
Belmont, CA 94002

YOUR GUIDE TO

Public Speaking

A CULTURAL PERSPECTIVE

by Clella Iles Jaffe

Your opportunity to make the cultural connection in public speaking

What comes to mind when you think about public speaking? Political speeches? Wedding toasts? Business presentations? Your images and expectations of public speaking are linked to your cultural experiences, and the same holds true for your listeners. *Public Speaking: A Cultural Perspective* is written to help you make the connection between culture and public speaking, ultimately preparing you to speak confidently in many different contexts. By learning the concepts and process of public speaking with an awareness of its cultural connection, you'll be ready to engage in dynamic, meaningful dialogues with your audiences. The following pages show you how you can learn the most from this book, and seize the opportunity to make this connection in public speaking.

Learn and Adapt Skills in Diverse Contexts

Norms for Speaking and Listening

There is a range of appropriate behaviors—both verbal and nonverbal—for communicative acts. The most common norms for U.S. public speaking are the subject of this text. For example, throughout this course, you will study the typical practices in listening, organizing a speech, selecting appropriate language, and delivering a speech. We judge speakers as *competent* or *incompetent*, based on their abilities to adapt to the verbal and nonverbal norms for public speaking in specific settings.

 In addition, cultural assumptions influence what we speak about and how we frame our arguments. For instance, a motivational speaker who was addressing an audience dominated by the Euro-American perspective would most likely stress individual effort, freedom, hard work, and choice. However, in a more collectivist culture, such as in Japan, that places a great deal of emphasis on the group, the speaker would emphasize group relationships, stressing the value of individual sacrifice in order to achieve group harmony and reminding listeners of their duties and responsibilities to one another.[19]

Note the icon. These icons visually alert you to points of cultural comparison or illustration.

The aim of this book is to help you become a skilled, confident speaker in a diverse world. Aided by the wide variety of examples in this book, you'll learn about the skills and process of public speaking. For instance, this particular section explains "Norms for Speaking and Listening" using illustrations from several different cultures. Through these comparative examples from Euro-American and Japanese cultures, you'll gain a solid grasp of what norms are, why they are important, and how they can vary between cultures and co-cultures.

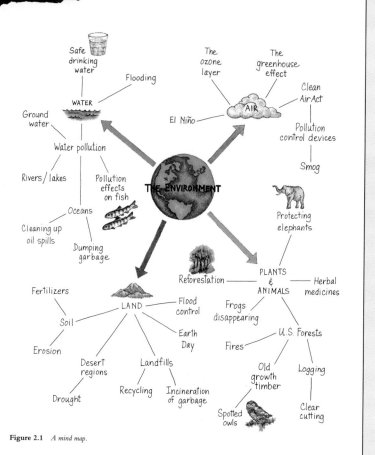

Figure 2.1 *A mind map.*

When you read about each individual concept or skill, think about it in relation to the total process of speaking, which you'll need to tailor to each situation. In Chapter 2 you'll find an overview of public speaking that will give you a clear sense of that process—from choosing a topic to delivering your speech. Studying this overview carefully will provide you with a framework for understanding the importance of each element to the final success of your speeches. You'll also find strategies in this chapter that will enable you to get started with public speaking right away. For instance, this "mind map" is one way you can go about selecting and refining a topic for a speech.

Figure 3.1 *Beliefs, values, attitudes, and actions.*

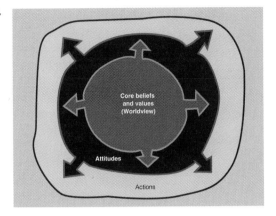

- *Perception of the world* Historically, those who are part of the dominant U.S. culture have believed that humans possess souls that set them apart from nature and make them unique from other animals. They have seen the physical world, in contrast, as a material reality that can be measured and quantified. Consequently, they see the universe as operating by rational rules with effects that are traceable to natural causes. The earth is a resource that can be conquered, owned, and used. In short, nature presents a series of problems to be solved through reasoning and application of technology.

- *Forms of activity* People in the United States tend to be action-oriented people who make things happen by defining and clarifying goals then moving to solve problems; they like to see measurable achievements. Competition serves as a motivating force. In their fast-paced lives, time is a resource to spend, save, or waste. Inactive people are sometimes called "free-loaders."

Co-Cultural Groups

Multicultural societies such as ours include many smaller groups that do not share the dominant culture's patterns in one or more areas. Some are *ethnic minorities* such as African Americans, Native Americans, Asian Americans, or Latinos, who come from different linguistic, historical, religious, and public

One of the key ideas behind this book, and behind effective speaking, is that a good speech really is a dialogue between the speaker and the audience. Therefore, you'll need to analyze the dynamics of each situation—from the audience's culturally based expectations and norms to your objectives as a speaker—in order to make your speeches a success. A careful reading of Chapter 3, Public Speaking and Culture, will give you a good handle on the ways in which culture influences public speaking, and vice versa. For instance, this section from Chapter 3 explains the interrelated beliefs, values, attitudes, and actions that each culture holds as its own, and that affect the nature of public speaking in that culture. Keep these points in mind as you build your speech skills and you'll find public speaking a much more rewarding experience—for you, and for your listeners.

Conquer Your Anxiety

Most students experience some form of Communication Apprehension (CA) when they deliver a classroom speech. The resulting effects may be internal (such as rapid heartbeat) and external (such as disrupted fluency).

If you're feeling a bit anxious about speaking in front of others, you're not alone. Even the best speakers can feel nervous. Chapter 4, Communicative Competence, will help you understand the reasons why you may feel nervous about public speaking, and how you can become a more confident speaker. This chapter also gives you some insights into culturally specific definitions of competence in public speaking. Knowing what your audience expects from a skilled speaker can help you prepare effectively and handle any nervousness you may feel.

dread or fear of having something negative happen to you as you communicate or because of your communication. These emotions cause some people to avoid or withdraw from communicating in contexts that they perceive to have potentially negative consequences.

Types of CA

Professor James McCroskey and his associates[14] have extensively studied communication apprehension. They have identified four major types of apprehension ranging from CA that is relatively enduring to a type that passes rather quickly. Some apprehension is linked to personality traits; other apprehension results from potentially threatening situations.

One type of communication appreh[...] "trait-like CA," which is triggered by all co[...] with innate traits of shyness and introversi[...] CA," where the speaker dreads commun[...] group based on previous negative experi[...] sion is "situational CA," where the speak[...] speech. Some people dread specific speak[...] exhibit "generalized-context CA." For m[...] public speaking. If you are in this categ[...] Public speaking has been called the number[...]

Examine the Case Studies

In selected chapters, you'll find case studies that reflect the real-life practice of public speaking and its relationship with culture. Each case is set up for you to walk through step-by-step and analyze for yourself. For instance, this case study asks you and your classmates to decide how a speaker should prepare a speech for three different audiences. Taking the time to think through cases like this one is a good way to deepen your practical understanding of speaking principles.

Persuasive Speaking **387**

CASE STUDY 16.1

Adapting a Topic to Different Audiences

Analyze the following public speaking situation: An anthropology major is going to present a speech on government funding for archaeological digs. Her claim is that the study of archaeology is important enough to receive government funding because knowing about other human cultures helps us better understand our own.

Divide into three groups within the classroom. Each group will discuss how the speaker should prepare for one of the following audiences:

1. A group of anthropology majors who agree with her and are highly positive toward her topic.

2. An audience that knows nothing about anthropology but is concerned about how their tax money is spent.

3. Listeners who feel that archaeology is a waste of time.

Questions

1. How will the speaker analyze the particular audience?

2. What purpose should she select for that group?

3. What specific strategies will she use to make her points?

4. What kind of reasoning and evidence should she use?

5. What should she emphasize and why?

KEY CONCEPT   Persuasive Purposes

Beliefs and actions What we believe affects how we act. Listeners are often unconvinced, unmotivated, or unfocused—and therefore inactive. Others are inconsistent when their actions do not match their beliefs. Still others consistently act on their beliefs. All these audiences require different speaking purposes and strategies.

Attitudes Listeners can have a positive, neutral, or negative attitude toward you and your topic. Generally, you attempt to strengthen positive attitudes and minimize negative ones.

Values When making value claims, establish criteria for the value judgment, link listeners with the topic emotionally, and appeal to authority when it is appropriate.

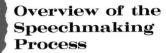

Overview of the Speechmaking Process

At the end of this chapter, you should be able to

- Identify two aspects of creativity
- Explain the five canons of rhetoric
- Choose and narrow a topic
- Identify both a general purpose and a specific purpose for a speech
- Write a central idea that states the main idea of the speech
- Identify some resources you may use in researching your speech topic
- Identify parts of the speech found in the canon of disposition
- Recognize the importance of language that is appropriate to the audience and the occasion
- Discuss the importance of rehearsal
- Deliver a short speech

The first page of every chapter highlights the objectives of that chapter and what you can expect to learn. Stop for a minute to absorb these objectives so you'll have a conceptual "frame of reference" as you read. It's easier to build a real body of knowledge about public speaking, rather than acquiring a mixed bag of ideas, if you create mental outlines for yourself and relate each new concept to the larger picture.

influences and is influenced by public speaking. For example, all people are free to speak, and we use persuasion as a means of another. The style of public speaking common in the United oriented, direct, explicit, personal, and informal. Moreover, des us with a range of appropriate behaviors both for speaking eeches. Similarly, public speaking affects culture. In addition to purposes of informing, persuading, and entertaining, we speak orce, repair, or change our listeners' beliefs, values, attitudes,

Not everyone in a pluralistic culture holds identical beliefs, values, and attitudes nor approves the same actions. Sometimes our cultural traditions are irreconcilable—we strongly accept ideas and behaviors that are strongly disbelieved or completely unacceptable to others around us. Similarly, attitudes and values can differ. As we encounter opposition, we respond in three common ways: defiance, accommodation, and surrender.

It is constantly a challenge in a pluralistic society to look to our values for guidance on ways to be civil to those with whom we disagree. Some cultural norms that promote ethical communication are courtesy, tolerance, and civility.

Student Speech

Jorge Oteiza

Ryan McGonigle, St. John's University

A tribute is a special kind of ceremonial speech that praises the characteristics of subjects who exemplify important cultural traits. [Note: Tributes can praise animals or actions of a group of people. For instance, in the "Gettysburg Address," President Abraham Lincoln praises an entire group of dead soldiers.] This sample speech—given by Ryan McGonigle, a student of Basque descent—praises the life of a famous Basque artist who is a cultural hero.

Ryan opens by introducing Oteiza, an artist revered in his cultural tradition, but unfamiliar to most of his listeners.

Since tributes praise cultural values, Ryan must explain some core ideals of the Basque people.

The name Jorge Oteiza may not exactly raise any eyebrows or provoke any curiosity amongst the American public, but to the Basque people and to me—an American of Basque descent—he is a living legend. Oteiza is arguably the greatest Basque artist and poet of the twentieth century.

Jorge Oteiza was born in Guipuzcoa Province in Spain, near the famous coastal Basque city of San Sebastian at the beginning of the twentieth century. As a child he was raised according to Basque tradition: Honor your father and mother; persevere under hardships; give generously to your neighbor; speak respectfully to others; and most of all, keep your word—which is better than gold. These ideals—centuries old—were later reflected in Oteiza's poetry and art.

One of the best ways you can learn about effective public speaking practices is to study the speeches and performances of others. This book includes a wide variety of speeches and speech outlines from professional and student speakers. This particular speech from the book was created by Ryan McGonigle, a student at St. John's University in New York. Annotations in the margins help you analyze his speech and the goals, audience considerations, strategies, and many other factors he considered in preparing it.

At critical points in each chapter you'll come across lists that summarize the key ideas in the material you have just read. For instance, this **Key Concept** section reviews the most important points to remember about Communicative Competence. Studying these Key Concept sections will help you increase your memory and understanding of these ideas because they immediately follow the related discussions.

Other ways to enhance your study: review the list of **Key Terms** and the **Summary** at the end of each chapter. In addition to the Key Concept sections throughout each chapter, these two review sections will also help deepen your knowledge and strengthen your memory of critical points.

appreciating and participating competently in your own ethnic speech community. In the following example, a Nigerian woman living in the United States explains how she accomplishes this:[13]

> *At work, . . . I raise my voice as loud as necessary to be heard in meetings. At conferences where I present papers on "Women from the Third World," I make serious arguments about the need for international intervention in countries where women are deprived of all rights. . . . Yet as easily as I switch from speaking English to Ibo [her African language], . . . I never confuse my two selves.*
>
> *Hundreds of thousands of women from the third world and other traditional societies share my experience. We straddle two cultures, cultures that are often in opposition. Mainstream America, the culture we embrace in our professional lives, dictates that we be assertive and independent—like men. Our traditional culture, dictated by religion and years of socialization, demands that we be docile and content in our roles as mothers and wives—careers or not.*

KEY CONCEPT   **Communicative Competence**

Personal effectiveness Because of individual differences between people, there is no single way to be an effective communicator, and a speaker chooses behaviors that are effective for his or her personality.

Social appropriateness Different speaking situations call for different presentational styles; rhetorically sensitive speakers adapt to a variety of speaking situations.

Personality variables Extroversion and introversion are two factors that influence a speaker's comfort.

Cultural variables Cultures have different public speaking traditions that may affect a speaker's comfort and competence.

> *Who speaks* In some cultures, only certain people speak publicly—often men who are elders in the group.
>
> *How they speak* Cultural variations include directness, indirectness, and fluency.
>
> *What is spoken* Cultures vary in topic selection and in public expression of opinions, feelings, and disagreements.

Communication Apprehension

Although many people learn to be competent speakers, they continue to experience anxiety about speaking. *Apprehension* is defined as the dread or fear of having something bad happen to you. *Communication apprehension (CA)*, then, is the

Check Out the Student Resource Workbook

You'll find even more help in becoming a better speaker in the Student Resource Workbook. Written by author Clella Jaffe, this resource book contains additional speeches and speech outlines from a diversity of professional and student speakers. The workbook also gives you guidance on the speech assignments from the text as well as tools for analyzing your own strengths and weaknesses as a speaker. To purchase your own copy of the Student Resource Workbook, please visit your local bookseller.

Public Speaking

Introduction to Public Speaking

At the end of this chapter, you should be able to

- Define public speaking
- Tell the difference between oral cultures, literate cultures, and electronic cultures
- Tell ways each type of culture educates public speakers
- Identify five concepts in a dialogical theory of communication
- Draw a common model of communication

Note
This chapter begins with an example to show how public speaking relates to real people. The first section of the chapter helps students connect the material in the course to their lives. Most of the chapter relates public speaking to our past, present, and future. Throughout, it introduces terminology and theoretical foundations for the rest of the book.

Teaching Idea
During the 1992 campaign, candidates Gore and Clinton said they wanted to be involved in a national conversation with voters. You can develop this idea with your students by discussing ways we "converse" nationally about such topics as record labeling, condom distribution in schools, and environmental pollution.

In January 1992, *Time* magazine reported, "Few people in any field have demonstrated the power of a single impassioned voice as well as Peggy Charren."[1] Mrs. Charren was an ordinary citizen who became concerned about a problem—the quality of children's television—and publicly spoke out for change. Through her organization, Action for Children's Television, she persuaded Congress to pass laws regulating programming for children. Peggy Charren, whom *Time* nicknamed "Mrs. KidVid," is part of a great tradition in U.S. society, in which ordinary individuals voice their concerns in order to make a difference about issues that matter to them.

Across the nation, people of all ages join in a *national conversation* in which they discuss people, events, and policies in political, educational, business, and social settings. They speak in many languages and dialects, in formal and informal public settings, for a variety of purposes—to inform, to persuade, to entertain, and to reinforce community values. Indeed, public speaking is vital in a free society where each person is valued and each citizen has the constitutional right to express ideas freely.

Not only do we have opportunities to speak and listen within the United States, we also can converse publicly with people from across the globe. Some enter our national conversation when they immigrate to the United States. At other times, Americans speak to international groups when they visit different countries or work in international organizations. Through television and radio, we have additional opportunities to hear international speakers.

You know from experience that a conversation requires both a speaker and a listener; consequently, the national conversation requires audience members as well as speakers. As they discuss issues that concern their common life, speakers interact with audiences to co-create mutual understandings and work toward commonly agreed-on goals. It is probable that you will be a public speaker in the future; however, it is almost guaranteed that you will be an audience member who hears and evaluates public messages. The skills needed for competence in these dual roles—speaking publicly and listening to speeches—are the focus of this book.

A major theme of this text is the relationship between culture and public speaking. Not only do cultures shape public speaking, public speaking shapes cultures. Cultures provide their members with resources that include a world view, beliefs, values, attitudes, and normative behaviors, and some of our speaking functions to transmit, maintain, and renew these resources. However, cultures are dynamic and changeable. The United States is a pluralistic society in which many groups live, and culturally diverse people offer alternative ways of believing and behaving. This results in public speaking that attempts to influence audiences to change their ideas and behaviors.

Culture also shapes the forms of public speaking, and speech forms, or *genres*, such as lecture, tribute, briefing, or sermon, have identifiable culturally influenced elements. A genre can vary over time and between cultural groups. For example, a sermon is not the same in Catholic, Southern Baptist, and

Pentecostal traditions; furthermore, today's sermons differ from those common in the eighteenth century. In your public speaking class, you will learn some of the common genres of public speaking used in the United States. You will also read about some contrasting norms from other nondominant cultural groups and from other societies across the globe.

This introductory chapter will provide you with an overview of three types of culture and the place of public speaking in each. Because public speaking has been and continues to be part of every society, we will examine the education of speakers in each type of culture. The chapter concludes with an emerging theory and a model that provide the bases for many of the ideas that will be developed throughout the text.

Public Speaking and You

Teaching Idea

Invite a guest speaker (or speakers) to discuss the importance of public speaking in occupations that are typical of the work your students plan to do in the future. Often, retired people are more than willing to come into the classroom. *Exercises 1, 2, and 3, found at the end of the chapter, are appropriate here.*

Although most people do not think of themselves as public speakers, chances are you have already spoken publicly at least once. *Public speaking* means that one person prepares and delivers a presentation to a group who listen, generally without interrupting the flow of ideas. For example, you may have presented a class report, given an inspirational talk in a club, or spoken out in a campus forum. Even making an announcement is a form of public speaking. Your experiences, combined with the abilities you have developed to do research and to organize ideas, give you a foundation on which to build competence in public speaking. Even if you have no public speaking experience prior to this class, you probably have developed some of the characteristics important for good public speaking.

Employment and Public Speaking

Teaching Idea

Hagge-Greenberg's research results are in the Instructor's Manual. Duplicate copies for your students. Discuss whether or not they think the study is still valid. What societal changes might make communication skills more or less important? What other skills on the list might be developed in this class?

In a society that depends on skilled communicators, verbal abilities are highly significant to employers. For example, in one survey of traits that employers considered desirable, researcher Lanna Hagge-Greenberg[2] found that verbal (oral) communication skills ranked first in importance with *both* employers who hire liberal arts graduates and those who do not. Both interpersonal and public speaking skills are valued. Thus, even if your major is a field such as accounting, engineering, or one of the sciences, your future employer will probably consider your verbal communication skills to be of great importance. Moreover, Hagge-Greenberg found that employers value other skills that you will develop and refine in this class—written skills, organizational skills, and to a lesser extent, selling and promoting skills.

Other research supports the conclusion that public speaking is valuable in most job settings, even in "ordinary" jobs done by "ordinary" people. A recent survey[3] showed that more than half of a randomly selected sample of ordinary people spoke to a group of ten or more persons at least once in the last two

Public speaking skills are highly valued in a wide variety of occupations.

For Further Reading

See D. B. Curtis, J. L. Windsor, and R. D. Stephens. (1989). National preferences in business and communication education. *Communication Education* 38, pp. 6–14. Teaching Note 1.1 in the Instructor's Manual summarizes this research.

years. Seventy percent of those gave four or more speeches during that time, often on topics related to their work. Many of the speeches were informative, given by teachers, nurses, police officers, or parents. This survey further showed that people with higher incomes spoke more than those with lower incomes, and people with higher educational levels spoke in public more than those with less education. Many people are in college because they are hoping for a career with a good income. If you are in this group, you will probably have many opportunities to speak in a variety of situations in the future.

Public Speaking in Oral, Literate, and Electronic Cultures

For Further Reading

W. Ong. (1982). *Orality and literacy: The technologizing of the word.* New York: Methuen.

As you begin to study public speaking, you become one link in a long chain of speakers, stretching back to the beginnings of human history, for in every human community, individuals have formulated mental ideas and communicated these ideas to other individuals through language. In this section, we discuss forms of communication in oral, literate, and electronic cultures.

Oral Cultures[4]

Although global literacy is widespread, a few cultures are still primarily oral, whereas others retain elements of orality. In a culture distinguished by *primary orality*, there is *no* writing; words exist only as they are spoken. There is no tech-

Note

Previously, such cultures were termed "illiterate," with the connotation that they were somehow not as good as literate cultures.

nology for recording and sending messages from one person to another. The result is that speakers and their audiences meet face to face, and the poems and fables, prayers and chants, proverbs and sayings, genealogies and stories they share are the only means available for members to pass on the values, beliefs, and history of the culture. Each new generation must learn the tribal lore and pass it on to succeeding generations.

In the book *Roots*,[5] a chronicle of one African-American family's history, author Alex Haley visits the oral culture of his ancestral African family. He tells of his encounter with the *griots* (storytellers), elders in the tribe who held the history of his people in their memories. In his first meeting with an elderly griot, Haley recounts how he sat, surrounded by a crowd of villagers:[6]

> *The* griot *would speak, . . . his words seeming almost physical objects. After a sentence or two, seeming to go limp, he would lean back, listening to an interpreter's translation. Spilling from the* griot's *head came an incredibly complex Kinte clan lineage that reached back across many generations: who married whom; who had what children; what children then married whom; then their offspring. It was all just unbelievable.*
>
> *The old* griot *had talked for nearly two hours up to then. "About this time . . . the eldest of [Omoro Kinte's] four sons, Kunta, went away from his village to chop wood . . . and he was never seen again." And the* griot *went on with his narrative.*
>
> *I sat as if I were carved of stone. My blood seemed to have congealed. This man whose lifetime had been in this back-country African village had no way in the world to know that he had just echoed what I had heard all through my boyhood years on my grandma's front porch in Henning, Tennessee . . . of an African who always had insisted that his name was "Kin-tay"; . . . who had been kidnapped into slavery while not far from his village, chopping wood, to make himself a drum.*

As the griot continued, Haley fumbled for his dufflebag and found the notebook in which he had recorded his grandmother's stories. And at that moment, the other listeners recognized him. Haley concludes his description of the event with an account of his joyful reunion with his African relatives.

In a culture without writing, griots housed the wisdom and the history of the tribe; they were the only link the living had to their past. In fact, Haley compared the death of a griot to a library being burned to the ground.

Although most cultures in the world are at least partially literate, traces of orality survive in every culture. There are remnants of oral traditions in American tales, proverbs, and sayings. The phrases "Once upon a time" and "They lived happily ever after" provide frames for "fairy tales" that contain moral lessons such as "Virtue and perseverance pay off in the end." People recite proverbs, such as "A stitch in time saves nine" or "A penny saved is a penny earned," long after they quit patching their clothing and pennies have little value. Additional traces of orality, such as nursery rhymes, folk stories, "old wives tales," and playground chants pass from generation to generation through the spoken word.

Members of this oral society in Delta Egypt rely on their village folksinger to memorize and transmit the history and traditions of the culture in story and song.

Teaching Idea

Working in small groups or as a whole class, elicit some urban or campus legends that students know. Or read some of these legends and let the class discuss them. For examples, see J. H. Brunvand. (1993). *The baby train and other lusty urban legends.* New York: W. W. Norton.

Speech Assignment

The Student Resource Workbook includes an assignment for telling a modern legend that students can use to introduce themselves. Because anxiety is often great at this stage, some instructors have their students sit in a circle to deliver this speech. *Exercise 4 correlates with this assignment.*

The creation of oral traditions is an ongoing process. Rap music, for instance, is a type of oral performance based in the verbal resources of the African-American community. Urban legends[7] are another ongoing oral form. For instance, did you ever hear the one about the lady who decided to speed up drying her poodle after a bath, so she put the dog in the microwave and blew it up? No one can ever tell you the name of the woman or where she lived, but many people repeat the story. It is one of the urban legends of our time, perhaps told as an expression of the latent fear people have of the many new technologies in the culture. Students have their own sets of legends—often about outwitting a professor—especially at test time.

Learning to Speak in Oral Cultures In oral cultures, speakers learn their craft by apprenticing under a master. The following example of traditional Japanese storytellers demonstrates the apprenticeship process:[8] There are two types of traditional storytellers in Japan—both are male. Those called *kodan* tell stories with historical themes. There are about 20 kodan masters in Tokyo. A larger group of masters (about 220) called *rakugo* specialize in short humorous episodes told to entertain their listeners. These master storytellers have their pupils repeat their tales word for word, while they imitate the actions of the master. Apprentices copy the master until they perfect the traditional forms; then they may add their own individual creativity and innovation in retelling the stories.

Haley[9] describes the training of African griots somewhat differently. A griot begins to learn his lore when he is still an adolescent. By the time he is a senior griot, he is usually about seventy years old, and he has been listening and learning for forty or fifty years. Each senior elder teaches a series of progressively younger apprentices. Griots and their pupils form a long line of chroniclers that extends back to the earliest tribal historians.

Although orality survives to a certain extent in every culture around the globe, pictographic and alphabetic writing systems predominate in the transmission of information in today's world. The shift from orality to literacy resulted in profound cultural changes.

Literate Cultures

The invention of writing was an important development in the history of communication. Literate people were no longer restricted to face-to-face interactions with their audiences, for writing allowed them to store their ideas in a permanent, linear form in books or scrolls and communicate them to audiences separated by both distance and time.

Although many written messages do not survive, other books or manuscripts outlive their authors. Consequently, you can still read the words of Confucius who wrote twenty-six centuries ago. Although African-American author W. E. B. DuBois has been dead for three decades, he can still "speak" to you through his written words.

In oral cultures, words exist only in the realm of sound. In contrast, with writing, words become visible "things" to define and store in dictionaries. Speakers in oral cultures typically use only a few thousand words; the vocabulary of English contains at least a million and a half words.

Literacy also changes the ways people think and reason. Writing makes it possible for readers (audience members) to stop and contemplate, to underline, read, and reread—which is impossible in orality. Since letters and words follow one another in a linear fashion, literate people begin to think in linear ways, tracing "lines" of thought and making outlines of their ideas. Reading audiences are analytical; they evaluate claims, weigh evidence, and construct rules and codes of logic.

Writing affects public speaking, as well. Literate speakers are not limited by what they remember about their subjects; rather, they can draw speech materials from the writings of others. Furthermore, writing frees speakers from memorizing their words and allows them to use notes or manuscripts as they speak. Finally, communicators can send messages through others. For example, President Thomas Jefferson did not personally give his State of the Union Address; rather, he wrote it and had a clerk deliver it to Congress. It was not until Woodrow Wilson was chief executive in the early 1900s that presidents personally delivered these addresses.[10]

 Learning to Speak in Western Literate Traditions Although public speaking texts often trace their history to the ancient Greeks, there are traces of well-developed public speaking traditions throughout the world. In ancient Mesopotamia[11] (2700–2550 B.C.), for instance, fragmentary evidence indicates a public speaking tradition involving an "Assembly of Elders" that judged cases and made

BOX 1.1

The Precepts of Kagemni and Ptah-hotep

The following principles from *The Precepts of Kagemni and Ptah-hotep* provide clues to the importance ancient Egyptians placed on effective speaking for both their sons and daughters. Here are some principles for both speaking and listening found in the writings:

1. Speak with exactness; however, there is a time for silence.

2. Listeners who lack "good fellowship" cannot be influenced by the speeches of others.

3. Speakers should not be proud of their learning.

4. It is wise to be silent in the face of a better debater, to refute the false arguments of an equal, and to let a weaker speaker's arguments confound themselves.

5. Do not pervert the truth.

6. Do not give or repeat extravagant speech that is heated by wrath.

7. Avoid speaking of that which you know nothing.

8. A speaker who is covetous lacks persuasiveness in speech.

deliberative and advisory decisions. Women probably participated in this assembly or had alternative courts of their own in which they reasoned and argued cases.

Speaking was also important in ancient Egypt. Fragments of the oldest book in existence, *The Precepts of Kagemni and Ptah-hotep*,[12] date to 2100 B.C., predating the Pyramid of Khufu. The principles in this text, written twenty-three centuries before Aristotle, instruct young Egyptian men and women in the wisdom of the culture. Not surprisingly, these writings stress the importance of public speaking and give some guidelines for communicating effectively. Box 1.1 lists some of the speaking principles found in this historical fragment.

In the fifth century B.C., Corax of Syracuse and his pupil Tisias began the systematic training of students in the principles of public speaking. A tyrant, who had usurped land from the common people, was driven from power. After his ouster, the people naturally wanted to reclaim their ancestral properties, but they lacked documents to prove their claims. Corax and Tisias, using forms of argument that already existed in the culture, taught these common citizens how to build their cases and provide evidence to support their claims. Although they did not invent the principles and rules they taught, these two are often credited as being the first instructors of public speaking in the Western tradition.

Classical Traditions During the next four centuries in Greece, *rhetoric*, the art of persuasive public speaking, was one of the most important subjects taught.

The principles of rhetoric established by orators in classical Greece and Rome still influence public speaking today.

Teaching Idea

Today, phrases such as "mere rhetoric" and "empty rhetoric" are common. Many think of rhetoric as a substitute for action. *Use exercise 5 to help students explore their attitudes toward the subject.*

Aristotle wrote an early public speaking text entitled *Rhetoric*. In it, he identified three arenas of speaking common in Greek society: (1) in *judicial* speaking, which took place in courts of law, disputants presented arguments for the prosecution and the defense; (2) in *legislative* speaking, citizens created the laws by which they governed the city state of Athens; (3) in *ceremonial* speaking, orators praised Athens' heroes and vilified her enemies. Aristotle's ideas continue to exert wide influence in public speaking courses and textbooks, including this one.

The study of rhetoric was also important in ancient Rome. Roman citizens conversed publicly and privately about justice, about governing, and about other issues and policies that were essential to the development of the city. Famous orators, like Cicero, wrote treatises on public speaking. After the dictatorial emperors came to power, ordinary citizen participation became less important in formulating Roman laws, but common people still spoke in public to pass on their cultural traditions.

These early teachers of rhetoric knew the inherent power of words. Consequently, they recognized the ethical implications of persuasive public speaking. They generally agreed that an effective speaker should be not only knowledgeable in many areas and skilled in speaking but a person of good character as well. The Latin phrase, *Vir bonum, dicendi peritus*—"The good person, skilled in speaking"—sums up their teaching.

Teaching Idea

Some instructors have students keep a notebook or journal. In it, students keep class notes, speech outlines, and self-evaluations or journal entries. Several end-of-the-chapter exercises would be suitable for journal entries.

Quintilian, a famous Roman educator, believed that good speakers should read, write, listen, and speak effectively. These four disciplines are components of most public speaking courses to this day. As you prepare your speeches, you will *read* your text as well as other printed sources. You will *write* notes and outlines as you organize your thoughts; you will also take notes on the speeches of classmates. You will *listen* to other speakers to learn what is effective and what is less effective. Finally, you will actually practice *speaking*—you will learn by doing.

Cross Reference

Chapter 2 presents an overview of the canons. Invention is the subject of Chapters 5, 7, 8, and 15. Chapters 9 and 16 discuss disposition. Style is found in Chapter 10, memory in Chapter 9, and delivery in Chapter 12.

To help their students become competent in the skills necessary for speaking, Roman orators developed the five *canons* of rhetoric. A canon is a body of principles, rules, standards, or norms. These canons are discussed in detail in the next chapter and throughout the text. The principles in them will guide you throughout your speech preparation. These are the five canons and a brief description of their principles:

1. *Invention* Decide on a topic and a purpose for your speech. After you select and narrow the topic, gather speech materials. Throughout your preparation, consider your audience. Develop reasonable and logical arguments, and select evidence that will keep listeners interested and motivated.

2. *Disposition* After you have gathered your speech materials, organize them into a pattern that enables the audience to understand your ideas. The canon of disposition includes the common patterns for introductions, bodies, and conclusions of speeches, as well.

3. *Style* To enliven your speech, select vivid wording that is appropriate, memorable, and interesting. Through language choices, you attempt to elicit mental pictures that remain with listeners after the speech.

4. *Memory* In literate cultures memory is sometimes called the "lost" canon. Modern speakers use note cards or a prepared manuscript, TelePrompTers, or cue cards.

5. *Delivery* Often your delivery "makes or breaks" your speech. This canon provides guidelines on nonverbal behaviors, including effective use of vocal variation, gestures, and eye contact.

Further Developments in Rhetoric Others besides Greeks and Romans contributed to our knowledge of effective speechmaking. Throughout the centuries, rhetoric was one of the original seven liberal arts, and scholars from Africa, Italy, England, France, and many other countries have clarified our understandings of public communication. They continue to do so. For instance, the emphasis on dialogical public speaking developed throughout this text draws from the work of two Germans, Martin Buber and Hellmut Geissner, the Russian Mikhail Bakhtin, the Swiss author Paul Tournier, and many others.

Every culture has its own unique resources for persuasive discourse. For example, when thousands of students in China gathered in Tiananmen Square to demand more freedom in 1989, student speakers supported their ideas using forms of reasoning and argumentation found within their culture. After the Soviet Union collapsed, speakers used evidence and reasoning strategies from Russian cultural public speaking traditions to convince their audiences of new ways of thinking and acting. We will look at many additional international public speaking traditions throughout this text.

When we look at the availability of printed materials, it is easy to see how literacy is dominant in this culture. Yet, because we are becoming increasingly influenced by the electronic media, it is likely that, instead of picking up a newspaper today, you turned on a radio or the television set to receive information. The electronic inventions of the twentieth century have led to cultures that are dominated by messages that rely on impressions formed from images and music as well as words.

Electronic Cultures

At the turn of the century, technicians began to wire our continent and our world. In the early 1900s, communicators sent telegraph messages over wires in Morse code. As technological developments continued, the telephone, radio, and tape recorders became common; these machines carried *voices* over great distances, making knowledge of the dot–dash Morse code unnecessary. New inventions such as moving pictures and television brought *voices*, *faces*, and *images* from around the globe into individual homes. The result is that we live in a culture in which the spoken word is supplemented by images; in some cases, visual impressions bypass words entirely.

In addition to visual and audio messages, print messages now arrive through electronic channels, such as e-mail or FAX machines. Ideas are now stored on floppy disks, in computer memory banks, on videotapes, CDs, and audiotapes. As forms of technology continue to evolve at a rapid pace, we can only guess what communication resources you will have in the future.

The electronic revolution is changing the thought patterns of the media generation in ways that scholars are currently investigating. The holistic impression formation that results from the combination of words, images, music, quick cuts, and edits may be replacing the structured outlines, lines of thought, and propositional thinking characteristic of literacy. Because of the differences in the ways ideas are presented in an electronic culture, scholars, such as Kathleen Hall Jamieson,[13] are exploring the effects that media messages have on speaking styles and on modes of thinking. Here are a few of her conclusions:

- Electronic messages are more conversational, personalized, and autobiographical. Narrative and drama are dominant, and audiences are persuaded by emotional appeals more than by extended reasoning.

- A political speech used to last for an hour or so; now political ideas are reduced to eight- to nine-second sound bites shown on the evening news. This reduces many complex political ideas to mere slogans.

- Previously, speakers used words to elicit mental images in their audiences; now words provide captions for pictures that communicate messages independently of language.

For Further Reading

K. H. Jamieson. (1988). *Eloquence in an electronic age.* New York: Oxford University Press. For a redefinition of the canons in an electronic age, see P. E. Corcoran. (1979). *Political language and rhetoric.* Austin: University of Texas Press.

Some students take courses to learn how to create effective public messages using electronic technology.

Just as the role of the audience changes in literate cultures, it also changes in electronic cultures. Some listeners accept electronic messages fairly uncritically, trusting television and radio announcers to convey the truth. The audience need not be entirely passive, however. Many viewers critically analyze and evaluate media messages, looking for the biases and agendas of the communicators. Some join the discussion of ideas by participating in radio call-in shows or by phoning or writing letters to their television station.

Although communication in the future will differ from that of the past, many of the principles presented throughout this text continue to provide the foundational ideas on which public speaking, even in an electronic culture, is based.

Learning to Speak in an Electronic Culture   As electronic media becomes more and more dominant in societies across the globe, educators are developing new ways of training communicators to create media messages, to evaluate the media messages of others, and to participate in national and international communication made possible by an electronically connected world. Because these media are relatively new, there is no 2,500-year tradition of instruction in media techniques. However, many colleges and universities do offer courses and majors in broadcasting and media production. These courses prepare students to write in the special form that is required for television and radio, to deliver their speeches using electronic devices, to work within rigid time limitations, and to understand the technical aspects of production, such as camera angles, lighting, cutting, editing, and splicing.

In short, although oral, literate, and electronic cultures differ in the ways they train public speakers, all three types of culture recognize the importance of public speaking and make provision to educate public communicators.

KEY CONCEPT

Public Speaking in Oral, Literate, and Electronic Cultures

Oral cultures Without any means for storing messages, people in oral cultures engage in face-to-face communication. They rely on proverbs and stories, formulas and patterns, to remember their ideas. Public speakers learn their craft during a long apprenticeship under a master storyteller. Traces of orality remain in every culture.

Literate cultures Because of print, the message originator can be separated from the receiver. This leads to analytical, linear thought patterns. Public speakers have access to written sources for their speeches and can use written notes or scripts as they speak. Public speakers learn their art by reading, writing, listening, and speaking. Aristotle's text and the Roman canons still exert a great deal of influence in modern speech courses.

Electronic cultures Emerging technologies are creating electronic cultures that rely on messages dominated by pictures as well as words with the result that audiences form holistic impressions from the images and sounds. Communicators must learn to work with the technology that aids them in the production of messages. Many universities offer courses and majors in media.

Contemporary Communication Theories

Contemporary scholars continue to study the process of communication, developing both explanatory theories and models. Communication research focuses on four interrelated components:[14]

- The *communicators* or producers of messages
- The *audiences* or interpreters of messages
- The *content* of the message itself
- The *situation* or context in which the communication occurs

However, theorists vary in the amount of attention they pay to each component. For example, *message-centered* research concentrates on the preparation and performance of the message itself. *Speaker-centered* research focuses on the speaker's intentions, communication apprehension, and the ethical implications of influencing others. A great deal of recent scholarship focuses on the *process* of communication. Most current theories and models emphasize the role of both speakers and listeners as they jointly and actively co-create meaning. We now turn to one such theory and then briefly look at a model of the communication process.

Theories

For Further Reading

M. McGuire and E. Slembek. (1987). An emerging critical rhetoric: Hellmut Geissner's Sprechwissenschaft. *Quarterly Journal of Speech* 73 (3), pp. 349–400.

Theories are explanations by which scholars provide the general or abstract principles of a field of study. Thus, theories related to speaking and listening aim to explain human communication in a variety of contexts. The German scholar Hellmut Geissner[15] proposes a speaker–audience theory based on conversation or dialogue ("Gespräch") as the *prototype* (or original form) of human speaking that provides the foundational pattern of all other speaking. Thus, for Geissner, communication is *the reciprocal process of speaking with one another.* It is (1) language based; (2) embodied, meaning that it is delivered by a speaker; (3) interpersonal; (4) formally defined; and (5) dependent on the situation for meaning. The last three of these major ideas are introduced here; all of his ideas are developed in greater detail in later chapters.

Cross Reference

The ideas introduced here are developed further in the text, especially in Chapters 5 and 6, which explore the relationship between speakers and listeners.

Communication Is Interpersonal   By recognizing the primacy of dialogue, Geissner focuses not on the speaker, the listener, or the message but on the relationship of all three. Speakers do not simply prepare messages that they "give" to a passive audience; listeners must also participate by actively wrestling with the ideas the speaker presents. Geissner emphasizes *respons*-ibility—the necessity of both speakers and listeners to respond to one another and come to mutual understandings. Although public speaking is different in many ways from interpersonal dialogue, competent speakers and listeners take a dialogical attitude toward one another. This idea is expanded in Chapter 5.

Communication Is Formally Defined   Each speech community has characteristic speech acts or genres that vary from simple requests to complex orations. Each of these speech acts has appropriate structures, functions, and lengths. Complex genres or forms include briefings, narratives, interviews, lectures, or courtroom defense summations. The Russian scholar Mikhail Bakhtin summarizes this point when he says, "We 'pour' our speech into ready-made forms or speech genres. These forms are given to us in the same ways in which our native language is given."[16] The major purpose of this text is to introduce you to some of the most common patterns used by public speakers within this culture.

Communication Depends on the Situation   Both objective factors and subjective factors influence the understandings that emerge from the speaking situation. *Objective factors* include the physical acts of speaking and listening, such as movements of the vocal cord or vibrations of the eardrum. They also include the gestures and other movements that both listeners and speakers use to convey meaning. *Subjective factors*, such as the intentions and underlying assumptions of both listeners and speakers, also play a necessary role. Thus, meaning depends, in Geissner's words, on "Who says what, where and when, why and for what, in what manner, with and for whom? . . . and who understands what, where and when, how, why, and for what, in what manner, with or from whom?"[17]

To illustrate, meanings depend on the situation in which a public speech takes place. For example, the same speech—one that explains a new health plan—can be made to two different groups in two different settings:

- One speech is given to the company's board of directors at a meeting immediately prior to the president's budgetary recommendations. It takes place in the walnut-paneled board room of the corporation. A young, female speaker addresses a group made up entirely of older men.

- The second speech is delivered to a casual gathering of young women who have recently signed on with the corporation. They are sitting on couches in a staff lounge, having coffee and doughnuts. The same speaker addresses them.

Objectively, the speaker has accomplished the same physical acts; she used her vocal cords to create sound waves; she gestured and made eye contact with her audience. Yet subjective factors, including her clothing, her age, her gender, and the needs of the listeners, led to different understandings and responses from each group.

Theories, in short, explain a phenomenon or process, and communication theories attempt to explain the process of communication. Geissner's theory emphasizes dialogical interactions in which speakers and audiences use culturally accepted speaking and listening patterns that are interpreted in specific, concrete situations. Theories, however, are generally abstract. Because of this, many people understand concepts better if they are made visible in models or drawings. We now turn to a common communication model.

Models

Models represent abstract concepts in concrete, visual form. For example, engineers make model cars before the automobile goes into production. Drawings or flow charts are other ways to represent abstract ideas and processes. You have probably seen drawings that represent atoms and molecules or flow charts that represent the organizational pattern of a corporation.

Figure 1.1

*Communication has been likened to (**a**) an arrow, (**b**) a circle, and (**c**) a helix.*

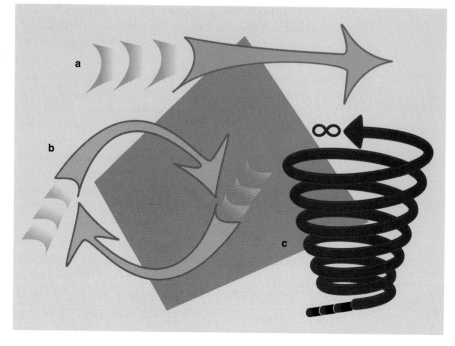

It is one thing to make a model or diagram that depicts something that is unchanging; it is quite another challenge to depict a process that constantly moves and changes. Thus, it is difficult to model or diagram the complex process of communication. Because communication moves in a forward direction, meaning that words once spoken can never be recalled, an arrow (Figure 1.1a) might be used to depict this progressive quality of communication.

However, an arrow does not capture the dialogical nature of communication. Both speakers and listeners must cooperate in creating meaning, and a good model should depict this interactional relationship. As a result, theorists have created complex circular models to show the give-and-take nature of communication. Figure 1.1b shows arrows that outline the circular model in its simplest form.

Communication professor Frank Dance[18] suggests that a helix or spiraling figure, depicted in Figure 1.1c, best represents communication. Dance explains that, as the helix starts from a point and progresses in "graceful turnings,"[19] so communication moves from one speaker (who becomes a listener) to a listener (who becomes a speaker) in a continuous interplay of messages. In addition, speakers loop back to build on experiences and ideas developed previously while they continue to move into the future. Each new curve of the spiral is fundamentally affected by the one from which it emerges, just as each new element of communication depends on what has come before. Since the process of communication is ongoing, the upper part of the figure ends in an infinity loop.

Teaching Idea

In this text, the discussion of models is intentionally simplified. This allows students to explore the model further through additional research. There is supplementary material in the Instructor's Manual. *Using exercise 5 at the end of the chapter, have students form into small groups or pairs and draw their own model of communication.*

In summary, communication is a complex, dynamic process. Themes and ideas that originate in speech are often encoded into print. This print, in turn, becomes the basis for more speech. If the topic is significant to a large number of people, the electronic media may pick up the continuing discussion and broadcast it to a larger audience. This may then lead to more discussion and more print as the cultural conversation continues, interweaving elements of orality with literacy and electronic technology. Both models and theories attempt to explain the many variables that affect the way humans cooperate with one another to create meanings.

KEY CONCEPT   ## Contemporary Communication Theories

Theories Theories are scholarly explanations of the general or abstract principles of a subject. Hellmut Geissner's theory explains all communication as a form of dialogue. In addition to being *language based* and *embodied*, or delivered by a speaker, communication is:

Interpersonal Both speakers and listeners take turns in sending and receiving messages; both take the *respons*-ibility for co-creating meaning.

Formally defined There are culturally determined patterns for different types of speeches.

Dependent on the situation Meaning depends on such factors as who speaks and who listens, how and why, where and when.

Models Models are representations of abstract concepts in visual form; one model depicts communication as a circular process, another uses a helix that continuously turns as it spirals onward, building on the past as it moves to the future.

Summary

This introductory chapter has given an overview of the place of communication, not only in the institutions in which you live and work but also in the various cultures around the world. You have seen that most employers cite the ability to communicate as vital, and good public speaking skills will probably help you gain and keep employment.

This chapter introduced the major theme of the book—that culture determines public speaking forms and that public speaking shapes culture. As members of a culture, we participate in a national conversation, an exchange of ideas in which our beliefs and values are strengthened, modified, and communicated to new generations. Public speaking is a special form of communication, developed historically and affected by the media of the culture; as a result, speakers and listeners interact differently in oral, literate, and electronic cultures. Citizens of a democracy speak in public to entertain, inform, persuade, and inspire one another. For this reason, effective public speaking is vital in most of the institutions of our society, including education, government, and business.

You join a long line of public speakers, who first belonged to oral cultures, then literate, and now electronic. Because public speaking is important in every society, all cultures make provisions to educate competent speakers. The academic study of public speaking in the Western tradition still draws heavily on important Greek and Roman contributions.

Scholars create both theories and models to illuminate the process of communication. Recent theories conceive of a speaker and listeners in a dialogical relationship, cooperating in the creation of meaning. One model of communication is the helix or spiral figure that depicts the idea that communication depends on the past as it moves into the future.

With this foundation, the next chapter will overview the entire speechmaking process. It focuses specifically on creativity and on the rhetorical principles that you can use to create your public speeches.

Questions and Exercises

1. To better understand the relationship between public speaking and occupations, make a list of well-paying, desirable, and prestigious occupations that do *not* require public speaking. List beside it those jobs in which addressing the public is vital. Which list is longer? Compare your list with those of your classmates.

2. Interview a person working in the field you hope to enter when you graduate. What opportunities exist for public speaking? Ask if and how public speaking is related to the higher-paying, more prestigious jobs within the field.

3. Sometimes people do not see themselves as public speakers because they define the word *public* too narrowly. They think of public speakers as politicians speaking at conventions rather than as homemakers testifying before a local school board hearing. Write your definition of "publics," then make a list of specific publics you have already addressed and those you may address someday.

4. Begin a collection of stories that you have only heard orally. Who are the "legends" in your family, your religious group, sports team, living group, or university? What lessons do these stories provide? What *kinds* of narratives are remembered and passed on? What values or actions do they help you remember and perpetuate?

5. The word *rhetoric* does not always enjoy a positive reputation. Read the essay entitled "Mere Law, Mere Medicine, Mere Rhetoric" in the Study Guide. Begin listening for the public use of the word *rhetoric* throughout the term. Make a note of the times you read or hear the word used in the news or in your research. Classify the references as positive, negative, or neutral. Note if any sources speak of rhetoric as essential in a free society.

6. Do further research to discover other common models that represent the process of communication. Using these models as a guide, work with a small group of your classmates to come up with your own pictorial representation.

Key Terms

genre
public speaking
oral culture
literate culture
electronic culture
Aristotle
rhetoric
canon
dialogue
communication
respons-ibility
objective factors
subjective factors
Hellmut Geissner

Notes

1. See Tynan, W. (1992, January 20). Ms. Kidvid calls it quits. *Time*, p. 52, and Waters, H. F. (1988, May 30). The Ms. Fixit of kidvid. *Newsweek*, p. 69.

2. Hagge-Greenberg, L. (1979). Report on the Liberal Arts Employer Survey: Opportunities for the liberal arts graduate. Midwest College Placement Association. See also Curtis, D. B., Windsor, J. L., & Stephens, R. D. (1989). National preferences in business and communication education. *Communication Education, 38*, 6–14.

3. Kendall, K. E. (1988). Does the public speak publicly? A survey. *World Communication, 17* (2), 279–290.

4. There is a large body of literature on orality and literacy. A good place to start is Ong, W. J. (1982). *Orality and literacy: The technologizing of the word.* New York: Methuen. See also Innis, H. (1951, 1971). *The bias of communication.* Toronto: University of Toronto Press; McLuhan, M. (1964). *Understanding media: The extensions of man* (2nd ed.). New York: Signet; and Goody J., & Watts, I. (1991). The consequences of literacy. In D. Crowley & P. Heyer (Eds.), *Communication in history: Technology, culture, society* (pp. 48–56). New York: Longman.

5. Haley, A. (1976). *Roots.* Garden City, NY: Doubleday.

6. Ibid., pp. 678–679.

7. Brunvand, J. H. (1993). *The baby train and other lusty urban legends.* New York: W. W. Norton.

8. Hrdlickova, V. (1976). Japanese professional storytellers. In D. Ben-Amos (Ed.), *Folklore genres* (pp.171–190). Austin: University of Texas Press.

9. Haley. (1976). Op. cit.

10. Podell, J., & Anzovin, S. (Eds.). (1988). *Speeches of the American presidents.* New York: H. W. Wilson.

11. For a discussion of Sumerian public speaking, see Wills, J. W. (1970). Speaking arenas in ancient Mesopotamia. *Quarterly Journal of Speech, 56,* 398–405.

12. For quotations from the Egyptian manuscripts, see Gray, G. W. (1946). The precepts of Kagemni and Ptah-hotep. *Quarterly Journal of Speech, 31,* 446–454.

13. Jamieson, K. H. (1988). *Eloquence in an electronic age.* New York: Oxford University Press.

14. Fearing, F. (1967). Toward a psychological theory of human communication. In F. W. Matson and A. Montague (Eds.), *The human dialogue: Perspectives on communication* (pp. 179–194). New York: The Free Press.

15. For a further explanation of Geissner's ideas, see Schwandt, B., & Soraya, S. (1992, August 13–15). *Ethnography of communication and "Sprechwissenschaft"—merging concepts.* Paper presented at the Ethnography of Communication Conference, Portland, OR; see also McGuire, M., & Slembek, E. (1987). An emerging critical rhetoric: Hellmut Geissner's Sprechwissenschaft. *Quarterly Journal of Speech, 73* (3), 349–400.

16. Bakhtin is quoted in Wierbicka, A. (1991). *Cross-cultural pragmatics: The semantics of human interaction* (p. 149). Berlin: Mouton de Gruyter.

17. Geissner is quoted in McGuire and Slembek (1987), Op. cit. p. 352.

18. Dance, F. E. X. (1967). Toward a theory of human communication. In F. E. X. Dance (Ed.), *Human communication theory* (pp. 288–309). New York: Holt, Rinehart, and Winston. This model is on p. 296.

19. Dance, F. E. X., & Zak-Dance, C. C. (1986). *Public speaking* (p. 9). New York: Harper & Row.

2

Overview of the Speechmaking Process

At the end of this chapter, you should be able to

- Identify two aspects of creativity
- Explain the five canons of rhetoric
- Choose and narrow a topic
- Identify both a general purpose and a specific purpose for a speech
- Write a central idea that states the main idea of the speech
- Identify some resources you may use in researching your speech topic
- Identify parts of the speech found in the canon of disposition
- Recognize the importance of language that is appropriate to the audience and the occasion
- Discuss the importance of rehearsal
- Deliver a short speech

Note

Since most instructors want their students to speak in the first few days of class, this chapter briefly previews the entire speech-making process. A major focus of the chapter is on selecting a speech topic and purpose. Introduce cultural concerns by suggesting that students look for topics relating to ethnic and international issues.

Chapter 1 pointed out that there are speechmakers in a variety of occupations and organizations across the globe. However, you may not yet see yourself as one of them. Nevertheless, you now find yourself in a speech class where *you* are a public speaker—for in the next few weeks, you will stand in front of your classmates and make four or five public presentations.

Successfully preparing and giving a public speech presents a challenge that sets into motion a creative process. A good public speech is a fitting response to a situation, a topic, and an audience. Think of it as a dialogue that involves you, the audience, and the topic within a specific setting.

This chapter begins with a look at creativity as it applies to speechmaking. Then, it provides a brief overview of the entire process of preparing and delivering a speech by examining the principles found in the five canons of rhetoric.

Creativity and Public Speaking

For Further Reading

R. W. Weisberg. (1986). *Creativity: Genius and other myths*. New York: W. H. Greenman, and N. Hermann. (1988). *The creative brain*. Lake Lure, NC: Brain Books.

In the United States, people typically think of life as a series of problems to be solved by creative people. Thus, public speaking assignments can be seen as challenges or problems that call for meaningful solutions. Researchers on creativity give two criteria for judging a creative response to a problem: the response must be novel, and it must truly solve the problem. Creative speechmakers, thus, provide a novel or unique speech for each situation, and the speech they give truly meets the requirements of the audience and the occasion.

Create a Novel Response[1]

"Novel" means that the speech is new both to you and to your listeners. That is, it is a specific response created for a specific audience on a specific occasion. Consider how professional financial planners create a novel response for each speech they make. They use the same organizational pattern for the speech and the same visual aids, yet each time, they alter the presentation slightly. They select specific illustrations and appeals for different ages, genders, and occupational levels. They shorten the speech on a very warm day or in a late evening meeting. They update each presentation with details from the current week's Dow Jones averages. Although parts of the speech remain constant, every presentation is a novel response to a unique situation.

A novel speech stands in stark contrast to a "generic" or "file" speech. For this reason, going back to a term paper you wrote in high school and simply reading it to your classroom audience is not novel. This does not mean that you cannot use topics you have previously researched; however, it means that, if you choose to use material from previous research, you rework it specifically for your classmates. Students occasionally reach into a file, such as a "frat file" of sample

Successful public speakers adapt their presentations to the specific topic, the setting, the audience, and the occasion in which they speak.

student speeches, pull out an old speech, and read it to their classmates. Not only is this dishonest, it is not a novel response to the assignment, for using someone else's old material does not account for the unique aspects of the present speaking situation.

Solve the Problem

Cross Reference

If you used the Hagge-Greenberg table found in the Instructor's Manual for Chapter 1, emphasize the value of effective problem solving to employers.

In addition to being novel, the solution—in this case, the speech—must solve a problem that involves several factors: your motivation or desire to share knowledge, beliefs, or information; your audience's need to know; and an occasion that draws you together. The text of your speech is a response to all these factors. The requirements of the assignment, thus, dictate or limit appropriate solutions. For instance, in business, people who are assigned to present an award fail to meet the needs of the audience and the occasion if they give a sales speech instead, even if it is a wonderful, novel presentation.

Classroom speeches are similarly evaluated according to whether or not they meet specific requirements. For example, many instructors assign a visual aids speech. If you fail to use visual aids, you have not solved the problem posed by the assignment. If the assignment is a narrative speech, a wonderful policy speech, however novel, does not fulfill the requirements. Generally, there is also a time limit inherent in a speech occasion, with classroom speeches usually lasting from five to seven minutes. To solve the problem posed by the occasion, successful speakers must abide within the time constraints.

Thus, a speech that is effective and creative solves the problem and provides a fitting response to the occasion, the audience, the speaker's need to speak, and the topic. For this reason, it is very important that you clearly understand your classroom assignment. Most instructors carefully go over specific details of each assignment. Don't hesitate to ask questions so that you clearly understand the requirements for each speech.

Teaching Idea

Supplementary material on creativity and public speaking is in the Instructor's Manual. It is suitable for transfer to a transparency for use in a lecture.

   **Creativity**

Create a novel response Rather than give a generic speech, each speech is new to you and your listeners.

Solve the problem The speech meets the requirements of the audience, the occasion, and the speaker.

Principles of Speaking

Teaching Idea

Develop the idea of the canons inductively by using Activity 2.1 in the Instructor's Manual.

To help their students become competent in the skills necessary for speaking, we saw in Chapter 1 that Roman orators developed the five canons of rhetoric: invention, disposition, style, memory, and delivery. In review, a *canon* is a body of principles, rules, standards, or norms. Here we will define the canons and show how you can use the principles in them to put together an effective public presentation.

Invention

Cross Reference

The terminology presented here is used throughout the text.

The canon of invention contains the principles that guide you as you consider your audience, decide on a topic and a purpose for your speech, gather information to support your ideas, develop reasonable and logical arguments, and select evidence to keep your listeners interested and motivated.

You can compare the process of "invention" in public speaking to other types of invention. For instance, Bob Maydew, a mechanical engineer, designed a valve specifically for oil wells. As an inventor, he went through a process similar to the one you go through in creating a speech. He first saw a need for a new product because the oil drilling rigs were not working efficiently. Then he used personal resources, such as knowledge and experience, which he combined with external resources, such as metals and tools, to design a valve that solved the problem. Like an inventor, you speak because you see a need—the need to discuss a particular topic. Then you take resources from within yourself and from outside sources to create a speech.

The following is a brief overview of what the Romans designated as the canon of invention. It includes the procedures you follow to find and narrow a topic, to identify a general and specific purpose for the speech, to write a central idea, and to gather information from research. Chapters 7, 8, and 15 discuss the canon of invention in further detail.

Choose a Topic   What shall I talk about? How do I find a topic that I know enough about to discuss, one that is interesting to the class as well? Many students find these questions to be among the most difficult aspects of classroom speaking because instructors generally do not assign specific topics. There are five things to consider as you choose an appropriate subject for your speech:

Need   The topic should be significant, one that needs to be discussed in order to bring about change, increase the audience's understanding, or maintain important cultural values and beliefs.[2] As you consider whether or not a topic is significant, think of what your audience knows. Some students select topics that are not significant because the listeners have no need to hear about them. For instance, one student showed her audience how to make a peanut butter and jelly sandwich. In the discussion that followed, her classmates agreed that she had wasted their time by presenting a trivial subject.

Audiences often vary in their motivation to listen to a topic. Most people want to hear about topics that affect their lives here and now—topics that relate to their interests and needs. Thus, they have a motive to hear about writing a resume when they are looking for a job because the topic fits with their goals, desires, and interests. However, other topics are further removed from daily concerns. Some such topics involve national issues. Let's say you choose the topic of "open" adoption. Why should your listeners have an interest in adoption laws? Your challenge is to link this topic to their perceived interests and needs. In this case, you might relate it to their need to know their biological roots, or you might link it to other family issues such as parental rights. Topics relating to international issues often seem further removed from the daily lives of audience members. If you choose such a topic, you must look for additional ways to motivate listeners. For instance, are U.S. tax dollars used to support the global enterprise? Can listeners identify with the plight of fellow humans who are

Teaching Idea

Activity 2.2 in the Instructor's Manual presents ideas for eliciting topics for speechmaking. Use newspapers, newsmagazines, TV schedules, and other course texts for topic ideas. Store the ideas for use later in this chapter and with Chapters 14 and 16.

For Further Reading

Lloyd F. Bitzer. (1968). The rhetorical situation. *Philosophy and Rhetoric*, 1, pp. 1–14.

Teaching Idea

Use the topics you elicited from the class in Activity 2.2. Have students evaluate whether or not there is a need to speak about specific subjects. Then have students select a topic on the list and identify ways to relate it to the interests and needs of the classroom audience. (This will prepare them for the information in Chapter 9 that discusses the introduction to the speech.)

caught in international conflicts? Does the topic tie into fundamental values, such as the desire for a world at peace or for freedom and justice for all?

As you can see, choosing a topic that meets an audience's need to know is a foundational principle in speechmaking. However, when audience members lack motivation to listen, you must take special care to link the topic to their interests and goals.

Personal Interests and Experiences   Generally, good public speakers are curious about the world around them. They want to know what is happening, and they are concerned about how these events and processes affect the lives of ordinary people. Use your natural curiosity to generate possible topics. What do you know and care about? What would you like to explore further? What is your major? Your future occupation? What have you read about or seen on television that you found interesting? What concerns you? What changes would you like to see in society? Here are ways some students used personal interests to create speeches:

- Paula once spent a summer in Israel; she spoke about concerns related to Israeli–Arab conflicts.
- Fadi feels that the homeless are not receiving enough attention; his speech advocated increased funding for low-cost housing.
- Peggy heard about the Bermuda Triangle and wanted to know more about it.
- Joshua built a telescope in high school; he explained the major constellations.
- Leah is a pre-med major, and she spoke on Tay-Sachs disease.

In addition, students select topics from their life experiences, including knowledge gained from their family backgrounds, their jobs, or their recreational interests. For instance, one student who fought forest fires spoke on containment of fires. Another discussed her experiences while white-water rafting. Some students draw from their personal experiences with educational challenges such as dyslexia. Others have discussed artists and writers from their ethnic group.

Speaking on topics that fascinate or concern you has obvious advantages. When you are truly interested in your subject, you will probably be more enthusiastic about it. This enthusiasm often helps you concentrate on the topic and your listeners' need to know rather than your insecurity as a speaker. In addition, audiences like to listen to speakers who care about their subjects instead of speakers who appear to be bored by their topics.

Other Courses   Students often find speech topics in other courses they are taking. For example, a student who is taking psychology looks at the table of contents

Many students find speech topics in subjects they research in other classes. For example, a student studying Asian cultures might speak on traditional Nepalese healers, known as jhankri.

in her psychology textbook. There, she finds potential topics such as Freud's theories of personality, defense mechanisms, memory, perception, and behaviorism. Giving a speech on an interesting topic from another class has the added advantage of helping the speaker learn material for that course.

Don't hesitate to use research you've done for other courses if the subject is an appropriate speech topic. For instance, as part of a nursing course, Jack wrote a paper on Cherokee Indian medical beliefs and practices. He used some of the same material in his classroom speech on Native American medicine.

Current Events   Newspapers, newsmagazines, and television shows are another excellent source of topics appropriate for public discourse. Skim headlines, jotting down current topics that interest you. Don't overlook television program guides as a source of topics. This list came from only one day of television programming:

multiple personalities	country music
the decade of the 1950s	the first Americans
dinosaurs	English villages
pool sharks	the Amish
rappelling	women who love felons
Brazil's national debt	unwanted pets
movie special-effects	Stalin
stalkers	vigilante justice
compatibility tests	doctors who sexually abuse patients
Africa	cutbacks in military funding
college sports	assassination investigations
the Gold Rush	Mount Vesuvius and Pompeii

Topics from current events usually meet a need in society. The fact that they are important enough to be discussed in print or electronic media means that they are significant in the lives of many people. In addition, since they are publicly discussed, it is often relatively easy to find further information that you can use in a speech.

Teaching Idea

Exercise 1 is appropriate here.

International Topics   Your public speaking classroom is a good place to expand your audience's understanding of global processes and events that affect their lives. You can often find international topics by exploring your own heritage and experiences. Thus, a person of Swedish ancestry might examine the tax structure in Sweden, comparing it to that in the United States. Someone who works at McDonald's might look at management styles in Japanese or Russian restaurants. In addition, newspapers, magazines, and television broadcasts regularly report on topics such as trade, global investments, or international crime that will be increasingly important to U.S. audiences in the twenty-first century.

Early in the term, plan to spend time brainstorming for possible topics. Make a list of subjects that interest you; then narrow your list to four or five major topics. If you select your topics early, you can be alert for information throughout the term to use in your speeches. Let's say you are looking for material on eating disorders; you can scan weekly TV schedules, looking for shows that feature the topic. You can also set up interviews with professionals as well as people who have experienced eating disorders. Because you have the topic clearly in mind, you have plenty of time to gather up-to-date materials to create a good speech. If you begin early enough, you can create a file for each speech, photocopying or clipping articles from newspapers or magazines, and taking notes on television programs or lectures. At speech time, you have available resources for a good presentation.

Narrow the Topic   Once you have selected a broad topic, you must narrow it enough to discuss it in the short time allotted for a classroom speech. Besides time constraints, several other considerations help you narrow your topic. One major consideration is the audience. As discussed earlier, anticipate what your listeners already know and what they need to know. In addition, be sensitive to their motivations to listen.

During the course of brainstorming, consider the value of using a mind map as a way of letting your ideas flow. Figure 2.1 illustrates how a student might start with a very broad topic—the environment—and narrow it to a series of topics that she can discuss within a classroom setting. Not only is there a need (or exigence) to discuss environmental issues, the student is also a biology major who plans to deal with related issues in the future. Some of her ideas come from her experiences, some from classes she is taking, and some from current events.

Because this student does careful work at the beginning of the term, she has several topics for use throughout the term. She gives an informative speech on the disappearance of frogs. Later, she discusses the controversial questions that some scientists have raised regarding the destruction of the ozone layer. In a third presentation, she urges listeners to buy a water-purifying system. Her narrative speech describes a flood that she has experienced.

Cross Reference

This refers to Geissner's point that communication depends on subjective factors in each speaking situation.

Select a Purpose   You do not speak in public by accident; rather, public speaking functions to accomplish specific goals. This is the "why" of public speaking, as described in Geissner's theory in Chapter 1. Before you speak, you should have a clear idea of what you are attempting to accomplish. Both at the outset, and as you work on your speech, identify a general purpose for your speech and begin to formulate a specific purpose. In addition, writing out a summarizing statement will help both you and your listeners understand the central idea of the speech.

General Purposes   Many rhetoric scholars have looked at what speakers attempt to accomplish in speeches. Almost 2,000 years ago, St. Augustine, who was a scholar of rhetoric, identified three purposes for speaking: to teach, to please, and to move.[3] In the sixteenth century, George Campbell identified four: to enlighten the understanding, to please the imagination, to move the passions, and to influence the will.[4] In this century, Alan Monroe said we attempt to inform, entertain, stimulate through emotion, or convince through reasoning.[5] Today, most speech texts identify these three general purposes:

- *To inform*, in which your intention is to explain, teach, describe, or provide a basis for knowledge.

- *To persuade*, in which your intention is either to change your audience's beliefs, values, attitudes, or actions or to maintain and intensify the practices your listeners already have.

- *To entertain*, in which you provide amusement and diversion, helping your audience release tensions and laugh as you take a humorous look at your subject.

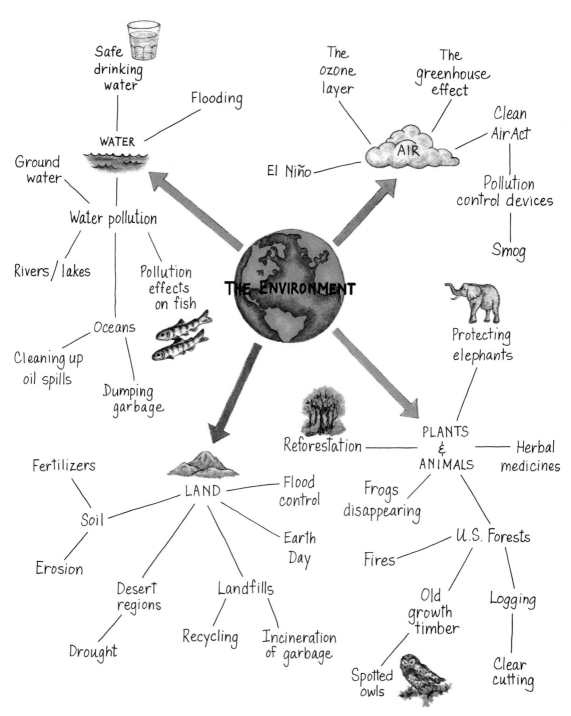

Figure 2.1 *A mind map.*

These intentions or purposes often overlap. A college recruiter may, for example, attempt to persuade her listeners to attend a specific college, but she does so by both informing them about the college and entertaining them with humorous accounts of campus life. In addition, there may be several audiences represented in the crowd, necessitating different purposes—she entertains the alumni with stories, informs the parents or spouses about financial aid, and persuades the prospective students to fill in application forms.

Cross Reference

There is more detailed information on speech purposes in Chapters 3, 14, and 16.

In the classroom, your instructor generally assigns a purpose for each speech. For instance, you may be assigned an informative speech. If this is so, your research will focus on discovering and presenting unbiased, factual material that will give your audience a better understanding of the subject. At other times, your purpose is to persuade. Then you select convincing and motivating materials that will help your listeners believe and act in the ways you desire. Chapters 3, 14, and 16 look further at ways speakers focus their speech purposes more narrowly.

Specific Purpose Because you speak intentionally, you desire to produce a response in your listeners. Often it helps to think of responses in cognitive, affective, or behavioral areas. When your aim is for *cognitive* outcomes, you intend through your speech to influence beliefs, understandings, and other mental processes. *Affective* outcomes are the emotional responses, the feelings you hope to arouse in listeners. *Behavioral* outcomes are the actions you want audience members to perform as a result of the speech.

Think about what you specifically want your listeners to think, feel, or do, and write that into a specific goal statement. Include your awareness of the listeners' desired response by using the words "my audience" within the goal statement. Here are a couple of specific purpose statements a student might formulate for her speech on dioxin, depending on her general speech purpose:

> *To inform my audience about the dangers of toxic byproducts such as dioxin caused by chlorine bleaching that can be eliminated by using alternative processes.*
>
> *To persuade my audience to change their shopping habits and thus create a demand for safer products that do not produce dioxin.*

Although most instructors have their students begin the specific purpose statement with the phrase "to inform my audience," some professors prefer that their students write the specific purpose as a statement of the outcome they want to produce in their listeners—one that specifies the desired audience response, like this:

> *As a result of my speech, my audience will* know *specific steps they can take to change their shopping habits and demand safer products that eliminate chlorine bleaching. (informative speech)*

As a result of my speech, my audience will change *their shopping habits and purchase safer products that eliminate chlorine bleaching. (persuasive speech)*

At this stage of her preparation, the speaker has this much of her speech formulated:

Topic:	Toxic Paper Products: Dioxin in Our Lives
General purpose:	To persuade
Specific purpose:	To persuade my audience to change their shopping habits by demanding safer paper products

She is now ready to begin formulating a statement that summarizes or captures the major idea of the speech. This is known as the central idea.

Teaching Idea

If you would like a paper-and-pencil activity that could be done individually or in pairs, the Student Resource Workbook has an assignment relating to speech purposes. *See also exercises 2 and 4 at the end of the chapter.*

Central Idea   The *central idea* is a summary statement of the main theme or idea of the speech. For this reason, it is also known as the *core idea* or *thesis statement.* It is stated in one declarative sentence such as this:

Chlorine bleaching creates dangerous byproducts, but consumers can improve the health of the environment by purchasing alternative products.

Begin to formulate your central idea early; however, don't be afraid to revise it during the speech preparation and organization as you do additional research and focus more clearly on the essence of your message.

It is important that you state the central idea in your speech, usually in the introduction. This helps your audience know what you are going to talk about, and it helps them prepare to listen. Look at how this speaker incorporated her central idea into the introduction of her speech in order to inform her audience directly of her purpose for speaking:[6]

Today, I want to explain why I think these products, as they are currently manufactured, are dangerous to our environment and possibly to our own health. I hope to encourage you to take action to solve this problem. I have found that in almost every case, alternatives to chlorine bleached products exist and work. By sharing what I have learned with you, I hope to convince you to change your own shopping habits—to use your consumer power to create a demand for safer products and to work to change legislation to protect our environment from the effects of chlorine bleaching processes.

In summary, topic and purpose selection is obviously a major part of invention—a process that frustrates many students. If you select a topic that interests you, narrow it to a manageable subtopic, and formulate your general and specific purposes for the speech, you will have the focus you need as you continue your preparation.

Interviewing a knowl-edgeable person is a good way to gather information for a speech.

Teaching Idea

Discuss the problem in exercise 3. If two students prepare a speech on the same subject, their first reaction is generally to panic. Help them see that, though some of their material may be similar, different indi-viduals consult different sources and prepare unique speeches.

Cross Reference

The theme of oral, print, and electronic cultures is introduced in Chapter 1.

Do Research Next, begin the process of gathering materials that provide the information that you will include in the speech itself. These materials come from several sources that will be developed further in Chapter 7. Here is a brief overview.

Personal Experience Draw examples and insights from your personal knowledge or experiences with your subject. For instance, Sara took a year off from school to be a nanny in Belgium. She drew from her experiences with an employment agency and her employers to discuss her overseas job.

Oral Sources Plan interviews with knowledgeable persons in one of two ways: a direct, face-to-face interview or a telephone interview. In either case, contact the person beforehand, set up an appropriate time for the interview, have spe-cific questions prepared, and be prompt to the interview. For her speech on car-jacking, Carol interviewed a police officer. In addition, she used materials from lecture notes she took in other classes.

Print Sources Find books, magazines, pamphlets, government documents, and other materials related to your topic. Sara supplemented her speech by using statistics from an article she read on nannies. In addition, she used a newspaper report for additional information on opportunities for nannies, both male and female, in Belgium as well as other European countries.

Electronically Stored Resources In addition to print sources, video and audio recordings provide information. Look for facts and examples from television programs or radio news broadcasts. Consult media libraries with extensive collections of tapes—both video and audio—on a wide variety of subjects. (You can also write away for transcripts of radio and television broadcasts.) Finally, if you have access to a computer with a modem, you can use it to download information from a variety of data banks instantly.

This is a brief overview of what the Romans designated as the canon of invention. It includes the procedures you follow to find and narrow a topic, to identify a general and specific purpose for the speech, to write a central idea, and to gather information from research. The next step in speechmaking is to put your ideas in order.

Disposition

Throughout the world, speechmakers organize their material into culturally meaningful patterns. The body of rules that contain the organizational patterns common in Western ways of speaking is called the canon of disposition. One dictionary definition of *disposition* is "orderly placement or distribution." For instance, the disposition of real property in an estate settlement is the orderly way that property is divided up and distributed among the survivors. Similarly, disposition of speech materials is the way the information is divided up and distributed in the speech. In this class, you will learn several speech patterns that are typical of speeches in U.S. institutions. Chapters 9 and 16 cover them in more detail.

Cross Reference

Chapter 9 gives the most common patterns. Chapter 16 adds patterns that are effective in persuasive speeches.

Most speeches in the Western speaking tradition have three major parts: the introduction, the body, and the conclusion. To be an effective speaker, you will first orient your audience toward the subject by introducing the topic and relating it to your listeners' lives. This leads to the body of the speech, the part that generally takes up most of the speaking time, where you explain and develop your major ideas. After the major points, you leave your listeners with a memorable conclusion. Taken as a whole, the outline looks like this:

Cross Reference

Quintilian was introduced in Chapter 1. Details on introductions, bodies, and conclusions are found in Chapter 9.

Introduction An introduction has these four major functions according to the Roman educator Quintilian:[7]

1. Orient the audience by drawing their attention to your subject.
2. Motivate them to listen by relating the topic to their concerns.

3. Demonstrate that you are a credible speaker on the subject by linking yourself with the topic.

4. Preview the major point of the speech by stating the central idea.

Speech Assignment

There is an assignment for a single point speech in the Student Resource Workbook. If students did not introduce themselves in Chapter 1, this speech can function as an introduction. Have students select one major characteristic of themselves or a classmate, then support that idea with three pieces of information.

Body   In the body, you will present your major ideas and develop each one using evidence for clarification and support. There are many ways to organize the body of the speech, and you can choose from common patterns such as problem–solution, causes–effects, and topical. This results in a linear pattern illustrated in this skeleton outline of a cause–effect speech:

    A. Causes
        a. First cause
            1. Support
            2. Support
        b. Second cause
            1. Support
            2. Support
    B. Effects
        a. First effect
            1. Support
            2. Support
        b. Second effect
            1. Support
            2. Support

Conclusion   To be most effective as a speaker, you will not end your speeches abruptly; instead, you provide a sense of closure that ties the ideas together and leaves your audience with something to take away from the speech. Conclusions often have these four parts:

1. A transition to the conclusion

2. A summary of the major ideas

3. A reference to the introduction

4. A final memorable statement

Connectives   In addition to introductions, bodies, and conclusions, you provide transitions between ideas—the connectives that tie the thoughts of the speech together and aid in a smooth flow from point to point. These connectives include words and phrases such as "Next," "Finally," or "We have looked at the arguments for spanking; now let's turn to the reasons some experts feel the practice is harmful to children." Connectives help your listeners keep their place in the speech by relating the various points to one another and to the speech as a whole.

Once you have the material (invention) and the general framework or organizational pattern for the speech (disposition), you can begin to refine the language of the speech and then put it into your memory so that you can deliver it effectively to an audience. The principles for these aspects of speechmaking are found in the final three canons: style, memory, and delivery.

Style

Many people think of style as the way a person walks, talks, and dresses. So if someone says, "I really like your style," he or she is probably referring to the way you present yourself. However, in rhetoric, style means *language*, and the canon of style contains the principles for using language effectively in speaking and writing as well. That is why you will find style manuals in writing classes that list the rules for presenting ideas clearly in words.

Put the finishing touches on your ideas by polishing the words you use to present your thoughts, always with an ear tuned to your listeners. Here are a few general guidelines for effective use of language in public speaking:

1. Choose appropriate vocabulary and grammar for both the occasion and the audience. This means that you adapt your vocabulary to audience characteristics such as occupation, age, or educational level.

2. Omit language that is offensive to some or all of your listeners. Eliminate swear words, as well as sexist, racist, or ageist language from your speeches.

3. Choose words that listeners understand—either define technical terms and jargon or eliminate those words.

4. Use fewer slang expressions. The language used in public speeches is generally more formal than the language used in everyday conversation.

More information on the canon of style is found in Chapter 11.

Memory

In literate cultures, memory is sometimes called the "lost" canon. Most modern speakers do not memorize their speeches; rather, they use note cards or a prepared manuscript, TelePrompTers, or cue cards. Chapters 4, 7, and 12 give you ideas to help you remember your speech.

Putting a speech into your memory does not mean that you memorize every word that you will say. In fact, doing so is highly risky for beginning speakers. Forgetting even a few simple words often leads to public embarrassment. Instead, your goal should be to remember your major ideas and the organizational pattern you have chosen for your speech. Thus, when you are in front of the audience, you clearly know your ideas, but you do not rely on exact memorization of single words or phrases. As you prepare, put your major ideas

Note

Many students consistently confuse the canon of style with delivery. It may help to bring a style manual to class and explain that, in the study of rhetoric, style relates to word choices, grammar, and so on.

Note

At some point, you may wish to distribute a list of criteria for grading. The Instructor's Manual has the criteria that members of the Speech Communication Association (SCA) developed. This lets students see how speech professors across the country evaluate speeches.

Rehearse so that you know the main ideas you intend to discuss instead of trying to memorize the specific wording of your speech.

on note cards. Rather than writing complete sentences, write only single words, concepts, and statistics that will jog your memory as you deliver your speech.

Adequate rehearsal is a vital part of the entire process. Go over the speech mentally; then find a quiet place where you can deliver it out loud, using your note cards. Plan to rehearse several times before the speech day and again just before you enter the classroom. Each time, select slightly different wording. Focus on looking away from your notes and communicating your ideas in a conversational manner.

Delivery

Teaching Idea

Exercise 5 summarizes this entire section. It would be an appropriate journal entry.

Finally, the day comes when you actually perform your speech before an audience. This is a major source of anxiety for most beginning speakers, and Chapter 4 is devoted to the apprehension that speakers—both amateurs and professionals—face. The canon of delivery provides guidelines on nonverbal behaviors, such as gestures, that make you an effective performer. Your presentation includes both the words you say and the manner in which you say them. Various aspects of delivery are covered in Chapter 12.

Briefly, your speech will be more effective if you make eye contact with your listeners, have pleasant facial expressions, and smile when it is appropriate. Throughout the delivery, visualize yourself as being in a dialogue or conversation with your listeners. Focus, not on giving something *to* them, but on creating something *with* them—which is the key to dialogical public speaking.

KEY CONCEPT Principles of Speaking: The Five Canons of Rhetoric

Invention Select a topic and purpose, and gather information to be used in the speech.

Disposition Organize the speech into an appropriate speech pattern. Most speeches have an introduction, a body, and a conclusion.

Style Select appropriate language for the audience and the occasion.

Memory Rehearse the major ideas of the speech.

Delivery Present the speech to an audience.

Summary

Preparing a speech is a creative process in which a unique work of verbal art is fashioned for a specific audience and occasion. Good speakers go through a process of preparation, and speakers in Western traditions use the principles in the five canons of rhetoric described by the Romans. These include invention, disposition, style, memory, and delivery.

It is not enough to simply get up in front of an audience and talk—good speaking requires a great deal of thought and preparation. One of the major challenges facing you as a beginning speaker is topic selection. Look for topics that interest you and are of importance to your listeners. After selecting a topic, focus on your intention or purpose for the speech and write out the specific responses you want from your listeners. Then, collect information, organize it into a pattern, select appropriate language for your ideas, rehearse, and deliver the speech.

This chapter has given you general principles that apply to speechmaking. Out of the principles, there are some simple ideas to remember for each speech:

1. Be sure you understand the assignment. For classroom speeches, know specific criteria on which your speech will be judged. In real-life settings, find out about the size of the group, the reason for the gathering, the purpose

for your speech, and the resources (such as chalkboards, microphones, and overhead projectors) that will be available to you.

2. Settle on a topic early and stay with it. This gives you enough time to gather sufficient information and to step back from your preparation to allow the ideas to come together.

3. Prepare well in advance. This can help control your nervousness.

4. Consider your audience throughout the speech. Think of your speech as a dialogue with your listeners. What do they know? What do they need to know? How do they feel about your subject?

Student Speech

Come Watch Lacrosse

by Andrés Lucero, St. John's University, New York

The following is an example of a single point speech. The speaker, Andrés Lucero, tries to convince his audience to attend a lacrosse game. He gives three reasons why they should do so: lacrosse is fast and exciting, it is hard hitting, and it requires strategy.

In the introduction, Andrés gains the audience's attention and relates his sport to something in their experience. After linking himself with the topic, he makes his single point.

Have you ever sat and watched a long, boring baseball game? You all know the deal: ball . . . strike . . . ball . . . strike . . . ten minutes later, a pop up. Well, if you've endured such "entertainment," and agree that there might be more exciting things to do with your time, you should try watching a sport created by Native Americans—one that is fast and exciting, hard hitting, and very strategic. A sport like lacrosse. As you may know, I play lacrosse for the university. Today, I will explain why you should watch a lacrosse game.

Here is his first reason to watch the game.

Lacrosse is fast and exciting. In fact, it is called the fastest sport in the world, because the clock runs constantly and only stops for a few seconds when the ball goes out of bounds. Unlike baseball or football, players never have time to rest. For that reason, there are many substitutions during the game. Since there is always action on the field, there is never a boring moment. Watching lacrosse is similar to watching a long rally in a tennis match, yet the game itself is as hard hitting as football.

Andrés uses the word *second* as a signpost to signal that he has moved to another point. His final sentence leads directly to his last point.

A second reason to watch lacrosse is because it is a very physical game. Since it is a contact sport, not surprisingly, there is lots of rough contact. If I am not careful, I can be seriously injured. I know this from experience. In my first month of college play, I had a painful introduction to Division I lacrosse. On too many occasions, I found myself lying flat on my back, with nothing but sky in view. I discovered that there are many lacrosse players who set up a kill and look to just cream a guy. However, a player does not have to be roughed up. Some players—myself included—try to use strategy to outsmart the opponent.

And this is another reason you should watch a lacrosse match. Good players and good teams do not just go out and run around the field, they plan what they will do; then they execute their plan. When you watch a game, you can see how the entire team works together to make goals. Most of the finesse teams, those who concentrate on strategy, win more often than those who look for ways to injure their opponents.

His conclusion reviews the main points, then ends memorably by referring to his opening scenario.

In conclusion, you now have three good reasons to watch a lacrosse game— it is a fast, hard-hitting sport that requires much strategy to win. So the next time you find yourself sitting in front of the TV watching a ball . . . then a strike . . . then a ball . . . then ten minutes later, a pop up, get up and go watch a lacrosse game—experience it first hand!

Questions and Exercises

1. Sit down with a piece of blank paper, and think of possible topics for classroom speeches. It may help to fold the paper into eight sections and label each using a different category, then think of possibilities for each category. Use categories such as people, places, issues, events, controversies, international topics, processes, or ideas.

   Consult your texts, a television guide, current newspapers and magazines, your experiences, and your interests for possible topics.

   After you have come up with several topic possibilities, select two or three that interest you and make a mind map that further subdivides the topic.

   File this paper for use during the term.

   To get a good start on your speechmaking assignments for the term, set up three or four files on different topics. Throughout the course, be alert for information in each subject area. When you hear a program or see information that relates to your subjects, clip, photocopy, or take notes and place them in the file.

2. Select a topic from the list you made in exercise 1. Then write the general purpose, the specific purpose, and the central idea for a speech on that subject.

3. Let's say that two people in the class, unbeknown to each other, get the same idea for a speech topic from reading the cover story of a current newsmagazine—hunting elephants to near extinction for their ivory tusks. Using what you know about creativity and the canon of invention, why should this not be a problem?

4. Formulate a general purpose and specific purpose statement for a speech on each of the following topics:

   - Shopping at resale (thrift) shops
   - The five stages of conflict
   - Donating blood
   - Vitamin C

5. Consider the five canons of rhetoric: invention, disposition, style, memory, and delivery. Rank them in order of difficulty for you personally. Which will be easiest? Most difficult? Why? What plans can you make at the outset of the course to work on the area or areas in which you anticipate the greatest challenge?

Key Terms

creativity
general purpose
specific purpose
cognitive outcomes
affective outcomes

behavioral outcomes
central idea
connectives
invention
disposition
style
memory
delivery

Notes

1. For a further discussion of creativity, see Weisberg, R. W. (1986). *Creativity: Genius and other myths*. New York: W. H. Greenman.
2. Bitzer, L. F. (1968). The rhetorical situation. *Philosophy and Rhetoric, 1,* 1–14.
3. Augustine. (1958). *On Christian doctrine: Book IV* (D. W. Robertson, Jr., Trans.). New York: Liberal Arts Press. (Original work written 416.)
4. Campbell, G. (1776, 1963). *The philosophy of rhetoric* (L. Bitzer, Ed.). Carbondale: Southern Illinois University Press.
5. Monroe, A. H. (1962). *Principles and types of speech* (5th ed.). Chicago: Scott, Foresman, & Co.
6. Place, M. F. (1992). Toxic paper products: Dioxin in our lives. Student speech, Oregon State University, Corvallis, Oregon.
7. Quintilian. (1920–1922). *The institutio oratoria of Quintilian* (4 Vols.). (H. E. Butler, Trans.) The Loeb Classical Library. Cambridge: Harvard University Press.

3

Public Speaking and Culture

At the end of this chapter, you should be able to

- Define culture
- Explain four core elements of culture as they relate to public speaking
- Tell how communication produces, reinforces, repairs, and changes cultural beliefs, values, attitudes, and actions
- Explain irreconcilable cultural differences
- Describe three ways of dealing with diversity
- List guidelines for ethical communication in a pluralistic culture

Note

This chapter is central to the general themes of the book: that culture influences and is influenced by public speaking and that other cultures have different public speaking traditions based on their core beliefs, values, and attitudes. It further explores ways that public speaking can help people who live in pluralistic cultures deal with differences that might otherwise divide them.

In the Crown Heights section of New York City in August of 1991, a car driven by a Hasidic Jew struck and killed a seven-year-old West Indian black child. That night, a group of young West Indians retaliated by stabbing a Jewish man. Three days of rioting followed these incidents. Fourteen months later, after a jury acquitted the teen who had twice confessed to the stabbing, a new round of furious accusations threatened the already fragile social fabric of the ethnically mixed community. In response to the charges and countercharges of Jews and blacks, Mayor David Dinkins made a televised speech in an attempt to heal the divisions. In his sixteen-minute appeal for "reason, respect, and reconciliation," the mayor reaffirmed community ideals. An excerpt from his speech demonstrates his central idea:

> *Those who would seek to split our city apart by race or religion or sexual orientation are delighted to suggest that we New Yorkers do not have the will or the way to continue to live side by side in peace. That groups in conflict will never recognize or embrace their shared history of persecution and enslavement. That in a city peopled by immigrants from every world culture and creed, there can only be chaos.*
>
> *I will not accept that poisonous philosophy. Our city will not be divided. Race-baiters and rabble-rousers do not understand our lives. Because every day and every night, on subways and buses, at work stations and in offices, at lunch counters and in libraries, in our parks and in our movie houses—New Yorkers live and work and learn and play, side by side and shoulder to shoulder.*[1]

For Further Reading

See J. W. Carey. (1989). *Communication as culture: Essays on media and society.* Boston: Unwin Hyman, and W. B. Pearce. (1989). *Communication and the human condition.* Carbondale: Southern Illinois University Press.

The mayor spoke *intentionally*. His purpose was to use words as a means, not only of encouraging community members with different cultural backgrounds to maintain their commitments to common values and goals, but also to repair the causes of distrust in the community. His speech is an example of the importance of rhetoric, or persuasive public speaking, in building and maintaining a cohesive society.

This chapter discusses the relationship between public speaking and culture. It shows the necessity of speechmaking as a way of creating, maintaining, and changing a society's beliefs and practices. After a definition of culture, it will focus on ways that culture influences public speaking. Then it discusses how purposive public speaking influences culture. It closes with ethical guidelines for communication among people from various cultural backgrounds.

Cultural Foundations for Public Speaking

Individuals who live in a society share a way of life—a culture. For a culture to survive and remain healthy, cultural patterns must be constantly constructed and reconstructed, and members of every culture continually transmit and reinforce their cultural beliefs and practices through public speaking.

A culture is a way of life that includes shared beliefs and values, predictable ways of behaving, and such things as food, language, and clothing styles. Within a larger culture, such as the United States, there are a number of smaller co-cultural groups.

Teaching Idea

To connect public speaking and culture for the students, point out how Mayor Dinkins's speech attempted to "reconstruct" the culture of Crown Heights after the riots.

A culture is commonly defined as the predictable patterns that make up both the visible and underlying characteristics of a society.[2] This includes external or visible patterns of dress, art, food, and language as well as implicit or subconscious core beliefs, attitudes, values, and other factors that affect the way its members view the world. Through public speaking, we attempt to influence culture. For example, speakers argue for "English-only" laws; others challenge cultural assumptions regarding "proper" roles for women and men.

Many of the cultural patterns of the United States reflect a middle-class orientation that derives largely from the literate tradition, predominantly established by European males. These patterns shape the major institutions of this society, including its educational, economic, and political systems. For these reasons, they are designated *Euro-American* or *dominant* patterns in this text.

Some of the most fundamental assumptions that members of a culture hold make up their *world view*.[3] A culture's world view consists of the assumptions inherent in the philosophical and religious traditions of the society. Simply put, it is derived from the culture's answers to the larger questions of life: Who are we? Where did we come from? Why are we here? What happens after we die? What is truth? How can we know it? What is important in life? What is the purpose of suffering? How should human beings relate to nature and material possessions?

The answers to such questions guide both how we speak publicly and what we consider important enough to be a speech topic. To illustrate, there are profound differences in topic choice and in what seem to be reasonable conclusions between cultures that see humans as apart from and in control of nature and those that see people as an integral part of nature—between those who believe in owning property and those who believe that land cannot be owned, between people who believe that we learn about the world through scientific experiments and linear logical reasoning and those who believe that we learn more through intuition.

Core Elements of Culture

Teaching Idea

Use the transparency in the Instructor's Manual, or refer to Figure 3.1 as a basis for defining this terminology. Emphasize that these are not isolated characteristics. Beliefs, values, attitudes, and actions overlap and influence one another. And they can change over time.

For Further Reading

See M. Rokeach. (1968, 1972). *Beliefs, attitudes, and values: A theory of organization and change.* San Francisco: Jossey-Bass, and M. Rokeach. (1973). *The nature of human values.* New York: The Free Press. See Teaching Note 3.1 in the Instructor's Manual for further elaboration.

Communication professor W. Barnett Pearce[4] explains that cultures provide their members with a pool of *resources* that he defines as "logics of meaning and action that define what is obligatory, legitimate, dubious, or prohibited."[5] These *cultural resources* include a system of beliefs, values, and attitudes as well as a set of predictable behaviors that provide a foundation for every area of life, including public speaking.

Beliefs   A belief is a mental acceptance that something is true or false, correct or incorrect, valid or invalid, and we often speak in public to change or to reaffirm our audience's beliefs.[6] Beliefs may be based on study or on investigation; in contrast, people hold beliefs—such as a conviction about the existence of life on other planets—without much factual information. Further, it is possible to believe something that is not true; that is, people have false beliefs or misconceptions.

We have hundreds of thousands of beliefs, ranging from general ("with hard work you can do anything") to specific ("with hard work you can get an A in this class"). Beliefs also range from inconsequential personal beliefs that are relatively easy to change ("German cars are better than Japanese cars") to core beliefs that are central to our mental system and are consequently difficult to change. Although individual beliefs vary from person to person, most of the members of a culture share some core cultural beliefs. For instance, most people in the United States accept the cultural belief in the importance of the individual. They would not easily change their minds and begin to think that one's family obligations or obligation to a group supersedes the individual. However, such beliefs regarding group obligations are common in collectivist societies, which compose 70 percent of global cultures.[7] Knowledge of your audience's shared beliefs is important in planning the content of your speeches.

Values   Values are the mental programs by which both individuals and cultures judge what is good and bad, right and wrong, moral and immoral, beautiful and ugly, kind and cruel, appropriate and inappropriate.[8] Simply put, the values of a culture are the ideas and ideals important to the members of that culture that provide the basis for its behaviors. According to Milton Rokeach,[9] we have only a few dozen values.

Although values vary from individual to individual, there are underlying value clusters that are characteristic of members of U.S. culture. Several years

Values help define a culture, for they are society's ideals of what is right, good, beautiful, and appropriate. Reaching out to others is one of several core American values that motivated these people to travel to the Midwest to help shore up Mississippi levees during a flood. Public speakers often appeal to shared values.

Teaching Idea

Have students compare their values with those of their classmates. Discuss (1) how (or if) they differ from their parents, and (2) how public speaking has led to changes in cultural values over a period of decades. *Use exercise 2 or the material "Explore Your Personal Values" found in the Student Resource Workbook.*

ago, speech scholars Edward Steele and Charles Redding[10] identified the following seven core values that they found emphasized in American political campaign speeches:

- *Individualism* Emphasis on individual choice and freedom, failure or success through personal efforts, the individual's right to participate in government.

- *Puritan and pioneer morality* Seeing the world as good and evil; casting issues as right and wrong, just or unjust; reaching out to help others in humanitarian ways.

- *Achievement and success* Emphasis on work, wealth, status, and material possessions.

- *Change and progress* Looking to the future, prizing what is new and different.

- *Equality of opportunity*   Ideals of equal treatment and justice for all.

- *Effort and optimism*   Belief that hard work will pay off and that we can triumph over obstacles; valuing a positive, upbeat, cheerful approach to life.

- *Efficiency, practicality, and pragmatism*   Valuing problem-solving inventions that are useful, quick, and workable.

Teaching Idea

Exercise 3 is appropriate here. If an awards ceremony is being broadcast on television around this time, you might videotape part of it and show it to the class as a whole. Look for the values and beliefs that are emphasized.

You can hear these values praised in one way or another as you listen to public speeches. For example, President Bush's final State of the Union message emphasized changes that will result from winning the cold war against communism (progress, pioneer morality). He praised the soldiers of the Gulf War for "their special style, their rambunctious, optimistic bravery, their do-or-die unity unhampered by class or race or religion" (individualism, success).[11] He urged an overhaul of government (efficiency), hard work by members of Congress to overcome the problems of the economy (effort and optimism), and opportunities for home ownership for the poor (equality of opportunity).

Attitudes   Think of attitudes as preferences—our likes and dislikes that are directed toward specific objects (including people and symbols) or situations (including events, issues, and behaviors). Attitudes have a *mental component* that involves beliefs, an *emotional component* that involves feelings, as well as a *behavioral component* that influences actions.[12]

Because attitudes are preferences, people often express their attitudes by stating an opinion, and you may hear statements like this: "I like eating out, but I strongly disapprove of having a tip automatically added onto my bill." Although there are many acceptable differences in attitudes among members of a culture—not everyone feels the same about jogging, for instance—on many basic issues members of the society tend to share certain core attitudes, and like core beliefs, core attitudes are difficult to change. When you appeal to a core attitude in a speech, you are more likely to be persuasive. Some characteristic attitudes that recur in speeches are:

- Positive toward democracy and negative toward communism

- Positive about education and negative toward ignorance

- Positive toward voter registration and negative toward stuffing the ballot box

Cross Reference

Chapter 16 discusses persuasive purposes when audience members' beliefs and attitudes are inconsistent with their actions.

Although attitudes influence actions, our behaviors may contradict our stated attitudes. Consequently, we may have a positive attitude about democracy and voting but neglect to go to the polls on election day. We like learning but neglect our own personal studies or vote against a school levy. Often, when our actions do not match our beliefs and attitudes, we feel hypocritical. A public speaker may then urge us to change our beliefs to match our behaviors—or to alter our behaviors to match our attitudes. For instance, if you generally have a positive attitude toward helping others (a core cultural attitude) but fail to do anything for those in need, you might respond to a speaker who urges you to act by providing you with specific information on how you can get involved.

Actions   Out of the wide range of actions that are physically possible, members of a culture select a narrowed group of behaviors that they consider appropriate and normal in specific situations, including public speaking. These are known as *conventional* or *normative* behaviors. Normative behaviors usually fall within a range of acceptable options. People who deviate from the normative range are considered highly individualistic or, if extreme, "deviant" or possibly criminal. Although actions vary from individual to individual, society's members act predictably in many areas. For instance, we agree—for safety's sake—to drive on the right side of the road. To maintain orderly interactions, we wait in lines until it is our turn to check out at a supermarket. Similarly, in communicative events, there are normative behaviors for speaking and listening in public, interpersonal, and group contexts.

We often speak to encourage audiences to act in ways that benefit society. For instance, you may urge people to donate blood, to write a letter to a congressional representative, or to protest against an injustice.

Basic Assumptions

Teaching Idea

To explore cultural issues, have students do exercise 4 here.

Beliefs, values, attitudes, and actions are not separate, as Figure 3.1 shows. They combine to form a set of core assumptions and behaviors that are characteristic of a culture and contribute to the way that members of the culture speak in public. Edward Stewart and Milton Bennett[13] have compared cultural patterns cross-culturally. Their book, *American Cultural Patterns*, outlines the following four clusters of core beliefs, attitudes, and values that form the foundation for much of the dominant U.S. culture.

- *Perception of the self*   The focus on the individual as a psychologically unique, singular member of the social order is "the integral assumption of the culture."[14] People influenced by the dominant culture view themselves as active, doing persons who draw on self-motivation, rather than fate or coercion by others, in order to achieve and make choices. They actively set personal goals and strive to accomplish them.

- *Forms of social relations*   A common tenet of the culture is that individuals are valuable and of worth simply because they are human. Since people are equal, each one deserves fair treatment; as a result, they often write out procedures and laws to ensure fairness. However, equality means equality of opportunity, rather than equality of ability, and people are expected to work for what they get. As a result, individuals receive differing rewards that correspond with their achievements.

Figure 3.1 *Beliefs, values, attitudes, and actions.*

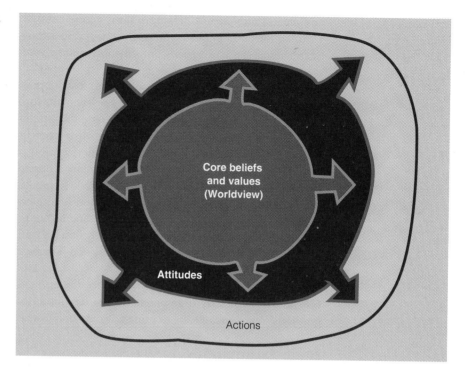

- *Perception of the world* Historically, those who are part of the dominant U.S. culture have believed that humans possess souls that set them apart from nature and make them unique from other animals. They have seen the physical world, in contrast, as a material reality that can be measured and quantified. Consequently, they see the universe as operating by rational rules with effects that are traceable to natural causes. The earth is a resource that can be conquered, owned, and used. In short, nature presents a series of problems to be solved through reasoning and application of technology.

- *Forms of activity* People in the United States tend to be action-oriented people who make things happen by defining and clarifying goals then moving to solve problems; they like to see measurable achievements. Competition serves as a motivating force. In their fast-paced lives, time is a resource to spend, save, or waste. Inactive people are sometimes called "free-loaders."

Co-Cultural Groups

Multicultural societies such as ours include many smaller groups that do not share the dominant culture's patterns in one or more areas. Some are *ethnic minorities* such as African Americans, Native Americans, Asian Americans, or Latinos, who come from different linguistic, historical, religious, and public speaking traditions. Others are *cognitive minorities*[15] whose world view or belief system sets them apart from the dominant culture. They include groups like Seventh Day Adventists or pacifists who hold to a set of beliefs that result in practices that differ from those of the majority. Speeches within those groups often emphasize alternative beliefs, values, and actions. Still others are members of *countercultural* groups who live out alternative lifestyles in a conscious rejection of mainstream patterns in one or more areas. The hippies of the 1960s and members of the youth culture fall within this category.

In spite of co-cultural differences, members of various groups often interact effectively in societal institutions such as corporations or universities because they share enough common beliefs and values to work together toward common goals. For instance, a Latino and a pacifist may have different ways of thinking and behaving in some areas of their lives. However, when individuals from these groups come together in public situations, they share enough common ground to communicate competently. At other times, however, cultural differences divide people, and history is full of civil wars, persecutions of minority groups, and ethnic unrest, both nationally and globally. Later in this chapter, we discuss what happens when groups have profound differences that are seemingly irreconcilable.

In short, members of a society share a basic cultural orientation, but cultures are made up of individuals who constantly negotiate and rethink aspects of their inherited culture. The result is that each individual is in a sense a culture maker[16] who inherits resources from dominant cultural patterns as well as from nondominant groups but who adapts and transforms them to fit his or her personal reality. Often effective public speaking contributes to these changes.

KEY CONCEPT   Cultural Foundations for Public Speaking

Core elements of culture   Each culture provides its members with resources that guide their beliefs and behaviors. These resources influence what we speak about as well as how we speak in public.

Beliefs   We have thousands of mental conceptions of what is true or false, correct or incorrect. Some are inconsequential; some are core beliefs that are difficult to change.

Values   We make judgments regarding what is right and wrong, moral and immoral, beautiful and ugly, and so on.

Attitudes   Our positive or negative feelings, directed toward specific objects and situations, include beliefs, feelings, and tendencies to respond.

Actions   We consider a range of behaviors to be normal in specific circumstances, including appropriate public speaking and listening behaviors.

Basic assumptions The dominant culture in the United States includes a set of core assumptions and behaviors that characterize this society and influence public speaking within it. They include an individualistic sense of self, a legalistic basis for social relations, a dualistic perception of the world, and an active approach to problem solving.

Co-cultural groups Within complex societies, there are groups that vary from the dominant culture in one or more areas. They include ethnic minorities, cognitive minorities, and countercultural groups.

Culture's Influence on Public Speaking

As we have seen, public speaking both affects and is affected by culture. External or visible aspects of culture determine the way we present messages, the appropriate forms of delivery, the technological resources such as visual aids that are available to us as we speak. Implicit culture, the subconscious assumptions we hold, determines what we consider to be reasonable, what counts as evidence. It also includes the assumptions we make about humans and human interaction that lead us to choose public speaking as a means of social influence. In short, there are many ways that Euro-American culture influences public speaking. This section discusses three: democratic forms of government, a communication style, and norms for speaking and listening.

Democratic Forms

As a result of the core beliefs, values, and behaviors identified earlier in this chapter, the United States has a democratic form of government. For instance, since we value freedom, ideally, we interact in ways that show respect for individuals, and we emphasize uncoerced choice. Additionally, we believe that individuals are intelligent, reasonable people who can make wise choices if they have adequate information. As a result of these assumptions, we choose persuasion rather than coercion as the dominant means of influencing people in this country.[17] In contrast, there are cultures with different core beliefs and values in which people are not allowed to express their ideas freely and where democracy is not the ruling form.

Another fundamental right that arises from our core ideas and ideals is freedom of speech. Since anyone in our society is free to speak, colleges and universities offer classes in public speaking so that ordinary citizens can learn to organize their ideas clearly, weigh the ideas of others, and contribute to discussion of public issues. Because of the principles of free speech, people are at liberty to say

In our democratic form of government, we allow a variety of viewpoints to be voiced, and individuals use their freedom of speech in an attempt to persuade others to believe as they do.

what they want, even if their ideas offend others. On the other hand, ethical public speakers take responsibility for their words and the effects their speeches have on their listeners.

Communication Style

In addition to a democratic form of government that gives ordinary citizens a right to express their opinions freely, our culture provides us with a style of communication that characterizes the way we conceptualize issues and organize ideas. Stewart and Bennett[18] studied the U.S. style of communication and identified these five components of the communication style that are most often seen in our public speaking:

1. *Problem oriented* Because of the assumption that the world is rational and ordered and that individuals are agents who can act on these problems to solve them, much of the speaking in this country is done to solve problems and resolve issues.

2. *Direct* In our action-oriented society, most speeches are linear and move in a logical line to an explicit conclusion without a lot of contextualization or digression.

3. *Explicit* Speechmakers use clear, concise language and say precisely what they mean rather than depending on nonverbal messages or more indirect allusions.

4. *Personal* In line with our forms of social relations, we relate to one another on the basis of personal experiences that we are willing to disclose. We look for common ground with our listeners in order to establish a relationship with an audience of peers.

Teaching Idea

To highlight how our culture influences our speaking, duplicate and distribute the table in the Instructor's Manual that compares Western and Eastern cultural patterns. Discuss the kinds of public speaking that you might expect in each of the cultural groups, given these core patterns. Or have the class do Activity 3.1 in the Instructor's Manual.

5. *Informal* Because we believe in equality and that no one is inherently better than others, we communicate informally rather than formally although our public speaking is more formal than communication within other contexts.

This direct, explicit style within the United States contrasts with the communication style of other cultural groups, both co-cultural and international, that approach problems more indirectly and more formally. Often, speakers from other groups are less direct and allow for more implicit approaches to problems or issues. A person who identifies with the U.S. communication style might wonder why the speaker does not get to the point and say what is on his or her mind.

Norms for Speaking and Listening

There is a range of appropriate behaviors—both verbal and nonverbal—for communicative acts. The most common norms for U.S. public speaking are the subject of this text. For example, throughout this course, you will study the typical practices in listening, organizing a speech, selecting appropriate language, and delivering a speech. We judge speakers as *competent* or *incompetent*, based on their abilities to adapt to the verbal and nonverbal norms for public speaking in specific settings.

In addition, cultural assumptions influence what we speak about and how we frame our arguments. For instance, a motivational speaker who was addressing an audience dominated by the Euro-American perspective would most likely stress individual effort, freedom, hard work, and choice. However, in a more collectivist culture, such as in Japan, that places a great deal of emphasis on the group, the speaker would emphasize group relationships, stressing the value of individual sacrifice in order to achieve group harmony and reminding listeners of their duties and responsibilities to one another.[19]

KEY CONCEPT

Culture's Influence on Public Speaking

Democratic forms Based on core cultural assumptions and values, all people in a democracy are free to speak, and we use persuasion as a means of influencing one another.

Communication style The style of public speaking common in the United States is problem oriented, direct, explicit, personal, and informal. This contrasts with other cultures' communication styles.

Norms for speaking and listening Cultures provide their members with a range of appropriate behaviors both for speaking and listening to speeches.

Public Speaking's Effect on Culture

Teaching Idea

Have students identify and discuss an area of public policy in which public speaking functioned to produce, maintain, repair, or change structures and laws. Examples include the Vietnam War, health care reform, welfare reform, gun control legislation, gays in the military. *Exercise 1 is appropriate to use with this section. The results of their interview could be a journal entry.*

Although cultures have predictable, discernible ways of thinking and behaving, they are *dynamic*, meaning that they change and evolve over time, as individuals and groups continue to shape and mold their societies, often through public speaking. The history of the United States is characterized by activism directed toward specific cultural changes. When slavery was legal and institutionalized, for instance, many reformers insisted that owning other humans was morally wrong and should be made illegal. Eventually, the legislatures and the courts abolished the institution of slavery. Today, many areas of our culture are changing rapidly as citizens actively and vocally critique society's institutions, attempting to change what they think is wrong or to improve what they believe needs improvement.

As we discussed in Chapter 2, there are three general speech purposes: to inform, to persuade, and to entertain. However, since perpetuating, shaping, and changing a culture is a complex process, we often narrow our speaking purposes even further, for in a dynamic culture we constantly need to:[20]

Speech Assignment

The Student Resource Workbook contains a speech assignment for a tribute. Tributes are speeches that praise cultural beliefs and values, attitudes, and actions. Have students read the sample student tribute at the end of the chapter and the "Tribute to the Dog" in the Student Resource Workbook and identify the values that each speaker is praising.

For Further Reading

R. Nadeau. (1952). The progymnasmata of Aphthonius: In translation. *Speech Monographs*, pp. 264–285.

- *Produce, transmit, or initiate* cultural resources—beliefs, values, attitudes, and actions—in people who do not currently hold them. For instance, through public messages, immigrants learn how to become U.S. citizens. Others who are uninformed about voting procedures learn how to register to vote and how to cast a ballot.

- *Reinforce or maintain* elements of culture in our existing communities. Examples include pep talks given by employers, coaches, and club leaders that encourage their listeners to "keep on keeping on" with the behaviors they are successfully doing.

- *Repair or restore* to a healthy state our cultural coherence when ruptures in our communities threaten to tear apart our society. David Dinkins's speech, cited at the beginning of this chapter, is an example of a speech given to repair rifts in a deeply divided community.

- *Change or transform* cultural beliefs, values, attitudes, and actions when the patterns that people currently hold no longer provide adequate explanations or behaviors. For instance, speakers who believe that people in the United States tend to value success and competition too highly may try to influence audiences to place more value on cooperation and community instead.

These four narrowed purposes—to produce, reinforce, repair, and change cultural realities—are more narrowly focused intentions or subcategories of the

Public Speaking and Your College or University

Not only are there cultural entities such as nations, it is possible to think of smaller organizations as miniature cultures, for each has predictable ways of believing and behaving that distinguish it from other institutions. These organizations were often brought into being by public speaking, and they depend on speechmaking for their existence. Colleges and universities are examples of such organizations. Using your own college or university as a case study, examine ways that public speaking served in the past and serves today to keep the culture of the institution alive and functioning.

The Culture of the Institution Is Produced

Your school began because an individual or group of people had a vision or idea for it.

Questions What was the founding purpose of your school? On what beliefs, values, attitudes, and actions did the originators build? How did the founders speak their vision into reality?

What do you know about early recruitment of students and faculty? Where did the land come from? How did buildings get erected? What was the role of public speaking in each of these areas?

The Culture of the Institution Is Maintained

After the initial buildings were constructed, faculty and students recruited, policies formulated, and the library set up, the college began to graduate students. In order to survive, participants had to recreate the institution anew by speaking their vision to successive generations of students, parents, donors, and faculty members.

Questions How does your school use public speaking to recruit new participants? How does it maintain its buildings and grounds? What parts of its initial vision does it maintain in the present? How? What role does ceremonial

---

Case Study

Use this case study as the basis for a class discussion of the importance of public speaking in creating, perpetuating, and changing a cultural institution. If possible, show a promotional film put out by the school to recruit new students, or invite a student recruiter or fundraiser to address the class and explain the importance of public speaking to the institution.

three general purposes. That is, producing belief may be informative, whereas reinforcing values may be persuasive as well as entertaining.

In summary, cultures are dynamic and changing. As a result, we focus on specific areas of cultural resources and narrow our speech purposes accordingly. Sometimes we attempt to produce cultural beliefs and behaviors in listeners who have little or no information, opinions, or experiences related to our subject; at other times we attempt to strengthen or reaffirm what our audience already knows or does. Third, we speak to repair various aspects of culture when they are in danger of breaking down, and finally, we make attempts to persuade audiences to change their beliefs, attitudes, values, or actions.

speaking have in maintaining the values of the institution?

The Culture of the Institution Is Repaired

The daily reality of school life does not always mesh with the ideals of the institution, and there may be a fraying of the social fabric of the organization. Buildings deteriorate, libraries go out of date; lab equipment breaks and becomes obsolete. Such problems as date rapes, out-of-control parties, and hate speech strain social relations. Funding cutbacks can be divisive as different groups argue over the allocation of scarce resources.

Questions What issues on campus threaten to divide students, faculty, administrators? How does your campus use public speaking to repair these rips in the social fabric? How might you personally speak out regarding the conflict?

In an age of monetary cutbacks or drops in student enrollment, how does your campus rethink its identity and its educational goals? Who determines which courses are discontinued, which majors are cut, which faculty positions are eliminated? How do groups and individuals struggle over competing visions of what is important and valuable, what should be eliminated, and what is nonnegotiable?

The Culture of the Institution Is Changed

As society changes, educational institutions evolve. Although they retain beliefs and values from the past, new educational visions and challenges confront educators as they look toward the twenty-first century.

Questions How is your campus different from the original vision of the founders? How is it preparing for the next century? What beliefs, values, attitudes, and actions are being altered to meet the challenge of the coming years? How does public speaking function to move your school from the present to the future?

 **KEY CONCEPT** ## Public Speaking's Effect on Culture

In addition to the three general purposes of informing, persuading, and entertaining, we narrow our purposes more specifically, and we speak publicly to:

Produce or transmit cultural beliefs, values, attitudes, and actions.

Reinforce or maintain elements of culture.

Repair or restore health to our societies when there are divisive clashes.

Change or transform cultural characteristics by advocating new ways of believing or behaving.

Ethical Considerations

Teaching Idea

The Instructor's Manual includes the Credo for Free and Responsible Communication in a Democratic Society. Duplicate it and use it as a basis for a class discussion.

As we have seen, as members of a culture we share much in common; however, we do not all agree on even the most fundamental issues. Ideally, we allow a variety of viewpoints to be spoken and heard; indeed, an often quoted saying articulates this ideal, "I don't agree with what you say, but I will defend to the death your right to say it." Noble as this sounds, we do not always live up to our highest values, suppressing some voices and shouting down others.

This raises ethical questions. How do we determine right and wrong in public speaking? Should some things be left unsaid? Who decides? How? This section will look at some challenges inherent in living in a multicultural world and present some principles for ethical speaking within this culture that arise out of core Euro-American beliefs and values.

Diversity[21]

Teaching Idea

Using Activity 3.2 in the Instructor's Manual, have students examine underlying core beliefs and values that create irreconcilable differences between people and groups, and explore ways they might seek common ground.

In a society—and in a world—with so many sources of information and belief, groups of people frequently believe and behave in ways that are diametrically opposed to one another. The differences are thus seemingly irreconcilable, and they often lead to tension between individuals and groups who otherwise share much in common. Unless the communicators can find ways to tolerate others who differ or to negotiate their disagreements on basic issues, they may have difficulties in creating a cohesive community. Almost all of our cultural resources can be challenged by those who will not accept them.

People hold irreconcilable beliefs about many issues, and different groups sometimes debate their ideas loudly in public. Debatable issues often relate to deeply held central beliefs. For example, people hold such varying ideas as these about the definition of personhood:

Cross Reference

The idea of common ground or identification is developed more fully in Chapter 15.

A person is a person

- From the moment of conception
- After the fetus has brain waves
- At birth
- When the child is named
- When the child has his or her first birthday

Issues such as these cannot be resolved by observation or by scientific studies. The definition of personhood, for example, depends on underlying assumptions in such areas as philosophy and religion. Nevertheless, individuals staunchly defend one position or another, sometimes condemning those who do not and cannot accept their beliefs.

Emphasizing different core values often leads people to adopt irreconcilable positions regarding issues such as abortion.

Teaching Idea

Broaden the focus to examine differences on an international level. *Use of exercise 5 is appropriate here.*

Similarly, our values sometimes clash with those of others. Because values are associated with what we consider good, appropriate, and moral, we often hold them deeply, and value conflicts are often laden with emotion. Think, for example, of times you have had intrapersonal value conflicts. Perhaps you had to choose between honesty and loyalty to a friend—both fundamental values. If you have experienced such internal value clashes, you know how upsetting these choices can be. For these reasons, value conflicts are some of the most difficult to resolve.

Often major public issues are framed as value conflicts. Take, for example, the abortion issue. Instead of arguing about maintaining or discontinuing a medical procedure, both sides generally claim to be protecting a value. One side identifies itself as PRO-*LIFE*, whereas the other claims to be PRO-*CHOICE*. Since both choice and life are fundamental values, it is difficult for either side to negotiate regarding the value they emphasize. In fact, some activists refer to the opposing side as either "anti-choice" or "baby-killers."

Since attitudes derive from beliefs and values, they also may differ to such an extent that they are irreconcilable. Thus, it is unlikely that those who fight for environmental protection will share loggers' attitudes toward a specific piece of environmental legislation that favors the clear cutting of forests. Of course, people may fundamentally disagree on major issues but have positive attitudes toward one another personally. During the 1992 presidential campaign, for instance, much was made of the fact that Mr. Bush's campaign spokeswoman was romantically involved with Mr. Clinton's campaign chairman; they eventually married. The two obviously had different attitudes toward many issues and people, but these irreconcilable attitudes did not prevent them from forming a personal relationship.

As with beliefs, values, and attitudes, actions may differ so greatly that they are potentially irreconcilable. For example, the resulting actions that arise out of people's political beliefs, values, and attitudes can create great tensions between groups. Soldiers who fought in World War II and Korea found it difficult to understand the actions of those who refused the draft during the Vietnam War, and this issue loomed large in the 1992 election. Male and female behavioral differences similarly create misunderstandings and tensions between the sexes; men and women often disagree about the behaviors that constitute sexual harassment. In addition, young people often act so differently from their elders that there may be a resulting "generation gap" with potential for misunderstandings.

Dealing with Diversity

Because our world has high mobility with many opportunities for people of various cultural groups to come in contact with one another, it is difficult to avoid people with competing world views and lifestyles. Individuals and groups respond in a variety of ways to those with whom they differ. Three common responses are resistance, assimilation, and accommodation.

Resistance   Resistance results when groups refuse to risk changing and either *attack* the cultural traditions of others or *defend* their own ways against competing ideas and behaviors. The sociologist Peter Berger[22] terms this response *defiance*. *Defensively* defiant people draw into their own communities and huddle with like-minded people in order to find support for their way of life. Some groups even create alternative institutions and networks—private schools, media networks, and publishing houses in which their views are respectfully heard. A milder form of resistance occurs within individuals who refuse to listen to the views of others and remain silent about their own views when they find themselves in the minority.

Teaching Idea

Focus on campus-level differences. *Use exercise 6 as the basis for a group discussion.*

At other times, resistant groups *actively* attack the ideas of others. This can happen verbally when public speakers directly confront their opponents' ideas by producing speeches to counter them. Others attempt to suppress and repress the voices and actions they dislike. Often they challenge conflicting belief systems and world views—using forms of intimidation that range from the extremes of repression, persecution, or intolerance to milder challenges in which minority ideas and ideals are ignored, discounted, or ridiculed. Sometimes they attack their opponents physically. History, as well as current newspapers, contains report after report of such attacks.

Assimilation   A second way of responding to cultural differences is to concede one's beliefs and lifestyles—that is, individuals reject or forfeit their own cultural

Some groups react to diversity by active resistance. Here, defiant right-wing Afrikaaners demand that whites be given separate territories following the South African election that gave power to the black majority.

ways and embrace the beliefs and practices of another group. Berger[23] termed this response *surrender*. An example might be a person from a home in which both parents are physicians who comes to reject the beliefs and practices of the medical establishment. Instead, she embraces alternative, holistic healing practices. However, though assimilation may be possible in one or more areas of belief or practice, people rarely change their ways entirely. As a result, the United States is not a "melting pot" because co-cultural groups do not simply "melt."

Accommodation   The third way of responding to diversity is to show a willingness to listen to and evaluate the views of other people and groups. As a result, people may have to bargain or rethink some of their own ideas—surrendering some traditions, modifying others, and keeping still others relatively intact.

Teaching Idea

Have students read and discuss Stephen Littlejohn's speech, "The Quest for Quality in Public Discourse," located in the Appendix.

In a book called *Transcultural Leadership*, George Simons, Carmen Vázquez, and Philip Harris[24] use the term *acculturation* to describe individuals who acknowledge real differences between groups but who learn enough about other cultures to communicate effectively while remaining rooted in the values and language of their own traditions. They actively look for shared cultural checking points with others and cooperate with different people and groups to adapt and create new forms that transcend the traditions and world view of a single culture.

The result is a *multivocal* society—one that actively seeks out a variety of voices. (Here, *voices* means ideas, opinions, and wishes of a person or group that are expressed openly and formally.) Henry Louis Gates, Jr.,[25] chair of Harvard University's Department of Afro-American Studies, summarizes the ideals of such a society in which co-cultural groups hold divided opinions, yet they use their unique views of the world to forge a civic culture that accommodates both differences and commonalities.

Ethical Resources

For Further Reading

K. R. Wallace. (1955). An ethical basis of communication. *The Speech Teacher* 4, pp. 1–9; V. Jensen. (1985). Teaching ethics in speech communication. *Communication Quarterly*, pp. 324–330; and R. G. Johnson. (1970). Teaching speech ethics in the basic course. *Speech Teacher* 19, pp. 58–61. See also R. L. Johannesen. (1990). *Ethics in human communication*, 3rd Ed. Prospect Heights, IL: Waveland Press; J. A. Jaksa and M. S. Pritchard. (1988). *Communication ethics: Methods of analysis.* Belmont, CA: Wadsworth; and H. Barrett. (1991). *Rhetoric and civility: Human development, narcissism, and the good audience.* Albany: State University of New York Press.

We return to the questions of ethics. How should we respond to competing and conflicting ideas? Who should speak? Who should decide? Fortunately, our culture provides us with principles that you can use to guide your thinking and decision making about ethical public speaking. In this section, we look at some ethical guidelines proposed by many professors of speech.

- *Courtesy* When you are actively considerate, courteous, or polite to others, you are showing respect for them. Because you respond courteously, however, does not mean that you must agree with all of their ideas; you can respectfully disagree.

- *Tolerance* The dictionary defines tolerance as the disposition to be patient and fair toward those whose opinions or practices differ from one's own. It suggests a liberal, open-minded spirit toward the views and actions of others. Tolerance is grounded in the understanding that all humans are imperfect; none have total truth, but all should be free to live their lives as they see fit.[26]

- *Civility* The communication scholar Harold Barrett[27] emphasizes the idea of civility as a social virtue. Civility involves self-control or moderation. It is widely valued by cultures across space and time—from ancient Greeks to modern Japanese and other Asian cultures. Its opposite is pride, insolence, and arrogance. According to Barrett, civil behaviors include persuading, soliciting, consulting, advising, bargaining, compromising, building coalitions, and so on. In contrast, uncivil speakers coerce, deceive, confront, and manipulate their audiences. Civility includes knowledge and awareness of various world views, belief-value-attitude systems, and so on. This awareness is combined with a willingness to speak and to listen in an effort to create shared meanings in an environment of respect.

Teaching Idea

This list is not exhaustive. Refer students to the readings given on p. 62 and have them report on additional ethical perspectives. *Exercise 7 is appropriate here; it could be a journal entry.*

This is by no means an exhaustive list of guidelines. However, it contains principles that are often articulated in public speech classes. Since we live in a society and a world where there are competing world views and cultural understandings, there will be differences among people. Whether we take up weapons or handle our differences through speech depends to an extent on whether or not we are willing to listen, to negotiate, to understand, and to accommodate ourselves to those who differ from us.

KEY CONCEPT   **Ethical Considerations**

Diversity Differences between the belief-attitude-value systems, world views, and actions of various individuals and cultural groups can be so profound that understanding and compromise is difficult.

Dealing with diversity There are three common ways to deal with diversity:

Resistance Here one group actively or passively defends its own cultural ways and sometimes attacks the ways of others.

Assimilation An individual or group concedes beliefs and values and adopts the ways of another culture.

Accommodation People are willing to listen to others and negotiate a culture that has differences and commonalities. However, they remain rooted in the values of their own culture.

Ethical resources A partial list of ethical guidelines includes courtesy, tolerance, and civility.

Summary

Culture, the way of life of a people, exists in the minds of its members and is created and recreated through communication. Cultures provide their members with certain beliefs, values, attitudes, and actions. These cultural traditions are not shared equally by all individuals or co-cultural groups, nor are they inflexible and unchanging. We can put our cultural traditions at risk, allowing them to be changed by accommodation or surrender as we encounter new ideas.

Our beliefs are what we accept as factual, correct, or valid. Our core beliefs and assumptions form the basis for values, our judgments of what is good, moral, beautiful—or the opposite. These values underlie the most basic practices of our public speaking. Values important in a democracy include respect for the individual, fairness, freedom, and uncoerced choice, tolerance, civility, and cooperation, which provide the bases for ethical public speaking. Because of beliefs and values, we form attitudes—likes and dislikes—that lead to specific actions. Our culture identifies normative verbal and nonverbal behaviors that are adapted to the settings in which we speak.

Culture both influences and is influenced by public speaking. For example, in a democracy, all people are free to speak, and we use persuasion as a means of influencing one another. The style of public speaking common in the United States is problem oriented, direct, explicit, personal, and informal. Moreover, our culture provides us with a range of appropriate behaviors both for speaking and listening to speeches. Similarly, public speaking affects culture. In addition to the three general purposes of informing, persuading, and entertaining, we speak to produce, reinforce, repair, or change our listeners' beliefs, values, attitudes, and actions.

Not everyone in a pluralistic culture holds identical beliefs, values, and attitudes nor approves the same actions. Sometimes our cultural traditions are irreconcilable—we strongly accept ideas and behaviors that are strongly disbelieved or completely unacceptable to others around us. Similarly, attitudes and values can differ. As we encounter opposition, we respond in three common ways: defiance, accommodation, and surrender.

It is constantly a challenge in a pluralistic society to look to our values for guidance on ways to be civil to those with whom we disagree. Some cultural norms that promote ethical communication are courtesy, tolerance, and civility.

Student Speech

Jorge Oteiza

Ryan McGonigle, St. John's University

A tribute is a special kind of ceremonial speech that praises the characteristics of subjects who exemplify important cultural traits. [Note: Tributes can praise animals or actions of a group of people. For instance, in the "Gettysburg Address," President Abraham Lincoln praises an entire group of dead soldiers.] This sample speech—given by Ryan McGonigle, a student of Basque descent—praises the life of a famous Basque artist who is a cultural hero.

Ryan opens by introducing Oteiza, an artist revered in his cultural tradition, but unfamiliar to most of his listeners.

Since tributes praise cultural values, Ryan must explain some core ideals of the Basque people.

The name Jorge Oteiza may not exactly raise any eyebrows or provoke any curiosity amongst the American public, but to the Basque people and to me—an American of Basque descent—he is a living legend. Oteiza is arguably the greatest Basque artist and poet of the twentieth century.

Jorge Oteiza was born in Guipuzcoa Province in Spain, near the famous coastal Basque city of San Sebastian at the beginning of the twentieth century. As a child he was raised according to Basque tradition: Honor your father and mother; persevere under hardships; give generously to your neighbor; speak respectfully to others; and most of all, keep your word—which is better than gold. These ideals—centuries old—were later reflected in Oteiza's poetry and art.

This section of the speech describes Oteiza's background and formal education.

Being the son of a sheepherder, Oteiza was accustomed to adversity. At home he worked what seemed to be eternities every day. At school he struggled to learn Castilian Spanish—which, by the way, no one in his family spoke. He had no choice in learning it, however. It was either learn it or get whipped by the teachers. Later, he would write poetry in this, his second language. Ironically, it was through that very same school system that he became interested in art—his first love.

Ryan includes these details to show Oteiza's conflict between keeping tradition and developing the art that made him famous.

Following the death of his father, he was obliged to continue in his father's footsteps as a sheepherder. Traditionally, in the Basque country, sons follow the family occupation. If your father was a fisherman, most likely you will be one, too. Breaking with tradition is not only very hard to do, but it is also dishonorable. Fortunately for Jorge, his sister soon married, and the sheep became part of the dowry given to his brother-in-law. This released Oteiza to realize his true potential as an artist. His style of sculpture became well known in the area, and soon Oteiza's work was in demand. He made sculptures for the city in which he lives—San Sebastian—as well as for other cities throughout the Basque area.

Ryan now describes good as well as bad events in Oteiza's life.

In the mid-1930s, during the Spanish Civil War, three major events occurred for Oteiza. One, he married Itziar Carrieco Etxeandia. Throughout his life, she was the inspiration for much of his work. Not only did she support him, she encouraged him to create both poetry and art. The second important event happened when the Basque country declared its independence from Spain. This resulted in a war, and his home came under fire. In the conflict, he lost his best friend—the photographer Nicolas de Lekuona. Finally, Oteiza was incarcerated in a mass roundup of Basque intellectuals, priests, and artists. He spent almost two years in jail.

It was in one of Spain's infamous prisons that Oteiza became a man worthy of his surname. "Oteiza" in the Guipuzcoan dialect of Basque sounds very much like the word that means "prickly bush," and like a thorn—or a prickly bush—in the side of the Spaniards, he caused a bit of irritation. In prison, he became nationalistic, and his later sculpture and poetry shows the positive and negative effects of his identification with the revolutionary Basque movement. He frequently put his neck on the line by sculpting pro-Basque and/or anti-Spain works. For example, some of his work portrays the hardships of the Basque people that resulted from the policies of the Spanish dictator, Franco. Eventually, the regime of Franco got to him, and he took a hiatus from sculpture to work on his poetry.

In his poetry, the pro-Basque theme or the Basque experience is prominent. One phrase recurs throughout his work—"Gora Euzkadi Ederra" or "Long live the beautiful Basque country." This is a strongly nationalistic phrase that arouses Basque emotions. It is somewhat similar to the African-American slogan from the 1960s—"Black Is Beautiful."

Some tributes compare and contrast the subject with another person.

During this time, he took on an apprentice—a man by the name of Eduardo Txillida.* Oteiza put all of his efforts into teaching Txillida his art form,

---

* Txillida is sometimes spelled Chillida.

but all Txillida could do was to copy or imitate his master. Eventually, the two split, and to this day Oteiza accuses his pupil of not being able to do anything original. All of Txillida's works resemble Oteiza's, just on a grander scale. The younger artist copied his master without permission; he didn't develop his own style. In Oteiza's eyes, he failed to keep his word.

In his conclusion, which summarizes the speech, Ryan reviews the cultural values his subject embodies.

Basque critics consider Oteiza to be a true master because he maintained traditional art forms. He received honors from the Basque School, Euskaetz Aindia, the official academy of the Basque people. He did not care so much about money or fame—although he has both. Instead, he cared about his people and their welfare. Throughout the long ordeal of the war and in the ensuing years, Jorge Oteiza persevered under hardships. For these reasons, he is the true master.

Questions and Exercises

1. To understand how rapidly culture has changed in the past few decades, interview a senior citizen, asking questions such as these: What cultural changes have you observed over the years? How do these changes make you feel? What changes have you made in your personal beliefs or actions? What influenced you to change? Did public speaking play any part in these changes?

2. In recent years, there has been much talk about family values. What are family values? List the values your family taught you about right and wrong, good and bad, appropriate and inappropriate, moral and immoral, important and not important. Compare this list with others in your class. Which of these values or ideals do you feel strongly enough about to emphasize in a speech?

3. Attend a ceremony such as a convocation, or watch an awards ceremony on television. Identify the cultural beliefs and ideals that are stressed by public speakers at the occasion.

4. Ask someone from another culture about his or her culture's view of the self, the world, social relations, and forms of activity. How is public speaking viewed in that culture?

5. Explore why differences in core beliefs result in profound misunderstandings and mistrust among nations. For example, take the belief in the importance of the individual. How might you feel toward a nation that believed that people are less important than the state? What if that nation were trying to influence the governments of other countries? What if it had a strong military?

On the other hand, what if you were from a nation that believed strongly in the importance of kinship and religious traditions. How would you feel about American ideas as portrayed in television and movies?

6. What issues on your campus provide opportunities for people with irreconcilable differences to encounter one another? Which of the three ways of dealing with differences do they most often use? Assess the ethics of their responses.

7. Using your personal values and beliefs for resources, what would you write as an ethical code for public speakers in this society?

Key Terms

culture
Euro-American patterns
world view
cultural resources
beliefs
values
attitudes

co-cultural groups
ethnic minorities
cognitive minorities
countercultural groups
irreconcilable differences
resistance
assimilation
accommodation
multivocal society
voices
courtesy
tolerance
civility

Notes

1. Dinkins, D. (1992, November 26). Excerpts from Mayor Dinkins's speech on Crown Hts. and race. *The New York Times,* p. B3.

2. A strong argument that society exists in communication is made by Carey, J. W. (1989). *Communication as culture: Essays on media and society.* Boston: Unwin Hyman; see also Pearce, W. B. (1989). *Communication and the human condition.* Carbondale: Southern Illinois University Press.

3. For further information on world view, see Skow, L., Samovar, L. A., & Hellweg, S. A. (1990, February). *World view: The second hidden dimension.* Paper presented to the Western Speech Communication Association, Sacramento, California. See also Porter, R. E., & Samovar, L. A. (1994). An introduction to intercultural communication. In L. A. Samovar and R. E. Porter (Eds.), *Intercultural communication: A reader* (7th ed., pp. 4–25). Belmont, CA: Wadsworth.

4. Pearce, W. B. (1989). Op. cit.

5. Ibid., p. 20.

6. See Rokeach, M. (1968, 1972). *Beliefs, attitudes, and values: A theory of organization and change.* San Francisco: Jossey-Bass; and Rokeach, M. (1973). *The nature of human values.* New York: The Free Press.

7. Hofstede, G. (1992). Cultural dimensions in management and planning. In W. B. Gudykunst and Y. Y. Kim (Eds.), *Readings on communicating with strangers: An approach to intercultural communication* (pp. 89–109). New York: McGraw-Hill.

8. Lustig, M. W. (1988). Value differences in intercultural communication. In L. A. Samovar and R. E. Porter (Eds.), *Intercultural communication: A reader* (5th ed., pp. 55–61). Belmont, CA: Wadsworth.

9. Rokeach. (1973). Op. cit.

10. Steele, E. D., & Redding, W. C. (1962). The American value system: Premises for persuasion. *Western Speech, 26,* 83–91.

11. President Bush's speech is reprinted in (1992, January 29). *The New York Times,* p. A16.

12. Rokeach. (1972). Op. cit.

13. See Stewart, E. C., & Bennett, M. J. (1991). *American cultural patterns: A cross-cultural perspective* (rev. ed.). Yarmouth, ME: Intercultural Press, Inc.

14. Ibid., p. 129.

15. Berger, P. (1969). *A rumor of angels. Modern society and the rediscovery of the supernatural.* Garden City, NY: Doubleday.

16. Ovando, C. (1979). Coming to terms with the individual as culture maker: A pluralistic perspective. In N. V. Overly (Ed.), *Lifelong learning: A human agenda* (pp. 152–161). Alexandria, VA: Association for Supervision and Curriculum Development.

17. See for example, Wallace, K. R. (1955). An ethical basis of communication. *The Speech Teacher, 4,* 1–9.

18. Stewart and Bennett. (1991). Op. cit.

19. Simons, G. F., Vázquez, C., & Harris, P. R. (1993). *Transcultural leadership: Empowering the diverse workforce.* Houston: Gulf Publishing Co.

20. See Pearce. (1989). Op. cit., and Carey. (1989). Op. cit.

21. Pearce. (1989). Op. cit.

22. Berger. (1969). Op. cit.

23. Ibid.

24. Simons, G. F., Vázquez, C., & Harris, P. R. (1993). Op. cit.

25. Gates, H. L. (1992). *Loose canons: Notes on the culture wars.* New York: Oxford University Press.

26. Gray, J. (1992, October 2). The virtue of tolerance. *National Review,* pp. 28+.

27. Barrett, J. (1991). *Rhetoric and civility: Human development, narcissism, and the good audience.* Albany: SUNY Press.

Communicative Competence

At the end of this chapter,
you should be able to

- Define communicative competence
- Name two personality variables that may affect your perception of your competence
- Show the relationship between cultural variables and communicative comfort
- Define communication apprehension
- Identify internal and external results of apprehension
- Put into practice strategies to control your nervousness

Note

At the outset of the course, students often identify fear of public speaking as their major concern. And many nonnative English speakers express concern about their ability to communicate publicly. Thus, this chapter is included early in the text. It focuses on competence as the product of knowledge as well as skills that are combined with the motivation to succeed. The emphasis is on understanding communication apprehension and planning strategies to deal effectively with it.

After George Washington delivered his first inaugural address, a senator reported that the president was "agitated and embarrassed more than he was ever by the leveled cannon or pointed musket. He trembled and several times could scarcely make out to read."[1] President Van Buren likewise experienced debilitating anxiety when he spoke in public; he had to stop in the middle of his first speech to Congress. Similarly, President Zachary Taylor read his inaugural address "in a very low voice and very badly as to his pronunciation and manner."[2] For these men, the power of the presidential office did little to overcome their fear of public speaking.

If you feel apprehensive at the thought of speaking in public, you are in good company. Many famous people have shared your fears, including Presidents Lincoln, Roosevelt, Kennedy, and Reagan. The entertainer Johnny Carson and the writer Susan Faludi have spoken of their reluctance to speak in front of groups. Although they may not have felt confident, they are all known as competent public communicators.

Competence is defined quite simply as the ability to succeed or to do something well. You are already a successful communicator in many contexts—at least some of the time. You probably speak effectively with family members, converse with your circle of close friends, and contribute intelligently to classroom discussions. Although you communicate successfully in many contexts, you may have entered this class wondering if you can transfer these competencies to a structured public speaking setting where you are required to prepare several rather formal messages and deliver them to an audience of relative strangers. If you are experiencing anxiety about speaking in this class, don't worry unduly. Though their emotions may argue otherwise, most people have the ability to succeed in public speaking. Remember that competence and confidence, though they may be related, are not the same. By practicing the skills that lead to competence, many speakers begin to experience the confidence that comes from experience.

This chapter will look at both communicative competence and communication apprehension (CA), or lack of confidence. It will first define communicative competence and then examine several factors that may affect a speaker's feelings of competence. This will be followed by a discussion of communication apprehension. The chapter will conclude with suggestions that have helped many student speakers overcome their reluctance to speak in public.

Communicative Competence

Teaching Idea

Exercise 1 can be used here.

Communicative competence is defined as the ability to communicate in a personally effective and socially appropriate manner.[3] Competent communicators have the motivation, the knowledge, and the skills needed to meet the goals they have set for the specific set of circumstances in which they speak.[4] Figure 4.1 illustrates this concept.

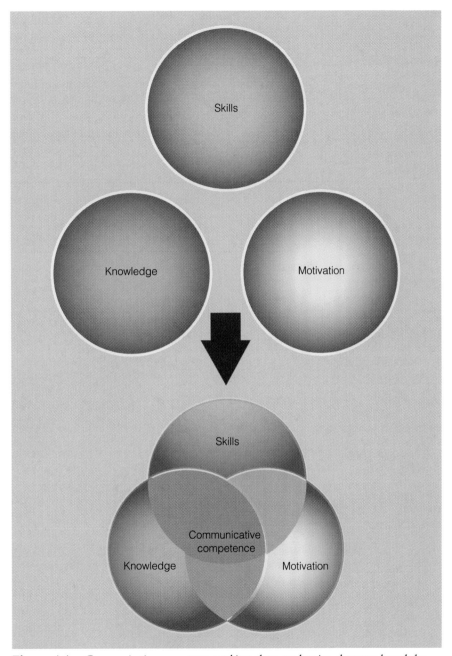

Figure 4.1   *Communicative competence combines three overlapping elements: knowledge about communication, skills in speaking and listening, and motivation to communicate.*

For Further Reading

See B. Spitzberg. (1983). Communicative competence as knowledge, skill, and impression. *Communication Education 32*, 323–329. See also W. H. Jones, J. M. Clark, and S. R. Briggs. (Eds.) (1986). *Shyness: Perspectives on research and treatment.* New York: Plenum Press.

Think of a past situation in which you communicated competently. You possessed both the knowledge and the necessary skills to act appropriately in the context; in addition, you were motivated to communicate. Your communication behaviors were both personally effective and socially appropriate. An example might be a successful conversation you had with a close friend. You have listening and conversational skills, and you know how to interact in a one-to-one conversation. You were motivated to talk with your friend. Your personal traits, such as a sense of humor or the ability to tell stories well, came through. You used language and ideas that were appropriate to the setting. For example, you probably used informal language with your friends that you would never use in classroom discussions. Similarly, the topics you chose to discuss, though appropriate in a friendly conversation, might not have been suitable for discussion in family gatherings or in public settings. Throughout the conversation, you were relaxed and felt comfortable.

Personal Effectiveness

Teaching Idea

Bring pictures or slides of a variety of recognizable speakers, such as Ronald Reagan, Whoopi Goldberg, or Hillary Rodham Clinton. Discuss how each, though different, is an effective speaker. Or show videotapes (or clips) of speeches. Elicit ways that each speaker uses personal traits to be effective in specific situations.

Just as there are many different behaviors that make a good conversationalist, there are a range of competent behaviors in public speaking that allow for a variety of personalities to succeed in this context. For example, Terry is personally most effective using a dramatic delivery—with lots of gestures and movement and a confident voice. Tyrone is more comfortable sitting on a stool, gesturing infrequently and speaking very informally and conversationally. Yolanda prepares carefully in advance and likes to stand behind a podium and use lots of visual aids when she speaks. All three are effective speakers because they allow their personal traits to work *for* them in the public speaking context.

Social Appropriateness

Competent speakers pay attention to the specific social setting in which they speak; this enables them to determine what is appropriate in that setting. These speakers are *rhetorically sensitive* people who "can adapt to diverse social situations and perform reasonably well in most of them."[5] Listeners have expectations for culturally appropriate behaviors in different contexts, and rhetorically sensitive speakers determine which presentational style is most effective with a given group of listeners; then they adapt to that style. This means they avoid using the same behaviors in every speech setting. Thus, even though Terry is a naturally dynamic speaker, he does not use dramatic, energetic delivery when he speaks at a funeral. Likewise, Tyrone gets off his stool and stands behind a podium when he addresses the Rotary Club. Yolanda moves away from the podium, uses more emotion in her voice, and gestures more frequently when she is at a political rally urging her friends to vote in an upcoming election. All three communicate competently in a variety of settings, adapting their personal style and selecting behaviors that their listeners see as appropriate in each social situation.

Many people such as Ann Richardson of Texas have extroverted personalities; however, most have a range of introverted to extro-verted characteristics that vary from situation to situation. Public speaking often causes people to feel shy.

Communicative competence—motivation, knowledge, and skills—depends on many variables. Two factors that might influence your motivation and your skills are personality variables and cultural variables. In the following sections, we look at each of these in turn.

Personality Variables

As we noted, not everyone feels comfortable speaking in public. Part of your comfort depends on personal characteristics that influence how you perceive your effectiveness as well as your competence. Extroversion and introversion[6] are two such traits.

In general, *extroverts* enjoy speaking and interacting, and they are relaxed and open around others. Since they have communicated competently in many contexts, many extroverts face public speaking with confidence.

Yet the characteristics associated with extroversion do not necessarily make them competent public speakers. For instance, stereotypical used car salespersons are outgoing people who speak very rapidly and confidently, yet listeners may perceive them as untrustworthy. President Clinton received his share of criticism for his verbal facility, and partly for this reason, some of his opponents dubbed him "Slick Willie." After his first press conference, *The New York Times* reported:

Quite simply, sometimes he can seem too smooth, too eloquent for his own good. Sometimes you want to check your wallet when he's done talking—just to make sure all your credit cards are still there.[7]

Introverted people, in contrast, tend to be private individuals who conceal many of their thoughts and emotions. However, introverts are often competent public speakers. Although they are less talkative in general, they are often excellent at formulating ideas and arguments and preparing speeches, and many reserved, reflective people are effective in public presentations. They may feel more comfortable, however, speaking from carefully prepared notes or from a manuscript rather than giving an impromptu speech. Most people have a range of extroverted-to-introverted traits. Ninety percent of people report shyness occasionally; 50 percent say that shyness is sometimes a significant problem.[8] These people say that new situations, strangers, authority figures, and people who impress them bring out their shy side.

Public speaking classes may trigger anxiety because public speaking is a new situation for most students and you may feel unsure of yourself. At the beginning of the course, your fellow students are mostly strangers to you, and you may feel anxious about revealing yourself and your ideas to them. What's more, your instructor is an authority figure who is grading your presentation. The good news is that most students report that speaking gets easier as the term progresses. This may be partly because the class is no longer made up of strangers. Through listening to one another's speeches, you begin to feel that you know your fellow students, and just as you want them to succeed, they are cheering you on as you speak.

Cultural Variables

Teaching Idea

Use Activity 4.1 in the Instructor's Manual to have students explore public speaking traditions within their cultural group.

As we pointed out in Chapter 3, your cultural background influences the beliefs, values, attitudes, and normative actions that you associate with public speaking. These, in turn, affect your communicative comfort and perhaps your competence in the public speaking context. Indeed, an intercultural communication scholar writes:

Speech is not equally valued in all societies, or even consistently throughout the United States. The qualities of cogency [the ability to be convincing], precision, and delivery which may be encouraged in speech communication classes in the United States may, in some other cultures, be regarded negatively.[9]

 Some cultures value silence—not revealing everything you know. For example, some Native Americans are comfortable with a lack of talk, even between friends. They do not consider a silent person to be necessarily shy. Similarly, Japanese culture associates silence with wisdom. In some Asian cultures, silence expresses power. A person who talks too much and self-discloses a great deal is

Although women and young people may have influence in private settings in a society such as Bahrain, they are expected to keep silent and let respected men speak in public. A Bahrainian woman who moved to the United States might find it very difficult to speak in public.

considered less powerful than one who keeps personal opinions and knowledge private.

Language concerns can also create anxiety for those who are not native speakers of English. For instance, Indera Ramjit's family was from India; she was born in Guyana and ended up in a university classroom in the United States. She explained:

> *I fear public speaking because I think that one of my weaknesses will be revealed. For example, proper usage of words, being able to pronounce the words correctly, and use proper English. Being from another country can create some of these hazards.*

Cultures vary not only in the value they place on public speaking but also in the *who*, *how*, and *what* they consider normative public speaking.

The Who of Public Speaking In the United States, all citizens have the First Amendment right to speak publicly though not all people take advantage of this right. In other cultures, only certain people are expected to address the entire community. In some societies, for instance, only adult men, sometimes just those who are considered very wise or knowledgeable, speak in public. Although they may speak among themselves, children, young people, nonexperts, and women are often expected to keep silent in public arenas.

The How of Public Speaking Within Euro-American culture, speaking one's mind and asserting one's views are traits of competent speakers—people even take workshops in "assertiveness training." In contrast, there are cultural groups where listeners expect to gain meaning from what is left unsaid, looking to nonverbal aspects of the message as well as what the speaker explicitly states. Speakers in such cultures choose less direct language, relying on metaphors and allusions to convey subtle meanings. Their word plays and elaborations on the message would be considered irrelevancies for those people who rely heavily on precise verbal messages.

Many African cultures greatly value fluency in public speaking. The Anang tribe, for example, admires verbally skilled individuals. In fact, the tribal name Anang means "the ability to speak wittily yet meaningfully upon any occasion."[10] This value on public speaking is shared by many people of African descent, who are often skilled speakers in the United States. A list of expressive and eloquent speakers includes the ex-Congresswoman Barbara Jordan; the entertainer Bill Cosby; and the religious and political leaders Martin Luther King, Jr., Jesse Jackson, and Malcolm X.

The What of Public Speaking Cultures differ in what is considered appropriate for public discussion. Speakers in the African-American tradition are expected to express their opinions and show their personalized, emotional involvement with their topics rather than approach the subject from an objective and distanced perspective.[11] However, in some other cultures, it is socially inappropriate to discuss personal feelings and viewpoints in public. Thus, the statement of personal opinions common in African-American discourse is uncommon in some Asian rhetorics.

In the United States, speakers and their words are considered separate. This means it is possible—even likely—that you can disagree with what someone says and still be friends with her or him. In China or Japan, it is inappropriate to argue publicly with a speaker. Carl Becker[12] has extensively studied Chinese communication. He links Chinese reluctance to engage in public confrontation to the Confucian idea of *hsin* in which words are inextricably related to the person who speaks them. Thus, if you disagree with someone's words, you cast doubt on the honesty of his or her character in general.

As you can see, factors from your ethnic background may determine how comfortable you feel in a public speaking classroom that teaches Euro-American cultural norms. What is considered competent in a classroom or board room in an institution of the dominant culture may be very different from the speaking norms your culture considers competent. If this is so, you can learn to be bi-cultural, knowing rules for competent speaking in the dominant culture while appreciating and participating competently in your own ethnic speech community. In the following example, a Nigerian woman living in the United States explains how she accomplishes this:[13]

> *At work, . . . I raise my voice as loud as necessary to be heard in meetings. At conferences where I present papers on "Women from the Third World," I make serious arguments about the need for international intervention in countries where women are deprived of all rights. . . . Yet as easily as I switch from speaking English to Ibo [her African language], . . . I never confuse my two selves.*
>
> *Hundreds of thousands of women from the third world and other traditional societies share my experience. We straddle two cultures, cultures that are often in opposition. Mainstream America, the culture we embrace in our professional lives, dictates that we be assertive and independent—like men. Our traditional culture, dictated by religion and years of socialization, demands that we be docile and content in our roles as mothers and wives—careers or not.*

KEY CONCEPT **Communicative Competence**

Personal effectiveness Because of individual differences between people, there is no single way to be an effective communicator, and a speaker chooses behaviors that are effective for his or her personality.

Social appropriateness Different speaking situations call for different presentational styles; rhetorically sensitive speakers adapt to a variety of speaking situations.

Personality variables Extroversion and introversion are two factors that influence a speaker's comfort.

Cultural variables Cultures have different public speaking traditions that may affect a speaker's comfort and competence.

> *Who speaks* In some cultures, only certain people speak publicly—often men who are elders in the group.
>
> *How they speak* Cultural variations include directness, indirectness, and fluency.
>
> *What is spoken* Cultures vary in topic selection and in public expression of opinions, feelings, and disagreements.

Communication Apprehension

Although many people learn to be competent speakers, they continue to experience anxiety about speaking. *Apprehension* is defined as the dread or fear of having something bad happen to you. *Communication apprehension (CA)*, then, is the

Most students experience some form of Communication Apprehension (CA) when they deliver a classroom speech. The resulting effects may be internal (such as rapid heartbeat) and external (such as disrupted fluency).

dread or fear of having something negative happen to you as you communicate or because of your communication. These emotions cause some people to avoid or withdraw from communicating in contexts that they perceive to have potentially negative consequences.

Types of CA

Teaching Idea

If you present this material in a lecture or discussion format, a transparency is included in the Instructor's Manual. *Exercise 2 is appropriate here. The test is found at the end of the chapter.*

Professor James McCroskey and his associates[14] have extensively studied communication apprehension. They have identified four major types of apprehension ranging from CA that is relatively enduring to a type that passes rather quickly. Some apprehension is linked to personality traits; other apprehension results from potentially threatening situations.

One type of communication apprehension that tends to be enduring is "trait-like CA," which is triggered by all communication events and is associated with innate traits of shyness and introversion. Also persistent is "person–group CA," where the speaker dreads communicating with a particular person or group based on previous negative experiences. A more transitory apprehension is "situational CA," where the speaker is anxious only about a particular speech. Some people dread specific speaking contexts over a long period and exhibit "generalized-context CA." For many people, the dreaded context is public speaking. If you are in this category of CA, relax—you are normal. Public speaking has been called the number-one fear of Americans.

Effects of CA

Regardless of the type of communication apprehension you experience, apprehension is an emotion, and like other emotions, it affects you both internally and externally.

Internal Effects   In any threatening situation, your body automatically prepares to save you by what is called the "fight or flight" mechanism. This means it energizes you either to fight against the threat or to run away from the dangerous situation. Unfortunately, your body does not distinguish between physically threatening situations, where you actually need the extra physical energy to make your escape, and emotionally or psychologically threatening experiences, where the mobilization strategies, such as increased heart rate, only add to your stress.

An increased heart rate is only one of many common physiological responses to apprehension. Your body also puts the activity of your digestive system on hold, causing your stomach muscles to contract. When this happens, you feel "butterflies" in your stomach. Even professional speakers experience this reaction. Veteran newscaster Edwin Newman once remarked, "The only difference between the pros and the novices is that the pros have trained the butterflies to fly in formation."[15] Other common responses are profuse perspiration, trembling in the knees and hands, throat constriction, dry mouth, warm face, and a red flush on your neck and cheeks.

External Effects   Although these internal effects are normal, they are mostly invisible to the audience. However, the distress they cause may lead to several common external or outward effects that listeners can see. Some people control their anxiety by *avoiding* the communication situation entirely—either bypassing opportunities to present their ideas publicly or choosing careers that do not require public presentations. Others *withdraw* by participating as minimally as possible—preparing short speeches and rushing through them. In another form of withdrawal, speakers disengage from the audience by looking almost exclusively at their outlines or over the heads of their listeners. A third group of speakers experience *disruption* in fluency—stumbling over words, finding their voices unnatural or shaky sounding, or forgetting their speeches. Occasionally, an anxious person, rather than avoiding or withdrawing from communicating, goes the other direction and *overcommunicates*. One student's six-minute prepared speech actually lasted fourteen minutes! He overexplained simple points and repeated his summary statement in three different ways.

Anxiety, in whatever form, can be frightening, and most beginning speakers look for ways to control their internal and external symptoms. In fact, one of the questions beginning students ask most often is, "What can I do so that I don't feel so panicky at the thought of giving a speech?" The remainder of this chapter addresses ways you can increase your confidence, and thus your competence, in public speaking.

KEY CONCEPT

Communication Apprehension (CA)

CA is the dread or fear of having something negative result as you communicate or from your communication.

Internal effects The body reacts to threats with the "fight or flight" mechanism.

External effects CA has several observable effects: avoidance, withdrawal, disruptions, and overcommunication.

Becoming Competent in Public Speaking

Teaching Idea

Pair up students who express apprehension and have them discuss their personal plans for improving their communicative competence. *Students can use exercise 4. It refers them to a checklist in the Student Resource Workbook. This checklist can serve as a self-report after their next speech.*

Communication professors and researchers have extensively studied methods to control apprehension in an effort to enable their students to relax and develop important competencies in public speaking. They have developed a number of practical exercises and guidelines for beginning speakers.

Know the Speechmaking Process

Fear of the unknown is one reason that people have anxiety. In public speaking, this translates into the fear of not knowing what to say or how to say it. To an extent, you can overcome this by learning the process of making a speech—how to go about selecting a topic and purpose for your speech, how to gather materials, organize your ideas, choose appropriate language, and so on.

People learn to communicate effectively by observation, study, and practice. As you observe other people speak, study the ways knowledgeable people prepare and give speeches, and actually speak to your classmates, you are learning how to create a public speech. You are also gaining a sense of what will "fit" with a particular audience. Eventually, when you are asked to give a speech, you won't panic, because speechmaking is familiar to you.

When you are learning any new skill, you follow the guidelines more closely in the beginning. Only after you have mastered the basics and feel more confident about the process do you begin to take more liberties. Remember when you first learned to drive a car? In the beginning, you concentrated on every decision you had to make; later, the process of shifting, steering, and braking became automatic. As you first learn to prepare speeches, your instructor may ask you to follow the guidelines and patterns very closely. However, after you have given many speeches, you will feel freer to be more creative in your preparation.

Think of your classroom as a small, safe environment in which you experiment and practice your speaking skills. Even professionals, like the comedian Lily Tomlin, practice in small settings before taking their show to larger audiences.

Know the Anxiety Process

For Further Reading

W. W. Brownell and R. A. Katula. (1984). The communication anxiety graph: A classroom tool for managing speech anxiety. *Communication Quarterly* 32, pp. 243–249.

Just as understanding the "how to" of creating a speech may reduce your anxiety, it may also help you know what you can reasonably expect about anxiety itself. In one study, Winifred Brownell and Richard Katula[16] found that students reported higher anxiety just before they spoke and during the first few minutes of the speech (see Figure 4.2). However, as speakers moved into the speech body, they began to feel more confident, becoming even more at ease during the conclusion. The students in the study reported the least amount of stress during the question–and–answer period immediately following the speech.

Knowing this process can help you take control of your nervousness, and Brownell and Katula suggest three tactics to ease anxiety. First plan a strong, compelling introduction to help carry you through the anxiety peak at the

Figure 4.2

Knowing that anxiety is greater in certain periods may help you control your nervousness by planning strategies that enable you to get through these periods effectively.

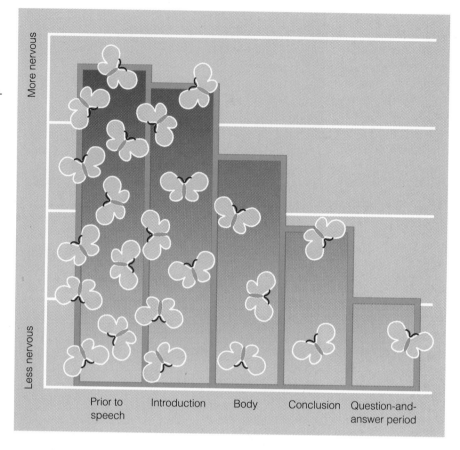

beginning of the speech. Second, use visual aids when appropriate, especially ones that work at the start of your speech. These ease tension since they give the audience something to look at besides you. Third, deliver your introduction from notes rather than reading it or reciting a memorized text. If you read a prepared text, you risk failing to engage your audience. A memorized introduction is hazardous since this is such a high-anxiety point in your speech.

Rehearse Wisely

Teaching Idea

Use the questions found in exercise 3 as a basis for a class discussion on the role of preparation in diminishing anxiety.

Many students worry about actually giving the speech—they are afraid they can't present their ideas competently. Often they underestimate what they will gain and overestimate what they will lose by participating in public speaking.[17] In addition to overanticipating the danger and harm, especially emotional or psychological harm that may come to them, many underestimate their ability to cope.[18] However, most people speak competently in the relative safety of their small classrooms after rehearsing their speeches carefully. They use suggestions from three different methods to control their apprehension: controlling internal monologue, visualization, and physical relaxation.

Controlling Internal Monologue While your mind makes frantic efforts to cope with what is unfamiliar, it tends to think the worst. Your internal voice says, "I don't know what I'm doing. I can't do this. I don't know if I'll remember. I probably won't get my ideas across. They will see my knees shake." Negative self-talk is called *Internal Monologue (I-M)*.[19] Such negative thinking adds to your discomfort and contributes to your communication anxiety. You can learn to control your negative self-talk by thinking positively in three areas: about the message, about the audience, and about yourself.

To think positively about the message, select a topic that interests you and is beneficial to your audience. Check the dictionary for the correct pronunciation of unfamiliar words, and take time to practice your speech. When you arrive in the classroom, silently repeat the goal of the speech, the main ideas, and your introduction so that you will start well.

To promote positive thoughts about the audience, remember that other students are probably as nervous as you when they speak, and they are not experts in your subject. Assume that they want you to succeed and focus on the purpose of your speech—to inform, reaffirm beliefs, or persuade.

Maintain a positive self-image about the things you do well. Remind yourself that your worth as a person is not related to your skill as a novice public speaker, and that competence develops with experience.

Visualization Not only do speakers rehearse out loud, they often find it helpful to visualize themselves successfully giving their speech. Professor Joel Ayers[20] and associates have developed visualization techniques that have been effective for students in their public speaking classes. They suggest that you find a quiet place and envision all the details from the beginning to the end of your speech. Mentally observe yourself as if you were a member of the audience watching a competent, well-prepared speaker. See yourself standing confidently. Listen to your voice as you stress words and pause effectively. Watch yourself making appropriate gestures. Finally, imagine your delight when the speech is over.

Physical Relaxation Often you can soothe prespeech anxiety with physical activities such as walking or running on the day of the speech. Limit sugar and caffeine if these substances make you feel wired. It may also help you to listen to soothing music or to meditate before class. Finally, breathe slowly and deeply just before you give your speech.

As you can see, controlling your self-talk and planning specific strategies to deal actively with potential stress is most helpful in developing a mindset of confidence. Finally, your competence is based on knowledge—knowing the basics of constructing a good speech and knowing the anxiety process.

For Further Reading

W. Howell. (1990). Coping with Internal-Monologue. In J. Stewart. (Ed.) *Bridges, not walls*, (5th Ed.) (pp. 128–138). New York: McGraw-Hill.

For Further Reading

J. Ayers and T. S. Hopf. (1985). Visualization: A means of reducing speech anxiety. *Communication Education* 34, pp. 318–323.

Teaching Idea

As a summarizing activity for this chapter, do exercise 5. Have students read Susan Faludi's report of her CA; then as a group, discuss the questions found after the excerpt from her essay.

During rehearsal, prepare yourself mentally by thinking positively about your message, your classroom audience, and your ability to give a speech successfully.

Becoming Competent in Public Speaking

Know the speechmaking process Competent speakers know "how to" put together a speech.

Know the anxiety process Take control of your anxiety during peak times—immediately prior to the speech and during the introduction; anxiety declines in the body and conclusion and is minimal during the question-and-answer period after the speech.

Rehearse wisely Competent speakers often use one or more of the following methods in rehearsal:

Controlling Internal Monologue (I-M) Minimize negative self-talk by substituting positive thoughts about the message, the audience, and yourself.

Visualization Mentally rehearse by imagining yourself successfully performing the speech.

Physical relaxation Exercise or use relaxation techniques to deal with pre-speech nervous energy.

Summary

The overriding goal of this text is to empower you to become a competent public communicator in the institutions of Euro-American culture. This chapter has defined competence as having the motivation, knowledge, and skills to communicate in a personally effective and socially appropriate manner. Competence develops over time as you learn the speechmaking process and learn to control your emotional responses to speaking before an audience.

Competence or success is affected by personal and cultural variables that lead to communication apprehension (CA) in many people, preventing some from entering the public speaking arena with confidence. Though CA is common, it can be very unnerving, as even professionals know. Although physiological responses are normal, you can take active control of your apprehension. One way is to learn thoroughly the process of creating a speech. In addition, you can help your performance by controlling Internal Monologue (I-M), rehearsing using visualization, relaxing, and understanding and taking charge of the anxiety process.

As we have seen, most people can learn to be effective public speakers. The key is to be rhetorically sensitive, varying your behaviors in different speech settings. In the next chapter, we focus on the most important reasons for communicating publicly—your listeners.

Essay

Speak for Yourself

Susan Faludi

Many famous people are anxious about speaking. In this excerpt from an article entitled, "Speak for Yourself," published in The New York Times Magazine *(January 26, 1992, pp. 10 ff),[21] Susan Faludi, author of* Backlash: The Undeclared War Against American Women, *shares her experiences with CA.*

"Oh, and then you'll be giving that speech at the Smithsonian Tuesday on the status of American women," my publisher's publicist reminded me as she rattled off the list of "appearances" for the week. "What?" I choked out. "I thought that was *at least* another month away." But the speech was distant only in my wishful consciousness, which pushed all such events into a mythical future when I would no longer lunge for smelling salts at the mention of public speaking.

Like many female writers with strong convictions but weak stomachs for direct confrontation, I write so forcefully precisely because I speak so tentatively.

"Isn't it wonderful that so many people want to hear what you have to say about women's rights?" the publicist prodded. I grimaced. "About as wonderful as walking down the street with no clothes on." Yes, I wanted people to hear what I had to say. But couldn't they just read what I wrote? Couldn't I just speak softly and carry a big book?

It has taken me a while to realize that my publicist is right. It's *not* the same—for my audience or for me. Public speech can be a horror for the shy person, but it can also be the ultimate act of liberation. For me, it became the moment where the public and the personal truly met.

While both sexes fear public speaking (pollsters tell us it's the public's greatest fear, rivaling even death), women—particularly women challenging the status quo—seem to be more afraid, and with good reason. We *do* have more at stake. Men risk a loss of face; women a loss of femininity. Men are chagrined if they blunder at the podium; women face humiliation either way. If we come across as commanding, our womanhood is called into question. If we reveal emotion, we are too hormonally driven to be taken seriously.

Public speech is a more powerful stimulus because it is more dangerous for the speaker. An almost physical act, it demands projecting one's voice, hurling it against the public ear. Writing, on the other hand, occurs at one remove. The writer asserts herself from behind the veil of the printed page.

The dreaded evening of the Smithsonian speech finally arrived. I stood knock-kneed and green-gilled before 300 people. Was it too late to plead a severe case of laryngitis? I am Woman, Hear Me Whisper.

I cleared my throat and, to my shock, a hush fell over the room. People were listening—with an intensity that strangely emboldened me. It was as if their attentive silence allowed me to make contact with my own muffled self. I began to speak. A stinging point induced a ripple of agreement. I told a joke and they laughed. My voice got surer, my delivery rising. A charge passed between me and the audience, uniting and igniting us both.

Afterward, it struck me that in some essential way I hadn't really proved myself a feminist until now. I knew public speaking was important to reform public life—but I hadn't realized the transformative effect it could have on the speaker herself. Women need to be heard not just to change the world, but to change themselves.

I can't say that this epiphany has made me any less anxious when approaching the lectern. But it has made me more determined to speak in spite of the jitters—and more hopeful that other women will do the same.

Questions and Exercises

1. Assess your communicative competence. Discuss with a group of classmates what motivates you to study public speaking. What skills and knowledge do you already have? What areas of skills, knowledge, or motivation do you need to improve?

2. Evaluate your emotional response to public speaking. When do you feel shy or apprehensive? Take the PRPSA test to determine your level of CA in a public speaking context. If your score is 120 or over, make an appointment with your instructor to discuss specific ways to overcome CA.

3. Consider the role of preparation and rehearsal in increasing your communicative competence. What effect does last-minute preparation have on competence? What effect does it have on CA? Knowing this, how do you plan to prepare for your next speech?

4. Develop a plan to become a more competent communicator. You may want to use the checklist found in your Student Resource Workbook to take control of your apprehension. Share your plan with at least one classmate.

5. Read Susan Faludi's essay on public speaking on pp. 85–86. As you read it, identify the types of CA she exhibited and the way she overcame her shyness to become a competent speaker by answering the following questions:

   - What kind(s) of CA did Ms. Faludi demonstrate?
   - What specifically did she do to deal with her apprehension?
   - What can you learn from her experiences about conquering your own apprehension?

Questionnaire for Use with Exercise 2

Personal Report of Public Speaking Apprehension (PRPSA)

PRPSA[22] is a self-test for CA. Mark whether you (1) strongly agree, (2) agree, (3) are undecided, (4) disagree, or (5) strongly disagree. Work quickly, recording your first impression.

_____ 1. While preparing for giving a speech, I feel tense and nervous.

_____ 2. I feel tense when I see the words *speech* and *public speech* on a course outline.

_____ 3. My thoughts become confused and jumbled when I am giving a speech.

_____ 4. Just after giving a speech, I feel that I have had a pleasant experience.

_____ 5. I get anxious when I think about a speech coming up.

_____ 6. I have no fear of giving a speech.

_____ 7. Although I am nervous just before starting a speech, I soon settle down after getting started and feel calm and comfortable.

_____ 8. I look forward to giving a speech.

_____ 9. When the instructor announces a speaking assignment in class, I can feel myself getting tense.

_____ 10. My hands tremble when I am giving a speech.

_____ 11. I feel relaxed while giving a speech.

_____ 12. I enjoy preparing for a speech.

_____ 13. I am in constant fear of forgetting what I prepared to say.

_____ 14. I get anxious if someone asks me something about my topic that I do not know.

_____ 15. I face the prospect of giving a speech with confidence.

_____ 16. I feel that I am in complete possession of myself while speaking.

_____ 17. My mind is clear when giving a speech.

_____ 18. I do not dread giving a speech.

_____ 19. I perspire just before starting a speech.

_____ **20.** My heart beats very fast just as I start a speech.

_____ **21.** I experience considerable anxiety while sitting in the room just before my speech starts.

_____ **22.** Certain parts of my body feel tense and rigid while I am giving a speech.

_____ **23.** Realizing that only a little time remains in a speech makes me very tense and anxious.

_____ **24.** While giving a speech, I can control my feelings of tension and stress.

_____ **25.** I breathe faster just before starting a speech.

_____ **26.** I feel comfortable and relaxed the hour or so before giving a speech.

_____ **27.** I do poorly on speeches because I am anxious.

_____ **28.** I feel anxious when the teacher announces the date of a speaking assignment.

_____ **29.** When I make a mistake while giving a speech, I find it hard to concentrate on the parts that follow.

_____ **30.** During an important speech, I experience a feeling of helplessness building up inside me.

_____ **31.** I have trouble falling asleep the night before a speech.

_____ **32.** My heart beats very fast while I present a speech.

_____ **33.** I feel anxious while waiting to give my speech.

_____ **34.** While giving a speech, I get so nervous I forget facts I really know.

Scoring

Step 1: Add the scores you assigned to items 1, 2, 3, 5, 9, 10, 13, 14, 19, 20, 21, 22, 23, 25, 27, 28, 29, 30, 31, 32, 33, 34.

Step 2: Then add the scores for items 4, 6, 7, 8, 11, 12, 15, 16, 17, 18, 24, 26.

Step 3: Add the total from Step 1 to the number 132. This is your subtotal.

Step 4: Subtract the total from Step 2 from the subtotal you derived from Step 3.

If your result is:	You have:
34–84	very low anxiety
85–92	moderately low anxiety
93–110	moderate anxiety
111–119	moderately high anxiety
120–170	very high anxiety

Key Terms

communicative competence
rhetorical sensitivity
extroversion
introversion
communication apprehension (CA)
trait-like CA
person–group CA
situational CA
generalized-context CA
fight or flight
avoidance
withdrawal
disruptions
overcommunication
the anxiety process
Internal Monologue (I–M)
visualization
physical relaxation

Notes

1. From Podell, J., & Angovin, S. (Eds.). (1988). *Speeches of the American Presidents*. New York:. H. W. Wilson.

2. Ibid.

3. See Treholm, S., & Jensen, A. (1992). *Interpersonal communication*, (2nd ed.). Belmont, CA: Wadsworth.

4. See the work of Brian Spitzberg. An example is (1983). Communicative competence as knowledge, skill, and impression. *Communication Education*, *32*, 323–329.

5. Hart, R. P., & Burks, D. O. (1972). Rhetorical sensitivity and social interaction. *Speech Monographs, 39*, 90.

6. Many authors are writing about introversion and extroversion based on the work of psychologist Carl Jung. See Kiersey, D., & Bates, M. (1984). *Please understand me: Character and temperament types.* Del Mar, CA: Prometheus Nemesis Book Co., and Krueger, O., & Thuesen, J. M. (1988). *Type talk.* New York: Delacorte Press, discuss these traits in detail.

7. Friedman, T. L. (1992, November 15). Now Clinton decides which promises come first. *The New York Times*, sec. 4, pp. 1, 2.

8. Many books are written on shyness. One that provides a collection of studies is Jones, W. H., Check, J. M., & Briggs, S. R. (Eds.). (1986). *Shyness: Perspectives on research and treatment.* New York: Plenum Press. See Hammerlie, F. M., & Montgomery, R. Self-perception theory and the treatment of shyness, in this collection.

9. Condon, J. C., Jr. (1978). Intercultural communication from a speech communication perspective. In F. C. Casmir (Ed.), *Intercultural and international communication* (pp. 383–406). Washington DC: University Press of America.

10. Messenger, J. (1960). Anang proverb riddles. *Journal of American Folklore, 73*, 235.

11. See Kochman, T. (1990). Cultural pluralism: Black and white styles. In D. Carbaugh (Ed.), *Cultural communication and intercultural contacts* (pp. 219–224). Hillsdale, NJ: Lawrence Erlbaum. See also Sullivan, P. A. (1993). Signification and African-American rhetoric: A case study of Jesse Jackson's "Common Ground and Common Sense" speech. *Communication Quarterly, 41*(1), 1–15. And Wierbicka, A. (1991). *Cross-cultural pragmatics: The semantics of human interaction.* Berlin: Mouton de Gruyter.

12. Becker, C. B. (1988). Reasons for the lack of argumentation and debate in the Far East. In L. A. Samovar and R. E. Porter (Eds.), *Intercultural communication: A reader* (5th ed., pp. 243–252). Belmont, CA: Wadsworth.

13. Ugwu-Oju, Dympna. (1993, November 14). Pursuit of happiness. *The New York Times Magazine*, pp. 40, 42.

14. McCroskey, J. C., & Beatty, M. J. (1986). Oral communication apprehension. In Jones, et al. (Eds.). Op. cit., pp. 179–194.

15. Edwin Newman is quoted in Ross, R. S. (1989). *Speech communication: The speechmaking system* (8th ed., p. 50). Englewood Cliffs, NJ: Prentice Hall.

16. Brownell, W. W., & Katula, R. A. (1984). The Communication Anxiety Graph: A classroom tool for managing speech anxiety. *Communication Quarterly, 32*, 243–249.

17. Phillips, G. (1991). *Communication incompetencies: A theory of training oral performance behavior.* Carbondale: Southern Illinois University Press.

18. Glass, C. R., & Shea, C. A. (1986). Cognitive therapy for shyness and social anxiety. In Jones, et al. (Eds.). Op. cit., pp. 315–327.

19. See Howell, W. (1982). *The Empathic communicator.* Prospect Heights, IL: Waveland Press. A chapter, Coping with Internal-Monologue, is found in Stewart, J. (Ed.). (1990). *Bridges, not walls* (5th ed., pp. 128–138). New York: McGraw-Hill.

20. Ayers, J., & Hopf, T. S. (1989). Visualization: Is it more than extra-attention?" *Communication Education, 38*, (1), pp. 1–5.

21. This article appeared in the 1/26/92 issue of *The New York Times Magazine*. It can be found on pp. 10 ff.

22. From *Communication: Apprehension, avoidance, and effectiveness* (4th ed.), by Richmond, McCroskey. Copyright by Gorsuch Scarisbrick, Publishers. (Scottsdale, Arizona). Used with permission.

5 Speakers and Pluralistic Audiences

At the end of this chapter, you should be able to

- Identify six types of audiences and tell specific challenges each poses
- Tell how demographic audience analysis helps you adapt your speech to the audience
- Identify elements of ethos, and describe how your audience's perception of you determines your ethos before and during your speech
- Contrast monological and dialogical roles that develop between you and your audience

Note

Instead of being subject centered, or speaker centered, speech classes are audience centered. This means that speakers focus on their listeners throughout the entire speechmaking process. Throughout, emphasize the importance of remembering that audiences are made up of individuals who come from different personal and cultural backgrounds. Although they may share some characteristics, each listener is distinctive. The chapter further elaborates on the idea of dialogical public speaking.

The front page of the July 12, 1992, *New York Times* ran this headline, "Perot Speech Gets Cool Reception at NAACP." A subheadline elaborated, "Listeners are startled as candidate refers to 'your people.'" In a campaign speech given to the delegates of the National Association for the Advancement of Colored People, one of the oldest African-American civil rights groups, businessman–presidential candidate H. Ross Perot surprised and angered listeners with two major speaking blunders:

> *As he talked about his childhood experiences with blacks in Texarkana, Texas, Mr. Perot quoted his father's saying, "Son, these are people too, and they have to live."*
>
> *When he discussed the country's economic situation, he blundered again with this statement, "Financially, at least, it's going to be a long, hot summer. I don't have to tell you who gets hurt first when this sort of thing happens, do I? You, your people do. Your people do. I know that and you know that."*

Most of the usually responsive convention delegates listened in stony silence. One later pronounced Perot "culturally out of touch with his audience"[1] for telling them blacks "are people too" and calling them "your people."

Perot himself seemed genuinely puzzled that he had offended his listeners. The headlines could have been different had Mr. Perot taken more time to consider his audience in advance and to prepare a speech that was culturally sensitive. As it was, these two miscalculations formed the basis for most of the next day's press coverage, largely obscuring other significant points he made.

Perot's error illustrates the importance of sensitivity to the audience at every step of the speechmaking process—from the initial step of topic selection through the question-and-answer period that follows the speech. Often speech professors call this subject "audience analysis" because you are, in fact, analyzing your audience and discovering resources by which you can most effectively communicate with a particular group. You may also find it satisfying to think in dialogical terms about yourself as a "listening speaker,"[2] who hears audience interests and concerns before, during, and after the speech.

Cross Reference

This develops Geissner's theory of communication as dialogue that occurs in a specific situation.

The relationship between speakers and their audiences is complex, involving interwoven sets of perceptions that they hold about themselves and one another. Understanding these perceptions helps underscore Hellmut Geissner's point presented at the end of Chapter 1: Meaning depends on who is speaking and listening, to whom, in what circumstances, and why. This chapter will examine the *why* of audiences by looking at motivations of six kinds of listeners. Then it will turn to the *who* of speakers and listeners, looking at three different sets of perceptions that develop throughout the speech.

Kinds of Audiences

Teaching Idea

Use Activity 5.1 in the Instructor's Manual to help students understand the types of audiences. *Exercises 1 and 2 are also appropriate with this section.*

Audiences gather for a variety of reasons. Their motivations result in meanings that depend in part on the answers to these questions: *why* do the listeners assemble? *why* do they stay attentive? *why* do they remain? Identifying the kind of audience you face may answer some of these questions and help you prepare more effectively for your speech. Several years ago, H. L. Hollingworth classified audiences into the following six types: pedestrian, passive, selected, concerted, organized, and absent.[3]

Pedestrian Audiences

Teaching Idea

If you present these ideas in a lecture, there is a teaching transparency in the Instructor's Manual.

This type of audience is made up of a random group of individuals who temporarily gather to listen to a speech; they are *accidental* or *nonintentional* listeners. Pedestrian audiences are not expecting to hear a speech at all, but for some reason, they are drawn to listen by something that attracts their attention—perhaps a dazzling visual demonstration or the impassioned voice of a speaker. A key factor that distinguishes such audiences is that members come and go.

Many people, for instance, are walking across campus when they impulsively stop to hear a student speaker in an outdoor forum; others gather around a speaker who is demonstrating a food processor in a department store; still others are members of a pedestrian audience when they pause to listen to a street corner preacher or entertainer.

Don't be surprised if you rarely speak to an accidental audience. Most public speakers do not attempt to create audiences out of passersby. However, since this type of audience does exist, you may some day find yourself in front of such a group. If so, your major challenges are to attract and maintain listener attention, spark interest, and draw in nonintentional listeners so that they will hear and respond to your message.

Passive Audiences

Members of passive audiences listen to speeches because doing so helps them accomplish other goals. They might be called *incidental* audiences because hearing the speech is only incidental to their other purposes. Employees, for instance, attend a workshop because their manager insists they do so. They are interested in neither the speech nor the speaker, but listening helps them keep their jobs—their major goal. The key feature of a passive audience is that the speech itself is only a secondary motivation.

This kind of audience is fairly common, and you will probably address a passive audience some day. In fact, some classmates may be passive listeners, especially if they reluctantly took the course because it is required. They attend class, not specifically to hear you speak, but because listening to you fulfills

*Because they must cre-
ate an audience out of
people who are not
intending to listen to a
speech, speakers some-
times use unusual
means to attract atten-
tion to their topic.*

course requirements, enabling them to receive credit and a grade—their primary goals.

Your foremost challenge with a passive audience is to make your material interesting and relevant to their perceived needs—a challenge that is inherent to all good speechmaking, and one that is emphasized throughout this course. In short, whatever your topic, you must enable the audience to understand why and how it affects their lives.

Selected Audiences

A third type of audience chooses to participate either because the members are interested in the topic or because they are interested in the speaker. In other words, these listeners select the speeches they will attend; their participation is voluntary. Their interest may be either positive or negative—that is, they may agree with or like the speaker personally, or they attend precisely because they disagree with the ideas they anticipate hearing, or they dislike the speaker personally. The key to selected audiences is that listening is *intentional*.

The topic itself can draw an audience. Consider the case of a speaker in New York City whose subject was the controversial school curriculum entitled, "Children of the Rainbow." This multicultural curriculum offered lessons on diversity, including discussions of homosexuality, in elementary schools. Both supporters of the lessons and those opposed to such teachings in the schools voluntarily assembled to hear the speech. In this case, their interest in the topic was more important than their interest in the speaker.

People also voluntarily gather to hear specific speakers, regardless of the topic. Politicians, civil rights leaders, activists, and other well-known figures regularly address large audiences who gather out of an interest in them—perhaps without even knowing the topic. For this reason, if newscaster Connie Chung came to campus, many people would go to hear her whether she spoke about her career in broadcasting or about a major policy issue. Not all popular speakers are nationally known; some are local figures. For instance, listeners may assemble to hear local members of the clergy who have reputations for presenting interesting, relevant messages, regardless of the topic.

An audience whose members are similar in their attitude toward a topic is called a *homogeneous* audience. A typical homogeneous audience gathers to hear about cancer prevention because they agree that preventing the disease is important, and they want to learn how to maintain good health. Homogeneous audiences can also be generally negative, even hostile, toward a topic. One made up of musicians is hostile when all its members disagree with a speaker who is urging the boycott of records.

Selected or voluntary audiences are common, and you may have many opportunities to address such a group, especially if you present seminars or workshops someday where your topic attracts interested people. In some ways this is the easiest type of audience to address—if the members are positive toward you and your topic. In these cases, you have to keep their attention and relate your subject to their interests, but their desire to hear you makes this comparatively easy. Your major concern is to develop your main ideas clearly so that listeners understand and accept your arguments.

Concerted Audiences

The fourth kind of audience chooses to be at a speech, and they more or less agree with one another and with the speaker about the importance of the subject. The key to a concerted audience is that, though positive toward the subject, they are not organized to act on their beliefs. Your purpose here is a persuasive one that aims to motivate listeners and then show them specific ways they can organize and act. Peggy Charren, mentioned in Chapter 1, is a good example of a speaker who worked with a concerted audience. When she began to discuss children's television publicly, audiences gathered because they believed in her cause, and they were interested in seeing changes brought about. Charren's challenge was to show them specific things *they* could do to be part of the change. This will, similarly, be your challenge with such audiences. When you know that members of your audience agree with one another and with you about your topic, first you attempt to motivate them to act, then you describe in detail the specific steps they can take to turn their convictions into actualities.

Organized Audiences

Organized audiences are made up of members who are motivated to act and already know their roles. Thus, your major task is to provide them with specific directions that enable them to carry out their tasks efficiently. Much of the speaking in the world of work is to organized audiences, and you may have opportunities to do this type of speaking in your future employment. In a business, for instance, members of a sales group already know their roles, but they assemble to hear updated information about new products and new marketing strategies. School teachers and staff personnel gather at regular meetings to hear about specific policies or other details related to their jobs. Volunteer coordinators speak to people who have assembled in an organization, such as a hospital, to do volunteer work. If you assume a leadership or management role in such a group, you will likely be the one who provides these directions.

Absent Audiences

Cross Reference

This relates to life in an electronic culture.

Sometimes a speaker communicates with listeners who are not physically present. These audiences most commonly hear the speech through a mediated channel such as radio, television, audiotape, or videotape. Generally, audience members are scattered, with each person listening separately or with just a few other people. For instance, an individual might listen to a tape while jogging, a small group might hear a speech through a video hookup, or a family might gather in the living room to watch a televised message. The distinguishing feature of an absent audience is that it is separated from the speaker, with the result that the speaker does not receive instant feedback from listeners. Generally, absent audiences are also selected audiences because members choose to turn on the program or play the tape.

If you speak to an absent audience, use conversational delivery, as if you were speaking to one listener at a time. Moreover, since listeners can easily switch off the message, strive to maintain their interest throughout the entire speech.

Audiences are not completely homogeneous. This means that, though most members of your audience may have one predominant motivation for assembling, you may in reality face a group of listeners with a variety of individual motivations. In a concerted audience, for instance, an incidental listener may tag along with a committed friend, not to hear you speak, but to maintain a relationship with the friend. Similarly, your classroom may contain both passive and voluntary audience members.

In short, since there are many types of audiences, you will be a more effective speaker in the future if you consider the *why* of your audience. Knowing their major motivation for gathering can help you more effectively plan a speech that is sensitive to their interests and needs.

KEY CONCEPT

Kinds of Audiences

Type of Audience	Characteristic Motivation of Listeners	The Speaker's Major Challenge
Pedestrian	Accidental or non-intentional	Attract and maintain attention
Passive	Listening is incidental to other goals	Make speech interesting and relevant
Selected	Choose to listen	Develop ideas clearly
Concerted	Motivated but unorganized	Provide specific steps listeners can take to accomplish their goals
Organized	Know their roles, motivated	Give specific, updated information
Absent	Choose to listen but separated from the speaker	Speak conversationally, maintain attention

Speaker—Listener Perceptions[4]

We have looked at six answers to the question asking *why* audiences gather. In this section, we examine issues regarding *who* is doing the interacting. It is important to know *who* is speaking, and *who* is listening, and how speakers and listeners perceive one another. The answers to these questions will help you understand how to select speech materials and how to communicate more effectively with your audiences.

Speakers and listeners bring perceptions not only of themselves but often of each other to the speech event. Because of this, before you even take the stage, you generally have some idea of who your listeners are and what they already know because you have analyzed them to a degree. Moreover, members of your audience have certain ideas about you. Further, during and after the speech, you continue to evaluate them, and they make judgments about you. However, these perceptions are only impressions. They may or may not be accurate, nor are they completely formed; yet these perceptions influence the meanings that result from the speech.

There are many interwoven aspects of this complex speaker–listener relationship. We will look at three: (1) your perception of your audience, (2) their perceptions of you, and (3) the perceptions you and your listeners hold regarding the relationship between you.

As you prepare your speech, consider salient aspects of your audience such as ethnicity, sex, age, region, and group affiliation.

Perception 1: Who You Think Your Listeners Are

Teaching Idea

Use a number of magazine ads as explained in Activity 5.2 in the Instructor's Manual to teach demographic audience analysis.

There are many ways to consider your audience. One of the most common is to engage in what is called *demographic audience analysis*. That is, you analyze or think about your listeners according to the cultural populations they represent. However, as you might expect, listeners' membership in groups becomes *salient*—meaning that it is significant or that it matters—in some situations; it is less salient in others.[5] For this reason, you must evaluate your listeners' identification with various groups *as it relates to the specific speaking situation*.

Although there are many considerations you make as you analyze audiences, the following categories are some of the most common: ethnicity, sex, age, region, and group affiliation.

 Ethnicity   Ethnicity refers to a group's common heritage and cultural traditions that usually stem from national and religious origins. A pluralistic nation such as the United States includes people from a variety of historical and geographical backgrounds that influence the ways they think and act to varying degrees. For example, the Russian Old Believers who live in the Willamette Valley of Oregon are a distinct ethnic group distinguished by language, clothing, cultural heroes, and religious traditions from their Anglo and Mexican-American neighbors. The Amish of Pennsylvania are another such group. Citizens of Japanese, German, Mexican, Italian, and Irish descent are just a few of the many ethnic groups that make up the United States. Urban areas are especially diverse. For instance, members of more than 150 ethnic groups (speaking 114 languages) reside in Queens, New York.

In many instances, ethnicity is related to religious traditions. Throughout your speech presentation, be sensitive to the possible range and intensity of religious beliefs of your audience. For example, some people may identify themselves as belonging to a particular faith yet see their religion as a peripheral part of their identity. For other people, religion is a central factor that influences many other areas of their lives.

Ethnic groups vary in the degree to which they have assimilated into the dominant society. Some groups, such as the Amish, resist assimilation, attempting to maintain their religious and ethnic identity. Others more readily adopt aspects of American culture, trading their traditional languages and customs for new ways. Additionally, individuals and families within ethnic groups vary in their degree of assimilation. Within the Mexican-American community, for example, some individuals and families are still quite traditional; others have become more Americanized.

Ethnicity is a complex concept. For one reason, many people have ancestors from more than one ethnic group. For instance, one listener may have a Japanese father and a Euro-American mother, another has a father of African descent and a mother who immigrated from Mexico, another is of German–English–French descent, and a fourth person is of Korean ancestry, adopted as an infant into a Euro-American family. These individuals filter their perceptions through a combination of cultural traditions.

Ethnic identity assumes salience in some contexts, whereas it is less important in others. It is generally salient if the group is fairly homogeneous in ethnicity. For example, an all-Irish group whose members are debating issues surrounding a St. Patrick's Day parade will probably identify closely with their Irish roots. In other instances, however, their ethnicity assumes less importance. An Irish student in a speech class with two ethnic Greeks, two Haitians, three Italian Americans, one Indonesian, and three African Americans probably considers her educational and occupational goals to be more important than her Irish ethnicity.

If your classroom is ethnically mixed, be aware of different cultural traditions, and don't assume that everyone shares your cultural perspectives. Further, if you work in a multinational organization in the future, the ethnic backgrounds of the various members will challenge you to be culturally sensitive in your speaking.

Sex   It is generally quite simple to distinguish people on the basis of sex—the biologically determined categories designated male and female. However, do not confuse these biological sexual differences with cultural gender differences. The concept of *gender* involves a cluster of traits that cultural groups label masculine, feminine, and androgynous (containing both masculine and feminine characteristics). In our rapidly changing society, we are continually examining and negotiating gender-associated characteristics, changing our notions of what constitutes "proper" behavior for men and for women.

For Further Reading

For information on cultural identity and salience regarding social identities, see M. J. Collier. (1994). Cultural identity and intercultural communication. In L. A. Samovar and R. E. Porter (Eds.), *Intercultural communication: A reader* (7th ed., pp. 36–45). Belmont, CA: Wadsworth.

Sexual orientation and sexual activity are additional factors to consider. When you speak before any audience, you cannot assume that all listeners are heterosexual, nor can you assume that all are sexually active. The point to remember is that if you make assumptions that a person will think or act in a certain way *because of his or her sex*, you are being *sexist*.

Some students demonstrate insensitivity to issues of gender, sexual orientation, and sexual activity when they speak. For example, on a campus with an active Greek system, one student spoke on how to get a date. He advised his listeners to attend a fraternity party, scope out interesting women, get one to drink heavily, then invite her to a bedroom upstairs to "look at the goldfish." Although many people in the audience laughed, others were offended by the assumptions he made about women, fraternities, drinking, and sexual behaviors.

Sometimes gender identity is salient to an audience. This is especially true at gender-exclusive conferences or retreats. Examples include a "Women in Science" conference or "Father's Weekend," a series of workshop presentations sponsored by a local boys' club. If you ever speak to such a group, you cannot ignore gender issues. At other times, however, you may speak to an all-male or all-female group, but gender identity is not particularly significant. An audience made up of females who gather to hear a political analyst discuss the deceptive use of images in political advertisements care less about gender than they do political affiliation, educational level, or some other factor.

Teaching Idea

Throughout this section on demographic audience analysis, refer to the magazine ads used in Activity 5.2. For example, you might contrast ads from *Modern Maturity* with those found in *Seventeen* or *Rolling Stone*.

Age   In his classic treatise on rhetoric, Aristotle[6] emphasized the importance of age as an influence on audience motivations and concerns because different generations have different perspectives that color their outlook on life. Globally, cultures distinguish between age groups, and ours is no exception. We categorize and label one another according to different ages. Because each generation has experienced different external social forces and events, their views of the world differ. For example:

People who came of age during World War II now make up the senior citizen population. When they were children, they had access to radio, but television was not available. Many in this generation remember outdoor plumbing. Their education included prayer in school, and students who chewed gum were a major problem for teachers.

People who were born from the mid-1940s to the early 1960s—called baby boomers—are the product of the post-World War II childbearing boom. They came of age in the late 1950s through the early 1970s. Older "boomers" participated in the national mourning that followed the assassinations of President Kennedy and Martin Luther King, Jr. Some members of this generation avoided the draft, experimented with drugs, and organized protests.

People born since 1961 are sometimes called generation X, *generation 13 (the thirteenth generation since Benjamin Franklin),* baby busters *(after the boom years),* or baby boomerangs *(returning to live with boomer parents).*[7] *They came of age in a media-dominated society, with television, CD players, portable radios, and computers. Socially, they grew up with high divorce rates, legalized abortion, and a huge national deficit. Their outlook on life, as well as their view of technology, is very different from that of senior citizens.*

Because people differ from generation to generation, they are moved by different appeals, and it is important to vary your speech materials for younger and older audiences. If your audience is fairly homogeneous in age, use generational interests in making such decisions as your speech purpose and the illustrations you select to support your major ideas. For example, if you give a speech on social security, your purpose, your emphases, and your supporting materials will vary for audiences made up of twenty-something, forty-something, or seventy-something individuals. In contrast, when you address audiences with a variety of ages, you must find topics that cut across generational lines, or you must develop the topic in such a way that it is not linked to a particular age.

In the classroom, be aware of age differences, and select topics that are important to the lives of everyone. Think back to the speech on campus dating in a fraternity setting. It was irrelevant to the thirty-five-year-old single mother of two who was taking the class in order to improve her communication skills to get a better paying job.

It is characteristic of U.S. culture to celebrate youth and actively look for young, fresh ideas. As a result, we listen to the ideas of younger people as well as those of more experienced speakers. However, in many cultures throughout the world, people respect the wisdom and experience that come only with age. Consequently, if you work in an international organization in the future, this is one of the cultural differences you must take into account as you communicate with international audiences. This may be especially true if you are much younger than your listeners.

For Further Reading

See Garreau. (1981). *The nine nations of North America.* Boston: Houghton Mifflin. See also P. A. Andersen, M. W. Lustig, and J. F. Andersen (1987). Regional patterns of communication in the United States: A theoretical perspective. *Communication Monographs* 54, pp. 128–144.

Region   We anticipate that speaking to audiences made up of Japanese or Nigerian listeners will require different speaking strategies, but what if we move from one geographical region to another in North America? Although people on this continent share many commonalities, author Joel Garreau[8] contends that North America contains not three nations but rather nine separate areas that differ in characteristic features (see Box 5.1). Each looks, feels, and sounds different; each has its own capital city. These nine areas do not correspond to the political boundary lines dividing Canada, the United States, and Mexico. According to Garreau, the climate, history, language, economic base, politics, and other such features influence the people who live in these regions. This can, therefore, influence audience interests and perceptions in public speaking situations.

BOX 5.1

The Nine Nations of North America

New England
Capital city: Boston. This area extends north of Maine into the coastal Canadian provinces. Its inhabitants pride themselves on their history of settlement and their traditions that value education and intellectual pursuits. The region lacks abundant raw materials and energy sources.

Quebec
Capital city: Quebec. The French-speaking area of Canada differs from its English-speaking neighbors not only in language but also in mindset. Its customs and traditions still retain distinctly French characteristics.

The Foundry
Capital city: Detroit. This section includes the middle eastern seaboard that extends into the industrial regions of the Great Lakes. The key factor in this region is the work ethic.

Dixie
Capital city: Atlanta. The "Deep South" has a slower pace of life that is linked to its agrarian history. The history of slavery and the Civil War also influenced the development of this region.

The Islands
Capital city: Miami. The southern tip of Florida and the Caribbean Islands form this Spanish-speaking nation that relies on tourism for much of its economy. A history of slavery also affects this region.

The Breadbasket
Capital city: Kansas City. This farming region stretches from parts of Texas into the middle of Canada. Garreau found this region to be most at peace with itself, and its people value stability and straightforwardness. Eighty percent of the land is used for farming.

Mexamerica
Capital city: Los Angeles. Mexico and southern parts of the United States are blending both languages and cultures in this region historically characterized by Spanish conquest. This nation contains distinct groups of Mexicans, Mexican Americans, and Americans who differ from one another in basic values.

The Empty Quarter
Capital city: Denver. This region includes mountainous and desert areas of the western United States and Canada, extending into Alaska. It is characterized by an abundance of minerals and a sparse population. In general, it lacks adequate water resources to sustain a large population.

Ecotopia
Capital city: San Francisco. The Pacific Rim runs from San Francisco to Anchorage, Alaska. This beautiful area has abundant natural resources, which its inhabitants want to preserve. Consequently, residents value working with nature by developing environmentally sound industries and policies.

Questions

Though not everyone agrees with Garreau's ideas, he emphasizes the importance of considering the audience's region of origin. In order to do so, ask yourself questions such as these:

1. What topics are more appropriate to Ecotopians? To residents of The Breadbasket?

2. In which regions is knowledge of a second language important? Where might you have to speak through a translator?

3. How might residents of The Empty Quarter and New England differ from Islanders on issues about the use of natural resources?

4. How do historical influences such as slavery and Spanish settlement in the southern "nations" and French and English settlements in northern "nations" affect public speaking?

Figure 5.1   *Thinking of North America by cultural region is in many ways more meaningful than by conventional political divisions.*

Group Affiliation   People often affiliate with others who share their occupations, interests, experiences, or hobbies. A few common groups are Veterans of Foreign Wars, the National Education Association, Young Republicans, Alcoholics Anonymous, the debate team, and the ski club. Often these groups invite guest speakers to regularly scheduled meetings. Since group identity is highly salient at such meetings, develop your speeches by drawing on common experiences and shared beliefs and values. For instance, the Young Republicans expect you to refer to Republican party heroes and to party goals and ideals. Members of an Alzheimer's caregiver's support group anticipate a speech that addresses their concerns.

It is common to address listeners who are all members of the same occupation, whether they be nurses, janitors, homemakers, stockbrokers, miners, professors, scientists, or any of a number of other groups. If you speak before such an audience in the future, select examples and proofs that relate to the shared interests and experiences of the group's members. When listeners gather as an occupational group, their job identity will probably be salient. For example, during the inservice meetings that precede the opening of each new school year, teachers gather to orient themselves to the coming year. In these meetings, their occupation as teachers—not so much their sex, age, or ethnicity—is what is salient to most. This is true whether the group is local, national, or international. Thus, in gatherings of local teachers, a national organization of teachers, or international educators, public speakers focus on issues and concerns to teachers.

Teaching Idea

As a culminating activity for this section, use exercise 3, or make a similar exercise for use with small discussion groups.

In summary, it is true that you form perceptions of your listeners partly on the basis of the demographic categories and groups to which they belong. Some of the generalizations you make are fairly accurate. However, many speakers—students and professionals alike—are less effective than they could be because they often make unwarranted assumptions about their audiences. Mr. Perot's audience criticized him for treating them as a racial group rather than as individuals who happened to be of African origin—although he surmised correctly that their racial identity was highly salient at the NAACP convention. Throughout your speech preparation, remember that audience members, while sharing certain features in common, are individuals who differ in significant ways. Your sensitivity in audience analysis will help you avoid an embarrassing public blunder.

KEY CONCEPT

Who You Think Your Listeners Are

Ethnicity Ethnic identity stems from historical heritage and tradition—usually national or religious in origin.

Sex Not only biological sex differences distinguish males and females, there are culturally influenced gender traits (masculine, feminine, or androgynous). Other facets of sexuality include sexual orientation and sexual activity.

While this ski instructor is assessing her audience's level of ability and physical conditioning, her listeners are evaluating her credibility. She will be more effective if she demonstrates that she is knowledgeable, trustworthy, enthusiastic, and concerned about their interests.

Age Members of different generations have different perspectives on life that influence their motivations and concerns. We often categorize people as senior citizens, baby boomers, and generation X (or one of a number of other names).

Region Regional differences create nine separate areas that share many things in common but vary in significant ways.

Group affiliation People affiliate with social and occupational groups, and this is often their reason for gathering as an audience.

Perception 2: Who Audience Members Think You Are

Note

Speakers' ideas about their listeners are important, but so are listeners' ideas about speakers. For this reason, the discussion of ethos or credibility—the speaker as seen through the eyes of the audience—is developed in this chapter more than in the chapter on reasoning, as is most common. (It is briefly reviewed in Chapter 15.)

Not only do you form impressions of your listeners, they also form perceptions of you that are their composite impressions about your character, your intentions, and your abilities. Aristotle used the Greek word *ethos*, which is often called *credibility*. He believed that ethos—your character as a speaker—is one of the most important "proofs" you use to give credence and support to your ideas. In short, when listeners believe in your good character, your intelligence and good judgment, and your positive feelings and intentions toward them, you are more likely to influence them. Quintilian, the first-century Roman teacher of rhetoric, phrased it like this:

A man [sic] who would have other men trust his judgment as to what is expedient and honourable, should possess and be regarded as possessing genuine wisdom and excellence of character.[9]

As you might imagine, ethos differs from culture to culture. Euro-Americans look at the speaker's knowledge of the subject and the evidence she or he presents, but other cultures judge speakers as credible on the basis of their character. It takes a person a long time in Chinese and Japanese cultures to develop credibility, for credibility is related to age, gender, social rank, and maturity more than it is to knowledge and expertise on a particular subject.[10] Similar values can also be seen in some Native-American cultures. When the occasion calls for "saying a few words," younger males and women seek out older males to speak for them. For example, Weider and Pratt[11] relate the story of a young Indian woman who spoke for herself and her husband on a public occasion. She was chastised by other members of her group for not knowing how to act.

There are two types of credibility: prior ethos and demonstrated ethos. Moreover, there are four characteristics of credible speakers: good sense, good character, goodwill, and dynamism.

Teaching Idea

Invite a guest speaker or speakers to class to discuss how she or he prepares for speeches. (Consider retirees who have spoken throughout their careers or invite student leaders who speak regularly.) In advance, give the speaker(s) an outline of the section on demographics and this section on ethos.

Types of Credibility   The first type of credibility is that which you bring with you to the speech because of who you are or because of your experiences with the subject. It is called *prior ethos* or *extrinsic credibility* because it is separate from the words of the speech itself. This means that, before you even take the stage, you may be seen as an expert for one reason or another. When the director of an art museum delivers a lecture on Egyptian art, the audience comes to the lecture expecting that she will know what she is talking about. She has prior ethos; that is, she brings with her the credibility that comes from her job and her title. Similarly, when an audience listens to a man whose son was murdered, they judge him as a credible speaker on victim's rights, based on his personal experience with the subject. However, you do not generally have prior ethos in the classroom, for you lack the credentials of education and experience that would make your classmates see you as an expert.

Because you lack prior ethos, you must demonstrate the second type of credibility in the course of speaking. This type of ethos is, not surprisingly, called *demonstrated ethos* or *intrinsic credibility* because it is evident from the information you present that you are knowledgeable about the topic. Even speakers with prior ethos must show within the speech that they are credible. Thus, the art director must demonstrate that she does, indeed, know her subject.

You can demonstrate your credibility in many ways. Probably the most important way is to be knowledgeable about your topic. Throughout the speech, define your terms, state your sources of information, give examples, and otherwise show that you have a thorough understanding of your subject. You may have further opportunity to demonstrate your expertise afterward in a question-and-answer period.

Characteristics of Ethos   According to Aristotle,[12] listeners see three traits as contributing to credibility: good sense, good character, and goodwill or friendliness of disposition. Modern researchers have added a fourth characteristic—dynamism—that consistently emerges in studies of ethos.

Good Sense   Good sense is a cluster of characteristics made up of several components. One aspect is *intelligence*. You demonstrate your intelligence by showing that you are knowledgeable; you understand your subject and provide up-to-date information about it. Moreover, you can discuss related historical developments and can link your topic to contemporary national and international issues. Listeners recognize that your knowledge is deep and thorough—that you are not "bluffing your way" through the speech.

Another aspect of good sense is *sound reasoning*. You demonstrate this by supporting your claims with trustworthy evidence and by making logical connections between ideas. For instance, one student gave a speech on good nutrition and urged the audience to eat carefully, choosing such nutritious foods as bananas, a food found in the dairy group. Audience members raised their eyebrows. After the speech, one listener asked if bananas were really in the dairy group. The speaker said, "Yes." The questioner then asked when bananas were reclassified from the fruit group into the dairy group. "Oh," the speaker said, "I saw this ad in a magazine that showed a glass of milk in a banana peel. So bananas are a dairy food." Audience members barely suppressed their laughter, and the speaker completely lost credibility (see Figure 5.2).

A third cue that often signals good sense is *composure*. Composure is the ability to remain calm in a stressful situation. When you remain calm under pressure, people have more confidence in you than when you lose your poise. For example, if you are highly agitated during one of your classroom presentations, your audience may feel that you are unable to control yourself adequately, and they lose confidence in you as a public speaker. However, if you are composed and controlled, they will perceive you more favorably. If you get angry at hostile questions and are rude to questioners, listeners may feel that you do not show adequate self-control because someone else caused you to "lose your cool."

In April 1993, U.S. Attorney General Janet Reno provided an excellent example of composure. She had only been in office about a month when the religious cult leader David Koresh and his followers died in a raging fire after a long standoff with federal officials. When Ms. Reno faced reporters as well as a congressional committee investigating the tragedy, she handled the stressful situation with composure, even when personal attacks were leveled against her and her officials. As a result, her credibility rose in public opinion polls for a time.

Although composure is important to credibility in Euro-American culture, other cultures have contrasting views of its significance. In an article entitled, "Force Fields in Black and White Communication,"[13] Thomas Kochman emphasized the emotional force expected of credible speakers in the African-American tradition. Good speakers are genuinely intense in their expressions,

Teaching Idea

Discuss speakers who have lost their composure with negative results or kept it under great stress, with positive results. Edmund Muskie, for example, was a presidential candidate until a reporter's question about his wife caused him to cry. Shortly thereafter, he dropped out of the race. Early in the 1992 campaign, Mr. and Mrs. Clinton maintained their composure in the face of Gennifer Flowers's accusations. Their campaign was successful.

Figure 5.2 *A student speaker lost credibility when she drew a faulty conclusion from an ad like this.*

When your potassium comes with dairy calcium, you don't need a bunch.

An 8-ounce glass of milk has about as much potassium as the average banana. And an 8-ounce cup of yogurt has even more. Dairy foods can be an excellent source of potassium. And many other essential nutrients as well. Including, of course, calcium.

Milk and yogurt, like all dairy foods, also come in a variety of lower fat alternatives. So build your family's diet on a firm foundation of dairy foods. It's the perfect way to avoid nutritional slip-ups.

Dairy Foods. The Basics of Good Nutrition.

© 1990 N.D.B.
National Dairy Board
America's Dairy Farmers

For Further Reading

See D. Carbaugh (Ed.) (1990). *Intercultural communication and intercultural contacts.* Hillsdale, NY: Lawrence Erlbaum. In that volume, see T. Kochman. Force fields in black and white communication, (pp. 193–217); and D. L. Weider and S. Pratt. On being a recognizable Indian, (pp. 45–64).

and sometimes their emotions threaten to override the order and procedure common in the Euro-American style of public speaking. For this reason, listeners from the Euro-American culture may consider them loud. Similarly, Janice Walker Anderson compared the expectations that Americans and Arabs have for "effective" speakers.[14] She found that, in contrast to the widely held U.S. value of objectivity and detachment, Arab listeners traditionally expect effective speakers to show emotion during their speeches.

Good Character   Audiences generally want to listen to speakers who have integrity—women and men who are honest, trustworthy, and unselfish. According to the dominant culture in the United States, you should provide ample documentation of your sources and give facts that square with what the audience knows to be true in order to be perceived as honest and worthy of trust. When you choose topics that matter to you, and stick by your convictions—even when they are unpopular—you demonstrate personal integrity. In contrast, speakers, such as politicians or executives, lose listener confidence if they change their positions from one day to another, depending on what the audience wants to hear. They pander to their audiences rather than stand up for their convictions.

Goodwill   When you demonstrate goodwill, you convey that you have your audience's interests at heart. Some related characteristics of goodwill are friendliness, openness, respect, and a spirit of mutual regard. Listeners feel that you see their perspective and understand their concerns when you find common ground with them and attempt to reach conclusions that are mutually satisfying. The terms *co-orientation* or *identification*[15] designate speakers who turn toward their listeners and identify with their interests in this way.

Teaching Idea

At the end of this section on ethos, have students do exercise 4. They can write a summary in their journal, or they can discuss their ethos with one other person.

Dynamism   Researchers have identified dynamism or forcefulness as a fourth trait that listeners perceive as making speakers more believable. As we see in Chapter 12, dynamism is linked to traits of extroversion, energy, and enthusiasm. This does not mean that you are not credible if you are not dynamic; however, when you visibly enjoy your topic and communicate your ideas with enthusiasm and liveliness, you may appear to be more believable to your audiences.

KEY CONCEPT   Who Audience Members Think You Are

Ethos   This is the credibility that results from the way the audience perceives you as a speaker.

Prior ethos   Also known as extrinsic credibility, this is the reputation you bring to the speech; it does not depend on the words of the speech.

Demonstrated ethos   Also known as intrinsic credibility, you appear credible during the speech through your obvious competence.

Speakers and audiences both have perceptions of their relationship to one another. This drill instructor is engaging in monological rather than dialogical communication with these recruits.

Characteristics of ethos:

Good sense Includes intelligence, sound reasoning, and composure.

Good character Includes integrity, honesty, and trustworthiness.

Goodwill Involves positive regard for the audience, often demonstrated by co-orientation or identification with them.

Dynamism Means the speech is delivered in a lively manner.

Perception 3: Perceptions of the Speaker– Audience Relationship

For Further Reading

See R. L. Johannesen. (1971). The emerging concept of communication as dialogue. *Quarterly Journal of Speech* 57, pp. 373–382. For a good summary of monologue and dialogue, see Chapter 4 (pp. 57–78) in Johannesen's 1990 text, *Ethics in human communication*, 3rd Ed. Prospect Heights, IL: Waveland Press.

You can relate to your audience in a variety of ways. You may relate in a *friend-to-friends* manner in which you share your ideas with an audience consisting of equals. You may also interact in a *teacher-to-students* relationship. There, you, the speaker-teacher, provide information for listener-students to learn. It is even possible to relate in a *puppet-master-to-puppets* role, as can be seen when speakers control the thoughts and actions of listeners who relinquish authority to them. Hitler is one example, as is David Koresh, leader of the religious group that burned its compound in Waco, Texas, in April 1993.

A common way of thinking about the speaker–listener relationship is to categorize it as either *monological* or *dialogical* in attitude and approach.[16] Monological speakers see their listeners as a collection of people to manipulate.

Audiences who participate in monologue allow speakers to dominate and control them. Instead of thinking their way through arguments and fighting for their personal conclusions, they allow themselves to be swayed by the words of the speaker. The puppet-master-to-puppets role illustrates this.

In contrast, dialogical speakers think of their speech as part of a longer interchange of ideas in which their listeners' viewpoints are also significant and worthy of a hearing. Paul Tournier, the Swiss psychologist, said,

> . . . one speaks quite differently if the audience is no longer an anonymous mass, if one seeks in it a few faces and exchanges glances with individuals, so that one's speech takes on the quality of a dialogue.[17]

Dialogical audience members respond by taking the words and ideas of the speaker and interacting with them mentally. They do this by performing a variety of mental operations, including weighing evidence, considering sources, drawing inferences, evaluating ideas in the light of their own experiences, and making judgments about the credibility of the speaker. The result is that, instead of being manipulated by speakers, they cooperate with them in producing mutually satisfying conclusions.

Teaching Idea

Have students discuss other monological speakers who use their rhetorical skills to advance their own agendas, regardless of their audience.

To understand the difference between these two attitudes, consider these contrasting scenes. In a *monologue*, a parent does all the talking to his teenager. "Now you listen to me," he says as he gives his opinions on how his child should think or behave. Most teens feel frustrated, even angry, manipulated, or coerced when they don't have a chance to say anything, and their perspective is not taken into account. A monological attitude can also be seen in the public speaking setting; for instance, a financial planner in Seattle convinced a group of limited-English-speaking Chinese investors to risk their savings on investments that he knew were shaky. He preyed on his listeners' desire for financial security in order to meet his personal desire for a financial profit.

In a *dialogue*, the parent has a definite point of view and clear ideas of what he wants his children to believe or do, but he talks *with* them, attempting to see the situation from their point of view as well as his, asking their opinion, perspective, and insights to reach a common ground. In the public speaking setting, dialogical speaking is an attitude, an intent, an awareness, a perspective rather than a series of rules for speakers or listeners. Dialogical speakers listen, as it were, to their audience before, during, and after the speech, trying to anticipate listener questions, understandings, interests, beliefs, attitudes, and goals, as well as their own.

Being dialogic does not mean that you have no personal biases or strong beliefs or that you cannot attempt to persuade people to share your viewpoints. Sometimes you may sincerely disagree with your audiences. However, rather than manipulate or trick your listeners, you honestly present the policies you think are in your listeners' best interests, and you use your best reasoning to support your ideas. Throughout your message, you are honest, noncoercive and nonmanipulative, and you truly allow your audiences to exercise free choice. A dialogical attitude is especially important in intercultural settings where listeners and speakers have different world views.

In public speeches that are dialogical, audiences take an active part in generating meaning. Therefore, you can use strategies that require active participation. One way is to ask rhetorical questions—where the listeners answer in their minds rather than out loud, such as, "Have you ever wondered why snowflakes are so perfectly symmetrical?" Or you can elicit mental images by directing listeners' thoughts, as in, "Think of a time you were really hungry." After the speech, inviting questions will open up the dialogue and also allow you to clarify your points and amplify your ideas.[18]

Professors John Stewart and Milt Thomas[19] summarize the traits of a dialogical attitude between speakers and their audiences:

1. Both the speaker and listeners value and build mutuality. That is, they realize that they have much to learn from one another.

2. Both are actively involved in the communication event. The speaker, of course, prepares and delivers the speech, gaining and holding the audience's attention. Audience members actively listen, evaluate, weigh information, and form their own conclusions.

3. Speaker and listeners are genuine and authentic. They are both open-minded and willing to change as a result of the speaking event.

4. They believe in synergy—a view that the whole is greater than the sum of the parts. That is, the knowledge generated by the cooperation of the speaker and audience is greater than the knowledge each could produce alone.

Cross Reference

Ethics is a recurring theme of this text.

In short, dialogical communicators are authentic, honest, and straightforward. They do not try to project a powerful "image" or facade. They risk personal involvement with their audiences and are willing to disclose some of their motivations and to accept the audience's reactions sincerely. Most people would probably evaluate dialogue as more ethical than monological communication because it allows people the freedom to come to their own meanings rather than imposing the speaker's views on them.

KEY CONCEPT

Perceptions of the Speaker—Audience Relationship

Monological Speakers talk *to* their audiences; they attempt to manipulate listeners, who allow them to do so.

Dialogical Speakers talk *with* their audiences; they consider themselves not only speakers who want to influence their audiences but also listeners who can be influenced by their audiences in turn.

Summary

Audiences approach speeches with a variety of motivations. Pedestrian audiences stop to listen to something that attracts their attention; they did not intend to hear a speech in the first place. Passive audiences listen to speeches because they are incidental to other goals, such as keeping a job. Selected audiences come out of an interest in either the topic or the speaker—an interest that can be either positive or negative. Concerted audiences are motivated to listen because they are concerned about a topic; they just do not know what to do about it. Organized audiences need specific details and instructions that will help them carry out their tasks more efficiently. Finally, absent audiences are separated from the speaker; they receive the speech through some form of media.

Throughout this chapter, we have seen that audiences and speakers are involved in an interactive process in which both form impressions of one another and of their relationship. You must consider your audience before you speak. You do this by assessing different demographic characteristics of listeners, such as age, ethnicity, and sex; and by considering their interests and group affiliations. However, you also realize that these characteristics are salient, meaning that they matter, at different times and in different circumstances.

Listeners, too, are actively involved in the speaking event. They sometimes evaluate you in advance of your speech—assessing your reputation with the subject. They also evaluate you during your speech. At these times, they form impressions of your ethos or credibility—using a combination of impressions regarding your good sense, your good character, your goodwill toward them, and your dynamism. The criteria for evaluating speaker credibility vary greatly among cultural groups. Whereas Euro-American society values composure and objectivity, African Americans and Arabs traditionally see speakers as credible when they are emotionally involved with their subjects. Native-American, Japanese, and Chinese listeners tend to view older speakers as wiser and more credible.

The relationship that forms between you and your audiences is important. In monological relationships, you try to impose your thoughts and ideas on others. In dialogical relationships, in contrast, you think of the audience as individuals who are involved with you in creating mutual meanings.

This is one of the most important chapters in this text. Presidential candidate Ross Perot found, to his chagrin, that sensitivity to a specific audience is not an option. It is essential to good speechmaking. Although both speakers and listeners have been the subject of the chapter, the major focus has been on the speaker's point of view. In Chapter 6, we look at the dialogical process from the listener's point of view.

Questions and Exercises

1. Identify different times when you have been a member of each type of audience: pedestrian, passive, voluntary, concerted, organized, and absent.

2. Discuss with a small group of your classmates the possibilities, if any, that might exist for you to address each type of audience in the future.

3. Using one of these topics, talk with a small group of your classmates about the different ways you would develop a speech for each of the following audiences:

   A. Topic: Your school's administrators are discussing a policy that will abolish all competitive sports on campus.

      Audiences: • Your classmates
      • A group of prospective students
      • Alumni who are consistent donors to the school
      • Basketball team members

   B. Topic: The United States should double its foreign aid budget.

      Audiences: • Senior citizens
      • A high school government class
      • The local chapter of the League of Women Voters

4. Try to see yourself as a member of the classroom audience would. At this point in the term, what prior ethos do you bring to each speech? How can you demonstrate ethos in subsequent speeches?

   Evaluate yourself on your good sense. How can you demonstrate to this audience that you are intelligent? That your reasoning is sound? That you are composed? In what ways might your good character be evidenced? How can you demonstrate goodwill toward your classmates? In what ways might you identify with them? Rate yourself on dynamism. How can you increase your dynamism (if needed)?

Key Terms

pedestrian audience
passive audience
selected audience
concerted audience
organized audience
absent audience
demographic
salient
ethnicity
gender
sexist
Nine Nations of North America
ethos
credibility
prior ethos (extrinsic credibility)
demonstrated ethos (intrinsic credibility)
composure
dialogical attitude
monological attitude

Notes

1. Applebome, P. (1992, July 12). Perot speech gets cool reception at N.A.A.C.P. *The New York Times*, p. A1.
2. Holtzman, P. (1970). *The psychology of speakers and audiences* (p. 111). Glenview, IL: Scott Foresman.
3. Hollingworth, H. L. (1935). *The psychology of audiences.* New York: American Book Company. See also Ross, R. S. (1989). *Speech communication: The speechmaking system* (8th ed.). Englewood Cliffs, NJ: Prentice-Hall.
4. The idea of complex relationships can be seen in Barnlund, D. C. (1990). Toward a meaning-centered philosophy of communication. In J. Stewart (Ed.), *Bridges not walls: A book about interpersonal communication* (5th ed., pp. 37–43). New York: McGraw-Hill. See also Watzlawich, P., Beavin, J. H., & Jackson, D. D. (1968). *Pragmatics of human communication.* New York: Norton.

5. Collier, M. J. (1994). Cultural identity and intercultural communication. In L. A. Samovar & R. E. Porter (Eds.), *Intercultural communication: A reader* (7th ed., pp. 36–45). Belmont, CA: Wadsworth.

6. Aristotle. (1954, 1984). *The rhetoric.* (W. R. Roberts, Trans.). New York: The Modern Library.

7. For terminology relating to this generation, see Israel, B. (1993, February 14). Lost in the name game. *The New York Times*, sec. 9, pp. 4, 9.

8. Garreau, J. L. (1981). *The nine nations of North America.* Boston: Houghton Mifflin. See also Andersen, P. A., Lustig, M. W., & Andersen, J. F. (1987). Regional patterns of communication in the United States: A theoretical perspective. *Communication Monographs, 54*, 128–144.

9. Quintilian. *Institutio Oratoria*, III, viii, 13. Quoted in E. P. J. Corbett. (1965). *Classical rhetoric for the modern student* (p. 80). New York: Oxford University Press.

10. Sitkaram, K. S., & Cogdell, R. T. (1976). *Foundations of intercultural communication.* Columbus, OH: Charles E. Merrill.

11. Weider, D. L., & Pratt, S. (1990). On being a recognizable Indian. In D. Carbaugh (Ed.), *Intercultural communication and intercultural contacts* (pp. 45–64). Hillsdale, NJ: Lawrence Erlbaum.

12. Aristotle. (1954, 1984). Op. cit.

13. Kochman, T. (1990). Force fields in black and white communication. In D. Carbaugh (Ed.), *Intercultural communication and intercultural contacts* (pp. 193–217). Hillsdale, NY: Lawrence Erlbaum.

14. Anderson, J. W. (1994). A comparison of Arab and American conceptions of "effective" persuasion. In L. A. Samovar & R. E. Porter (Eds.), *Intercultural communication: A reader* (7th ed.). Belmont, CA: Wadsworth.

15. See Burke, K. (1950). *A rhetoric of motives.* New York: Prentice-Hall. See also Lumsden, G., & Lumsden, D. (1993). *Communicating in groups and teams: Sharing leadership.* Belmont, CA: Wadsworth.

16. Many authors are writing about dialogical communication. In addition to Geissner and Bakhtin cited in Chapter 1, see Montague, A., & Matson, F. (Eds.). (1967). *The human dialogue: Perspectives on communication.* New York: The Free Press; Howe, R. L. (1963). *The miracle of dialogue.* New York: Seabury Press; Johannesen, R. L. (1971). The emerging concept of communication as dialogue. *Quarterly Journal of Speech, 57*, 373–382; and Buber, M. (1967). Between man and man: The realms. In Montague & Matson, pp. 113–117.

17. Tournier, P. (1990). The world of things and the world of persons. In J. Stewart (Ed.), *Bridges not walls: A book about interpersonal communication* (5th ed., pp. 163–167). New York: McGraw-Hill. The quotation is found on p. 165.

18. Martel, M. (1984). *Before you say a word: The executive's guide to effective communication.* Englewood Cliffs, NJ: Prentice-Hall.

19. Stewart, J., & Thomas, M. (1990). Dialogic listening: Sculpting mutual meanings. In J. Stewart (Ed.). Ibid., pp. 192–210.

Listening

At the end of this chapter, you should be able to

- Explain ways that linguistic factors and cultural factors influence listening
- Tell how listening schemas can aid you in listening more effectively
- Describe cultural variations in expectations about listening
- Explain how nonverbal aspects of posture, distance, and movements can help both you and the speaker
- Define eight types of questions
- Tell the role of nonquery responses in co-creating meaning
- Discuss ethical responsibilities of listeners

Note

Since most of our time is spent in listening, this chapter focuses on our roles as listeners. Studies show that we spend about 80% of our waking time in communication activities: 45% is spent in listening, 30% in speaking, 16% in reading, and 9% in writing. Although we learn to listen before we learn to speak, read, or write, schools spend more time teaching reading and writing and less time teaching speaking and listening. This chapter identifies barriers to listening, and ways to listen more effectively. Throughout, it refers to cultural factors that affect listening. It also develops the theme of dialogue.

Cross Reference

Quintilian's fourfold emphasis, presented in Chapter 1, establishes the importance of this chapter.

Teaching Idea

There is supplementary material on listening in the Instructor's Manual, including transparencies for use in a lecture format.

Imagine your worst member-of-the-audience nightmare. You decide to go to a speech event because you are interested in the announced topic or you are required to go for some reason. There are several speakers. The first shuffles to the front, obviously unprepared. He reads his entire speech—too softly to be heard. He has nervous mannerisms; you feel embarrassed for him. The next speaker uses biased information and highly emotional appeals to try to convince you to agree with her argument; you feel manipulated. The final speaker is arrogant. His vocabulary is too technical for you to understand; in fact, he talks down to you, acting as if you are incapable of thinking on your own. His speech does not connect with any of your interests or experiences; you feel annoyed at his self-centeredness. Most of us would dread listening to such speakers.

Now, imagine your worst speaking nightmare. You are standing in front of an audience. As you talk, you realize that hardly anyone is looking at you. One person is asleep in the back row, his head leaned against the wall. Two are whispering and chuckling at their own private conversation. One looks at you, leaning back in her chair, with her arms folded. Another turns toward the window, waving to a passing friend. Three stare vacantly; you recognize the glazed, "I-am-planning-what-I-will-do-after-this-speech" look. One seems to be listening intently, but he frowns and shakes his head in disagreement after each of your main points. One person walks out. During your final point, someone shouts, "That's stupid." Most of us would feel terror at the prospect of facing such an audience.

Think of one final scene in which you are an audience member. A speaker carefully prepares a speech presenting ideas she truly believes—realizing that not everyone shares her convictions. Before the speech, she has considered the questions you might have about her topic, and she has chosen evidence specifically to answer these questions. In the speech, she documents the sources of her evidence. She uses language that you understand. Her delivery is natural and spontaneous. Even as she argues for her ideas, she shows respect for your differing viewpoints and your ability to choose. You, in turn, respect her right to speak. You hear her out—leaning forward in your seat, other audience members are taking notes, some listeners nod in support, others frown as they struggle to understand her point of view. Two shake their heads in disagreement. After she speaks, three listeners ask questions. Two ask for more information.

These are not entirely imaginary scenes; such gatherings take place weekly in public speaking settings across the United States. Obviously, much ineffective speaking and listening exists side by side with effective public communication, raising questions such as these: What do we owe one another as speakers and listeners? If two of these scenes are nightmares, how can the third be characterized? What does it mean to be a competent listener in a society where you hear many voices proposing a variety of viewpoints?

In the last chapter, we saw how the speaker is, in many ways, a listener. This chapter will focus on the ways listeners become active participants in the speech event. Most of your time, even in a public speaking class, is not spent in speaking; it is spent in listening to other speakers—whether to your instructor or to your classmates. Since listening is so much a part of your life, the major focus of this chapter is what you can do, both verbally and nonverbally, to be a dialogical listener in a public speaking setting.

Cultural Influences on Understanding

Obviously, understanding the speaker's message is important in communication; however, understanding can be both hindered and helped by cultural factors. Two obstacles—linguistic factors and cultural factors—may hinder you from comprehending the speaker's words and ideas. As a result, you cannot critically evaluate the messages and come to informed conclusions. In contrast, culturally influenced listening schemas enable you to listen more effectively.

Linguistic Factors

Teaching Idea

If your classroom has many speakers who speak English as a second language, confront the issue of accent directly. Let's face it, it is difficult to pay attention to a speaker who is difficult to understand. If there are few nonnative speakers of English in the classroom, students can still hear such speakers on television.

A shared language is a vital factor in whether or not you understand a speaker, for it is impossible to understand a message given in a language you do not comprehend unless there is a translator to mediate between the two languages. Even then, since languages and the ideas embodied in them are so different, you will probably not be able to understand everything the speaker is saying.

At other times, you share a language with a speaker, but an accent or other linguistic variation of the speaker makes understanding difficult. Sometimes the resulting misunderstandings can be humorous. In the 1992 movie comedy "My Cousin Vinny," a Brooklyn lawyer—the Vinny in the title—argues a case before a judge in Alabama. In one scene, Vinny asks a witness (using a Brooklyn pronunciation) if he had observed the "two yutes" who were on trial.

The judge stops Vinny and asks, "Two what? . . . Did you say 'yutes'?"

When Vinny realizes that his pronunciation has made the words unrecognizable, he carefully sounds out the word, "you-*ths*."

Cross Reference

Accents are further discussed in Chapters 11 and 12. Jargon is addressed in Chapter 11.

In classrooms across the United States, many students speak with accents—regional accents, ethnic group accents, or accents influenced by their first language. When you listen to such a speaker, you may have to be particularly attentive in order to discriminate between words. Some people with an accent pronounce sounds in a different way. For instance, an international student gave a speech on "beerd watching." His instructor was puzzled and wondered who watched beards. It turned out that the speaker was pronouncing the vowel sound in "bird" with a heavy accent. At other times, nonnative English speakers accent syllables differently. A French speaker pronounced the word *atmosphere* as "at-MOS-feer." His listeners had to concentrate very carefully on each word he said in order to understand his message.

In addition to language and accent differences, misunderstandings can occur if you do not share the speaker's vocabulary. This may occur for a variety of reasons. For example, the speaker may use a highly technical jargon common to a particular field of study. A scholar at a convention read a paper with this sentence:

> *Urging a dialogue between neurology and culturaology, Turner suggests that the rhythmic activity of ritual, aided by sonic, visual, photic, and other kinds of "driving" may lead to specific neuronal activity that leads to social cohesion and feelings beyond verbalization.*[1]

Her vocabulary was appropriate to the community of scholars who listened to her paper, but a nonexpert would probably find it very difficult to comprehend what she was saying.

In addition to technical jargon, people vary in the number of words they understand. Some people have studied Latin or Greek, two languages that provide the roots for almost 80 percent of English words. Others have read widely and learned new words through literature. Still others have used a self-help book, such as *Thirty Days to a More Powerful Vocabulary*, to increase the number of words they know. Listeners who do not understand a speaker's vocabulary choices will obviously not fully understand the speech. For instance, in her speech to the 1992 Democratic National Convention, Barbara Jordan, former representative from Texas, said:

> *We must frankly acknowledge our complicity in the creation of the unconscionable budget deficits, acknowledge our complicity and recognize, painful though it may be, that in order to seriously address the budget deficits, we must address the question of entitlements, also. That's not easy, but we have to do it. We have to do it, because . . . the baby boomers and their progeny are entitled to a secure future.*[2]

Because she was speaking to a relatively well-educated audience, most of the attendees could figure out what she was talking about, but some listeners, both those in the convention hall and those watching the speech on television, would be hard pressed to define such words as "complicity," "unconscionable," and "progeny."

Cultural Factors

Another cause of misunderstanding comes when listeners simply do not understand the cultural allusions the speaker makes. Some speakers, for instance, allude to specific cultural events. For example, a student speaker discussing the Amish said that the 1985 movie "Witness" had drawn many tourists to Lancaster County, Pennsylvania, bringing unwanted attention to the group. Unless she explained that the movie depicted a man who was hidden among the Amish as he

Teaching Idea

Find a speech that was delivered in the 1940s or one that was given by a member of an ethnic group to other members of the same group. Identify cultural allusions that are understandable to the audience but are difficult for members of the class to comprehend.

waited to testify against crime figures, listeners who had not seen or heard of the movie would not fully understand the connection she drew between tourism and the film.

Often speakers draw allusions from historical, literary, and religious sources. Listeners who are unfamiliar with the original source will probably not understand the depth of meaning supplied in the allusion. Ronald Reagan occasionally referred to America as a "shining city on a hill." He was echoing the words of the Puritan leader John Winthrop, written in 1630, "we shall be as a City upon a Hill," a model for other colonies to emulate. (Winthrop was referring to a biblical passage, "Ye are the light of the world. A city that is set on an hill cannot be hid.") Listeners who were familiar with those sayings had the context necessary for a deeper interpretation of Reagan's metaphor. However, at the 1984 Democratic Convention, Governor Mario Cuomo of New York offered a competing image:

> *The President is right, in many ways we are "a shining city on a hill." But the hard truth is that not everyone is sharing in this city's splendor and glory. . . . In fact, Mr. President, this nation is more a "Tale of Two Cities" than it is a "Shining City on a Hill."*[3]

Again, most listeners would understand the literal meaning of the words Mr. Cuomo used. However, some listeners knew Charles Dickens's novel titled *A Tale of Two Cities* with its opening line, "It was the best of times, it was the worst of times, . . . it was the season of light, it was the season of darkness, it was the spring of hope, it was the winter of despair, we had everything before us, we had nothing before us."[4] These people would understand his challenge to the president on a deeper level than someone who was unfamiliar with the literary allusion.

In a pluralistic society and multicultural world, each group has different historical events, cultural heroes, literary or oral traditions, and religious resources that provide their speakers with sources for allusions. In pluralistic audiences, some listeners may not be familiar with culture-specific references. Sensitive speakers will explain these or will refer to areas of common knowledge.

Teaching Idea

Exercise 1 is appropriate here. If students are keeping a journal, this could be an entry.

For Further Reading

M. Fitch-Hauser. (1990). Making sense of data constructs, schemas, and concepts. In R. N. Bostrom (Ed.). *Listening behavior: Measurement and application* (pp. 76–90). New York: Guilford.

Listening Schemas

So far, we have looked at two factors that can hinder listening and understanding. In contrast, a set of cultural expectations, called *listening schemas*, can facilitate comprehension—helping you organize and comprehend the messages that you hear. Margaret Fitch-Hauser[5] explains that schemas are mental plans, blueprints, or models that people use, first to perceive incoming information, then to interpret, store, and recall it. Think of how you listen to a story. If you are typical, you interpret it within the context or mental model of what a story should be like. Then you know how to perceive the material—whether or not

As we gain experience from hearing a variety of speeches, we form mental schemas that help us know how to listen and interpret what we hear. We have different schemas for a news broadcast than, for example, a classroom lecture.

to take it seriously, how to draw lessons from it, what parts are worth remembering, and so on. However, you listen to a news report quite differently because the information it contains and the purposes you have for hearing it are not the same.

You formulate these cultural speech schemas as you listen to numerous examples of different types of speeches. For instance, after you have heard many college lectures, you have a pretty good idea of what to expect from a lecture because these presentations follow a somewhat predictable pattern. Similarly, you probably know what to expect from a demonstration speech, an entertaining story, a funeral eulogy, or an announcement since you have heard a number of speeches in each category.

KEY CONCEPT

Cultural Influences on Understanding

Linguistic factors Barriers of language, accent, or vocabulary can make it difficult to understand a speaker.

Cultural factors Failure to understand historical, literary, religious, and other cultural allusions results in a failure to discern meanings in a speech.

Listening schemas In contrast to cultural barriers that hinder understanding, cultures provide us with mental plans, models, and patterns that assist us in knowing how to perceive and interpret a speech.

Figure 6.1 *The Chinese character that translates as* listening *combines the symbols for ears, eyes, and heart.*

Eyes

Ears

Heart

Listening

Active Listening

Listening, which Robert Bolton[6] defines as a "combination of hearing what the other says and a suspenseful waiting, an intense psychological involvement with the other," involves you actively. The Chinese character for listening (Figure 6.1) depicts this concept. Throughout the speech, you are also sending messages, but your messages are mainly nonverbal. Yet there are times when you, as an audience member, have opportunities to interact verbally with the speaker. In this section, we look at both nonverbal and verbal interactions. As you read, remember that cultural expectations influence what are appropriate listening behaviors, and different groups have different norms, as Box 6.1 explains.

Nonverbal Interactions

When you pay close attention to a person or an object, your whole body is involved, and actual physiological changes take place. The blood vessels in your head dilate, there is a slight change in your rhythm of breathing, your pupils dilate—these and other bodily changes prepare you physically to take in information more effectively.[7] Along with these involuntary physiological changes, you can enhance your attending skills by adjusting your physical motions.

This section looks at attending skills that Bolton identifies to help you improve your listening competence. Although he mostly wrote about listening in an interpersonal context, you can apply many of the skills he identified to the public speaking context.

Teaching Idea

Use Figure 6.1 to reinforce the chapter's ideas. In addition to "ears" (hearing), discuss how their "hearts" are involved. How can listening be emotionally satisfying and enjoyable? How does dialogical listening create emotional involvement with the speaker? How does seeing the speaker or making eye contact affect dialogical interaction? *Exercise 2 is appropriate here.*

Note

Nonverbal communication is a way of sending messages without words. The nonverbal systems developed here are: posture, distance, and movements.

BOX 6.1

Cultural Differences in Expectations About Listening

The differences in world view and behaviors between members of the dominant U.S. culture and other cultural groups leads to differences in the way listeners approach the public speaking event.

Asians[8]

Although there is not one Asian culture, many Asian groups see nature as a unifying force of which humans are a part. As a consequence of this emphasis on unity, listeners expect speakers to develop oneness with them rather than present ideas that might be divisive. Speaker and audiences see themselves as partners who are equally responsible for making communication successful.

Asians display respect for one another in ceremonial and highly ritualistic speaking. As part of the ritual, the speaker may bow and offer flowers to the audience before giving the speech. In addition, audience members may give a garland of flowers to the speaker before the speech—a man to a male speaker, a woman to a female. To express humility, the speaker removes the garland. If not, the audience will laugh.

Some Asian audiences listen in absolute silence, for noise breaks their thought and concentration, and a great speech is an event requiring the concentration of audience members. In some cultures, applause signals suspicion—similar to "booing" by an audience in the United States. Some do not even applaud at the end of the speech because speaker modesty is a virtue.

In contrast to most Asians, listeners on the island of Java repeat phrases they like to a neighbor. This results in a buzz of voices throughout the audience, demonstrating to the speaker that the speech is being well received.[9]

African Americans[10]

Within the African-American community, a speech tends to be an interactive event, in which the entire audience responds in a nearly continuous response to the words of the speaker. This pattern, which reflects traditional cultural patterns from Africa, is termed "call and response." In this tradition, the speaker's statements (calls) are punctuated by the listeners' reactions to them (response), with the result that the audience is, in a real sense, talking back to the speaker. Since there is not a sharp line that distinguishes speakers and listeners, both cooperate to create the message.

For Further Reading

R. Bolton. (1990). Active listening. In J. Stewart (Ed.). *Bridges not walls: A book about interpersonal communication*, (5th ed., pp. 175–190). New York: McGraw-Hill.

- *Posture* Your posture both communicates involvement and helps you focus your attention. Face the speaker squarely. Even if you sit in the corner of the room, you can turn so that you face the speaker more directly. Incline your body toward the speaker. When you are thoroughly engrossed in a speech, this is a natural posture; you are "on the edge of your seat." In addition, let your body assume a relaxed, open position.

Look at each audience from the point of view of both the listeners and the speaker. How do you think listeners feel about the speaker and the message in each case? What messages are individual listeners sending to the speakers? How would you feel if you were confronted with each type of audience?

Teaching Idea

Use the questions in the caption for the three photographs as a basis for class discussion.

- *Distance* Think about the differences sitting in the back row or sitting closer to the front makes in your attentiveness. Your placement sends messages to speakers on how you feel about them or their topics. In addition, where you sit can affect your comprehension. One study[11] found that instructors interacted more regularly with students who sit within the triangular area shown in Figure 6.2. Arguably, those who interact more understand and remember more.

- *Movements* When listening to a speaker, avoid such distracting behavior as fidgeting, shuffling papers, or drumming your fingers on the desk. You can support the speaker by making eye contact, which also helps focus your attention. Smiling at an amusing anecdote, nodding in support of a major point, or applauding when appropriate also increases your involvement and assists the speaker.

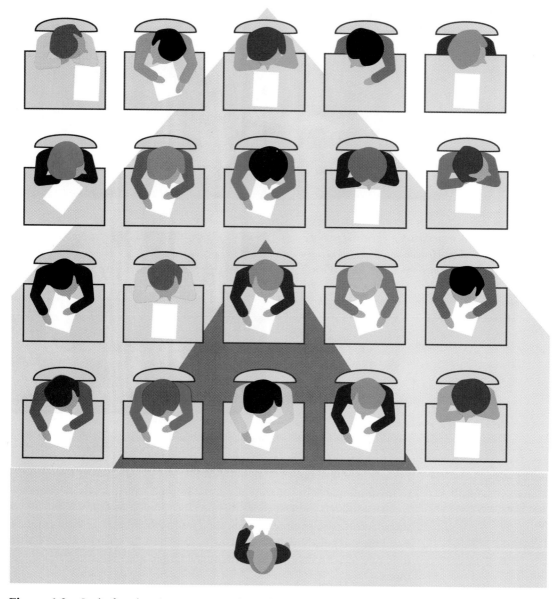

Figure 6.2   *In the formal seating arrangement depicted in this classroom diagram, the "action zone" is shaded red. Students who sit in this zone interact more with the instructor. Those in the area shaded yellow interact less frequently, and those in the unshaded area have the fewest number of reactions.*

Not only do your nonverbal messages help you concentrate, they also help the speaker feel that you are interested in the speech. It is arguable that obvious listener attention actually helps some speakers become more interesting. An often told story relates how a boring professor only stood at the lectern and read from his notes. His students decided to act *as if* he were a fascinating lecturer. Whenever he moved away from his notes, ever so slightly, they all shifted their posture into a more involved orientation, made eye contact, and used supportive motions. According to the story, the professor was eventually walking back and forth across the front of the room, lecturing animatedly to an audience that followed his every word.

Verbal Interactions with Speakers

For Further Reading

G. Goodman and G. Esterly. (1990). Questions: The most popular piece of language. In J. Stewart (Ed.). *Bridges not walls: A book about interpersonal communication,* (5th ed. pp. 69–77). New York: McGraw-Hill.

In addition to nonverbal interactions, which you always have a chance to communicate, you are often given an opportunity to interact verbally with a speaker. Prepare for verbal interactions by thinking of questions that the speech raises. You might question the speaker's sources of information, want to know where to write for further information, or dispute how a particular word is being defined. Jot down your questions, and ask them during the question-and-answer period that follows the speech.

Types of Questions   Questions are used not only for gathering information; they sometimes function as a way for listeners to give their own opinions or to demonstrate their own knowledge.[12] Thus, an audience member who asks, "Do you agree with me that gun control legislation is necessary?" is giving her personal opinion as well as asking for information from the speaker. Similarly, a listener who wants to know, "Have you read Plato's dialogue, *The Gorgias,* in which Plato takes on the whole business of rhetoric, painting an unflattering picture of speechmakers?" is probably trying to show off his knowledge as much as he is trying to get information from the speaker. Here are a few of the most common types of questions:

Loaded Questions   Sometimes questioners put speakers on the defensive because of the way they ask their questions and because of the implicit assumptions in them. For example, at the end of the speech, a reporter might ask the president, "When are you going to start keeping your promises about reforming the welfare system?" The question implies (1) that the president made the promise and (2) that he is failing to keep it. In addition, the question itself, "when?" is not really asking for a time. That is, the answer is not, "Well, I thought I'd start that on the morning of June 16, just before lunch."

Closed Questions   Closed questions ask for specific, brief answers. You use them when you seek additional information or want to verify your understanding. "Did you read Alex Haley's entire book?" "When did the Mexican government ratify the treaty?" "Where can I write for more information?" "Did I hear you correctly when you said that some scientists do not believe that the HIV virus causes AIDS?"

Open Questions   Open questions invite more lengthy responses in which speakers can elaborate on a point or give their opinions on information presented in their speeches. "How do you think the governor will respond to the proposal?" "I liked your proposal; how realistic do you think it is?"

Disclosing Questions   Questioners who ask disclosing questions provide information about their own knowledge, attitudes, values. Sometimes they don't really ask the speaker to respond; they merely indicate their own feelings and responses to information in the speech. Some examples are "Do you mean to tell us that you think this proposal will solve health care issues in our society?" "You expect us to believe that?" "Who do you think we are?"

Teaching Idea

Exercise 6 can be used with this section.

Clarification Questions   When you are confused or unsure that you have understood the ideas clearly, you often ask for more information. "Could you explain the difference between the Russian Old Believers and the Molokan Russians?" "What did you mean when you said that without gays in the military we might not have been born?"

Requests for Specific Information   Sometimes you want to know details or facts that speakers probably know but that they omitted from the speech. "Where do I go on campus to have my blood pressure checked?" "Do you have any statistics on the number of Jewish children who suffer from Tay-Sachs disease?"

Requests for Elaboration   Sometimes you ask a question in an attempt to get speakers to further expand on their ideas. "You told us that marijuana had medicinal uses; could you elaborate on that?" "Can you tell us more about the Asian Americans' press coverage of the boycott of Korean storeowners?"

Nonquery Responses   Instead of questioning speakers, you can elaborate on their ideas. Since speakers are generally not the only ones with information about the topic, audience members often provide additional information from their own research and experiences. For instance, after a speech on bulimia, one audience member added a statistic that she had heard on a television special on the subject. Another listener, who had a bulimic sister, briefly shared a story about her sister's treatment.

Besides adding information, you may disagree with ideas presented in the speech. If, for example, the speaker says something you know is incorrect, you might present correct information. You might also know of an example that further explains a point the speaker did not adequately explain. These responses are part of the co-creation of meaning that involves both speakers and participating audiences.

Teaching Idea

Discuss ways that the differences in questioning patterns between U.S. Americans and Japanese and Chinese might affect international interactions.

Cultural Differences in Verbal Interactions   Question-and-answer periods are not found within all cultural groups. In traditional Chinese and Japanese public speaking contexts, for instance, listeners are supposed to understand speakers. Asking a question is an admission that the listener was not intelligent enough to decipher the shades of meaning the speaker intends. In addition, questions reflect on the speaker's ability to communicate effectively, for if there are questions, the speaker failed to communicate. Finally, in order to preserve the speaker's "face," it is considered highly inappropriate to question a speaker's information—and thus, his character—in front of many other people.[13]

KEY CONCEPT   ## Active Listening

Nonverbal interactions   You can increase your attention and provide feedback to the speaker through your posture, distance, and movements.

Questions   Asking questions is a way to seek further information from the speaker.

> *Loaded questions*   Put speakers on the defensive because of implicit assumptions.
>
> *Closed questions*   Ask for specific, brief answers.
>
> *Open questions*   Invite longer responses, elaborations, and opinions.
>
> *Disclosing questions*   Allow the questioner to provide information about himself or herself.
>
> *Clarification questions*   Ask the speaker to clarify or explain confusing ideas in more detail.
>
> *Requests for specific information*   Ask for additional details or facts.
>
> *Requests for elaboration*   Invite speakers to provide supplementary information.

Nonquery responses   These add additional information to the message; sometimes listeners correct speakers who give inaccurate information.

Cultural factors.   Cultural norms determine whether or not questioning the speaker is appropriate.

Responsible Listening

Cross Reference

There is an emphasis on ethics throughout this text.

Listening has social and ethical implications. This means that good listening is essential for the establishment of cooperative and interdependent relationships among people who live in communities. Certainly you cannot listen to everyone; you simply do not have time for that. But when you choose not to listen to speakers when you are in the position to do so, they may feel that their ideas are not significant and that they are not worth your time. In contrast, choosing to listen to other individuals empowers them, giving them an opportunity to voice their ideas so that others can evaluate and learn from them.

Student Assignment

There is a listening self-evaluation form in the Student Resource Workbook. It guides students as they listen—before, during, and after a speech. *Exercise 5 goes with Box 6.2.*

There are many ways to silence speakers. Have you ever tried to talk to someone, only to have him say "I don't want to hear it" and walk away? You probably felt frustrated at the rejection. The same thing can happen in the classroom or in other public speaking settings. As Box 6.2 indicates, listeners tune out speeches for a variety of other reasons. Not only do individual listeners ignore speakers, sometimes two or more members of the audience sit together—often in the back row—whispering and laughing throughout the speech. They are doing two things: (1) indicating disrespect for speakers and their ideas and (2) being disrespectful of their fellow listeners who might want to hear the speeches. Other listeners refuse to listen and walk out in the middle of the speech. Finally, some choose not to listen and try to keep others from hearing the speaker's ideas by heckling the speaker.

Though you may not agree with speakers' ideas, allowing them to speak recognizes them as significant persons who are presenting thoughts and ideas they find important. Remember how good you feel when someone you know disagrees with you yet takes the time to ask you what you believe and how you came to your beliefs? Or how in the classroom, an audience listens respectfully and asks you questions following your speech on a controversial topic? Maybe the questions were tough, but they were not meant as personal attacks against you. You can similarly listen to speakers within your classroom.

What do you do if speakers say something you know to be false? Do you confront them in front of others? Do you plan a speech to counter their ideas and present more accurate information? Do you ask questions that enable other listeners to detect the misinformation? These are all responses that various listeners have made in such a situation. The point is that sometimes as a listener you are faced with ethical dilemmas in which you have to balance speakers' rights to free speech against other listeners' needs for accurate information within the light of your own beliefs and values.

Teaching Idea

Use the questions in this section as a basis for a class discussion of listeners' responsibilities. *Exercises 7 and 8 are appropriate here. They could be the basis for a journal entry.*

As you think about your responsibilities as a listener, ask yourself these questions regarding your listening habits:

1. In a society in which issues are decided by informed people, do I expose myself to available persuasion, or do I listen only to one side of arguments—the side I already agree with?

2. Do I fulfill my ethical responsibilities to other listeners, allowing them to hear points of view with which I disagree?

3. Do I encourage speakers to meet ethical standards? This may mean that I ask for further information about their sources or that I point out relevant information the speakers omit.[14]

BOX 6.2

Obstacles to Good Listening

People fail to listen well because they are distracted for a variety of reasons. In addition to external distractions such as those shown in the picture, Gerard Egan[15] identified the following:

1. *Self-consciousness* These persons are distracted by internal preoccupations such as worries about a test in the following class or concerns about their upcoming speech.

2. *Dreaming* A dreamer is off on a tangent, following thoughts triggered by something the speaker said ten minutes earlier.

3. *Message anxiety* Some listeners feel anxiety about certain topics, especially if they take a position that is different from that of the speaker. For this reason, they avoid hearing about these topics as much as possible.

4. *Long speeches* It is easy to get lost in the middle of a long speech, especially one that is not well-organized or is full of boring details. As a result, it takes special effort to focus on the speech and identify the major ideas in it.

5. *Black-or-white evaluations* Rather than listen to what a speaker says, the listener classifies the speech as "good" and stops listening critically or as "bad" and stops listening at all.

It is difficult to listen when there are obvious distractions. For example, during the inaugural speech given by incoming mayor of New York, Rudy Guliani, listeners found their attention drawn to his young son, who stood beside his father, making distracting motions.

6. *Categorizing* Listeners can relegate a speech to a category in a couple of ways. They lump the message with others of its kind and ignore it as "just another appeal for funds." Or they link it with others given by the same speaker and dismiss it by thinking, "Oh, him again!"

KEY CONCEPT   **Responsible Listening**

Ethical listeners have a responsibility to speakers, to other listeners, and to accuracy or truth in the message itself.

Heckling[16]

In March 1992, Governor Bill Clinton was campaigning in New York City. As he spoke, Bob Rafsky, a member of the activist AIDS group Act Up, began to interrupt. Here are some excerpts from that exchange:

Rafsky This is the center of the AIDS epidemic, what are you going to do? Are you going to start a war on AIDS? Are you going to just go on and ignore it? Are you going to declare war on AIDS? Are you going to put someone in charge? Are you going to do more than you did as the governor of Arkansas? We're dying in this state. What are you going to do about AIDS?

Clinton Can we talk now?

Rafsky Go ahead and talk.

Clinton Most places where I go, nobody wants to talk. They want us to listen to them. I'm listening. You can talk. I know how it hurts. I've got friends who've died of AIDS.

Rafsky Bill, we're not dying of AIDS as much as we are from eleven years of government neglect.

Clinton And that's why I'm running for president, to do something about it. I'll tell you what I'll do, I'll tell you what I'll do. First of all, I would not just talk about it in campaign speeches; it would become a part of my obsession as president. There are two AIDS Commission reports gathering dust somewhere in the White House, presented by commissions appointed by a Republican president. There's some good recommendations in there. I would implement the recommendations of the AIDS Commission. I would broaden the HIV definition to include women and IV drug users, for more research and development and treatment purposes.

Rafsky (interrupting, unintelligible) . . . you know it's true.

Clinton Would you just calm down?

Rafsky You're dying of (unintelligible) . . .

Clinton Let me tell you something. If I were dying of ambition, I wouldn't have stood up

Case Study

For a discussion of the ethics of radical confrontation, see S. D. Alinsky. (1971). *Rules for radicals: A practical primer for realistic radicals.* New York: Random House. R. Johannesen summarizes Alinsky's rules in (1990). *Ethics in human communication,* (3rd ed., pp. 82–85). Prospect Heights, IL: Waveland.

Summary

As a listener, you actively participate in the co-creation of meaning by assuming a dialogical relationship with the speaker. Culture affects our listening in many ways. First, some factors hinder effective listening. For instance, linguistic barriers often make it difficult to make sense of messages. Further, misunderstanding vocabulary or not knowing cultural allusions means that you do not fully understand the speech. However, cultural listening schemas aid you in listening more effectively. These mental blueprints or models help you understand how to perceive and interpret a speaker's words.

Active listening means that you are psychologically involved with the speaker and the message, and you can indicate this involvement in both nonverbal and here and put up with all the crap I've put up with for the last six months. I'm fighting to change this country. And let me tell you something else, let me tell you something else. You do not have the right to treat any human being, including me, with no respect because of what you're worried about. I did not cause it, I'm trying to do something about it. I have treated you and all the people who've interrupted my rally with . . . more respect than you've treated me, and it's time you started thinking about that. . . . If you want something to be done, you ask me a question and you listen. If you don't agree with me, go support somebody for president but quit talking to me like that. This is not a matter of personal attack, it's a matter of human wrong. . . . Do not stand up here at my rally, where other people paid to come, and insult me without—listen, that's fine, I'll give you your money back if you want it, out of my own pocket.

Questions

1. List the verbal responses that Rafsky makes; then identify what type of question or non-query response each is.

2. What do you think were Rafsky's motivations for attending the speech; that is, what were his listening purposes?

3. What ethical responsibilities does Rafsky have toward Bill Clinton? Toward the other listeners? Toward his cause? Which do you think should assume the most importance in this setting?

4. Is there ever a place for heckling? If so, when or where might it be appropriate? If not, why not?

5. In what ways, if any, could Rafsky have phrased his questions in order to participate in the creation of understanding between himself and the candidate?

verbal ways. First, your nonverbal actions can communicate that you are interested in the speech. They can also assist you in paying attention. These include posture that communicates involvement, maintaining an appropriate distance from the speaker, and moving appropriately throughout the speech. Then, you often have an opportunity to interact verbally with speakers. You do this either by asking questions or by providing additional information in nonquery responses.

Finally, listening is a social activity that calls for responsible actions from listeners. Allowing people to speak empowers them, giving them a voice and allowing others to hear their ideas. However, when speakers present incorrect or misleading information, you are faced with ethical decisions in which you must weigh your knowledge, beliefs, and values against the rights of the speakers and other listeners.

Questions and Exercises

1. Identify a time or times when your listening was less effective because of linguistic factors and cultural factors. What, if anything, did you do in order to comprehend the message better?

2. Think about the Chinese symbol that stands for listening (see page 123). In what way do you use your ears, eyes, and heart when you listen to your classmates? Your professors? A speaker whose ideas support your own opinions? A speaker with whom you totally disagree?

3. Compare the listening styles of various international and co-cultural groups. In a discussion with your classmates, add any information you have about the listening expectations common in co-cultural groups to which you belong.

4. Practice the nonverbal skills of active listening in one of your courses. That is, use posture, space, and movement to help focus your attention on the lecture. Afterward, evaluate whether or not your nonverbal behaviors helped you pay attention and remember the lecture material better.

5. Using the information in Box 6.2, identify and discuss times you have encountered each of the obstacles to good listening. That is, when have you been self-conscious or a dreamer? What topics create anxiety? When did a long-winded speaker "lose" you? When did black-and-white evaluations or categorizing cause you to tune out a speaker?

6. In the next group of classroom speeches, select one speech after which you will verbally interact with a speaker. During the speech, jot down several different types of questions that you will ask.

7. Listen to a speaker who takes a position that differs from the one you hold strongly; you may find such a speaker broadcast over radio or television channels. (Examples: a person whose lifestyle differs from yours; one who disagrees on an issue, such as capital punishment; a radio talk show host with a different political perspective from yours; someone with different religious beliefs.)

8. Evaluate yourself as a responsible listener. How do you avoid silencing speakers? Use the questions on page 130 to guide your self-evaluation.

Key Terms

listening schemas
active listening
loaded questions
closed questions
open questions
disclosing questions
clarification questions
nonquery responses

Notes

1. Delroy, K.-K. (1992, August 13–15). *Ritual studies as a medium for communication.* Paper presented at the Ethnography of Communication Conference, Portland, OR. p. 6.
2. Jordan, B. (1992, July 14). Excerpts from addresses by keynote speakers at Democratic convention. *The New York Times*, p. A12.
3. M. Cuomo's 1984 keynote address to the Democratic National Convention can be found in R. L. Johannesen, R. R. Allen, & W. A. Linkugel (Eds.). (1988). *Contemporary American speeches* (6th ed., pp. 307–315). Dubuque, IA: Kendall/Hunt.
4. Dickens, C. (1932). *Tale of two cities.* In T. H. Briggs, et al. (Eds), *Romance* (p. 249). Boston: Houghton Mifflin.
5. Fitch-Hauser, M. (1990). Making sense of data constructs, schemas, and concepts. In R. N. Bostrom (Ed), *Listening behavior: Measurement and application* (pp. 76–90). New York: Guilford.
6. R. Bolton. (1990). Active listening. In J. Stewart (Ed.), *Bridges not walls: A book about interpersonal communication* (5th ed., pp. 175–190). New York: McGraw-Hill.

7. Travers, R. M. W. (1982). *Essentials of learning: The new cognitive learning for students of education* (5th ed.). New York: Macmillian.

8. Sitkaram, K. S., & Cogdell, R. T. (1976). *Foundations of intercultural communication.* Columbus, OH: Charles E. Merrill.

9. Tannen, D. (1989). *Talking voices: Repetition, dialogue, and imagery in conversational discourse.* Cambridge: Cambridge University Press.

10. Smith, A. L. (Molefi Asanti). (1970). Sociohistorical perspectives of black oratory. *Quarterly Journal of Speech, 61,* 264–269. Daniel, J. L., & Smitherman, G. (1990). How I got over: Communication dynamics in the black community. In D. Carbaugh (Ed.), *Cultural communication and intercultural contacts.* Hillsdale, NJ: Lawrence Erlbaum.

11. The results of this study are reported in Hybels, S., & Weaver, R. L. (1992). *Communicating effectively* (3rd ed., p. 118). New York: McGraw-Hill.

12. Goodman, G., & Esterly, G. (1990). Questions—The most popular piece of language. In J. Stewart (Ed.). Op. cit., pp. 69–79.

13. See Becker, C. B. (1991). Reasons for the lack of argumentation and debate in the Far East. In L. A. Samovar & R. E. Porter (Eds.), *Intercultural communication: A reader* (6th ed., pp. 234–243). Belmont, CA: Wadsworth.

14. Additional guidelines for ethical listening can be found in Holtzman, P. (1970). *The psychology of speakers and audiences.* Glenview, IL: Scott Foresman.

15. Egan, G. (1977). Listening as emphatic support. In J. Stewart (Ed.), *Bridges not walls: A book about interpersonal communication* (2nd ed., pp. 228–232). Reading, MA: Addison-Wesley.

16. Transcript. (1992, March 28). Heckler stirs Clinton anger: Excerpts from the exchange. *The New York Times*, p. A9.

Researching
the Speech

- Distinguish between primary and secondary sources
- Know how to use personal experience as a speech resource
- Effectively use oral, print, and electronically stored resources in your research
- Include ethnic and international sources in your research
- Record your information in a way that is suited to your learning style
- Give examples of two kinds of unethical research

Note

Finding appropriate materials is an important skill for any speaker. This chapter presents a variety of resources that students can consult during the research process.

Most students are not experts in the topics they choose for classroom speeches. For example, Noreen spoke on patterns of communication in the family; Andre informed his audience about foods high in antioxidants; and Steve discussed ways to resolve conflict in interpersonal relationships. All these speakers had some experience with their topics, but none could be considered as expert on the subject. As they prepared their speeches, the challenge that faced them is the one that faces you once you have selected your topic: You must gather information that you will be able to use to support your ideas.

Gathering effective supporting materials is part of the canon that the Romans called *invention*. It combines several skills that contribute to your developing competence in the process of speechmaking. As you select materials for use in your speech, you:

- Know how to find the data needed to support your ideas
- Record your findings in a systematic way
- Recognize and avoid unethical research practices

This chapter will present information on the research process: how to find speech materials in a variety of sources, how to record the information you discover, and how to acknowledge your sources and maintain ethical research practices.

Gathering Material for Your Speech

Once you decide on a topic and refine your purpose for the speech, you begin to gather materials to present to your listeners. For informative and persuasive speeches, instructors usually recommend that you consult from three to seven sources. This gives you several different perspectives on your subject. Generally, a great deal of information is available on most topics, if you know how to find it. You can use both primary and secondary materials, from sources that are found in oral, print, or electronic data.

Teaching Idea

Bring examples of various sources to class and have students classify them into the categories discussed in the text, for example, an autobiography, a CD or tape of music, a videotape of a commencement speaker, a clay pot from Mexico, an academic journal, a textbook, *The New York Times Review of Books*.

Primary and Secondary Sources

Primary sources are documents and other works written or otherwise created by individuals and groups who are directly involved in events at the time they take place. There are several categories of primary sources. *Original documents*, such as letters, news footage, and minutes of meetings, were written or created by insiders who were personally involved in events. *Creative works* include books, paintings, poems, and dance performances. *Relics* or *artifacts* are cultural objects such as jewelry, tools, buildings, and other created items.

You can often gain access to primary sources by visiting a museum and observing creative works or artifacts that are displayed there.

Secondary sources are a step away from the actual persons or events under study. They are written by nonparticipants who summarize and interpret these same people and events. Although they may have been produced as the events occurred, they are not necessarily contemporaneous and may appear months, decades, even centuries later. Examples include history books, critical reviews of dance performances, and scholarly articles.

It is important to distinguish between primary and secondary sources. Although both are useful, you can appreciate the difference between information that comes from an eyewitness account or material that is an outsider's summary or interpretation of the same occurrence.

Cross Reference

The chapter develops the theme of oral, print, and electronic cultures that was introduced in Chapter 1. It also emphasizes cultural diversity by showing how to look for sources that reflect a variety of viewpoints.

In the research process, there are several ways to gather both primary and secondary materials for your speeches. Three sources correspond to the three types of cultures we saw in Chapter 1. You can collect information orally in face-to-face interactions with both primary and secondary sources; you can discover speech materials in print; and you can find data through media channels. In addition, many people draw speech materials from their own experiences.

Personal Experiences

Often speakers choose topics because they have developed expertise in the subject through personal knowledge and experience. In the world of work, speakers almost always select topics that are familiar to them. For instance, accountants speak about audits rather than the psychological impact a new procedure will have on workers. Instead, the organization's personnel director gives that speech.

Similarly, students often choose familiar speech topics from their life experiences. For example, a student who spoke about Type II Diabetes learned about the disease when she was diagnosed with it. As a result of her medical condition, she visited the doctor, listened to medical prognoses, read brochures, watched videos prepared for patients' families, learned to give injections, and adjusted her diet to deal with her diabetes. If you follow her example and choose a topic from your personal experiences, you may already have books, pamphlets, personal stories, and other materials that are readily available to be incorporated into your speech.

Teaching Idea

Ask students to tell areas in which they are "experts." Help them see how they can use this information as evidence in speeches.

Oral Sources

You consult oral sources when you get information in face-to-face interactions, including those that are one-on-one, as in a personal interview, or one-to-many, as in a lecture. Information from oral sources is direct. However, you need to record this information in some form, and it is generally helpful to take written notes or make audiotapes or videotapes.

Interviews   Many times you can talk with a knowledgeable person by conducting either a face-to-face interview or by speaking to your informant over the telephone. A well-planned interview gives you the advantage of being able to clarify confusing ideas by asking questions of someone with first-hand knowledge of your subject. There are two types of people whom you can use as sources of information: experts and laypeople.

Someone who has detailed knowledge about a subject due to in-depth study and experience is an *expert*. These people are often willing to speak with you personally. For example, if you were examining relationships within families, you might interview a professor on campus who is a well-known scholar on family systems. Students have interviewed chiropractors, police officers, park rangers, construction workers, and other people whose work experiences make them experts.

You can also interview *lay* or *peer informants*—ordinary people who have formulated opinions and gained insights into a topic through normal living rather than research. Thus, when you interview couples who have been successfully married for fifty-five years, you get information that differs from the kind received from experts. These insights, though not considered scholarly, often contain practical wisdom.

Most people in our society live active lives, with busy schedules. When you ask for an interview, you are asking for a portion of their time. Because the interviewed person is doing you a favor by acting as an informant, there are several important factors to consider when you set up an interview:

1. When you initially schedule the interview, give the interviewee an idea of your speech topic and the kind of information you are seeking. This is especially important if you are interviewing someone from another culture whose first language is not English. These interviewees may want you to submit written questions in advance of the appointment. This allows them to think through your question carefully and to prepare their answers in English.

2. Be aware of the importance of time. When you set up an appointment, give the person an idea of the amount of time the interview will take, then stay within those limits. Although different cultural groups have different norms regarding punctuality, be on time. If anyone is late, let it be the interviewee. If you find you cannot keep an appointment, notify the person well in advance.

3. Prepare in advance. Write down your questions so that when you are in the actual interview, you remember everything you want to ask. Written questions also help you keep your focus on the topic.

4. Take careful notes. Then, in order to be sure you have understood correctly, read your notes back to the interviewee and let him or her make corrections or additions. Ask questions such as these: "Is this what you said?" and "Am I understanding you correctly when you said . . . ?"

5. Aim to understand your topic from your interviewee's perspective. It is possible that, on some subjects, you may interview someone whose ideas and actions clash with yours. The interview, however, is not the time to confront your differences.

6. If you want to tape the interview in order to quote your source verbatim, ask in advance. Put the recorder in full view of the subject. Do not tape without permission.

If you are unable to schedule a face-to-face interview, you can often speak with your informant over the telephone. Follow the same guidelines regarding

It is not always necessary to conduct an interview in a face-to-face setting. However, if you tape the interview, as this student is doing through a recorder attached to the telephone, be sure to get the interviewee's permission in advance.

questions, advance preparation, and punctuality. Although it may take a little more time to schedule and conduct an interview, either in person or over the telephone, the information you gain from both experts and laypeople often provides excellent speech materials.

Lectures and Oral Performances In addition to one-on-one interviews, you can often hear an expert by attending a lecture or an oral performance such as a poetry reading. Many students, for example, use lecture notes from classes or from lectures given on campus or in the community as sources of information. The key for effective use of material gained in lectures or performances is to take careful notes. If you wish to use a tape recorder, get permission in advance. Some popular lecturers are syndicated, and their contracts do not allow listeners to record them; however, such speakers often sell tapes of their most popular lectures before and after they speak.

Print Sources

You will probably find most of your information in books, magazines, brochures, and similar print resources. The library is the place to gain access to these materials. Since each library is different, visit or tour the one in which you will do most of your research. In most libraries, professional librarians have prepared

Teaching Idea
A surprising number of students do not know how to use the college or university library. Activity 7.1 in the Instructor's Manual gives several suggestions for teaching students how to use their library. *Exercises 1 and 2 go with this section.*

"how to" pamphlets and brochures to enable students to find information readily. Since these librarians are paid to assist you in your research, don't hesitate to consult them.

Most modern libraries have converted to on-line computerized programs that assist researchers in locating information quickly and easily. These programs are user-friendly in that the computer itself provides on-screen instruction in how to use it effectively. If you have not done so already, plan to spend some time becoming familiar with your library's filing system. The research principles that follow apply both to libraries with a card catalog and those with a computerized system.

Books   Each book in the library is catalogued in three ways: by subject, author, and title. In libraries with card catalogs alone, each book can be found on three separate cards all filed in a single alphabet. Thus, Doris Paul's book, *The Navajo Code Talkers*, can be found under the author Paul, Doris, under the title, *Navajo Code Talkers*, and under the subject, Navajo Indians.

Computerized programs similarly list books in at least three ways. Let's say a student wants to research a speech on lying. She can request information in a number of ways, including subject, author, and title. Since she saw a television show featuring the philosopher Sissela Bok, who writes extensively about lying, she decides to see if any of Professor Bok's works are in the library by typing Bok Sissela. The computer screen displays a list of all the titles of books by Sissela Bok that are in the library.

If, however, the student saw the professor on TV, can't remember her name, but remembered she wrote a book entitled *Lying*, she can still locate Dr. Bok's book by typing in the title, *Lying*. The screen will list every book entitled *Lying*, whether or not Sissela Bok wrote it.

If the student knows neither an author nor a title, she can search for the topic by typing in words related to the subject, such as "lying" or "ethics speaking." The computer searches its files and comes up with a list of titles on the subject she has chosen.

As you do research, look carefully at the copyright date, which appears not only in the front of the book but also in catalog information. It is important to select up-to-date materials on some topics. For example, a recent book on health care will provide current information, whereas a book from the 1940s will be outdated. However, other subjects do not demand such current materials. For instance, when you speak about an issue that deals with ethics, you may draw from philosophical, religious, and cultural traditions that go back thousands of years. Because the subject of lying has ethical implications, a book on honesty and dishonesty from 1910 may still be as credible as one written in the 1990s.

Encyclopedias   General encyclopedias, such as *The Encyclopedia Americana* and *Collier's Encyclopedia*, collect and summarize information on thousands of topics. Many students consult them in the early stages of their research because they provide an overview of the topic. The English encyclopedia, *Encyclopædia Britannica*, is especially useful for articles on international topics. To find your subject, consult the encyclopedia's index; it is likely to guide you to several related topics. All these reference books provide a bibliography at the end of each article that can direct you to other sources of information.

In addition to general encyclopedias, look in the reference section of your library for specialized encyclopedias. They provide information in many subject areas, including organic gardening, science and technology, music, architecture, birds, ethics, computer software, and psychological depression.

Dictionaries Dictionaries provide definitions of words, as you know. However, detailed dictionaries also provide other interesting information about words, including the historical source of the word and its synonyms and antonyms. Most people are familiar with this kind of dictionary. However, many are less familiar with all the other dictionaries located in the reference section of the library, including those devoted to American slang, to psychotherapy, and even to pianists!

Sources for Statistics Consult the *Statistical Abstract of the United States* (a government document) for U.S. statistics on a variety of topics such as population, health, education, crime, government finance, employment, elections, and defense. This book shows historical trends as well as current statistics. In addition, almanacs such as *The World Almanac* are a rich source of statistical information.

Magazines and Journals There are many kinds of periodicals—from popular or general interest magazines, such as *Time, Sports Illustrated*, and *MacLean's* (from Canada), to more specialized periodicals, such as *Vital Speeches of the Day*, that reprint only recent public speeches. Popular magazines are usually easy to understand and have many contemporary examples, up-to-date statistics, and quotations from both expert and peer interviews.

In addition to these general interest magazines, libraries house trade or professional journals. Journals such as the *Quarterly Journal of Speech* contain the research findings of scholars writing in academic areas. Some of the material is too technical for use in classroom speeches. However, other articles are very understandable and provide excellent materials for speeches.

Congressional Digest This is an independent monthly periodical, not produced by the government, devoted to current controversies being discussed in Congress. Each issue features only one current issue. It provides background information on the topic, then presents the pro and con arguments given by four to ten members of Congress. Many students find it helpful as they prepare speech assignments on controversial topics.

Indexes   You can easily locate articles from both scholarly journals and popular magazines by using indexes to periodicals and journals. They are found in books or in computerized files, such as the ERIC index that provides specialized references in the field of education. *The Readers' Guide to Periodical Literature* is an invaluable tool for many speech students since it indexes articles from hundreds of popular magazines. The editors list each article in alphabetical order according to subject, author, and topic. Broad topics, such as privacy issues, are also indexed, as this sample entry demonstrates:

> **Right of Privacy**
> *E-mail: the boss is watching, D. Bjerklie. il* Technology Review *v96 p14-15 Ap 93.*
> *The politics of privacy, right and left. A Wolfe.* Harper's *v286 p18+ My 93.*

Each entry tells you the title, author's name, magazine where it is located, volume, and page number. The 18+ in the second article indicates that the story begins on page 18, but it is continued on later pages in the magazine.

Newspapers   Newspapers are valuable sources for material concerning important contemporary issues. A newspaper covers current events in greater depth than that usually offered on radio or television news broadcasts. Besides reports on current issues and events, newspapers furnish opinion pieces by syndicated columnists, editorialists, and amateur writers who voice opinions to the editors. Many newspapers also print humorous articles; obituaries; human interest pieces; and critical evaluations of plays, books, art exhibits, and musical performances.

There are many varieties of newspapers, including dailies, weeklies, and monthlies. Papers also range in size from a larger city paper down to smaller papers published by student organizations. Some are specifically targeted toward various cultural and ethnic groups. A few are dubbed "the elite media" because they are known for excellent, detailed coverage of stories, and they are widely used as sources for stories by smaller, less widely circulated papers. Two major newspapers in this category are *The New York Times* and *The Washington Post*. Most school libraries carry at least one of these elite papers. If you do not regularly read such a paper, you might find it profitable to browse through an edition and compare it to the same day's news found in local newspapers.

The New York Times is additionally an excellent source of primary documents because it reprints a number of them, in part or the whole. Consequently, if you want to read the text of one of Richard Nixon's inaugural addresses, you can find it in its entirety by reading a microfilmed copy of the *Times*. It often prints excerpts of testimony given at Senate hearings or of presidential remarks made at press conferences. Thus, if you want to know exactly what the president said about a specific policy, consult the *Times*. Further, it prints excerpts of both the majority and the dissenting opinions on significant Supreme Court decisions, so you can use it to read what the justices actually said regarding the issues that concern you.

Teaching Idea

Exercise 3 is appropriate here. Students may respond in a journal entry.

International and Ethnic Presses   In addition to local, regional, and national books, periodicals, and papers, many libraries carry printed information from other countries. Similarly, you may find works that reflect the views of a nondominant cultural group in the United States. These are excellent sources for gaining a different perspective—for hearing other "voices"—from those found in local or national print sources. For example, instead of reading only the American press's coverage of European issues, you can read European views on the same topic by consulting foreign newspapers. Many libraries carry materials from Canada, England, Malaysia, Japan, Mexico, Pakistan, Israel, Kenya, Saudi Arabia, and Iran, among other places. Many of these sources are printed in English. Some are written in languages such as Spanish, French, German, and Chinese. Consult your library to see what international sources are available to you.

Another useful source for an international perspective is the *World Press Review: News and Views from Around the World*. This monthly publication comprises materials excerpted from the press outside the United States. The articles are translated and edited for use in the periodical. The editors also classify the articles by the bias of the newspapers and journals in which they were first printed. Thus, if you read an article from a newspaper in Mexico, you know if the paper is considered conservative or liberal. This publication is indexed in *The Readers' Guide to Periodical Literature*.

In addition to foreign papers and magazines, libraries carry materials representing diverse perspectives in the United States. Some are written from a stated liberal or conservative orientation. For example, *The New Republic* is a well-known liberal magazine; whereas the *National Review* is avowedly conservative. Newspapers such as the radical *The Socialist Worker* are also available in libraries and at many newsstands, especially in urban areas. For the views of organized labor, consult *AFL-CIO News*. African Americans, gays and lesbians, and religious groups such as Catholics and Muslims all publish their own newspapers and magazines. Other ethnic groups produce periodicals that reflect their interests and perspectives. Consult your local or campus library for such diverse sources.

Newspaper Indexes   Major papers, such as *The New York Times*, provide tools to aid researchers in locating specific articles. *The New York Times Index* helps you find the date, page, and column location of almost every news article that has appeared in its pages since 1851. The index lists articles alphabetically under one of four basic types of headings: subject headings, geographic name headings, organization headings, and personal name headings. Since 1962, the foreword of the annual index has also provided a summary of the year's important events.

In order to develop the skills necessary to find information in print resources, it is important to become familiar with your campus library.

The index includes a brief summary of articles that can be a source of information in themselves when you want brief answers to questions such as "How many rhinoceroses are left?" Here is an example of an entry in the *Times Index*.

Rhinoceroses

Article focuses on action by conservationists to establish well-guarded and extensively managed sanctuaries or "metazoos" for rhinoceroses in last ditch effort to save the world's remaining species, whose population has dwindled to fewer than 11,000 in past few years; some conservationists say current population may not be large enough to maintain long-term genetic health; say species are being crowded out of natural habitats by development and slaughtered for their horns; drawings; photos (M), My 7, C, 1:1.

This entry came from the 1991 *Times Index*. It is a medium-length (M) article, meaning it is up to two columns long. The article is found in the May 7, 1991, paper; it is in section C, page one, column one.

Electronically Stored Resources

In addition to oral and print resources, we in the electronic age have access to a great deal of material stored electronically on film, audiotapes, CDs, records, computer data banks, and computer CDs. These resources will undoubtedly increase in the future. For example, *Time Magazine* is now available in on-line

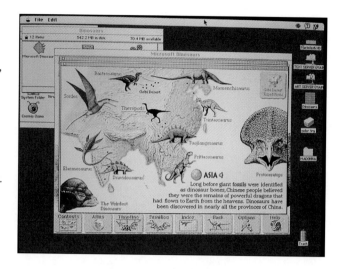

Take advantage of the information available in electronically stored resources. For example, in an encyclopedia stored on CD-ROM, you can find articles, charts, and pictures as well as sound clips, speeches, movie segments, and animations.

computer subscription form. Moreover, many software companies offer encyclopedias on CD-ROM. Microsoft Encarta is one that contains 25,000 articles, and hundreds of sound clips, speeches, movie segments, and animations. There are more than 7,000 digitized photos, maps, and other illustrations. Many of the charts are interactive—you can click on them with the mouse and bring forth greater detail. In addition to audio and video clips, Compton's Multimedia Encyclopedia lets you view several articles simultaneously. It also includes a note taker word processor.[1]

Audiovisual resources are often well worth your time. For instance, instead of reading Martin Luther King's most famous speech, "I Have a Dream," you can actually watch Dr. King deliver the speech. Instead of reading Sissela Bok's book alone, you may supplement it by watching the interview Bill Moyers had with her on public television.

Some electronic sources are already in your home. You can use news reports—on radio or on television—or watch a news program such as "60 Minutes" for speech materials. In fact, if you know that your topic is very current and will certainly be discussed on the news, plan to take notes, tape the portion of the program in which the topic is discussed, or purchase a videotape or a transcript of the program that provides the information you need. That way, you can play back the tape or read the transcript carefully to check the accuracy of your information.

As you watch or listen, remember the distinction between primary sources and secondary sources. Be sure that you distinguish between factual news reporting and editorial opinion. Both can be a source of information, but they should be distinguished from each other. For example, the "MacNeil-Lehrer

News Hour" on public broadcasting stations, usually begins coverage of a subject with factual information. Then the anchors assemble a group of experts who discuss the subject in depth for as long as fifteen minutes. This part of the broadcast consists of opinions and interpretations rather than factual reporting. Some of the people who appear in these segments, such as a representative of the Jordanian government, are primary sources. Others, like a U.S. professor of Middle Eastern studies, are secondary sources.

Teaching Idea

Exercise 4 is a culminating activity for this entire section.

You can go to many other places for electronically stored information. Many organizations circulate recordings and tapes of lectures, another good source for research information. For example, medical organizations circulate tapes of such topics as ethical treatment of patients with highly contagious diseases. Political action groups of all kinds offer audiotaped and videotaped information about the issues that concern them. Other sources are as close as your local video store.

KEY CONCEPT

Gathering Material for Your Speech

Primary sources These sources are direct and first-hand.

Secondary sources A step removed from primary sources, secondary sources interpret and evaluate the events.

Personal experiences Use your knowledge that comes from first-hand living with your subject.

Oral sources Interviews are conducted with both experts and lay or peer informants in one-on-one interactions. Lectures and performances provide information in one-to-many interactions.

Print sources Print sources include books, magazines, journals, and newspapers, some with international and ethnic "voices."

Electronically stored resources Electronically stored resources consist of videotapes, audiotapes, CDs, and other recorded information that provide images and sounds as well as words.

Recording Your Information

Note

The material in this section acknowledges the diversity in learning styles among students.

Select a way or ways to record the results of your research so that when you sit down to put your speech together, you have the necessary information at your fingertips and can easily classify your ideas into themes and patterns. Students use three common methods to record the materials they discover in the process of investigation: note cards, photocopied materials, and mind maps.

Note Cards

Many students find it helpful to record their research information on 3-by-5-inch or 4-by-6-inch cards. This method has many advantages. The cards are small enough to handle easily. By copying information and citing the source on a card, you can remember the facts you uncover in the research process. Finally, information is easily classified and sorted into major categories. There are two basic kinds of note cards: source cards and information cards.

Source Cards   If you choose the note card method, begin by making a separate card for each source consulted, writing each in correct bibliographic form. Source citations generally include author, date, title, place of publication (for books), or newspaper or magazine title, followed by the page number. You may find it useful to annotate your bibliography, meaning that you write a brief description of the materials that you found in the book or article. Source cards are also made for materials gathered from interviews, films, and other sources. Figure 7.1 shows examples of source cards from a student speech by Jill Nagaue on Hawaiian sovereignty. (See the speech outline at the end of Chapter 9.)

Information Cards   After Jill makes separate source cards, she copies down important information, creating a separate card for each different idea, statistic, quotation, example, and so on. On the top of each card, she writes a heading that classifies the information into a category that she may later use as a major idea in the speech. In addition, she labels the card with an abbreviated source citation so that when she uses the material in the speech, she can cite its source. Figure 7.2 shows examples of information cards Jill made to record material found in the articles by Twigg-Smith and Akaka.

After she has gathered all of her materials, she can easily place all the cards with arguments *for* Hawaiian sovereignty in one pile and the cards with arguments *against* sovereignty in another. After putting them into these broad categories, she can determine major ideas and identify supporting material for each idea. This structured, linear way of organizing material works well for many students.

Photocopied Materials

Other students, in contrast, find that they do not like such a structured approach to note taking. Although they recognize the importance of recording the ideas they discover in research, they like a more holistic approach to the research process. If you are in this category, take advantage of the many copier machines that are available in most libraries to copy articles from books, newspapers, and periodicals for this one-time use. Write bibliographic information directly onto

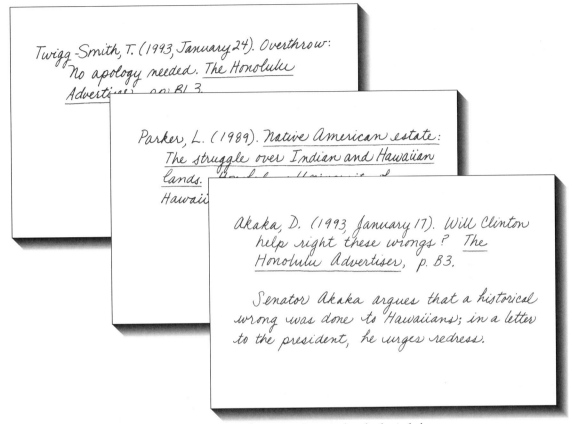

Figure 7.1   *Source cards contain bibliographic information. Annotated cards also include a brief summary of the material found in the source.*

your photocopies. Then, as you read through the articles, use highlighters to classify major ideas and to emphasize the important information you intend to use in your speech.

To see how this works, consider Jill's speech again. Instead of using note cards, Jill can photocopy pages from books and newspaper articles. (She can also clip articles from papers and magazines, if she, rather than the library, owns them.) At the top of each page, she makes sure that the entire reference is copied. Then, she uses one color of pen to highlight arguments for sovereignty and a second color to highlight arguments against the notion. When she is finally ready to organize and outline her ideas, she simply spreads out her photocopied and highlighted articles and weaves the elements together into a coherent speech.

Figure 7.2 *Use a different information card for each idea, and classify each card according to the major idea the information supports. Include an abbreviated source citation on each card.*

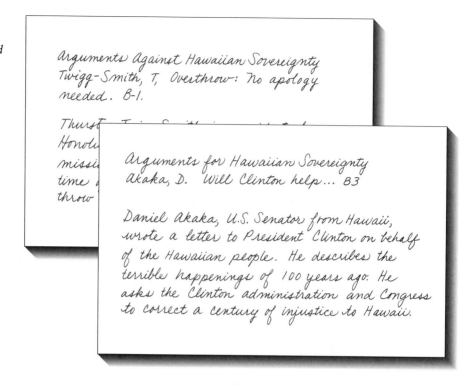

Arguments against Hawaiian Sovereignty
Twigg-Smith, T, Overthrow: No apology
needed. B-1.

Thurst...
Honolu...
missi...
time ...
throw ...

Arguments for Hawaiian Sovereignty
Akaka, D. Will Clinton help... B3

Daniel Akaka, U.S. Senator from Hawaii,
wrote a letter to President Clinton on behalf
of the Hawaiian people. He describes the
terrible happenings of 100 years ago. He
asks the Clinton administration and Congress
to correct a century of injustice to Hawaii.

Mind Maps

Teaching Idea

If you want students to work with mind maps, have groups of three select a topic, and have each member of the group bring to class an article related to the subject. Then, have them use information found in their articles to map information.

For Further Reading

T. Buzan. (1974). *Use both sides of your brain.* New York: E. P. Dutton, and J. Wycoff. (1991). *Mind-mapping: Your personal guide to exploring creativity and problem-solving.* New York: Berkley Books.

Another group of student researchers likes to use a third approach that is also less linear and more holistic. They make a mind map of their material. In Chapter 2, you saw how mind maps are useful for generating speech topics. You can use the same process for recording the information you discover from your sources. First, identify the subject of your speech in the center of the page—using a diagram or drawing. Then, as you gather information, draw a separate line for each subtopic out from this center. Show further subdivisions of your ideas by drawing a number of radiating lines. If there is a great deal of material, you may even make a separate page for each major point. See Figure 7.3 for an example of a mind map for the Hawaiian sovereignty speech.

As in every other method, it is important for you to list the sources of your information. If there is room on your mind map, you can write your references directly onto it. However, space is sometimes limited, and you may choose to make source cards; or you can list your references on a separate piece of paper.

One advantage of this method is that you can classify and subdivide the material as you gather it. This makes it very easy for you to pull your speech together when you finally sit down to organize your ideas.

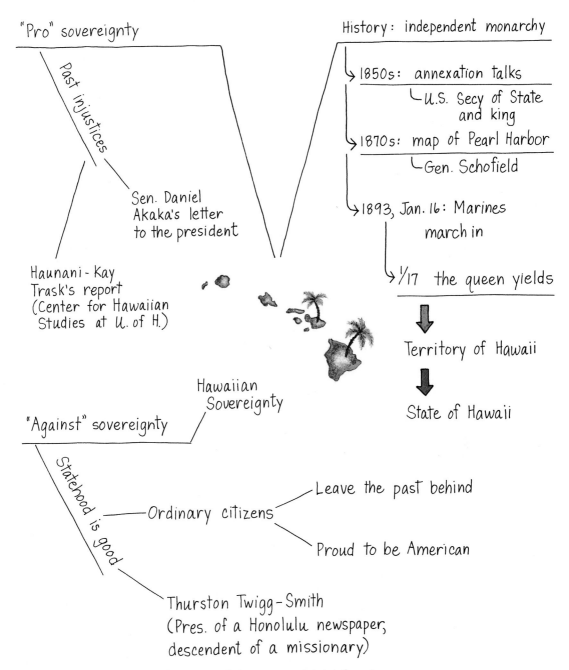

"Pro" sovereignty

Past injustices

Sen. Daniel
Akaka's letter
to the president

Haunani-Kay
Trask's report
(Center for Hawaiian
Studies at U. of H.)

History: independent monarchy

1850s: annexation talks
└ U.S. Secy of State
and king

1870s: map of Pearl Harbor
└ Gen. Schofield

1893, Jan. 16: Marines
march in

1/17 the queen yields

Territory of Hawaii

State of Hawaii

Hawaiian
Sovereignty

"Against" sovereignty

Statehood is good

Ordinary citizens

Leave the past behind

Proud to be American

Thurston Twigg-Smith
(Pres. of a Honolulu newspaper,
descendent of a missionary)

Figure 7.3   *Some students prefer to use a mind map to record their information.*

In summary, an important part of the research process is recording information so that it is readily available when you put your speech together. There are several ways to do this effectively. If you like very structured, linear types of research, you may find that you like to use note cards. In contrast, if you approach the research task with a more holistic approach, you may find it more useful to photocopy your materials, spread them out on a table, and mark them with different colors to represent different subtopics. Finally, you may organize your information better when you make mind maps of your ideas, using images as well as words as you record the results of your research.

Teaching Idea

Exercise 5 enables students to apply the material in this section.

KEY CONCEPT   **Recording Your Information**

Note cards In this linear approach to recording information, you write information onto a series of cards, with a separate card for each topic.

Photocopied materials Here you photocopy your materials, and then mark them with different colors to represent different subtopics.

Mind maps Using this visual method, you combine pictures with words for a more holistic way of recording ideas.

Ethics in Research

Cross Reference

Ethical considerations are developed throughout the text.

In 1987, Senator Joseph Biden was a Democratic primary candidate for the presidency of the United States. During several campaign speeches, he plagiarized other speakers by quoting phrases, sentences, and longer passages from their speeches.[2] The senator also fabricated information, falsely claiming that he had three undergraduate degrees and that he had attended law school on a full academic scholarship. When journalists exposed the truth about his plagiarism and his fabrications, the senator withdrew from the campaign. In order to avoid these ethical mistakes, it is important that you understand just what plagiarism and fabrication are.

Plagiarism

Teaching Idea

On some campuses, plagiarism is a problem; members of living groups announce to incoming freshmen that there are files of speeches if they need them. The Instructor's Manual provides Activity 7.2 for teaching plagiarism.

A public speaker who plagiarizes the ideas and words of others offers them as his or her own without giving credit to originators. This is akin to stealing. This has happened in public speaking classrooms in several ways. First, students occasionally use speeches given by other students in the past, presenting those speeches as if they were their own work. Because this is considered a serious ethical breach, colleges and universities generally have rules against plagiarism written in the student handbook, complete with penalties for students whose plagiarism is discovered.

In addition to using the speeches of others, students sometimes quote the words and ideas of others without giving credit to the source either in the speech itself or in the outline. Often this is done out of ignorance, as in the following case. One student spoke on cryonics, the process of deep freezing a live object then thawing it and bringing it back to life. He gave a vivid description of a dog that had been frozen and revived using this process. Throughout his speech his instructor kept thinking, "I've heard this before," and she suspected that the student was using a "frat file" speech. After class, she went to her files of student outlines and pulled out one on cryonics submitted by a student in a previous term. As she examined the outlines side by side, she found that, though the two speeches were markedly different, both contained the identical passage on the frozen dog. She concluded that, although the second student was clearly not giving a frat file speech, he had used one source the previous speaker also used, and although both speakers lifted the word-for-word description, neither gave credit to the original source.

To avoid plagiarism in your speeches, properly credit your sources within your speech. If you are using a direct quotation, introduce it as such. Here are some examples of acceptable source information from student speeches:

> *Faith Smith, President of the Native American Educational Services College in Chicago, argues that using Native American symbols in sports is derogatory, stereotypical, and often blatantly racist.*

> *According to an article in* The Wall Street Journal, *women in state and local governments held only 31 percent of the top administrative jobs.*

> Rolling Stone *admits drum machines have "taken over Top Forty," and* High Fidelity Magazine *describes them as having "come of age."*

Teaching Idea

There is a worksheet on source citations in the Student Resource Workbook.

In addition, when you write your outline, include a list of your sources at the end of the outline. Refer to Box 7.1 to see how to cite your sources properly in written documents. (At least two major bibliographic systems are widely used for source citations. This text presents the American Psychological Association [APA] method. Some instructors, however, ask their students to use the Modern Language Association [MLA] method. Check with your instructor for specific details.)

Fabrication

Besides using the words and ideas of others, some speakers make up information. Some guess at numbers, then present them as factual. Others cite references they do not consult. However, most students do not make up materials for their speeches. A greater hazard is that they will pass along rumors or unsubstantiated information from other sources. For instance, rumor mills report alleged face-lifts of famous entertainers—allegations the stars deny as fabrications. It

BOX 7.1

Crediting Your Sources

In order to avoid plagiarism, give credit to the sources of your material. At the end of the outline, list your sources using a standard bibliographic form. Here are some of the most common source citations in the American Psychological Association (APA) method; consult the manual for additional information.

Book, single author Ong, W. J. (1982). *Orality and literacy: The technologizing of the word.* London: Methuen.

Book, two editors Andersen, M. L., & Collins, P. H. (Eds.). (1992). *Race, class, and gender: An anthology.* Belmont, CA: Wadsworth.

Chapter in an edited book Deloria, V. (1992). Indian humor. In M. L. Andersen & P. H. Collins (Eds.), *Race, class, and gender: An anthology* (pp. 341–346). Belmont, CA: Wadsworth.

Book, no author or editor *Webster's Seventh New Collegiate Dictionary.* (1967). Springfield, MA: G & C Merriam.

Encyclopedia entry Woodroof, J. G. (1987). Peanut. In *McGraw-Hill Encyclopedia of Science and Technology,* 6th ed. (Vol. 13, pp. 169–172). New York: McGraw-Hill.

Journal article Wills, J. W. (1970). Speaking arenas of ancient Mesopotamia. *The Quarterly Journal of Speech,* 56(4), 398–405.

Magazine article Hughes, R. (1992, February 3). The fraying of America. *Time,* pp. 44–49.

Magazine article, no author named (Alphabetize by the first word in the title.) Swastika Season. (1992, May 18). *Newsweek,* p. 6.

Newspaper article Kristof, N. D. (1993, April 25). China's crackdown on births: A stunning, and harsh, success. *The New York Times,* pp. 1, 12.

Interview Johnson, C. (1994, May 15). Telephone interview.

Live speech or lecture Davidson, J. (1992, November 12). Overworked Americans or overwhelmed Americans? You cannot handle everything. Speech delivered before U.S. Treasury Executive Institute, Washington, DC.

Film Maas, J. B. (Producer), & Gluck, D. H. (Director). (1979). *Deeper into hypnosis* [Film]. Englewood Cliffs, NJ: Prentice-Hall.

Cassette recording Clark, K. B. (Speaker). (1976). *Problems of freedom and behavior modification* (Cassette Recording No. 7612). Washington, DC: American Psychological Association.

would be easy for a student who was researching the topic of plastic surgery to discover one of these rumors and use it as an example; however, to do so would perpetuate a falsehood. The best way to avoid fabrications is to use a number of different sources for information and to be alert for conflicting information. Check any discrepant facts thoroughly before you present them in your speech as factual.

Exaggerated Statistics

Kilolo is researching the topic of breast cancer. She finds several sources that say women have a 1 in 9 chance of developing the disease. As she does more extensive research, however, she discovers a *New York Times* article that calls this figure "faulty,"[3] stating that, if a woman lives to be 110, then, yes, the cumulative probability that she will develop this type of cancer is 1 in 9. However, even 80-year-old women are not at that high level of risk. The chances are closer to 1 in 1,000 for women under 50. A spokesperson for the American Cancer Society admits that the figure is more metaphor than fact, but she argues that it is used for good ends—it

makes women aware and concerned enough to seek early detection. Some physicians, in contrast, point to an "epidemic of fear" created by the inflated numbers.

Questions

1. Should Kilolo use the 1 in 9 figure? Why or why not?

2. What do you think of the American Cancer Society's decision to continue using the figure when they know it is inaccurate? Is this ethical?

Case Study

Use the case study to discuss the speaker's responsibilities to use unbiased material that does not deceive listeners.

In short, speakers face ethical issues as they prepare speeches. And ethical speakers take the responsibility of presenting their own ideas, giving credit to the ideas of others, and making sure that their information is as accurate as possible.

Ethics in Research

Plagiarism This breech of ethics involves passing off the ideas of someone else as one's own without giving proper credit to the source.

Fabrication It is unethical to make up or falsify information.

Summary

Part of your competence in speechmaking is your ability to gather materials for use in your speeches. Supporting material comes from two major sources: primary and secondary. Primary sources are original documents and other materials that provide first-hand information. Secondary sources provide interpretations, explanations, and evaluations of the subject.

Both kinds of sources are found in materials gained from face-to-face inter-actions—in interviews as well as lectures and oral performances, from print sources such as books, periodicals, and newspapers, and from a wide variety of visual and audio materials. Throughout the research process, consult a variety of resources, including those with international, ethnic, and alternative perspectives.

You can record the materials you discover in research by using note cards, photocopies, or mind maps—or by combining the three methods.

As you present your materials, be sure to cite sources and check a variety of sources to avoid ethical problems of plagiarism or fabrication. Plagiarism occurs when you use the ideas or words of another person as your own, without giving credit to the original source. Fabrication occurs when you willingly present something as factual when it is not.

In this chapter, we reviewed some of the major sources you consult for information. The next chapter will discuss the kinds of supporting materials you should look for in the course of your search.

Questions and Exercises

1. If you have not already done so, visit your campus library. Locate the reference books, the newspapers and periodicals, and the indexes and guides to them.

2. Make a file containing handouts that have been prepared by the librarians in the library where you will most often conduct your research. Use these to assist you in your research. (Examples: HOW TO: Locate U.S. Government Documents. HOW TO: Cite References According to the APA Manual. Periodicals Collection: A Service Guide.)

3. Make a list of library resources that provide an alternative perspective on subjects. That is, discover what subscriptions your library has to international, ethnic, and alternative newspapers and magazines. Read an article in at least one of the resources.

4. Select a current event, then find a book, a magazine article, and a newspaper article about it. In addition, list a possible interviewee and locate at least one electronic source that will provide additional information relating to your subject.

5. Think about the way or ways you collect information. Which method—note cards, photocopies, or mind maps—would you most likely use? Which would you least likely use? When might you combine methods? Discuss your research style with a classmate.

Key Terms

primary sources
secondary sources
oral sources
expert informants
peer or lay informants
print sources
electronically stored resources
note cards
source cards
information cards
plagiarism
fabrication

Notes

1. Machrone, B. (1993, Fall). Ziff–Davis/Personal computing. Advertising supplement to *The New York Times.*

2. Johannesen, R. L. (1990). *Ethics in human communication* (3rd ed.). Prospect Heights, IL: Waveland Press.

3. Blakeslee, S. (1992, March 15). Faulty math heightens fears of breast cancer. *The New York Times,* Sec. 4, pp. 1–2.

Supporting
Materials

At the end of this chapter, you should be able to

- Distinguish between fact and opinion and know how to test factual data
- Use examples effectively in public speaking
- Choose quotations and testimony that support your ideas
- Select numbers, including statistics and percentages, that meet the standards for use of quantified data
- Distinguish between literal and figurative comparisons

Teaching Idea

If you wish to use a visual aid to present the material in this chapter, there are transparencies in the Instructor's Manual.

Cross Reference

Cultural expectations determine what we accept as support for our ideas. For instance, oral cultures rely on narratives, proverbs (or quotations), and comparisons or analogies. They do not rely on statistical evidence.

Think about how you make decisions. How did you decide to attend this college or university? Did you read a promotional brochure? Did you talk to a friend or a high school teacher? Did you go by the reputation of the school? Most people select a school only after they ask questions such as, "Why should I go there? What does it cost? What's so great about that place?" They want evidence—facts, figures, examples, recommendations from other people—to support their decision to enroll. So it is with other decisions we make. We want support for our actions and our ideas. Because of this, both when we make speeches and when we listen to the speeches of others, we expect some kind of backing for the ideas presented.

Each culture has its own rules that determine what is acceptable as evidence. In the United States, we generally look for facts, examples, testimony and quotations, quantification, and comparison to support our ideas. Rather than accept all the information at face value, however, we follow cultural standards for weighing and evaluating evidence, accepting some support as valid and rejecting other data as inadequate, irrelevant, or inaccurate. For these reasons we will look, in turn, at typical kinds of supporting evidence used as speech materials. Following each type of evidence, you will find a list of tests you can use to evaluate the reasonableness of the data or evidence—both when you select materials for your own speeches and when you listen to the speeches of others.

Facts

Probably most of the information you discover about your subject will be factual, and in Euro-American culture, people like to have facts before they accept an idea or proposal as valid. Factual information is data that can be verified by observation, and established facts are those consistently validated by many observers as true or correct. Facts include explanations, descriptions, and definitions that are generally accepted by members of a society. Facts, thus, consist of information that you judge as true or false, correct or incorrect. They derive from a variety of sources, as these examples reveal:

- A certain football player checked into training camp weighing 275 pounds. [Source: measurement by a precision instrument]

- The racehorse Secretariat won the Triple Crown of racing in 1973. [Source: racetrack records]

- Cigarette smoking is statistically correlated with heart disease. [Source: empirical research studies conducted by scientists]

Here is an example of factual material discovered through research on marketing techniques. Researchers derived the facts from direct observation in supermarkets and from professional surveys and studies that examined the practices of grocers and the habits of their customers:

- Grocery stores are laid out with customers' buying behaviors in mind.
- Items sell more quickly when they are displayed on an end aisle.
- Some items—called loss leaders—are sold below cost.
- Marketers use loss leaders to attract customers whom they hope will buy grocery items with a higher markup.
- Cross-merchandising is a technique in which grocers place high-priced items near more basic items—placing expensive salad dressings near lettuce, for example.

Nonexperts can verify many of these facts by simply walking into a supermarket. There they will see salad dressing next to lettuce, sale items on end-aisle displays, and advertisements for "bargains" (loss leaders) in printed promotional flyers. Through talking with grocers, they can verify the effectiveness of these marketing strategies, that some of these bargains are indeed sold below cost in the hopes of attracting customers, and conclude that these facts are generally true.

In reporting factual material, speakers often interject personal opinion along with the data. Stating personal opinion—either yours or that of other people—adds a subjective interpretation that is not factual and is open to question. For instance, all the following statements include words or phrases that give interpretive or evaluative opinions alongside the facts:

- The *slob* checked into training camp weighing 275 pounds.
- Secretariat, *the greatest horse who ever raced,* won the Triple Crown in 1973.
- Grocers use *questionable* means to market their wares.

As you can see, the words in italics are opinions rather than direct observations. Another speaker might dispute any of these interpretations. Because of this, be careful, when reporting facts, not to interject personal opinions without letting your listeners know that it is your opinion.

There are two major ways to test the validity of facts:

1. Are the supposed facts accurate? Are they verified by more than one observer or source?

2. Are the facts up to date? Do they reflect contemporary reality?

Teaching Idea

There is a fact–opinion worksheet in the Student Resource Workbook.

Teaching Idea

The Instructor's Manual contains a number of examples in each category.

Saying that grocers offer some products below cost to attract customers is a fact. Saying that this is a questionable means of marketing is a statement of opinion.

KEY CONCEPT **Facts**

Factual information can be verified by observation; established facts are verified consistently over time. Facts should be distinguished from opinions.

Examples

Have you ever listened to a speech that seemed abstract and unrelated to your life? Then, the speaker used an example showing how the topic affected someone like you? Chances are your interest increased because of the illustration. In this culture, as well as in others, we often use examples to support our ideas. For instance, instead of simply saying, "Farm accidents are harming children across the land," illustrate your factual statement with examples of children who were injured by farming equipment in Iowa, Florida, and Idaho. The specific instances you choose as examples function to illustrate how the facts apply to people in real situations.

Cross Reference

Narrative reasoning is covered in Chapter 13.

Examples have many advantages. First, they attract attention. Narrative theorists argue that we listen for the examples and stories[1] that make abstract concepts and ideas more concrete and relevant. Second, hearing concrete illustrations helps listeners identify emotionally with the subject. When the example rings true to their personal experience, listeners respond with internal dialogue something like this: "Yes, I've known someone like that." Or "I've seen that happen. This seems real." Additionally, use of examples can enhance your personal credibility. Your listeners want to know that you are involved in the world of experience. Consequently, when you use illustrations, your audience can see that you understand the practical implications of your ideas.

Teaching Idea

You may want to correlate this section with Chapter 15, which explicitly discusses use of examples as a characteristic of reasoning by women and speakers from some ethnic groups.

There are two major types of examples: real and hypothetical. Both types can be further differentiated by length. Some are very brief; others extend into longer narratives.

Real examples recount actual happenings that you can use to illustrate your ideas—the experiences of people, as well as happenings in institutions, countries, and so on. For instance, you might illustrate a speech about study-abroad programs with examples of innovative programs from several different universities. Your speech on ethnic wars might include the generalization that such wars are not new, a conclusion you support by using examples from ancient Africa, medieval Europe, and the Middle East. For a speech on freedom of speech, you might use examples of Supreme Court rulings that protect this fundamental right. Because the examples actually occurred, provide specific details of names, dates, and places.

Sometimes you may instead use a *hypothetical* example—this means that the specific incident recounted did not really occur, but something like it did happen or could happen. Often hypothetical examples are composite representations of a typical person that include elements of several different stories. Thus, in an example of a teen suicide, instead of revealing details about a specific person, you might combine elements from the lives and deaths of various teens to create a typical victim.

Indeed, hypothetical examples may be more appropriate than real examples when the topic deals with sensitive issues such as mental illness or sexual behaviors. For this reason, speakers whose work involves a lot of confidentiality—physicians, ministers, counselors, or teachers, to name a few—often use hypothetical examples. Family counselors who present workshops on parenting, for example, provide hypothetical examples of good and bad parenting skills, without revealing exact incidents from the lives of clients whose real predicaments are confidential. Hypothetical examples are effective in informative speeches; however, when your intention is persuasion, it is best if you select a real example.

Examples do not have to be long; in fact, you may find that short illustrations are very effective in supporting your major points. Rather than using one brief illustration, you may find it effective to string together a series of short examples—most often three—such as these on the topic of deadbeat parents.[2]

John Lock went to court recently to explain why he still owes more than $160,000 in child support for his four children. The ex-dentist amassed that total despite more than 100 hearings related to the divorce and child support payments.

Frederick Grimaldi, a deputy sheriff, owes $22,144 in back payments. He disagrees. He figures he is only behind $19,000.

Delores Podhorn ended up $72,395 in debt after she lost custody of her four children.

These three individuals are participants in fierce struggles raging in broken families across America. These battles over child support leave no winners.

In contrast, speakers sometimes provide longer examples that include many details. They often tell entire stories, called narratives, to provide most of the material in the speech. As we will see in Chapter 13, skillful use of details make the listeners more apt to identify emotionally with the story. Look at how the details in this illustration make the story more compelling. The subject is marketing of tobacco products throughout the world.[3]

Stephen Asante gasps for breath in a hospital in Ghana. For months, he has been losing weight, and X-rays show that his lungs are filling with fluid. His doctors are pessimistic. Asante, however, is determined to conquer his tobacco-related lung disease, because his family's survival depends on his health. Without his steady income, his wife will be without economic resources; his children cannot pay their school fees. "Deciding to smoke was the biggest mistake I ever made," Asante tells a friend as he celebrates his 55th birthday from his hospital bed. A day later, Asante suffers a relapse and dies. His family's financial security dies with him.

Teaching Idea

Have students divide into topical interest groups, and have each bring to class an article on the subject—for example, AIDS, welfare, international investments, campus issues, repressed memories, guns. Have them work in groups to find examples and apply the tests for each kind of evidence.

Because of the details—Ghana, the hospital, the X-rays, the birthday, the school fees—listeners have many points with which to identify with Mr. Asante's plight. This increases their emotional involvement in his situation. Because they provide more points that engage listeners, extended examples are more compelling.

As you select examples and as you evaluate the examples that you hear in speeches, consider the following tests:

1. Are these examples representative or typical? That is, do they represent normal people or typical institutions in the population being discussed? Or are they extreme cases? This test relates to the *probability* of occurrence. Although the examples may be possible, how probable are they?

2. Are they sufficient? Are there enough cases presented to support the major idea adequately? Listeners should be able to see that the issue that you discuss is extensive, affecting a lot of people.

3. Are they true? Or if they are hypothetical, do they ring true to what we know about the world and the way it operates?

A topic, such as the marketing of tobacco products throughout the world, can be more interesting and meaningful if you use a specific, detailed example of a real person who suffered as a result of the practice.

KEY CONCEPT **Examples**

Examples are specific instances that illustrate an idea; they recount real or hypothetical happenings. Some are brief; others are extended with many details. Narratives can comprise the entire speech.

Testimony and Quotations

Teaching Idea

Explore with students their core beliefs regarding authoritative sources. Whose words and ideas do they trust?

Because we look to authorities as sources for belief and knowledge, speakers often support their ideas by citing the opinions of authoritative sources. This is often called *testimony*. Quoting well-recognized sources can be especially valuable to you when you are generally not considered an expert on your topic. Using support from authoritative sources shows that you are not alone in your ideas—knowledgeable, experienced people agree with your conclusions. When you quote the exact words of the expert, you are using a *direct quotation*.

However, when the material is extensive, it is often better to summarize the quotation in a *paraphrase*.

Cross Reference

See core beliefs about authority in Chapter 3. Teacher's Note 3.1 in the Instructor's Manual explains types of belief in detail.

There are two kinds of authorities—experts and laypeople (or peers) who understand a subject because of experiences they have with it. To convince listeners that the testimony of your source is credible, you must state in your speech just who these authorities are, why you believe their testimony, and why the audience should believe them.

Expert Testimony

We often quote the opinions of experts—people whom we consider credible because they know about a topic from study or from work-related experiences. Expert testimony comes from scholars, elected officials, practitioners such as doctors or stockbrokers, journalists, and others like them. Here is the way expert testimony could be cited in a speech about cults in America.[4]

> *Cults are normally small, fringe groups whose members look to a single, charismatic individual for their identity and their purpose. Some are destructive groups that "manipulate, mistreat and exploit their followers and misrepresent themselves both to their followers and to the outside society," according to Marcia Rudin, director of the International Cult Education Program in New York. The most troubling groups are armed. Destructive but non-violent cults control their members' behavior closely. Rudin notes their "psychological hold, imprisonment, and control over people's lives."*

Since most people in the audience have probably never heard of Ms. Rudin, it is important that the speaker provide enough information about her so that listeners can decide for themselves if she is a credible source. You can see from the information provided that she works with cults. From her words, you might also assume that she has studied cults extensively.

Sometimes well-known people hold opinions that differ from what we might expect. That is, we commonly expect people to agree with the "conventional wisdom" of others who are similar to them in some way. For instance, William F. Buckley, Jr., a well-known conservative writer and journalist, supports legalization of drugs—a position not generally associated with conservatives. In much the same way, Nat Hentoff, a writer and editor who has been associated for many years with the liberal New York newspaper *The Village Voice*, takes a pro-life position, one that is surprising to many readers of the *Voice*. Using unexpected testimony such as this can be very powerful as evidence in persuasive speeches. This is so because listeners reason that persons who go against their peers have thought their opinions through carefully.

Peer or Lay Testimony

Not all people gain their knowledge through study or professional experience; some authoritative sources know about a subject from first-hand experiences with it. They might not know scientific facts and related theories, but they know how it feels to be personally involved as a participant. Here is an example paraphrasing the words of someone who knows about teen-age gambling from personal experience.

> *Bob spoke to a television reporter about the lure of gambling for teens. Why are so many young people found at the racetrack? Bob says it's for the money, obviously. With a regular job at minimum wage, he makes $4.25 an hour. But on a good day at the track, he can win $400 to $500 in the same period of time.*

Quotations

Speakers not only quote contemporary experts, they also look to authoritative sources from the past, whose words are often recorded in books of proverbs or in other written texts. Within any culture, speakers quote cultural heroes as authoritative sources, when their words still have relevance for contemporary situations. For example, this text includes quotations from Aristotle, whose writings have influenced rhetorical theories for thousands of years.

Authorities are not always well-known individuals. You can also quote authoritative figures in your own life, as this speech excerpt illustrates.[5]

> *I was brought up with a positive self-image, and although my parents never met Eleanor Roosevelt, they echoed her sentiments when she said, "No one can make you feel inferior without your consent."*
>
> *My parents—and especially my father—taught me to draw an invisible line. He said to me, "Farah, you decide how you want other people to treat you, and if somebody crosses that line and it's unacceptable to you, just walk away from it. Don't let people treat you the way that they feel you should be treated. Have people treat you the way you feel you should be treated."*
>
> *That was good advice then. It is good advice now.*

Some of the sources for quotations are religious and philosophical writings. The evangelist Billy Graham, for example, is famous for saying, "The Bible says . . . " Muslims quote from the Koran; many Asians quote the sayings of Confucius for authoritative guidance regarding present situations. Such quotations are meaningful only if your audience accepts the source of the quotation as valid.

As with other kinds of evidence, there are tests for testimony. Consider the following guidelines for evaluating this type of evidence:

1. What is the person's expertise? Is it in the subject under discussion?
2. Is the person recognized as an expert by others?
3. Is the person stating an opinion commonly held by others like him or her? In other words, is it a typical or representative view?

Billy Graham is famous for the phrase, "The Bible says. . . ." Biblical quotations provide effective support for his ideas to listeners who accept the text as authoritative.

4. Are the words taken out of context? That is, do they fairly represent the speaker's intended meaning? Words can be so distorted that the quoted person appears to hold a position she or he does not, in fact, hold.

5. When using quotations, make sure the audience accepts the source of the quotation as authoritative.

KEY CONCEPT **Testimony and Quotations**

Testimony Quote or paraphrase the knowledge and opinions of authoritative sources, whether they be experts who know about a topic through study or work, or peers or laypeople who know about a topic through first-hand experience.

Quotations Quotations can be taken from written works as well as the sayings of famous and not-so-famous individuals.

Quantification

We commonly use information in the form of numbers to enable us to understand the extent of an issue or problem or to predict the probability of some future happening. People in this society like numbers. We begin measuring and counting in kindergarten. We print the results of opinion polls and statistical research. We tend to accept numbers and measurements as credible and trust-worthy, as "hard" facts and evidence. Because of this, speakers who use numbers effectively may increase their credibility, appearing competent and knowledge-able. In general, however, statistics do not involve the feelings of listeners; thus, they are short on emotional appeal, and too many in a speech may bore your audience.

We use numbers in many ways, including enumeration and statistics.

Enumeration

Enumeration simply means counting. Providing a count helps the audience understand the extent of a problem or issue. The result is that you will hear speakers give numbers of people injured in accidents annually, those diagnosed with a disease, institutions that have adopted a particular textbook, and so on.

It is generally best to round a number up or down for two reasons. First, lis-teners find it hard to remember exact large numbers. Thus, instead of saying "251,342 people were diagnosed with this disease in 1993," a wise speaker might say, "More than a quarter of a million people," or "More than 250,000 people received this diagnosis in 1993." Another reason to round numbers is that, when they are related to current topics, they are likely to change rapidly. For instance, AIDS activists announced that 129,001 lives had been lost as a result of the dis-ease since 1981. However, that number was out of date even before it was announced, for a look at the day's obituaries showed that several more people had died of AIDS-related diseases the previous day.

Because numbers can be boring, it is often helpful to make them come alive for listeners by comparing them to something already in their experience. Look at how Representative Bob Whittaker of Kansas helped his audience under-stand the numbers he presented. In an October 1990 speech to antitobacco ac-tivists and church leaders from Washington, D.C., Representative Whittaker explained:[6]

> Of the 2.5 million people globally who die from the effects of tobacco, 390,000 are Americans. This figure is equal to the number who would die if three 747 jumbo jets, loaded with passengers, crashed 365 days a year. However, in February, the Centers for Disease Control said that this figure is too low; actually closer to 434,000 pre-ventable deaths occur annually. That is an 11 percent increase over the initial esti-mate—more than two additional plane crashes each weekend.

By showing his listeners what the number meant in relation to something they could visualize, Whittaker kept their attention and helped them relate more emotionally to the subject. It is hard to imagine 390,000 people. It is easier to feel the shocking effect three plane crashes each day of the year would have.

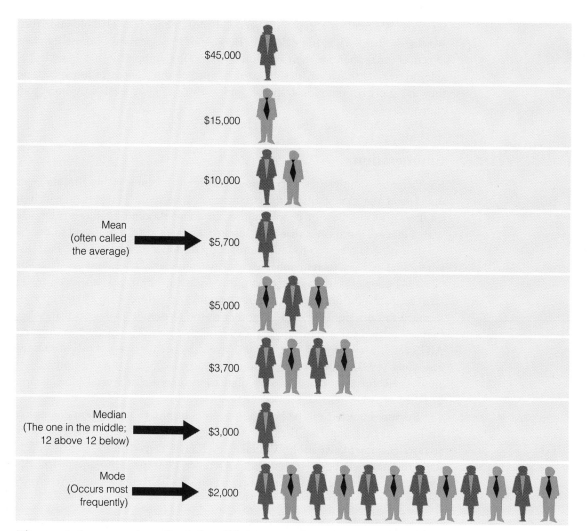

$45,000

$15,000

$10,000

Mean
(often called
the average) → $5,700

$5,000

$3,700

Median
(The one in the middle;
12 above 12 below) → $3,000

Mode
(Occurs most
frequently) → $2,000

The mean is the average; the median is the middle instance. When a few extreme instances might lead to unrealistic conclusions, the median is often a more useful statistic.

Statistics

For Further Reading

D. Huff. (1954). *How to lie with statistics*. New York: Norton.

The statistics commonly used in speeches include means, medians, percentages, and ratios.

Mean   The mean is the average of a group of numbers. To calculate the mean, add up all the cases or instances, then divide by the total number of cases. For example, you might discuss the mean SAT scores of students at your school who are going into education, then compare these scores with those of pharmacy students. However, if there are extreme figures at either end of the range, the average is skewed, and the statistic then becomes less useful.

Median   The median is the middle number in a set of numbers that have been arranged into a ranked order; half the numbers lie above it and half fall below it. This statistic is often used when a very high or very low number would skew the data. For this reason, you will hear the median age at which people marry or the median score on a class examination.

Percentages   Percentages are used to show the relationship of a part to the whole, which is represented by the number 100. Public speakers commonly use percentages such as these, which can be effectively displayed by using a map of the United States.[7]

> *During the forty years from 1880 to 1920, at least 12 million immigrants fleeing poverty and persecution in European countries flocked to the United States. Since 1965, when the immigration laws were changed, at least that many more have entered the United States—both legally and illegally. Of legal immigrants, 79 percent go to one of seven states, as this map shows:*

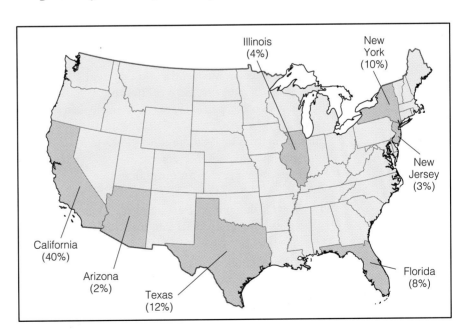

Often, you will find the percentage stated as a *rate of increase or decrease*, which compares growth or decline during a period to a baseline figure from an earlier period. Treat these rates with caution, for unless you know the baseline number, the rate of increase or decrease is relatively meaningless. Case in point: If a company employs two people in the year 1993 and adds an additional employee in the year 1994, the *rate of increase* is 50 percent (1/2 = 50 percent). However, if a company employs 100 people in 1993 and adds an additional employee in the year 1994, the number of new employees is the same, but the *rate of increase* in the larger organization is only 1 percent (1/100 = 1 percent). The reverse is also true. If the small company lost one employee, it would decrease by 50 percent. As you can see, when baseline numbers are initially very low, the rate of increase is potentially astonishing.

Public speakers often use such rates when they present information, as this example demonstrates.

Teaching Idea

Discuss the ethical implications of using statistics that slant the issues. When does slanting become distortion? What responsibilities do listeners have to interpret statistics?

An AIDS activist spoke at a small town in a rural county of a western state. He announced that AIDS increased by 34 percent in rural areas, whereas its rate of increase was only 5 percent in cities. However, he failed to show how that rate applied to the county in which he spoke. The total number of cases in the entire county was 8. A 34 percent increase meant that there were 6 cases the previous year. However, a 5 percent increase in a city with 10,000 cases meant that 500 additional people were afflicted with the disease.

Ratios   Often, we present relationships between numbers as a ratio rather than as a percentage; consequently, you may find 10 percent and 1 in 10 used interchangeably. Twenty-five percent, similarly, is stated as 1 out of 4. Ratios are most helpful when the percentage is very small such as 1 case in 100,000 (.000001 percent). As a result, it is more effective to say, "18 per 100,000 teens died of gunshot injuries in 1989, up from the 12 per 100,000 recorded in 1979," than it is to give the figures as percentages.

Here are some tests for quantification.

1.   What is the source of the numbers? Does the source have an interest such as a possibility of financial gain that would make high or low numbers more desirable?

2.   Are the numbers up to date? As you can imagine, using a count or a percentage that is old is generally not applicable to current conditions.

3.   Before you use startling rates of increase, look at the baseline figures that form the basis for the percentages. Note any other relevant factors that might affect this rate.

KEY CONCEPT   # Quantification

Quantification is information in the form of numbers.

Enumeration Enumeration is numbering or counting.

Statistics Statistics are common in speeches.

> *Mean* The mean is the average of a group of numbers.
>
> *Median* The median is the middle number in a group of numbers put in ranked order.
>
> *Percentages* Percentages show the relationship of the part to the whole, which is represented by the number 100. The rate of increase or decrease shows changes in comparison to a baseline figure; use such ratios with caution.
>
> *Ratios* This type of quantification shows numbers in relationship to one another. Ratios are often used if a corresponding percentage is very small.

Comparison and Contrast

Cross Reference

Comparison–contrast evidence is related to reasoning by analogy, covered in Chapter 15. It is a common form of reasoning in all cultural groups.

When we learn new information or encounter new ideas, we often find it helpful to compare and contrast the new to something familiar. *Comparison* points out the similarities between the two things; *contrast* highlights the differences. This sort of evidence is often called *analogy*. Comparisons and contrasts can be literal or figurative.

Literal Comparison

Some evidence compares or contrasts two actual things that are alike in some ways. Thus, a speaker who argues that Joe Montana is the greatest quarterback who has ever played the game might compare him to other quarterbacks whom the audience considers great. By literally comparing and contrasting rushing yards, games won, passing yards, touchdown passes, and so on, the speaker demonstrates that Montana meets or exceeds the performance of every other quarterback.

In a speech on the pros and cons of fetal-cell transplantation, both sides of the controversial issue literally compare the dead fetus to other dead bodies.[8]

> *Supporters of transplantation believe that the fetus is essentially a cadaver. They feel this cadaver should be used to develop more effective methods of treating debilitating diseases. Those who use this justification for fetal cell research argue that adult cadavers are used in research with consent of their families. So why shouldn't fetal cadavers*

be used the same way? John Robertson, a law professor at the University of Texas, says that the dead fetus is essentially an organ donor and that its usable organs should be used to treat horrible diseases.

. . . Critics of fetal tissue research and transplantation believe that the fetus is essentially a victim. They ask, "Should we do harm so that good may come?" Their answer is, "No." Arthur Caplan, Director of the Center for Biomedical Ethics at the University of Minnesota, argues against using a victim to save the lives of others, "Society will not tolerate killing one life for another."

Not only do speakers use comparison, they also show contrasts or differences between one lesser known thing and one that is better known. Thus, a speaker explaining the Japanese educational system shows not only its similarities to schooling in the United States but also its differences.

The major test for literal comparisons requires that the two items being compared are alike in essential details. Thus, though the jobs of a police officer in Houston, Texas, and another in Sioux Falls, South Dakota, are alike in many ways, they are not alike in essential details. Because of this, comparing the Houston officer to one in Los Angeles or Miami is more appropriate because all three are urban settings with a large number of immigrants. Sioux Falls officers, on the other hand, have more in common with officers in small cities in Michigan and Nebraska.

Figurative Comparison

In contrast to comparisons between two similar things, figurative comparisons or *figurative analogies*, point out similarities between dissimilar things. Using analogies requires listeners to use their imaginations to integrate and synthesize likenesses between two otherwise different things or ideas. For example, one student's entire speech explained an analogy that is commonly used in the business community—the "glass ceiling." In this introduction, she explains what the ceiling is and mentions another common organizational analogy, "the corporate ladder."[9]

When I say the words "the glass ceiling," what comes to your mind? Probably nothing, because most students do not know what it is. It is not a brand new architectural design that lets in more light. In contrast, it describes a barrier—a clear barrier in which the top area is visible but cannot be reached. The phrase is used to describe an invisible barrier that appears to block those who are perceived as "not fitting in" from climbing the corporate ladder. The height of the ceiling varies among different companies.

Teaching Idea

As a summarizing activity, have students do exercises 1 and 2. (In exercise 2, each example may contain more than one kind of evidence.)

In short, analogies are useful to connect what is familiar to listeners—in this case, ceilings—to what is lesser known—the inability of individuals and groups to reach high levels of power and influence within organizations. The use of metaphor does not require the same type of tests as other forms of evidence. However, the metaphors must be clear and make sense so that listeners can make the mental connection.

KEY CONCEPT | **Comparison and Contrast**

You can use likenesses (comparisons) and differences (contrasts) to illustrate a point; comparisons are often called analogies.

Literal comparison These analogies compare actual things.

Figurative comparison These imaginative analogies point out similarities between otherwise dissimilar things.

Summary

It is vital to support your ideas with evidence that listeners can understand so that they see reasons for your major points. Select facts that can be verified by a number of sources. In addition, select facts that are up to date. Further, during your research, distinguish factual material from opinions.

Most listeners like examples, and these specific incidences function to make abstract concepts more concrete and relevant. In addition, illustrations help listeners identify emotionally with your topic. Examples can be real or hypothetical, brief or extended. To be effective, examples should be representative, sufficient in number, and plausible.

The use of testimony and quotations can enhance your credibility if you are not considered an expert on a topic. Quote or paraphrase the opinions of experts and lay or peer sources. In addition, you can quote cultural proverbs, written texts, and words of wisdom from relatively unknown sources.

In a society that tends to be impressed by quantification, the judicious use of enumeration and statistics may increase your audience's acceptance of your ideas. Be sure that your numerical support is understandable, up to date, and used in ways that do not create misleading impressions.

Finally, comparison (analogy) and contrast are two additional forms of support. Literal analogies compare or contrast two actual things; figurative analogies compare two things that are generally considered different, but share a likeness in one specific way.

As you interweave facts, examples, numbers, testimony, and figurative and literal comparisons, you give your listeners more reasons to accept the conclusions you present.

Questions and Exercises

1. Bring to class a current issue of a newsmagazine or newspaper. With your classmates, decide upon an issue that appears in the week's news. Collect and display information by dividing the chalkboard into sections—one for each kind of evidence. Contribute information from your magazine or paper, cooperating with your classmates to fill the board. Evaluate the evidence using the tests presented in this chapter.

2. With a small group of your classmates, evaluate the effectiveness of the following pieces of evidence taken from student speeches. What kind (or kinds) of evidence does each excerpt represent? Is the evidence specific or vague? Does the speaker cite the source of the evidence adequately? Does it meet the tests for the type of evidence it represents?

A recent study showed that at least three out of four black children who were placed in white homes are happy and have been successfully incorporated into their families and communities.

According to The Natural History of Whales and Dolphins, *dolphins communicate through a system of whistles, clicks, rattles, and squeaks. These clicking sounds are not only used for navigation in the deep waters, but may also be used to convey messages. Pulsed squeaks can indicate distress, whereas buzzing clicks may indicate aggression.*

As far as deaths [from killer bees] are concerned, Mexican officials report that only sixteen people have died in the last three years as a result of their stings. That number is similar to the number who die of sharkbite. As one Texan put it, "The killer bee will be no more a threat to us than the rattlesnake."

According to New Jersey congressman Frank Guarini, "American families play amusement ride roulette every time they go on an outing to an amusement park."

As reported by the World Press Review Magazine, *the Japanese use of disposable chopsticks has resulted in the destruction of half of the hardwood forests in the Philippines and one-third of the forests in Indonesia. This trend will likely continue as long as the Japanese use 12 billion pairs of throw-away chopsticks a year, which is enough wood to build 12,000 average-sized family homes.*

In 1988, fetal brain cells were implanted deep into the brain of a 52-year-old Parkinson's victim. Traditional treatments all failed this person. Now, he reports that his voice is much stronger, his mind is sharper and not confused, and he can walk without cane or crutches.

Key Terms

facts
examples
hypothetical examples
direct quotation
paraphrase
expert testimony
peer or lay testimony
quantification
enumeration
mean
median
percentages
ratios
rate of increase
rate of decrease
comparison
contrast
analogies
literal comparisons
figurative comparisons

Notes

1. Narrative theory is covered in Chapter 15 of this text. See A. MacIntyre. (1981). *After virtue: A study in moral reasoning* (2nd ed.). South Bend, IN: University of Notre Dame Press.

2. Waldman, S. (1992, May 4). Deadbeat dads. *Newsweek*, pp. 46–52.

3. Thompson, B. (1991, April–May). The sun never sets on the Marlboro Man. *World Vision*, pp. 4–8.

4. Marcia Rudin is quoted in Woodward, K. L. (1993, March 15). Cultic America: A Tower of Babel. *Newsweek*, pp. 60–61.

5. Walters, F. M. (1992, November 15). In celebration of options: Respect each other's differences. *Vital Speeches of the Day*, pp. 265–269.

6. Bob Whittaker's speech is reported in Scriven, C. (1991). Why the Marlboro Man Wants Your Kids, in *Christianity Today,* April 8, pp. 33–35.

7. This information came from Morganthau, T. (1993, August 9). America: Still a melting pot? *Newsweek*, pp. 16–23.

8. Patti, C. (1991, November 11). Fetal cell transplantation. Student speech. St. John's University. Jamaica, New York.

9. Li, V. (1992, April 27). The glass ceiling. Student speech. St. John's University. Jamaica, New York.

9 Organizing the Speech

At the end of this chapter, you should be able to

- Organize the body of your speech by using a number of patterns, including topical, chronological, spatial, causal, pro-con, and problem-solution
- Identify and use alternative patterns when they are appropriate, including the wave, the spiral, and the star
- Develop an introduction for your speech that gains attention, motivates the audience to listen, establishes your credibility, and previews the speech
- List a number of ways to gain and maintain attention in a speech
- Develop a conclusion for your speech that signals the end, provides a summarizing statement, provides psychological closure, and ends with impact
- Link the parts of the speech to one another through skillful use of connectives such as signposts, transitions, internal previews, and internal summaries
- Outline the contents of your speech in a linear form
- Put a speaking outline onto note cards for use during delivery of your speech

Note

After speakers collect information, it is important to for them to organize their thoughts into culturally appropriate patterns. The principles for doing so are found in the canon of disposition or organization. This chapter begins with the body of the speech, for that is where students should begin. It then moves to introductions, conclusions, and transition statements. It concludes by showing students the standard forms of outlining.

In October 1991, President George Bush responded to a question on tax cuts in this way: "I think it's understandable, when you have a bad—economic numbers come in from time to time, mixed, I must happily say, with some reasonably good ones, other people get concerned. I'm concerned. But I don't want to do—take—I don't want to say to them, 'Well, you shouldn't come forward with proposals.'"[1] Many people found it difficult to understand the president because his thoughts were so disorganized. Afterward, many wondered, "What'd he just say?"

Good speakers, after they collect speech materials through research, find ways to organize their thoughts and present their ideas in patterns that their listeners can follow and remember. This is what the Romans called the canon of *disposition*. This chapter identifies and explains predictable patterns of organization that will help you order your thoughts and focus your listeners' attention on your major ideas. Detailed information on introductions, conclusions, and the connectives that bind the entire speech together follows. The chapter concludes with a section on outlining, including a sample student outline.

The Body of the Speech

Cross Reference

The diversity theme is emphasized by presenting previously unpublished material on alternative organizational patterns commonly used by women and members of ethnic groups.

The part of the speech in which you present the material you discovered during the research process is called the body of the speech. Although it is the middle part of the speech, it is the part that you plan first. Afterward, you plan an introduction that orients your listeners to the subject, then you select material for a conclusion that leaves your audience with something to remember. First, this section looks at some of the more common organizational patterns used in Euro-American speeches. Then it considers alternative patterns that are common in other cultural groups.

Topical Organization

Teaching Idea

These are standard organizational patterns. Illustrate each type by using examples. If you have access to a file of old student speech outlines, read the preview statements of a number of speeches, and ask students to identify the organizational pattern of each speech. Activity 9.1 in the Instructor's Manual provides some examples of previews.

The most widely used organizational pattern is one that classifies major points into topics or subdivisions, each of which is part of the whole. Although every point contributes to an understanding of the subject, the points themselves do not have to occur in any particular order. For instance, when Professor Joan Aitken spoke to a group of parents about communicating with children, she used this topical organizational pattern.[2]

> *There are four important things to remember when communicating with children.*
> *A. Communicate by having fun.*
> *B. Communicate by nurturing self-esteem.*
> *C. Communicate by your actions.*
> *D. Use music to communicate.*

Dr. Aitken could easily have presented her ideas in a different order. Indeed, other speakers would have chosen the point about self-esteem as their starting point, then ended with the idea of having fun.

Chronological Organization

A second way of organizing material is to relate the points to one another in a time pattern. In this pattern, the sequencing—what comes first and what follows in a given order—is vital. Because this pattern develops an idea as it occurs over a period, chronological organization is useful in biographical speeches, those that recount historical events, and those that explain processes or cycles.

It stands to reason that the points of a biographical speech are often developed chronologically because an individual's life unfolds over a period of years. Here is a sketch of the main points of a speech about a person's life, organized chronologically.

Mahatma Gandhi was a hero in the nonviolence movement.

A. His early life in South Africa
B. His public career teaching nonviolence
C. His subsequent assassination

Chronological organizational patterns also function effectively when speakers describe historical events because they also occur in a time sequence.

The Civil War cost more lives than any other war.

A. Events preceding the war
B. The war years
C. Reconstruction of the South

Process speeches are another type that generally feature a chronological pattern. In such a speech, a sequence of steps or stages follow one another in fairly predictable patterns. People speak about natural as well as social processes. This skeleton outline shows the chronological organization of a natural process.

The death of a star

A. The star's early years
B. One thousand years before its death
C. The final year
D. The star's collapse
E. One year later

Many social, psychological, or personal processes also occur in patterned sequences or cycles. Here is the way one student organized her speech on grief.

Chronology is a commonly used organizational pattern that presents ideas in a sequence or time pattern.

There are five stages in the grief process.

A. First is a period of denial.
B. Anger follows.
C. This is replaced by bargaining.
D. Depression follows.
E. Finally, there is acceptance.

The key to chronological speeches is that events *must* occur in a sequence, and there is a clear "first, next, finally" pattern. In a disease, for instance, symptoms follow, rather than precede, infection with a virus. Occasionally, however, speakers vary the pattern by beginning with the final point before showing the events that led up to it. For instance, the speaker could first describe Gandhi's assassination then go back and provide details from his early life and his career that led up to the killing.

Spatial Organization

A third pattern organizes points of the speech by place or location. This pattern is less commonly used than some of the others, but it is good for speeches about places or about objects that are made up of several parts. Speakers who inform their listeners on how to use the library, for instance, usually provide a map and describe what is located on each floor. Generally, they begin with the ground floor and work their way to higher floors. Speakers who describe the effects of alcohol on the human body sometimes move from the brain downward to the heart and other organs. The order in which you present your points does not matter with some topics, as this speech outline demonstrates; it is divided by geographic regions.

Major global earthquake areas

A. Eastern European fault lines
B. The Pacific "Ring of Fire"
C. The Rift Valley in Africa

A spatial pattern is often used to organize speeches about places. For example, a speaker discussing Greece might begin with the southern peninsula and work her way northeast, describing each peninsula in turn.

Other subjects that can be handled spatially are objects that speakers describe from top to bottom, bottom to top, or side to side. For example, since dams are constructed in layers, students who explain the process of dam building usually begin with the bottom layer and move to the top of the dam. Similarly, an exercise instructor who begins with head and neck exercises and works down the body organizes the speech spatially.

Causal Organization

Because of basic Euro-American thought patterns, people in this culture tend to look for causes that underlie events. For this reason, cause–effect patterns are common when a problem can be discussed by examining the reasons for it (the causes) and the implications it has for individuals or for society at large (the effects). There are two basic causal organizational patterns: cause to effect and effect to cause. Here is a cause-to-effect outline.

Amusement park tragedies injure thousands of people annually.
A. Causes
   1. Equipment failure
   2. Operator failure
   3. Rider behavior
B. Effects
   1. Personal risks
   2. Needless tragedies

Conversely, speakers may begin by looking at the effects a problem has on an individual or group; then they explore the reasons or causes of the problem. This is an effects-to-cause organizational pattern.

> The lack of available organs for donation affects many people in our society, and there are many reasons for this shortage.
>
> A. Effects
>   1. Scarcity of organs
>   2. Length of waiting lists
>   3. Deaths due to scarcity
> B. Causes
>   1. Potential donor's fears
>   2. The family's fears
>   3. Health care provider's fears

Pro–Con Organization

It is common to debate controversial issues, looking at both the arguments for and those against a question or issue. If you give a speech that summarizes both sides of an issue, you may find the pro–con organizational pattern to be useful. Classify all the arguments *in favor of* the issue under the pro label, then list the arguments *against* it under the con label, as this student did.

> Fetal cell transplantation is a controversial medical procedure with both proponents and opponents.
>
> A. Arguments in favor of fetal cell transplantation
>   1. Research is promising.
>   2. A fetus is like a cadaver.
>   3. This is a choice issue.
> B. Arguments against fetal cell transplantation
>   1. It will lead to an industry of profit.
>   2. A fetus is a victim.
>   3. More abortions will occur.

This organizational pattern works best in informative speeches, when the speaker is attempting to enlighten people on the nature of an issue. By presenting both sides, listeners can weigh the evidence and evaluate the arguments for themselves. Speakers whose purpose is persuasive, those who advocate one set of arguments rather than another, do not generally choose this pattern.

Problem–Solution Organization

Because of core beliefs that life presents a series of problems to be solved, members of this society often approach global and national issues as well as personal problems as challenges to understand and solve through knowledge and effort.

(Some cultures, in contrast, believe that it is futile to fight fate.) Thus, a problem–solution organizational pattern is common. Not surprisingly, speakers who choose this pattern first look at the problem, sometimes examining its causes and effects; then they propose solutions. Here is an example of an outline for an informative speech on elder abuse.

Elder abuse is an increasing problem in our society.

A. Causes of the problem
B. Effects of the problem

Several solutions have been proposed.

A. Day care for adults
B. Support groups
C. Senior advocates

Theme

The linear patterns in this section are not the only way to organize good speeches. Some students may find it easier to visualize the organization of their speeches by using a pictorial representation of the speech. The following section introduces original work on these alternative patterns that has been done by Cheryl Jorgensen-Earp of Lynchburg College.

Some speakers choose to present problem–solution approaches to personal as well as national or international topics. This outline shows the major points in a speech about a personal issue.

Many women, as well as men, experience hair loss.

A. Causes of the problem
B. Effects of the problem

There are several solutions on the market.

A. Medications
B. Hairpieces
C. Bonding techniques
D. Transplants

If the purpose of the speech is informative, speakers inform their listeners of a variety of solutions. In persuasive speeches, however, they propose several solutions, then narrow the list to the one best solution that they argue should be implemented. We discuss this persuasive pattern in more detail in Chapter 16.

Other Patterns

In addition to these traditional patterns usually taught in public speaking classes, researchers are looking at other organizational patterns commonly used by women and ethnic speakers. For example, Cheryl Jorgensen-Earp[3] is exploring a number of alternative patterns that women have used historically. She argues that many speakers are uncomfortable with the standard organizational patterns because of cultural backgrounds or personal inclinations. As alternatives, she proposes several less direct and more "organic" patterns that provide a clear structure for a speech but have a less linear form. Jorgensen-Earp uses diagrams

BOX 9.1

Speaking in Madagascar[4]

In many areas of the world, speakers choose patterns that are very different from those presented in this text. For instance, elders in the Merina tribe of Madagascar use a four-part organizational pattern when they speak.

1. First is a period of excuses in which the speaker expresses his humility and reluctance to speak. He uses standard phrases such as, "I am a child, a younger brother." He sometimes relates well-known stories and proverbs.

2. He follows this by thanking the authorities for letting him speak at all. He uses a formula that thanks God, the president of the republic, government ministers, the village headman, major elders, and finally the people in the audience.

3. In the third section, he uses proverbs, illustrations, and short poems as he makes his proposal.

4. He closes his speech by thanking and blessing his listeners.

or pictures to describe these patterns, comparing them to a wave, a spiral, and a star. (We present a fourth pattern often used in narrative speeches, the infinity loop, in Chapter 13.)

The Wave Pattern   In this pattern, illustrated in Figure 9.1, the speaker uses repetitions and variations of themes and ideas. The major points of the speech come at the crest of the wave. She follows these with a variety of examples leading up to another crest where she repeats the theme or makes another major point. There are two types of conclusions: One "winds down" and leads the audience gradually from the topic; the other makes a transition to a conclusion and rebuilds so that the conclusion is a dramatic "peak." African Americans as well as women often use this pattern in speeches.

Teaching Idea

Show a videotape of a speech that uses a wave pattern. *Exercise 4 is appropriate here.*

Perhaps the most famous speech that illustrates this pattern is Martin Luther King, Jr.'s "I Have a Dream." King used this memorable line as the crest of a wave that he followed with examples of what he saw in his dream; then he repeated the line. He ended with a "peak" conclusion that emerged from the final wave in the speech—repetition and variation on the phrase "Let freedom ring."

And when this happens, when we allow freedom to ring—when we let it ring from every village and every hamlet, from every state and every city—we will be able to speed up that day when all of God's children, black men and white men, Jews and

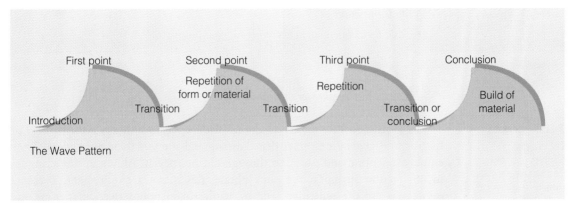

Figure 9.1

Gentiles, Protestants and Catholics, will be able to join hands and sing, in the words of the old Negro spiritual, "Free at last! Free at last! Thank God almighty, we are free at last!"[5]

An excerpt from Sojourner Truth's "Ain't I a Woman?"[6] speech also illustrates this pattern.

That man over there says that women need to be helped into carriages, and lifted over ditches, and to have the best place everywhere. Nobody ever helps me into carriages, or over mud-puddles, or gives me any best place!

And ain't I a woman?

Look at me! Look at my arm! I have ploughed and planted, and gathered into barns, and no man could head me!

And ain't I a woman?

I could work as much and eat as much as a man—when I could get it—and bear the lash as well!

And ain't I a woman?

I have borne thirteen children, and seen them most all sold off to slavery, and when I cried out with my mother's grief, none but Jesus heard me!

And ain't I a woman?

One African-American man used the following outline to introduce a speaker:

Who is this man?

- Example of his accomplishments
- Example of personal characteristics

Who is this man?

- *Additional information about his accomplishments*
- *Another example of personal characteristics*

Who is this man? . . .

He's . . . [our speaker for the evening]

Teaching Idea

The excerpt from Elizabeth Cady Stanton's speech in the Appendix includes Jorgensen-Earp's analysis of the wave organizational pattern. *Exercise 6 is appropriate here.*

In short, between the major points of the speech, speakers use a barrage of specific and general examples that illustrate and support their main ideas. They employ repetition and variation throughout the speech. Although the examples in this section all repeat the same phrase, this is not a requirement. Speakers sometimes use the repetitive style by stating main points that differ from one another. (An example of this type of repetition—an excerpt from Elizabeth Cady Stanton's "The Solitude of Self"—is included in the Appendix.)

Cross Reference

This pattern can also be used with narrative speeches (Chapter 13).

The Spiral Pattern A repetition pattern that builds in intensity may be easier to visualize as a spiral than a wave. This pattern, illustrated in Figure 9.2, is similar to a wave pattern, but since each major point is more important—or more dramatic—than the preceding point, the speech builds to a climax.

One way to use the spiral pattern is to repeat a narrative with several variations. Let's say a speaker chooses the subject of selecting a college. She establishes a hypothetical student, Todd, who appears in three scenarios. First, she narrates his experiences if he decides to go to a local community college. In a second instance, Todd goes out of town but stays within the state. In the final scene, he attends a school that is across the continent from where he lives. Each succeeding instance requires more money and places him at a greater distance from home.

The spiral pattern is often useful for speeches on controversial topics, such as euthanasia. A speaker might establish a narrative around a hypothetical character named Jake who suffers from painful terminal cancer. In the first scenario, Jake dies in a hospice where he is heavily sedated at the end. In the second, he is given less medication with the result that he suffers a great deal. In the final scenario, members of his family assist him in committing suicide. Each scene builds in tension with the most controversial scenario reserved for the final spiral.

Patterns that use repetition can provide valuable organizational schemes. It may help you to compare them with the form that is common in songs. Each verse of the song provides a different development of the song's theme, but the lyrics are repeated exactly in the chorus. Keep in mind throughout your preparation that these patterns require as much organizational planning as the other more linear formats.

Note

Although some of these patterns are arguably topical, it helps many students who are more visually oriented learners to think of diagrams rather than use a linear outline.

The Star Pattern Each point in a star pattern speech, illustrated in Figure 9.3, is relatively equally weighted within a theme that ties the whole together. Speakers who use this variation on the topical pattern often present the same

Figure 9.2

The spiral pattern

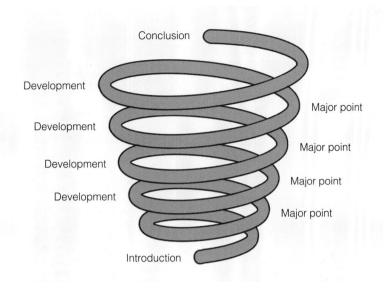

speech to a number of audiences. By visualizing the points of their speech as a star, they have the flexibility of choosing where to start and what to emphasize, depending on what is relevant for a specific audience. To illustrate, speakers may choose to begin with a point the audience understands or agrees with, then progressively move to points that challenge their understanding and agreement. For inattentive audiences, they may begin with their most dramatic point. For hostile audiences, it is often best to begin with the most conciliatory point. This pattern has the advantage of allowing a speaker to make such audience adaptations quickly and still have the speech work effectively.

There are two ways to develop the points of the speech: Speakers can state the point, support or develop it, then provide a transition to the next point; or they can develop each point fully before they state it. These decisions depend on the type of audience and the nature of the various points.

The final element in the pattern is a thematic circle that binds all the points together. Although the points of the speech are connected individually, each point rests comfortably within the overall theme. By the close of the speech, listeners should feel that the circle is completed and the theme fulfilled.

For instance, a speaker who presents seminars on investment management might have the general theme of financial security, with points on retirement plans, medical insurance, growth investments, and global funds. With some audiences, she may cover all the points briefly; with others, she concentrates more on retirement plans and global investments. This pattern is common in election speeches. For instance, one might use the underlying theme of Vote for me! However, the candidate chooses a different ordering or development of points and issues depending on the audience.

Cross Reference

Chapter 16 has a section on hostile audiences.

Figure 9.3

The star pattern

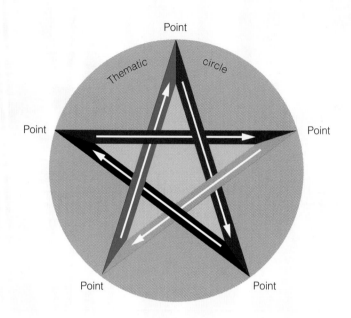

Teaching Idea

Using exercise 1, have students identify a second pattern that could be used—e.g., types of dogs could be topical or spatial (Asian dogs, African dogs, and so on).

Thus, we see that there are several common patterns that you can use to provide the form or shape of the body of your speeches. These include topical, chronological, spatial, causal, pro–con, and problem–solution. In addition, speakers—often women and members of minority groups—use the wave, spiral, and star patterns to organize and present their ideas.

KEY CONCEPT   The Body of the Speech

Topical organization This organizational pattern classifies major points according to subdivisions, and the order in which they occur in the speech is not essential.

Chronological organization This organizational pattern arranges major points into a time or sequential pattern.

Spatial organization The speaker arranges the points according to their place or geographic location.

Causal organization This pattern contains two major points: causes and effects; they can be arranged causes to effects or effects to causes.

Pro–con organization The speaker presents arguments in favor of a proposal or a controversial issue and arguments against it.

Problem–solution organization This pattern develops the issues related to the problem and explains the proposed solution or solutions.

Other patterns

The wave pattern The crests of the waves are the major points that are developed through a series of examples; repetition and variation are two key components of this pattern.

The spiral pattern This repetitive pattern presents a series of points that increase in drama or intensity.

The star pattern A theme ties together a series of relatively equally weighted points; the sequencing of points does not matter.

Introducing the Speech

Teaching Idea

If you wish to use an overhead projector to present the parts of an introduction, there is a transparency in the Instructor's Manual. It presents the introduction as a way to orient the audience to the subject of the speech by answering some of the questions listeners may have as the speaker begins.

Once you have planned and outlined the body of your speech, you can begin to complete the speech by working on the introduction, the conclusion, and the transition statements that make your ideas flow smoothly. According to the Roman educator Quintilian, there are four purposes for an introduction.

1. To draw the listeners' attention to the topic
2. To motivate them to listen
3. To establish yourself as knowledgeable on the topic
4. To preview the major ideas of the speech

In addition, it is important to include essential definitions or background information on your topic that listeners will need to understand your speech. If you include these in your introduction, you will answer these basic listener questions at the very outset of the speech: What's this all about? Why should I listen? Why should I listen to you? What will you be covering? We look at each of these questions, in turn, in this section.

Gain Attention

Teaching Idea

Activity 9.2 in the Instructor's Manual gives ideas for introducing this section.

Gaining attention is the first step in the listening and understanding process; so as you begin, it is important to introduce your topic and draw your listeners' attention to it. Some speakers, students as well as professionals, simply announce their subject like this: "Today, my speech is about polar bears." This does introduce the topic, but it is not a very creative way to gain attention. Good speakers use more effective techniques. Here are a few of them.

Cross Reference

This section continues the
dialogical theme of the
book.

Ask a Question   There are two types of questions, rhetorical and participatory. Rhetorical questions are the kind listeners answer in their mind; participatory ones, in contrast, call for an overt response, such as a show of hands or a verbal answer. Here is an example of a rhetorical question that a professional speaker used as an interesting twist to open his speech, "Overworked Americans or Overwhelmed Americans? You Cannot Handle Everything."[7]

> *Here is a multiple-choice question. Which word best describes the typical working American today:*
>
> A. *Overworked.*
> B. *Underworked.*
> C. *Energetic.*
> D. *Lazy.*
>
> *While much has been written of late as to whether A, B, C, or D is correct, the most appropriate answer may well be, "None of the above." . . . The best answer may well be that the majority of Americans are overwhelmed.*

The audience responds internally to this rhetorical question by thinking of their own work-related experiences. Moreover, because they encountered multiple-choice questions in their schooling, the famous "none of the above" option adds a touch of humor.

In contrast to rhetorical questions, there are times when you want a visible response from your listeners. You must make it clear to them if you want them to respond physically. For instance, ask for a show of hands or call on a member of the audience to answer a question you pose, as this example demonstrates.[8]

> *Where do you think the following situations take place? Every person who leaves the house must carry a rifle. Every house has at least one gun easily accessible. No one leaves home after dark unless it is an emergency.*
> *(Pause—ask one or two people to venture an answer.)*
> *No, it's not Harlem or Bed-Stuyvestant,[9] but a quaint Arctic town in Canada called Churchill, Manitoba. And what these people fear is the polar bear.*

For a question to capture the audience's attention, however, it must be sufficiently intriguing. Here are two examples of ineffective questions. The first is too broad; the second is too specific to relate to most people.

> *How many of you have ever purchased an album, cassette, or a compact disk?*
>
> *Have you ever had your finger almost sliced off and left hanging by a small piece of skin?*

Both types of questions, rhetorical and participatory, contribute to the establishment of dialogue between speakers and listeners because they invite audience response, whether mental or physical.

Provide a Vivid Description Draw the audience's attention to the subject by describing a scene in such vivid language that listeners are compelled to visualize it mentally. The scene can be real or imaginary. Here is the opening for a speech on sharks.[10]

> *We have all seen it before—the ominous fin cutting through the water as the panic-stricken swimmer tries desperately to escape. With a flash of teeth, the predator hungrily devours its prey—and all that is left is a pool of blood on the surface of the water. This is an all-too-common, worldwide view of an animal that has been given a terrible, undeserved reputation—the shark.*

Begin with a Quotation You can often gain listener attention with a quotation or a familiar cultural proverb. These quotations can be *about* a subject or, in the case of a biographical speech, *by* the subject. When you use quotations, select one that encapsulates the overall theme of the speech. It is usually helpful to give the source of the quotation. The sayings do not have to be from real people, as this opening for a speech on computerized drums illustrates.

> *According to a record producer in the cartoon strip Doonesbury, "Drummers are extinct."*

Quotations can also come from song lyrics or poems. For instance, a student speech on toy weapons began with this rhyme.[11]

> *Major Bludd says,*
> *   "When you're feeling low and woozy,*
> *   Slap a fresh clip in your Uzi!*
> *   Assume the proper firing stance*
> *   And make the suckers jump and dance."*
> *Major Bludd is a figure created by Hasbro toys, and an Uzi is a play submachine gun manufactured for children. They are an example of toy weapons I discovered when researching what kind of effect these toys may have on children.*

Quotations may originate in family sayings or in memorable words spoken by someone such as a high school soccer coach. For instance, for a speech on perseverance, one such opening might be, "My grandmother used to say, 'It's a great life if you don't weaken.'"

Tell a Joke or Funny Story Professional speakers often begin by telling a joke, setting an informal, humorous atmosphere at the outset of the speech. Many speakers tell jokes and humorous stories successfully; however, many others embarrass themselves by beginning with a joke that flops. It is important that the joke relates to the topic of the speech. Otherwise, you are perhaps gaining attention, but you are not drawing it to your subject. The following riddle could be used to begin a speech on learning a second language:

You know the word for a person who knows three languages? It's tri-lingual.

What's the word for a person who knows two languages? Right, it's bi-lingual. What do you call a person who knows only one language?

The correct answer is, "An American!"

While most of the students in the rest of the world gain a measure of proficiency in English as well as their own languages, most students who graduate from high schools in the United States know only English.

Refer to a Current Event   In an effort to identify with listeners and establish common ground, speakers often refer to well-known current happenings. For example, this professional speaker spoke on communication with children just a few weeks after the 1993 presidential inauguration. She referred to that occasion in her speech opening.[12]

How interesting that you have given me three times as long to speak as President Clinton had for his Inaugural Address. I've been trying to figure out the significance of this fact. Could it be because the importance of good communication with our children is three times more important than the communication of a new president to the world? Actually, I believe it is, especially when we consider the potential of what we say: how our words affect the sense of self, how a smile can inspire learning, how a nod can influence personality, how our words can shape lives.

Begin with an Example   Examples provide your listeners with the opportunity to become emotionally involved with the topic. Most everyone likes a good story, and when we hear of real people involved in real situations, we generally become more attentive. This example from a speech on amusement park injuries demonstrates the power of an example in drawing listener attention to a topic.[13]

On October 17, 1983, two brothers—Wade Phillips, who was 19, and Tim Phillips, who was 21—boarded a ride called "The Enterprise" at the Texas State Fair in Dallas. The Enterprise is similar to a ferris wheel with gondolas that first spin horizontally, then tip vertically. Soon after the ride began, the gondola holding the brothers snapped off of the giant machine's main frame. It plunged to the ground and skidded 40 feet before coming to rest in the fair's congested midway. Miraculously, no one on the ground was injured. However, Tim Phillips suffered a broken leg and internal injuries, and Wade died of multiple injuries.

Start with Startling Numbers   Numbers and statistics can be dry; however, they can capture and hold your listeners' attention if they are shocking enough, as this example illustrates.

Look at your watch. Before the hour is over, approximately 3,000 puppies and kittens will have been born. The result is that nearly 8 million unwanted animals must be euthanized annually.

It is important to draw listeners' attention to your topic at the outset of your speech. One effective attention-gaining strategy is to use a visual aid.

Use an Audio or Visual Aid   You can use posters, charts, tape recordings, and other visual and audio materials successfully in drawing attention to your topic. If you like humor, consider using an overhead projector to display a relevant cartoon that has been transferred to a transparency. Begin a speech on buying a car by displaying a large poster of an automobile. One student played seven seconds of a tape recording of sounds made by humpback whales, and then began her speech.

> *What do you think makes this gentle sound? Do you think of a 50-foot-long, 4-ton giant? Well, the source of this sound is just that: a humpback whale.*

Teaching Idea

Exercise 2 is a culminating activity for this section.

Although this is not an exhaustive list of successful openings for speeches, it provides you with examples of openings commonly used by public speakers in a variety of settings. The purpose of an introduction is not simply to gain attention. It must draw attention to the topic. A few speakers have ignored this rule and done something startling like slapping the podium loudly and then saying, "Now that I have your attention, I am going to talk about animal overpopulation." Obviously, this introduction failed because, even though it attracted attention, it was not relevant to the subject.

Motivate the Audience to Listen

Cross Reference

Chapter 2 discusses the importance of tying in to audience interests. The importance of this is additionally developed in Chapters 5 and 14. Jill's speech is also discussed in Chapter 7.

Once you have drawn your listeners' attention to the topic, it is important to answer their question, why should I listen to this speech? Often speakers are excited about their topics, thinking they are important and interesting, but they realize that most listeners have never thought much about the subject, which they see as irrelevant. For example, Jill Nagaue was a student at Oregon State University when she gave a speech on Hawaiian sovereignty. (See the outline later in this chapter.) Most OSU students had never heard of the controversy over returning Hawaii to Hawaiian rule, and it was remote from their everyday lives. Jill's purpose in her introduction, which will be your purpose as well, was to give listeners a reason to listen by relating her topic to their interests.

Often speakers frame their topic within a larger issue; for instance, caller ID is a privacy issue, and elder abuse is part of a nationwide problem of violence against the helpless. A speech on polar bears does not directly relate to listeners in most classrooms. However, treatment of polar bears is connected to larger issues such as animal rights and animal overpopulation. Here is one way to relate such a topic to an audience.

> *At this point, you may be curious about polar bears, but you may not think much about them. After all, the only polar bears in New York are in the zoo. However, the problem with polar bears in Canada is similar to problems here on Long Island with a deer population that is getting out of control. What do we do with animals that live close to humans?*

One of the important characteristics of humans is their ability to learn new things. And at times you give speeches to increase your audience's knowledge. For instance, few people in the classroom will ever encounter a shark; however, many or most of the students have misconceptions about them due to the publicity in the media. This speaker appealed to his audience's need to have more accurate information about sharks.

Cross Reference

There are additional excerpts from this speech on sharks in Chapter 14.

> *I'm guessing that most people in this room share this basic opinion of sharks—that they are voracious man-eaters. This way of thinking is really incorrect, and is basically supported by overexaggerated films you may have seen and sensationalistic stories you may have read.*

Many issues that do not have a direct impact on the lives of your listeners actually affect their pocketbooks, whether or not they know it, because they cost tax dollars to support. For instance, students may never watch public television

It is important that your listeners know why you are qualified to speak about your subject. For instance, people paid attention when Marc Klaas spoke out regarding crime, because they knew that his daughter, Polly, had been kidnapped and brutally murdered.

Teaching Idea

Provide a list of topics, and have students discuss ways to relate each to the classroom audience. For example, the topic of cosmetic surgery can tie into larger cultural issues on beauty. Other topics: recycling plastics, tuition increases, the history of community colleges, loss of rainforests, vitamin therapy.

or listen to National Public Radio, and these media seem far removed from their lives until they realize how many federal dollars go to subsidize them. Consequently, for a speech on public broadcasting, you might refer to your listeners' financial concerns by showing how much public broadcasting costs taxpayers annually.

You can also appeal to audience curiosity. In a speech on Atlantis, for instance, one student appealed to the audience's natural love of a mystery. In Chapter 15, we look in greater detail at some of the needs, wants, emotions, and values that lead people to listen to speeches.

Establish Credibility

After you have the audience's attention and have given them a reason to listen to a speech on your topic, you must give them a reason to listen to *you*. At this point in your introduction, link yourself to the topic. Speakers typically do this by briefly sharing their experiences, interests, and research findings. In the classroom, you can mention your major, courses you have taken, television shows that first interested you, and so on. This speaker linked himself to the topic of sharks through his personal experiences.

I first became interested in sharks when I was about twelve years old, and I was fishing at my uncle's house in the Florida Keys. There for the first time, I encountered a shark in the wild. At first I experienced the normal anxiety people feel when they see

*a shark almost the size of the boat, but as I observed it further, my fascination grew.
Since then, I have been snorkeling many years, and I have seen sharks from under-
water as well.*

In a speech on "the glass ceiling," the invisible barrier that prevents women
and minorities from rising to the top in organizations, the student speaker, an
American of Chinese descent, linked herself to the topic in this way:

I became interested in this topic when I read an article in Newsday *about Charlotte
Beers, a woman who broke through the barrier to become the first woman to hold a
top position in a multi-billion-dollar advertising agency. I realized that this is the barrier I have personally encountered in a variety of managerial positions I have held at
various firms.*

Cross Reference

Relate this material to
prior ethos in Chapter 5.

This part of the introduction is sometimes optional for several reasons.
Many speakers are introduced by someone else who links the speaker with the
topic. Also, professional speakers generally have credibility, and well-known experts on a topic do not need to establish their credibility in the introduction.
However, if professionals speak on a topic outside their area of expertise, they
might do well to link themselves with the topic. For instance, if a psychologist is
testifying before a group of lawmakers on the need for a traffic light at a particular corner, her expertise as a psychologist is not particularly important. Instead,
the fact that she is a resident of the neighborhood who has narrowly escaped
injury on that corner makes her more credible on that subject.

Preview the Speech

Note

Presenting information three
times helps audien-
ces remember the major
ideas. Thus, a preview of the
main points, their development in the body, and a
brief summary or restate-
ment of them is
recommended.

There's an old saying, "Tell them what you're going to say; say it; then tell them
what you said." The preview serves the first function. It is the short transition
statement you make between the introduction and the body of your speech in
which you state some form of your central idea. This speaker previewed the two
major points he intended to develop in his topical speech in this way:

*Today I will show you that the reputation given the shark is based on stereotypes and
misinformation and that we harm sharks more than they harm us.*

For Further Reading

"The cumulative" three
is a persistent, "half-
instinctive mode of reasoning" that dates to earliest
human logic. See V. Hopper
(1938). *Medieval number
symbolism.* New York:
Columbia University Press,
p. 15.

Here is a sample introduction that pulls together all the elements of a good
opening. The speech is about human–dolphin communication, and all four parts
of the introduction are easily identifiable.[14]

1. *"Hoop-right-frisbee-in." Although you know the words I just used, I doubt if
    most of you really understood what I said. But if you were a dolphin trained in
    communicating with humans, you would have known exactly what I meant.*

2. *In the world today, we sometimes forget that humans are not the only life form on the earth. The barrier of language that separates humans from other animals can create many problems in our understanding of the life outside our "human" world. But researchers are currently showing that communication between humans and dolphins is possible. Their studies specifically involve the bottlenose dolphin.*

3. *I became interested in the dolphin's ability to understand and communicate with humans after I read an article for a writing course. While researching this topic, I found several magazine articles and books related to dolphin communication.*

4. *Today, I would like to explain to you the concept of dolphin intelligence, communication methods these animals use among themselves, and communication they have developed with humans.*

This introduction successfully meets the requirements of a good speech opening. In it, the speaker (1) draws attention to her topic, (2) relates it to her listeners through an appeal to curiosity, (3) links herself to the subject through both interest and research, and (4) finishes by previewing the major ideas in her topical speech.

KEY CONCEPT   ## Introducing the Speech

Gain attention Introduce the topic by focusing your audience's attention on the subject in an interesting way.

Motivate the audience to listen Give listeners a reason to listen by making your subject relevant to their lives and interests.

Establish credibility Give your audience a reason to listen to you by linking yourself with the topic through interest, experience, and research.

Preview the speech State the central idea of the speech so that listeners will have a brief overview of your major ideas.

Concluding the Speech

A good speech does not end abruptly after the main points are made; polished speakers provide closure through a final summary and a satisfying or challenging closing statement. Since the major function of the conclusion is to bring the speech to an end, do not add new information in the conclusion. In your preparation, think your speech through to the final phrase, for that will be your audience's final impression of both you and your subject. Appearing disorganized at the end can negate positive impressions the audience held during the speech.

Like the introduction, the conclusion has several important parts: to signal the end, summarize the main points, refer to the introduction, and end with an impact.

Signal the End

Just as the preview provides a transition to the body of the speech, speakers often provide a sentence or phrase that signals a transition to the conclusion. The most common phrase, used by both beginning speakers and professionals, is "In conclusion." However, polished speakers often use more creative phrases in their transition to the conclusion, such as this:

> *We have now looked at an important issue facing Americans today, that of Japan bashing.*

You can also use nonverbal actions to signal that your speech is coming to an end. Many speakers, for instance, use a pause and shift their posture. Some take a step away from the podium. Speakers also make slight changes in their rate and volume, slowing down a bit and speaking more softly. Verbal and nonverbal transitions are not mutually exclusive, and you will see speakers use nonverbal cues along with the spoken transition phrases.

Summarize the Main Points

The summary or recapping of the main points of the speech is the "Tell them what you said" part of the phrase. It *briefly* reviews the major points that were developed in the speech. These two examples show how students combined the transition statement with a summary of the major ideas.

> *Now that we have looked at the shark as it really is [transition phrase], maybe you now realize that its reputation is really inaccurate and that humans present a greater threat to the shark than sharks present to humans [restatement of the central idea].*
>
> *Today we have taken a look at the opponents' and supporters' views concerning Native American symbols being used as nicknames and mascots for schools and sports teams. We also looked at where this debate stands today.*

Refer to the Introduction

To provide a sense of psychological closure for listeners, speakers often refer to something they said in the introduction. For instance, someone who begins with an example, returns to complete it in the conclusion. Other speakers refer to startling statistics or to quotations they presented in the opening. Here is the way the student returned to her story of amusement park tragedies.

Effective speakers conclude with a short summary, provide a sense of closure to the speech, and leave listeners with a memorable thought.

Once we understand the causes and effects of amusement park tragedies, we can begin to take serious action to eliminate the thousands of accident victims each year—people like Wade Phillips and his brother Tim.

End with an Impact

Finally, leave your listeners with a memorable final impression. During the few minutes you are speaking, audience members are focusing their attention on your subject. When you are finished, however, each listener will return to his or her own thoughts, moving away from the mental images created throughout the speech. Leave them with something that they will remember. There are many ways to create this positive memory, including some of the same types of material you used to gain attention in the beginning, as this partial list demonstrates.

- End with humor.
- Ask a thought-provoking question.

- Use a quotation.
- Issue a challenge.
- Tie the subject to a larger cultural theme or value.

Cross Reference

For example, a speech on organ donation might tie into the cultural value of generosity; one on new trends in computers is related to the U.S. value on progress. See Chapter 3.

Here is the entire conclusion for the speech on toy weapons mentioned earlier.

1. *Altogether, there are some widely contrasting views on the safety of toy weapons.*
2. *Some feel they have a negative effect physically and emotionally, because the border line between fantasy and reality is blurred for children. On the other hand, others see toy weapons as a stage of growing up for children, a way for them to release anxiety.*
3. *Through everything, we can count on Major Bludd and his Uzi being followed by more and more advanced toy weapons and ammunition.*
4. *To consider the effects of these toys on the mind of a child is to make a decision for the children of tomorrow.*

Teaching Idea

Exercise 3 enables students to apply the material in this section.

You can see that this speaker (1) provides a transition to the conclusion, (2) summarizes her major points, (3) refers to the introduction, and (4) finishes with a thought-provoking closing statement that ties into cultural values on families and the future.

KEY CONCEPT   **Concluding the Speech**

Signal the end Use both verbal and nonverbal cues to signal that the speech is coming to an end.

Summarize the main points This is the part of the speech when you "tell them what you said" by briefly reviewing the major ideas in the speech.

Refer to the introduction Provide your listeners with a sense of psychological closure by returning to something from the introduction.

End with an impact End strongly with something that the audience will remember after your speech is over.

Connecting the Parts of the Speech

After the speech body is planned and the introduction and conclusion are formulated, you will add the final touches to polish your speech. These are the connectives—the words, phrases, and sentences that lead from one idea to

Teaching Idea

For a paper-and-pencil activity, there is a worksheet on connectives in the Student Resource Workbook. Have students work in pairs to write words, phrases, and sentences that tie the speech together.

another and tie the various parts of the speech together smoothly. They function as the tendons or ligaments, as it were, that hold the speech together and help listeners keep their place as you talk. The most common types of connectives are signposts, transitions, internal previews, and internal summaries.

Signposts

These simple connectives are like signs along a highway. As highway signposts help drivers know how far they've come and how far they have to go, so signposts within a speech help listeners orient themselves to their place in the speech. Words such as *first, now,* and *finally* introduce each new point and let listeners sense the flow of the speech.

Transitions

Technically, a transition summarizes where you have been and where you are going in the speech. A simple transition for a pro–con speech, for example, sounds like this: "We have seen the major arguments for dental implants; now let's turn to the arguments opponents make against this type of dental work." Transitions can also lead from subpoint to subpoint within a major idea. Thus, under causes for amusement park tragedies, a transition sounds like this: "While both equipment and operator failure cause accidents, a number of tragedies are additionally caused by rider behavior."

Internal Previews

Internal previews occur within the body of the speech. Speakers briefly summarize the subpoints that they will develop under a major point in the speech. For instance, a speaker could say:

> *Experts agree that there are three main causes of amusement park tragedies: equipment failure, operator failure, and rider behavior.*

This preview helps audience members organize their listening as the speaker proceeds to develop each point.

Internal Summaries

Sometimes, speakers summarize subpoints after they have made them, *before* they move to another major point. Thus, the speaker could have summarized the section on causes, before moving on to the effects of amusement park accidents, like this:

> *In short, we have seen that equipment failure, operator failure, and rider behavior combine to create thousands of tragedies annually.*

Connectives, then, are words, phrases, and complete sentences that connect your ideas to one another and to the speech as a whole. They serve to introduce points, to preview and summarize material within a point, and to help listeners keep their place in the speech.

KEY CONCEPT

Connecting the Parts of the Speech

Signposts Simple words and phrases, such as *first* and *next*, help listeners keep their place in the speech.

Transitions Transition sentences briefly summarize the point just covered and lead into the next point.

Internal previews Previews within the body of the speech identify subpoints that will be developed under a major point.

Internal summaries These summaries of a major point are given within the body of the speech.

Outlining the Speech

In Chapter 1, we pointed out that reading, writing, and listening have been an integral part of public speaking for more than two thousand years. In Chapter 7, we looked at the relationship between reading and public speaking by examining the print sources that you consult during the course of your research. Throughout this chapter, you have seen how writing is also an important part of public speaking since it helps you organize your ideas and connect your thoughts to one another.

Note

This linear outline form is common in the businesses and institutions of U.S. society.

For these reasons, most instructors require students to submit written outlines. These outlines do not contain the exact words that you will use in your speech; instead, they show the major ideas of the speech, written in relationship to one another, in a skeleton form. Outlines are written in a linear form in this basic format:

    A. Major idea
        1. Supporting information
           a. Specific information
           b. Specific information
        2. Second piece of supporting information for first major idea
    B. Second major idea
        1. Supporting information
           a. Specific information
           b. Specific information

       1) Very detailed information
       2) More detailed information
    2. Second piece of supporting information for second major idea

Content Outline

Teaching Idea

The requirements for outlines differ across speech departments. Provide specific instructions for your students if your department's guidelines differ from the example shown here. The outline is presented with annotations that explain it.

The heading has four elements:

In the heading, state what you explicitly hope to accomplish through your speech.

Letters and numbers alternate with a separate letter for each major part of the introduction.

Point C is necessary for background information.

Jill has included all the essential elements of an introduction.

The signpost *first* serves as a transition to the body of the speech.

Some instructors ask their students to write out both the introduction and the conclusion, and outline only the body of the speech. Most instructors ask for a list of references at the end of the outline. Your instructor will give you specific details that he or she requires. Read through Jill Nagaue's outline carefully, noting the specific details she considered as she organized and wrote down her ideas.

Topic:	Hawaiian Sovereignty
General Purpose:	To persuade
Specific Purpose:	To persuade my audience that, although many Hawaiians want sovereignty, Hawaii should remain a state.
Central Idea:	Supporters of Hawaiian sovereignty argue that Americans should redress wrongs done to them over a century ago; however, this would not be a good thing.

I. Introduction
   A. Imagine living on a peaceful island ruled by a queen; then imagine that the queen is replaced by a takeover.
   B. This happened in Hawaii, and although you may not be aware of the issue of Hawaiian sovereignty, you may someday vote on whether or not to allow Hawaiians to again be a sovereign nation.
   C. Hawaii was once an independent nation, ruled by kings and queens.
      1. One day, the United States seized control of the tiny nation.
      2. Some Hawaiians want to restore the monarchy.
   D. Because I am a Hawaiian, I followed the discussion that took place during the centennial remembrance of these events.
   E. Today I will explain the American takeover, the plan of some Hawaiians to regain their nation, and the reasons many people, including me, feel that sovereignty would be a mistake.
II. Body
   A. First, let's look at what took place a hundred years ago in Hawaii.
      1. According to Haunani-Kay Trask, head of the Center for Hawaiian Studies at the University of Hawaii, on January 16, 1893, Marines surrounded Iolani Palace, Queen Liliuokalani's residence.

This point is developed chronologically.

2. The next day, the Queen yielded her throne to "avoid any collision of armed forces and perhaps the loss of life."
3. The United States created a Provisional Government, the Territory of Hawaii, which transferred its power to the present-day State of Hawaii.
4. The takeover was part of a plan for annexation that had been in the works for forty years.

Use one sentence for each point.

   a. In the 1850s, the U.S. Secretary of State tried to buy Hawaii.
   b. On several occasions, the United States tried for annexation.
   c. Hoping for eventual annexation, in the 1870s, the United States surveyed and mapped Pearl Harbor.

Content outlines include main points, subpoints, and supporting materials.

B. Now, some Hawaiians want to gain sovereignty and restore the Hawaiian monarchy.
   1. The Office of Hawaiian Affairs has proposed a constitutional convention with Hawaiian delegates.

These are very specific supporting details.

      a. They will develop a document for a new Hawaiian nation that voters would ratify or defeat.
      b. If ratified, Hawaiians, and probably other U.S. citizens, including you, would determine the form and substance of Hawaiian sovereignty.

In this very linear pattern, all the points line up precisely.

   2. Daniel Akaka, U.S. Senator from Hawaii, wrote President Clinton to correct this century of injustice.

Transition Statement: We have looked at the history of Hawaiian statehood and have seen that some want sovereignty restored; now let's turn to a different perspective.

Here is the third major point.

C. After the overthrow, Hawaiians were initially furious, but today many can say that it was a good idea, and they are proud to be part of the United States.
   1. Thurston Twigg-Smith, newspaper president and descendent of a missionary, believes "the overthrow of the monarchy and subsequent relationship with the U.S. are the best things that ever happened to Hawaii and its people. These events were neither illegal nor do they call for apology by anyone."

She cites the source of her information.

   2. According to the *Honolulu Advertiser*, "few present day Hawaiians would benefit from a return to a monarchial form of sovereignty" because American citizenship leaves Hawaiians better off economically overall.

This is peer opinion.

   3. One resident believes we should leave past history and work toward a future.
   4. Another resident asks if sovereignty is really possible; he believes the vast majority of Hawaiians are proud of their islands and like their way of life.

Here is the signpost.

She *briefly* summarizes.

This refers to the introduction.

She ends with impact.

III. Conclusion
    A. As you can see, there are mixed thoughts and feelings about what is best for Hawaii.
    B. Although many Hawaiians are working for sovereignty, many others believe that, because they cannot change their past, they should work for a strong tomorrow for their children.
    C. Although the issue of Hawaiian sovereignty may seem distant, you or your elected officials may someday vote on the issue.
    D. And whether you are a surfer from Hawaii, a farmer in Idaho, or a stockbroker in New York, *Ku like pu mai kakou,* "Let us stand together."

Cross Reference

Refer students to Chapter 7 for information on bibliographic form.

References

Akaka, D. (1993, January 17). Will Clinton help right these wrongs? *The Honolulu Advertiser,* p. B3.

Budnick, R. (1993, January 24). Annexation was plotted for 40 years. *The Honolulu Advertiser,* p. B1.

Office of Hawaiian Affairs. *Makua: Sovereignty in practice.* Honolulu: Office of Hawaiian Affairs.

Parker, L. (1989). *Native American estate: The struggle over Indian and Hawaiian lands.* Honolulu: University of Hawaii Press.

Trask, H.-K. (1993, January 17). Money cannot substitute for Hawaiian land base. *The Honolulu Advertiser,* pp. B1, 3.

Twigg-Smith, T. (1993, January 24). Overthrow: No apology needed. *The Honolulu Advertiser,* pp. B1, 3.

Watson, K. (1993, January 22). Annexation was a blessing. *The Honolulu Advertiser,* p. A11.

Teaching Idea

Have students outline one of their classmates' speeches as suggested in exercise 5.

Throughout the outline, you can see that Jill uses alternating letters and numbers, as well as linear spacing, to show the relationship of her ideas to one another. She designates major ideas by capital letters, shows the first level of supporting material by numerals, and uses lowercase letters for detailed support. Although Jill didn't use it, the next level of material would be indicated by a numeral followed by a right parenthesis—that is, 1), 2). This outline is typical of the format that most instructors require. To assist you in the correct spacing, some word processing software has a stylesheet that sets up the outline form for you. If you do not have software with this feature, consult your campus computer center.

Speaking Outline

Although content outlines are useful because they help you organize your ideas and visualize them in relationship to one another, they are not the outlines you take to the podium. Your speaking outline differs from content outlines in several ways. First, you do not use full sentences in speaking outlines except in two

Teaching Idea

Many students write full-sentence outlines on their note cards, then read their speeches. To help them get away from this, ask to look at their speaking notes on the class period before they speak. This requires them to prepare enough so that they have adequate time for rehearsal.

places: transition statements and direct quotations. Rather, you create a *key word* outline, using only enough of the important words to jog your memory when you are in front of your listeners. Write the key words onto note cards from which you speak. Figure 9.4 to illustrates Jill's speaking outline.

By speaking from these brief notes, rather than reading from an outline or trying to memorize her speech, Jill will be able to remember the major ideas and supporting materials for her speech. Moreover, she can maintain eye contact with her listeners, while she has the security of knowing that, if she loses her train of thought, she can easily glance at her notes to regain her place in the speech.

Outlines for Alternative Patterns

If you are using one of the alternative patterns, such as the wave, spiral, or star, your outline will be less conventional. However, you can still design an appropriate representation of your ideas and their relationship to one another. First, decide on the pattern that you will use to organize your materials; you may find it useful to sketch the diagram. Then, write out your main points. With your pattern in mind, indicate what you will use for developmental material, placing this material where it will be in relation to your points. Write the thematic grounding statement that will hold the entire speech together. Indicate how you plan to begin and end your speech; then, write out key transition statements.

As you develop the ideas in your speech, you may find it helpful to use the standard indentation and numbering pattern presented in Jill's outline. Throughout your work, use complete sentences, just as you would in a standard content outline.

KEY CONCEPT   ## Outlining the Speech

Content outline   Content outlines are written in full sentences that show the major ideas of the speech in relationship with one another.

Speaking outline   Speaking outlines contain key words to help you remember the speech.

Outlines for alternative patterns   Using the visual diagram, arrange your ideas in a design that indicates their relationship to one another. Write out the thematic statement, introduction, and conclusion.

Summary

After you gather information for your speech, you must organize it into a pattern. Begin with the body of the speech, and choose from the many patterns that speakers use to organize their major points. Common organizational frameworks

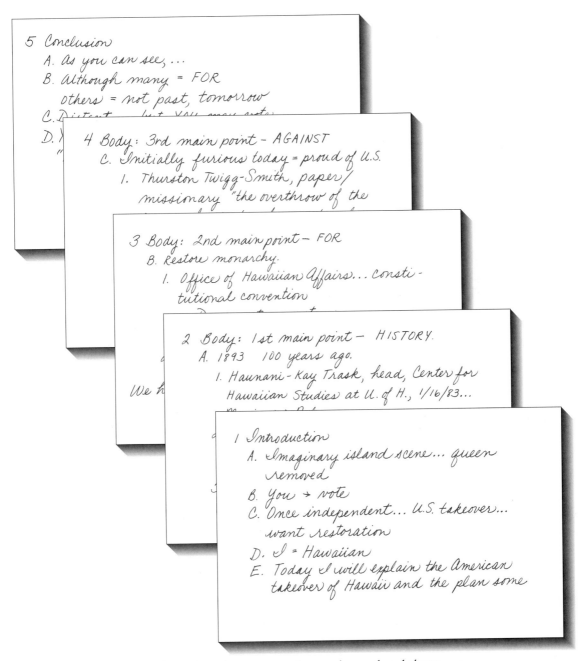

Figure 9.4   *A speaking outline—shown here on note cards—uses key words and phrases that jog the speaker's memory.*

include the cause–effect, chronological, topical, pro–con, problem–solution, and spatial patterns as well as the wave, spiral, and star patterns traditionally used in speeches given by women and ethnic speakers.

After the body of the speech is organized, plan an introduction that will take your listeners from their various mental worlds and move them into the world of your speech. In addition, plan a conclusion that leaves your listeners with a challenge or memorable saying. Throughout the entire speech, use connectives—the words, phrases, and sentences that connect the parts of the speech, weaving points and subpoints into a whole unit.

As part of the speechmaking process, instructors hope to have their students understand and show the ways that points and subpoints relate to one another. For this reason, most instructors ask their students to outline their ideas in a linear form, using alternating letters and numbers and careful spacing for their points. However, this is not the outline they use when they speak. Speaking outlines consist only of key words, which enable speakers to remember their main points but prevent them from reading their speeches verbatim.

Questions and Exercises

1. Identify the organizational pattern that would probably work best for a speech on:

   - Types of dogs
   - Gun control legislation
   - The worldwide spread of tuberculosis
   - How to fill out an income tax form

2. Find introductions to three different published speeches. One of the best sources for such speeches is *Vital Speeches of the Day*, a bi-weekly periodical available in most libraries. Consider the effectiveness of each introduction by answering these questions:

   - How does it gain attention? Do you think this is effective for the specific audience being addressed?

   - In what way or ways does the speaker relate the speech to audience interests and needs in the introduction? Is this effectively done?

   - Does the speaker establish his or her own credibility? If so, how? (Most of the speakers were probably introduced by someone who stated their areas of expertise.)

   - Does the speaker effectively preview the speech? How?

3. Look at the conclusions to the speeches you examined in Exercise 2. Can you find all the elements that should be included in a conclusion? How effective is the conclusion?

4. Read or listen to a recording of a speech by an African-American speaker such as Vernon Jordan, Malcolm X, or Martin Luther King, Jr. (*Vital Speeches of the Day* often reprints such speeches. Malcolm X's can be found in his biography.) What basic organizational pattern does the speaker use? Can you find examples of the wave pattern within the speech?

5. Outline a speech given by one of your classmates. Evaluate the effectiveness of the introduction and conclusion. Is the organizational pattern easy to discern? What suggestions, if any, could you give the speaker?

6. Read the excerpt and analysis of Elizabeth Cady Stanton's speech "The Solitude of Self" that is found in the Appendix.

Key Terms

topical organization
chronological organization
spatial organization
pro–con organization
problem–solution organization
the wave
the spiral
the star
rhetorical questions
preview
signposts
transitions
internal previews
internal summaries
content outline
speaking outline

Notes

1. Mr. Bush's remarks are quoted in R. W. Apple, Jr. (1992, November 13). In command of language. *The New York Times*, p. A19.
2. Aitken, J. (1993, March 6). Light the fire: Communicate with your child. *Vital Speeches of the Day, 59*, 473–476.
3. Jorgensen-Earp, C. (1993, September 28). Telephone interview. Also (n.d.) Making other arrangements: Alternative patterns of disposition. Unpublished paper. Karen Zediker presented Professor Jorgensen-Earp's work in (1993, February). *Rediscovering the tradition: Women's history with a relational approach to the basic public speaking course*. Panel presentation at the Western States Communication Association, Albuquerque, NM.
4. Bloch, M. (1975). *Political language and oratory in traditional society*. London: Academic Press.
5. King, M. L., Jr. (1963, August 28). I have a dream. Speech given at the march on Washington, Washington, D.C.
6. Truth, S. Ain't I a woman? In *Norton's Anthology of Women's Literature* (p. 253).
7. Davidson, J. (1993, March 6). Overworked Americans or overwhelmed Americans? You cannot handle everything. *Vital Speeches of the Day, 59*, 470–473.
8. Burke, M. B. (1992). Polar bears. Student speech, St. John's University, Jamaica, New York.
9. This speech was given by a student in a beginning speech class in New York. These are two areas of the city known for high crime statistics.
10. Abt, J. (1991, December 4). Sharks. Student speech, St. John's University, Jamaica, New York.
11. Bartlett, A. (1990). Toy weapons. Student speech, Oregon State University, Corvallis, Oregon.
12. Aitken, J. (1993). Op. cit.
13. Jurgens, T. (1990, May 7). Amusement park tragedies. Student speech, Oregon State University, Corvallis, Oregon.
14. Moser, T. (1992, April 23). Dolphins' communication with humans. Student speech, Oregon State University, Corvallis, Oregon.

Audiovisual Resources

At the end of this chapter, you should be able to

- Explain the value of audiovisual support in your public speeches
- Tell advantages and disadvantages of using various means of displaying visuals, including overhead projectors, boards, hand-outs, posterboard, and slides
- Provide examples of each type of three-dimensional visuals: objects, persons, models
- Distinguish between lists, tables, and charts
- Know how to use photographs, drawings, and maps effectively
- Identify four types of graphs: line, bar, pie, and pictograph
- Know the advantages and disadvantages of using audiotapes, films, and videotapes
- Explain the value of computer-generated visuals
- Give guidelines for using audiovisual aids

Note

Because the technological means for reproducing and transmitting visual and audio information is expanding greatly, today's students live in a world where information is conveyed by pictures as well as words. Look, for instance, at the difference between this text and one that was written in the 1950s and 1960s. They have no pictures; this text has many full-color photographs and diagrams.

Teaching Idea

Using the opening examples, elicit more ways that speakers use visuals. Or invite a guest speaker to discuss the visuals used in his or her work.

Student Assignment

Because the use of VAs is so important, most instructors require that students use visuals with at least one speech. An assignment for an informative speech using a VA can be found in the Student Resource Workbook. There is a sample speech at the end of this chapter.

Imagine an architect who comes before a university's board of trustees with her firm's proposal for a new building on the campus. She describes in vivid language the layout of the building. She asks the trustees to picture in their minds the design of doors and windows, the type of brick that will go into the building, the interesting architectural features. At a different university, another architect presents his firm's design. He enhances his speech with large drawings of the proposed building. He projects a map of the floor plan onto a screen. On a table beside the podium, he displays a model of the campus with the new building in its projected location, enabling listeners to see how the design fits with existing buildings. Because of his visual support, his presentation is far more interesting and understandable than that of the first speaker.

This hypothetical contrast is ridiculous. It would be hard to imagine the first speaker trying to communicate her vision and her ideas only through words. Her employers would not send her out to represent them without visual support. Use of audiovisual (AV) supporting materials is important in illustrating ideas, keeping the audience's interest, and making abstract concepts clear.

You will probably use audiovisual aids when you make public presentations. Here are a few examples of speakers who routinely use such supporting materials:

- A representative of a pharmaceutical company who brings samples of the product to sales meetings. She also has drawings, graphs, and brochures that further explain the product.

- A weight-loss nurse who shows before-and-after videos of clients who have used his program. These supplement the packet of handouts he provides prospective clients.

- The benefits officer of a corporation who gives new employees a packet of handouts and brochures that she uses to explain the various benefits options available in their new job. She supplements her lecture by projecting charts and graphs copied onto transparencies.

- A dance instructor who teaches a new dance step, using his body to demonstrate the moves.

This chapter will discuss the importance of audiovisual support. Then it will give some common types of media used for displaying audiovisual aids, followed by the most common kinds of visual support used by speakers. A special section is devoted to visuals made by computers. The chapter concludes with pointers for more effective use of audiovisual aids.

The Value of Audiovisual Support

As a result of the increasing role of technology and media in modern life, all the children born in the United States now are born into a culture that is highly saturated by the media. Even older people who were born before the advent of

Cross Reference

The impact of electronic technology on public speaking is found in Chapters 1, 7, and 12.

Teaching Idea

Use the question at the end of this paragraph to generate a class discussion.

Teaching Idea

Ask a representative of the campus media center to demonstrate this equipment or discuss the use of multimedia presentations. If possible, have him or her show several examples of computer manuals for presentation packages such as Harvard Graphics or Delta Graph.

Note

This section is presented first so that students do not confuse the equipment with the visual. An "overhead" is not a visual; it is simply one way to present a visual.

television and home computers are influenced by technological developments. Similarly, across the globe, mediated pictures and sounds communicate messages to international audiences. Because of this, audiences are becoming much more visually oriented, depending on images as well as words for meaning.

Walter Ong,[1] longtime professor at St. Louis University, terms this development in communication *secondary orality*. In a secondarily oral culture, print exists side by side with visual and audio materials that, like print, function to inform, persuade, and entertain. Professor Ong believes that people in these cultures think differently from people in oral or literate cultures. As we saw in Chapter 1, the linear, analytic thought characteristic of what Ong calls "deeply interiorized literacy" is replaced by thoughts formed from impressions and images. The result is that, if you learn to use visual and auditory resources effectively, you will be empowered in a culture and a world dominated by the media.

Despite a proliferation of media in this century, the use of visual aids is not new. Visual support has always been part of effective communication. In oral cultures, speakers used objects as well as words to clarify their ideas and help their listeners better understand abstract concepts. As far back as the sixth century B.C., the Jewish prophet Jeremiah used a ruined linen belt as an object lesson to symbolize the decay that would come to the kingdom of Judah as a result of disobeying God.[2] In addition to clarifying ideas, people learn and remember better when they use more than one sense to take in information. Think of your own experiences listening to speakers. Do you learn more and remember more from those who use posters, charts, models, maps, objects, and graphs than from those who do not even use the chalkboard?

Although visuals are not new, the amount and kinds available are different from those used even fifty years ago. And there is the promise of even greater diversity and combinations of media in the future. Multimedia presentations—those involving text, audio, still images, and video—are becoming common in education and other institutions. Software analyst Anusha Fernando says, "Multimedia is a revolution in communication, education, and in media itself."[3] She terms it "the next wave of computing" in which sound effects, music, color pictures, motion video, and special graphics can be added to lectures or presentations. Because of this, Fernando concludes, "Multimedia is here to stay."[4]

Visual Resources

There are several types of visuals you can choose to support your presentations. These, in turn, can be displayed in a number of ways. For example, one type of visual representation is a graph. You can display graphs drawn on posters or chalkboards, project them by using an overhead projector, photocopy them onto a handout, or show them on a slide. This section will first present various means of display; then a discussion of a variety of common visuals will follow.

Displaying Visual Aids

You can probably list a number of ways good speakers display their visuals. Most use one or a combination of several common means to display visual aids, each with advantages and disadvantages.

Overhead Projectors   Overhead projectors are machines found in classrooms, businesses, and other organizations throughout the United States and across the globe. They have the advantage of allowing you to display an image so that it can be seen on the wall or on a screen even in a large auditorium. The transparencies on which you imprint the images have many advantages, including these:

1. They are simple to make.

2. They are inexpensive and readily available in many campus bookstores, print shops, and office supply stores.

3. They are easily stored and easily carried from place to place.

4. They come in many colors, and you can use special colored pens on them. These overhead pens come either in permanent or washable inks.

5. Professional-looking transparencies are easily made using a computer or by photocopying a professionally made visual.

6. You can write directly onto a blank transparency while you speak, using it as you would a chalkboard, without having to turn your back to your audience.

Once you have decided on the type of visual you want, it is easy to transfer it to a transparency because whatever can be drawn or printed on a piece of paper can be easily imprinted on these thin plastic sheets. You can draw freehand directly onto the transparency or trace a cartoon, map, or other drawing from any printed copy. For a more professional-looking copy, use a copier machine to transfer a printed image to the sheet of plastic. Simply put a plastic transparency in the paper bin on top of the pile of paper before you press PRINT. You can also overlay transparencies by simply placing one on top of another.

Skillful use of an overhead projector greatly adds to your ethos—your audience's perception of your competence. However, unskillful use can have the opposite effect. For best results, before you begin your introduction, turn the machine on and adjust the focus of your transparency. If you are using a list of words on a transparency, cover all but the heading with a sheet of paper; uncover each new point only as you refer to it in the speech. If you want to draw your listeners' attention to some part of your visual, point to your transparency

Teaching Idea

Throughout your discussion, model the correct way to use an overhead projector. Also show negative models—that is, do it "wrong" so they can see how distracting and unprofessional poor use of the equipment can be. Teaching Note 9.1 in the Instructor's Manual summarizes research on using positive and negative instances in teaching.

Teaching Idea

Have a variety of visuals available on transparencies. For example, enlarge a map, a political cartoon, a drawing, and a graph taken from a printed source. Transfer these enlargements to a transparency. Also show examples of hand-lettered transparencies. You can even copy colored photographs onto transparencies (though quality is sometimes uneven). Have some (or all) of the transparencies in frames. Consult your campus media center for additional examples.

Learning to use an overhead projector effectively is an important skill; this equipment is widely available and transparencies are easy to make.

instead of the screen. Unfortunately, if you are very nervous, your trembling hands will show. Use a pointed object, placing it where you want your listeners to focus, then move your hand away from the projector.

Teaching Idea

Since boards are so common, this is the one display medium that most students will use at one time or another. Help students understand both their advantages and disadvantages. Many instructors discourage (or prohibit) their students from using boards during the visual aid speech.

Boards   Chalkboards are very convenient, and they are part of the standard equipment in most educational settings. Chalkboards are commonly black or green. Other more high-tech boards are made of white plastic, requiring the use of special colored pens and erasers. Some boards are magnetic.

Chalkboards have several advantages. Since most classrooms across the country have at least one board, this display medium is almost always available for your classroom speeches. They are excellent for explanations of unfolding processes, such as the working of a mathematical problem. They also encourage a level of informality that is appropriate in some public speaking settings. Finally, they are useful in settings that include speaker–audience interactions, such as brainstorming sessions.

However, although many instructors use chalkboards for lectures, the boards have three major drawbacks that make them less suitable for many student speeches within the classroom.

1. You cannot prepare your visual in your leisure before the speech. Having an unprepared visual creates additional anxiety for some beginning speakers, who like to have everything, down to the visuals, ready and rehearsed in advance.

2. When you write on the board, your back is turned to your audience, and you are talking to the board. This is probably the major drawback of boards in general.

3. Most people do not write well on chalkboards. This visual aid, then, does not look professional.

Boards continue to evolve. Really sophisticated boards, the kind that will probably be common in the future, allow the speaker to write or draw on the board and then press a button on a copier machine at the board's base. The attached machine copies what was written on the board onto an $8\frac{1}{2}$-by-11-inch piece of paper that can then be made into handouts. In addition, electronically linked magnetic blackboards can be set up in several sites for use during a teleconference session. With this technology, for example, what is drawn or written on a board in Seattle can appear simultaneously on boards in Hong Kong, São Paolo, and Cairo.[5]

Teaching Idea

Bring, or have students bring, examples of handouts to class. Go to the student health service, for instance, and find examples of informative brochures. Or get a packet from campus recruiters; have the class discuss the effect such handouts would have on potential students. Contrast to the effect of not distributing handouts at all.

Handouts   A third way to display material is to provide each listener with brochures, pamphlets, photocopies, or other visual handouts. For example, if you do a speech on a health-related issue, you can often get a number of professional brochures from campus health services or from doctors' offices. For other speeches, you can prepare a handout for each listener by photocopying maps, charts, lists, photographs, and other materials.

Although handouts may not be common in the classroom, they are very common in businesses and other institutions in society. Companies, for example, generally provide their sales representatives with brochures and other handouts for potential customers. Participants in board meetings or staff meetings often have an entire book of reports and visuals.

When you use handouts, your primary challenge is to let them supplement your message, not replace it. For this reason, do not distribute handouts and expect your audience to pay attention to you until they have finished reading the material contained in them. Follow these suggestions for a more polished use of handouts.

1. One of the most effective ways to use a handout is to distribute it, turned face down, at the beginning of your speech; then, at the point you discuss the material on it, ask your audience to turn it over.

2. Mark the points you want to emphasize with a letter or number so that you can easily direct your listeners to specific places on it. For instance, if you have a map showing an entire state, but you want to talk about three areas, mark the first with an A, the second with a B, and the third with a C. Then at the appropriate moment, draw your listeners' attention to point A.

3. When you are using handouts to supplement informative lectures, consider leaving some of the words blank, and have your listeners fill them in as you discuss them in the speech.

Note

A surprising number of professionals use posters. For example, one financial planner sets up three easels and has eight to ten posters showing various charts and graphs on each. Each audience member also has a booklet with copies of the charts and graphs. Students commonly display their visuals on posterboard.

Posterboard   Another fairly inexpensive and convenient way to display visuals is by using large sheets of posterboard, available in a variety of weights and colors at most campus bookstores or art supply stores. You can use felt pens or press-on letters to make words or to draw pictures on the poster. The poster itself is usually set up on either a table easel or a free-standing easel.

If you ever watched Ross Perot's paid political speeches, you saw a major public figure use posterboards regularly to display his charts and graphs. Speakers who make the same speech over and over, such as financial planners, regularly use professionally prepared posters to display charts and graphs. Students commonly use them in classroom speeches.

Make posters with care. As with transparencies, it is easy for posters to have a "loving hands at home" look. Here are a few tips that will enable you to make more professional-looking posters.

1. Use rulers or yardsticks to ensure straight lines.

2. Consider the effect of using more than one color to attract and hold audience interest.[6]

3. If you plan to use the poster more than once, stick-on letters will make it look more professional.

4. Protect your poster from becoming bent or soiled. Cover it with plastic when you transport it to the classroom. If you use the same posters repeatedly, carry them in a poster-sized portfolio.

Teaching Idea

Give students a chance to evaluate the effectiveness of various posters; use Activity 9.1 in the Instructor's Manual.

Posters are especially effective with relatively small audiences when other means of display are not available. At greater distances, they are often difficult to see.

Slides   Slides are similar to overhead transparencies in that you can project them onto a screen where fairly large audiences can see them. However, they have the disadvantage of being less visible in well-lit rooms. You can make slides from photographs; in addition, with a number of special computer programs, you can make slides directly from a personal computer. This type of aid is more effective if you have several images to show.

Teaching Idea

Exercises 1 and 2 are culminating activities for this section.

Common slide projectors have a carousel-type tray in which you place your slides in order. Then, use a hand-held control and press it each time you want to project a different slide. For a professional presentation, put a black slide between sections of content so that you can pause to talk with your audience while avoiding a blast of white light or having a picture or diagram up so long that it is distracting or boring.

KEY CONCEPT   # Displaying Visual Aids

Type of Display	Advantages	Disadvantages
Overhead projectors	Availability, can be used in large room	Minimal noise of machine
	Transparencies are easy to make	Initial cost of equipment
	Easy to get a professional look	
Boards	Availability, informality	Can't prepare in advance
	Good for unfolding processes	Speaker's back to audience
		Often messy
Handouts	Can be professionally made	May replace the speech
Posterboard	Good for repeated speeches	Not effective in large rooms
Slides	Good for large rooms	Require dimmed lights

Types of Visuals

Teaching Idea

Have plenty of examples of each type of visual. Ask other instructors in the department to describe some of the most successful instances they have seen of students using each type of VA.

Overhead projectors, boards, handouts, posterboard, and slides are all ways to display visuals, yet *they are not the visual itself.* So far, we have looked only at the *how* of presenting your visuals; now, we will turn to the variety of visuals—the *what* you actually show your audiences using the equipment mentioned.

There are two major kinds of visuals—three dimensional and two dimensional. Three-dimensional visuals are material objects, such as a model or the object itself, whereas two-dimensional visuals are charts, graphs, and the like. Both provide support for your ideas though sometimes you can present your idea better by using one instead of the other. Throughout your speaking career, you will probably have the opportunity to experiment with presenting both kinds of visuals.

Objects

Imagine a basketball coach trying to tell his team the finer points of making a free-throw without using a basketball to demonstrate. Or think of an origami instructor trying to communicate how to fold a crane without actually showing the process with origami paper. These scenes are hard to visualize because people need to see for themselves as well as hear verbal descriptions of some subjects. For this reason, many speakers use actual objects, especially in speeches of demonstration where they show their listeners a process.

Your topic determines whether or not an object is a realistic choice for a visual aid. What object could you use for a speech about the Bermuda Triangle? How could you objectify black holes? It would be nearly impossible. In addition, some objects, such as firearms, are prohibited by law in classrooms. Other objects are difficult or impossible to bring to the listeners. Live animals are often in this category. One student brought a wolf-dog into a classroom; the animal was so nervous that it detracted from his speech. In addition, nervous animals sometimes pose a danger to the students in the class. Another student wanted to demonstrate how to ride a motorcycle, but he could not think of a way to bring the machine into the classroom. The class solved his problem by walking to a nearby parking lot where he gave his speech, seated on his motorcycle. Finally, objects should be large enough for everyone in the room to see. This eliminates many small items—unless the speaker is able to provide each listener with an individual object. In short, objects must be applicable, legal, accessible, and practical.

Some objects pass all the tests and contribute successfully to student speeches. One student showed beekeeping equipment in his speech on honey production. A lacrosse player brought the equipment used in his sport. A veterinary major brought syringes used to inoculate both large and small animals for her speech on preventive health care for animals. Another student brought clothing for her speech on how clothing could change a person's image.

Teaching Idea

Occasionally, students incorporate other senses into their speeches. Again, bring out the list of topics your students made in Chapter 2, and help students identify possible topics where they might use objects or sensory resources.

You can even bring in objects that communicate your point through touch, smell, or taste. For instance, Shelly gave each listener a tuft of unprocessed wool and a piece of yarn to feel for her discussion of yarn making. Melissa provided small samples of freshly ground coffee to smell for her talk on coffee-roasting procedures, and Jonathan had his classmates chewing on sticks of gum while he talked about the origins and evolution of gum.

One word of caution if you use an object in your speech rather than samples for each listener: *Do not pass the object around.* If you do, some members of the audience will focus their attention on the object rather than on your speech. Often, by the time everyone actually gets the object, you will have completed the speech.

People

Sometimes speakers use their friends or volunteers from the audience to demonstrate a movement or a concept. In addition, they sometimes use themselves as a visual aid, especially speakers who are experts in some area. While describing it verbally, a dancer or a cheerleader shows how to make a move. A first aid instructor demonstrates how to find pressure points using her own body to show the location of major arteries.

Teaching Idea

Again, use of positive and negative instances are appropriate throughout this section.

Speakers often use individual members of the audience or the audience as a whole. One student began his speech on apartheid by having his listeners stand and separate themselves into groups by ethnicity. He then explained that such separation, enforced by law, was the principle underlying apartheid. On other occasions, students bring cooperative friends who assist them in their speeches. One student, who wanted to point out the problems inherent in judging people by looks only, introduced her friend to the class. Then, during the course of the speech, she used makeup, hair gel, and black clothing to transform her friend from a "preppy" into a "punk" in just a few moments.

Models

When it is impossible to bring actual objects into the classroom, you may use a model instead. Scaled-down models can be made of larger objects, like the model of the building used by the architect at the beginning of this chapter. Enlarged models can show very small objects. Have you seen models of an atom? Teachers often use models of skeletons, brains, or hearts because they cannot bring the real objects into their classrooms. People learning CPR practice on models rather than on real persons. Sometimes you can make your own model, or you can borrow one for a classroom speech.

One student explained his summer job as a pyrotechnician, or fireworks display technician. Since federal regulations prevented him from bringing explosives into the classroom, he made a model of the spherical explosive device, complete with a fuse. He also brought the actual cylinder into which he drops these lit explosives. Finally, he wore the jumpsuit and displayed the helmet that he wears for safety's sake.

In this section, we have looked at three types of three-dimensional visuals: objects, people, and models. In certain types of speeches, especially in speeches of demonstration, they are almost indispensable. However, there are occasions when three-dimensional visuals are impossible to use. Then you turn to two-dimensional resources, including tables, lists, charts, photographs, drawings and maps, and graphs.

This professor uses an enlarged model of the human ear for her lectures on audiology. Occasionally students borrow such models for classroom speeches.

Tables

Tables are good for situations in which you present data in columns and rows. They are easy to put on posterboard, transparencies, or handouts. For instance, one student used an overhead projector to display a table—shown in Figure 10.1a—comparing the average salaries of child care workers with average salaries of other men and women.

Lists

Speakers commonly use lists. You can easily make into a list anything that is done in stages or that occurs in steps. For this reason, they are popular for speeches that have a chronological pattern. For instance, a speech on the stages of grief might include a list of the main points, as shown in Figure 10.1b.

Moreover, you can use lists to summarize the main points of a topical speech in words, phrases, or sentences, briefly encapsulating the key points of

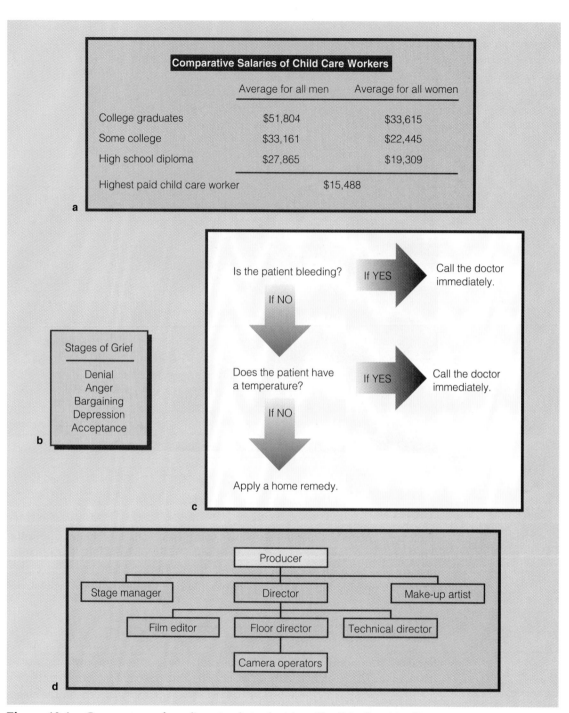

Figure 10.1   *Common types of two-dimensional visuals: (a) a table, (b) a list, (c) a flow chart, and (d) an organizational chart.*

more detailed material. Because they are summaries, they often help your listeners organize and remember ideas. However, it is important not to put too much information in the list. If you do, your listeners may simply read the list, discover the information in your speech, then stop listening. As a general guideline, follow the six-by-six rule: Use no more than six lines and no more than six words per line.

Charts

Although many people refer to lists and tables as charts, technically, charts differ from both. There are two basic types of charts: *flow charts* and *organizational charts*. Flow charts show the order in which processes occur. You can often recognize them by the use of arrows indicating a directional flow. Flow charts can include drawings (pictorial flow charts), or they may simply be a series of labeled shapes and arrows. Figure 10.1c illustrates a portion of a flow chart.

Organizational charts show hierarchies and relationships. A family tree, for example, is an organizational chart showing the relationships among family members. The chart in Figure 10.1d shows the relationship among various individuals involved in television production.

Photographs

Although photographs provide an actual view of objects, persons, or scenes, the saying "A picture is worth a thousand words" is not necessarily true in classroom speeches. Photographs are of little use to audiences unless they are large enough to be seen. Because of this, any photo you show to the class as a whole should be poster size. This ensures that each audience member can see the details of the picture.

However, since it is difficult to get enlargements of pictures, and since prints themselves are generally too small to be seen in even the smallest classrooms, students who feel that a photograph is essential visual support must think of the best way to display the picture. Here are three ways that they have effectively displayed photographs.

1. Tricia gave a speech about Harry Truman. She found four pictures of him at various stages of his life. She cut and taped them onto one piece of paper; then she made a photocopied handout for each of her classmates.

2. Alene transferred a black-and-white photograph of a newborn baby to a transparency; then she used an overhead projector to project it onto a plain wall in the classroom. Throughout her speech on fetal development, the image of the baby framed her presentation.

3. Bunnasakh wanted to show her American classmates what her country looked like. So she brought six carefully selected slides to introduce Thailand.

Despite some successes, many students use photographs ineffectively. Generally, the most common mistake students make is to pass a series of prints around. As you can imagine, the person closest to the speaker sees all the pictures as the speaker describes them, but the person at the farthest corner of the room gets the final photograph after the speaker has been seated for three minutes. Another mistake is to try to show a picture from a book. For instance, John showed famous cathedrals in France by opening a book of photographs and walking back and forth across the front of the room displaying the pictures. The book didn't open completely; the pictures were too small to be seen by everyone at once; and holding the book put John in an awkward posture. This was not an effective way to present his pictures.

Drawings and Maps

Teaching Idea

To draw the distinction between types of visuals and means of display, ask students how they would best display a drawing in a large auditorium, a classroom, a speech given outdoors, or a presentation in someone's living room. (Several means may be appropriate.)

Drawings can be invaluable to speakers. Drawings not only stand alone, they can also be added to lists or other visuals as decorative or supplementary support. Speakers usually display them on posterboard, photocopied onto a handout, or by using an overhead projector. They are easily made by drawing an original work or by tracing or photocopying a commercial drawing onto a transparency or handout. Furthermore, most computer graphics packages have extensive clip-art files of prepared drawings that you can easily add to your visuals. This partial list gives you some idea of how speakers use drawings.

1. Students draw guns because actual guns are illegal in the classroom. They show drawings of car engines—objects too large to bring into classrooms. They use cutaway drawings to show interior regions of buildings. An architect's drawing, for example, can show part of a wall removed so that the interior of a room is visible. Similarly, a cross-section of a human heart reveals its inner chambers.

2. Cartoons are another type of drawing often incorporated into speeches when one perfectly illustrates the point of the speech and adds humor to the talk.

3. Diagrams are line drawings or graphic designs that serve to explain rather than realistically depict an object or a process. One student, for instance, did a diagram of the acid rain cycle, depicting emissions from a factory and a car that rise to form clouds that drop polluted rain.

Maps are drawings that visually represent spaces. We map the heavens as well as the earth; we map weather, and we even talk about mind maps—maps of information. There are several different kinds of maps.

1. Political maps show the borders between nations and states. Such maps are easily outdated in a rapidly changing world. For instance, any world map

Figure 10.2

A floor plan of a building is one type of map.

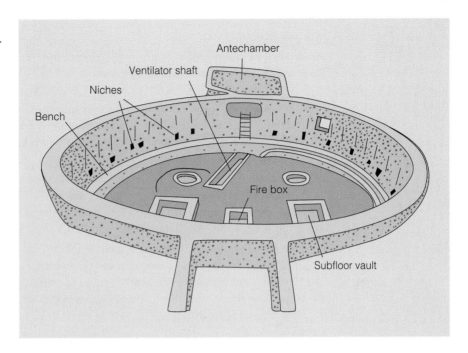

dated before 1990 is obsolete; since then, a number of countries, including the Soviet Union and Yugoslavia, have been dismantled; consequently, new political boundaries have been drawn.

2. Geographic maps—those showing mountains, deserts, lowlands, and other natural features—do not go out of date.

3. Maps also include blueprints and floor plans of buildings, maps of routes between two points, city maps, campus maps—the list goes on. Figure 10.2 depicts a map of a Native-American kiva.

Because details on maps may be difficult to see at a distance, transparencies or handouts are often the best means of display. As mentioned earlier, if you want to draw your listeners' attention to specific features on the map, mark the spot with a letter or number. Then, during the speech, ask listeners to focus on that specific feature.

Graphs

Have you ever heard a speech in which the speaker bombarded you with statistics? You probably found the speech boring, difficult to follow, and impossible to remember. Contrast that speech to one in which the speaker presents you with graphs that represent the statistical data in diagram form. Since statistics are often difficult to envision or to remember, representing your material in a graph allows your listeners to "see" how numbers relate to one another. They are common in public speeches, both in the classroom and in professional settings. There are at least four major kinds of graphs.

1. *Pie graphs* (see Figure 10.3a) are circular graphs that are especially good for showing divisions of a population or parts of the whole. This pie graph, which depicts the way typical Americans get to work, could be used in speeches about carpooling or public transportation.

2. *Bar graphs* are useful for comparing data from several different groups. For instance, the information comparing the salary of child care workers to other workers, shown in Figure 10.1a, could have been displayed on a bar graph, such as the one depicted in Figure 10.3b.

3. *Line graphs* are best for showing a variable that fluctuates over time, such as the changes in patterns of international trade during the 1980s. Moreover, they are good for showing the relationship of two or more such variables— comparing food, cars, travel, and consumer goods traded during the time period (see Figure 10.3c).

4. *Picture graphs,* or *pictographs,* the least common of the four types, can be very effective for certain kinds of data, especially those that relate to objects or people. Each picture represents a certain number of individual cases, as Figure 10.3d demonstrates.

Visuals are used daily in hundreds of settings as speakers attempt to illuminate their ideas by bringing in actual objects or two-dimensional representations of the subject under discussion. They make ideas clear, give audiences ways to organize and remember material, and present abstract concepts in concrete form. They are indispensable in a visually oriented society. However, in some cases, speakers turn to audio sources—sometimes combined with visuals—to lend further support to their ideas.

KEY CONCEPT   **Types of Visuals**

Objects You can use three-dimensional material objects such as sports equipment or art supplies.

People People sometimes assist in a speech. Speakers often act as their own visual aids by demonstrating with their bodies.

Models You can use scaled-down models of large objects or enlarged models of small objects when actual objects are not available.

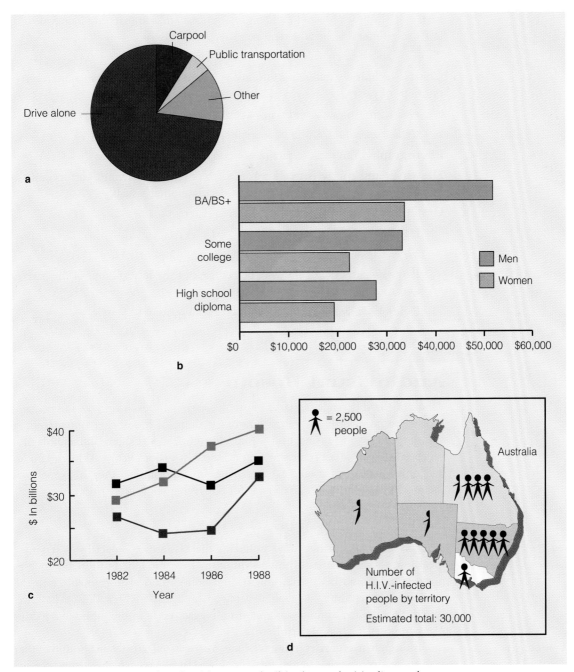

Figure 10.3 *Major types of graphs: (**a**) a pie graph, (**b**) a bar graph, (**c**) a line graph, and (**d**) a pictograph.*

Lists Use lists for ordering the steps of a process and summarizing major ideas in words, phrases, or brief sentences.

Tables Tables present numerical data in columns and rows.

Charts Technically different from lists or tables; they show ordering and relationships of parts.

> *Flow charts* show the order in which processes occur.
>
> *Organizational charts* show hierarchies and relationships.

Photographs You can use pictures of people, objects, or scenes.

Drawings and maps Artwork in the form of realistic drawings, cartoons, diagrams, and maps illustrate your point or decorate other visuals.

Graphs Graphs represent statistical data in diagram form.

> *Line graphs* best show one or more variables over time.
>
> *Bar graphs* are useful for comparing several groups of data.
>
> *Pie graphs* are best for showing percentages or the relationships of the parts to the whole.
>
> *Picture graphs or pictographs* are good for data relating to people.

Audiovisual Resources

Think of the difference it makes between hearing a speech on jazz and actually hearing some recordings of jazz music. Or think of the greater understanding you get when you see and hear a film clip showing the sights and sounds of a rodeo compared to a poster showing a list of its major events. Although audio and audiovisual support take extra preparation and planning, they are sometimes the most effective means you can use for conveying your information.

Audio Support

Students have successfully used sound in the classroom, especially when they speak on a topic related to music. Musicians have brought instruments such as portable electronic keyboards, guitars, and ethnic musical instruments into the classroom. In addition, they often bring in tapes to let the audience hear the sounds they are explaining—ranging from reggae music to the music of a particular composer, such as Hector Berlioz.

Cross Reference

This speech is mentioned in Chapter 9.

Although it is less commonly done, you can effectively use sounds other than music to provide support for your ideas. In her speech on whales, for instance, Mary Beth gained the audience's attention by playing a tape of a whale song and asking listeners to identify the source of the sound.

Films and Videotapes

Films and videos are widely used in persuasive and informative presentations in institutions across the United States and around the world. For instance, college recruiters visit high school campuses and show films of the campus, complete with background music and interviews with administration, faculty, and students. In many cases, the film itself provides most of the message. The recruiter simply introduces it, then fields questions afterward.

With the proliferation and accessibility of video recordings, you have access to massive amounts of audiovisual resources—some of which can be used in classroom speeches. Exercise caution about using both pictures and sounds, however. In your speeches, use only carefully selected clips that illustrate, rather than substitute for, your own words. Plan carefully so that you know exactly when to start and stop the tape.

Despite the challenges of audiovisual support, many students have used videotapes effectively in the classroom. Here are a few examples.

Teaching Idea
If you saved the lists of topics that the class brainstormed in Chapter 2, bring them out now. Have students identify topics in which audio support or films and videotapes are appropriate. Then, as a culminating activity for the entire section of the chapter, identify where a list or table, chart or graph might be appropriate. *Exercises 3 and 4 are appropriate here.*

Lisa made the Guinness Book of Records *for being part of the largest tap dancing group ever assembled at one time for a performance. In her speech explaining ways to get listed in the famous record book, she used a fifteen-second clip from a tape of the event filmed with her mother's camcorder.*

Mary Beth's whale speech ended with a ten-second clip taken from a television program, showing a number of whales playfully leaping in and out of the water.

Andrew discussed the difference between men's and women's gestures. To illustrate, he brought in a fifteen-second commercial showing a male and female interacting. As he introduced his topic, he played the tape. Then as he discussed each point, he again played the tape—this time with the sound turned off—pausing the tape at various places to illustrate the point he was making.

It is obvious that supporting materials enabling listeners to see or hear are important in many public speaking settings today. Indeed, they are almost necessary in some presentations such as demonstrations. Skillful construction and use of visuals often distinguishes good speakers from adequate ones, and as you learn to work with visuals, your competence will increase. In the next section, we present an easy way to make high-quality visuals using computers.

KEY CONCEPT   Audiovisual Resources

Audio support You can use music and other sounds to support your ideas.

Films and videotapes Short clips of moving images as well as sounds can be used as supporting materials.

Computer-Generated Visuals

Note

The use of computer-generated visuals is becoming so important that we might be doing our students a favor by requiring that, sometime during the term, they use a computer-generated visual in a speech.

Computers are tools that enable you to generate high-quality, professional visuals quickly and easily. Software packages currently on the market are very sophisticated compared to the software widely used even a decade ago. In addition, software engineers continue to design even more high-tech but easy-to-use products that enable an ordinary speaker to turn a presentation into an extraordinary one with both visual and audio support.[7]

Word Processors

The simplest way to use the computer to create a visual is by using a word processing program to display the information that you will eventually transfer to a handout or a transparency. You can use a single font and a single size to create a clean, clear visual. However, you can easily change a plain list into a more visually appealing one by experimenting with fonts, sizes, and formats.

Graphics Programs

Not only do word processing programs help you create lists and charts, special computer graphics programs help you convert your statistical data into graphs. Some of the better known programs are Harvard Graphics, StatView, Delta Graph, and Freelance Graphics. You do not have to be a genius or a computer whiz to use these packages successfully.

Typical *presentation programs*—those written to create a total package of lists, tables, and graphs for public speakers—allow you to type in your data and end up having professional-looking visuals with backgrounds, different typefaces, and colors in place, all coordinated. Once you type in a few easy directions, the computer will create line, bar, and pie graphs. You can also select graphics from almost 200 pieces of clipart. When you finish your series of visuals, the computer prints them onto paper, transparencies, or slides.[8]

KEY CONCEPT   **Computer-Generated Visuals**

Word processors By using a word processor and varying fonts, print sizes, and formats, you can create unique visuals.

Graphics programs These software packages help turn statistical data into bar, line, and pie graphs. Presentation programs allow you to create a set of charts and graphs that you can print onto paper, transparencies, or slides.

Guidelines for Using Audiovisual Aids

Teaching Idea

Before you teach this section, ask your students, working in pairs or small groups, to come up with a list of guidelines for using visual aids. Allow class notes but not the text. (Some students may have read the text, but others will be drawing generalizations from the specific instances they have seen.)

Although each type of audiovisual aid has specific techniques for successful use, there are some general principles for using these aids that apply to several types of visuals and displays. In this concluding section, we look at guidelines for audiovisual aids in general.

1. Be sure visuals can be seen. This generally eliminates posters and small objects if you're speaking in a large auditorium. In addition, make sure words and lines on the visuals are dark enough to be clear.

2. Consider using color. The Bureau of Advertising[9] credits color visuals with four advantages: they attract and hold audience interest; they increase learning, retention, and recall; they are more persuasive; they additionally increase audience motivation and participation.

3. Keep visuals neat and simple. Eliminate clutter. Use words and phrases rather than long sentences or whole paragraphs. Keep details in drawings and maps to a minimum.

4. Let the visuals enhance, not replace, your speech. For that reason, do not put too many words on the handout; otherwise, your listeners will read the handout rather than listen to your speech. Carefully edit audiotapes and films, incorporating only short clips into your presentation.

5. Display visuals only when you discuss them. Thus, have listeners keep their handouts face down on their desks, turning them over only when you are ready to use them. Turn the overhead projector light on and off as you use the transparency. Cover posters when they are not in use.

6. Talk to the audience, not to the visual.

7. Rehearse using your audiovisuals. This is easy to do with objects and models but sometimes more difficult with posters and transparencies because you do not always have access to projectors and easels when you practice your speech. However, you can use a table as a "projector" in practice. In addition, you can visualize how you will use your posters or transparencies, where you will stand in relationship to them, how you will point out specific features on them.

Cross Reference

Ethos is discussed in Chapters 5 and 15.

8. Do not violate the norms or expectations of your audience to the point where listeners are so shocked, offended, revolted, or angered that you lose their attention. One student speaker did this by killing, skinning, and cleaning a live fish in front of a horrified class. Another showed pornographic photographs to illustrate her speech about pornography. When you shock or violate expectations so severely, you may never regain attention, and your ethos—especially in the area of good sense—suffers as a result.

BOX 10.1

If Your First Language Is Not English

One of the biggest worries that nonnative speakers of English have when addressing a group of American classmates is that their English will not be understood or that they will make mistakes. For nonnative speakers, however, visuals provide the following advantages:

1. By putting key words on your visual, even if you have accented English, your listeners can see as well as hear the word. This will enable them to understand you more clearly.

2. By providing something for your audience to see, their focus—at least part of the time—will be on your visual rather than on you. This may help you overcome some of the anxiety that you face.

3. Using visuals also helps you remember your speech. The words written on a list, for instance, help you remember your main points. Pictures in a flow chart function in the same way.

9. When using mechanical audiovisuals, have a plan B in case the machine does not work. Imagine what will happen if the slide projector does not work properly, the light on the overhead projector burns out, or the videotape machine eats your tape. An alternate plan, usually in the form of a handout, would save your speech. Demonstrating your composure in case of equipment failure is another way to enhance your credibility.

Summary

As a speaker in a visually oriented world, it is to your advantage to learn to use audiovisual support effectively. This type of support serves three functions: visuals illustrate your ideas, keep your audience focused on your speech, and make abstract ideas more concrete. Although AVs are nothing new, the amount and kind of support is continually evolving. In this chapter, we concentrated mostly on visuals that your listeners can hear and see though there are occasions and topics where touch, smell, and taste can be incorporated into your presentation.

There are several ways to display your visuals, using different kinds of equipment. Perhaps the easiest method to use is an overhead projector. They are advantageous because they are easy to operate, the transparencies are simple and inexpensive to make, and they allow the image to be enlarged enough to be seen by a large audience.

Chalkboards, handouts, posterboard, and slides are additional ways to present your visual aids. All have their advantages and disadvantages, and you should take care to have a plan B in case of equipment failure. These are all ways to display your visuals, but they are not the visuals themselves.

There are two types of visuals: three dimensional and two dimensional. Three-dimensional visuals include objects, persons, or models that you use in the course of your presentation. The six common types of two-dimensional visuals include lists, tables, charts, photographs, drawings and maps, and graphs. You can use audio support when speaking about sounds or music; in addition, videos are widely available from a number of sources.

Emerging technologies, led by advances in computer engineering, are guiding us into a century in which you will have access to even more sophisticated presentational equipment. The high-tech boards that can be connected globally are but one example. Even now, you can use word processing programs, graphics packages, and presentation packages to help you create professional-looking visuals.

When preparing your visuals, remember that audiovisual support should enhance, rather than replace, your speech. For this reason, display visuals only when you are discussing them, and talk—not to them—but to the audience. Carefully edit audio and audiovisual materials to short excerpts. Further, in order to be effective, they must be visible or audible. Consequently, make sure visuals are large enough and clear enough for all of your listeners to see; similarly, ensure that audio messages are loud enough to be heard.

In conclusion, do not overlook the importance of competent use of visual materials as a way to enhance your credibility. As you make any visuals, therefore, keep in mind that professional-looking ones create more positive impressions than those that appear to be scribbled out just minutes before your presentation. Further, the disastrous case of equipment failure may actually increase your credibility, if your listeners see you handle the stressful situation with composure. Finally, demonstrate your good sense by selecting and presenting visual support that does not violate your listeners' expectations.

Student Speech

Japanese Writing

Ariko Iso

This speech was given by Ariko Iso,[10] a student from Japan for whom English is a second language. Imagine, if you can, how the speech would be different if she had used no visual support.

Ariko distributed the handout illustrated in Figure 10.4 before she spoke, asking her listeners to leave it face down until she told them to turn it over.

Figure 10.4 *She uses her handout to get her audience members actively involved.*

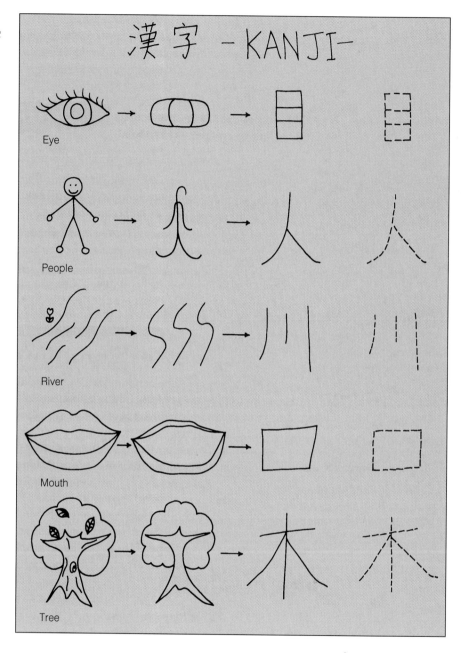

One of her primary challenges is to enable her audience to see how this topic relates to them, so Ariko begins her speech by linking her subject to familiar objects.

How many of you have tee shirts that have writing in a foreign language? Can you understand the meaning of the words or symbols? Many of you raised your hands, because recently, foreign words have become part of fashionable clothing. Have you seen a Pepsi can recently? You may have noticed that the word "Pepsi" is written in several languages. Although English is spoken throughout the world, it is good to know many languages and writing systems. By knowing about other languages, we can know the different cultures directly by ourselves.

After I came to America, some of my friends asked me to write their names in Japanese. I can write down their names very easily, but if they ask me about my language in detail, I am confused myself, because Japanese has three kinds of characters. Each of them has its own characteristics and its own usage.

She previews her speech.

Today, I will explain the three kinds of Japanese characters. I will especially focus on those that came from Chinese characters and show you how they are made.

She begins with an overview of the topic.

First, let's look at Japanese writing in general. Japanese writing has three kinds of characters—*kanji*, or Chinese characters, *hiragana* or Japanese characters, and *katakana* or Japanese characters used to distinguish words that came from foreign countries. Chinese characters are the basic ones. We imported Chinese characters to Japan in 600 A.D. However, the Japanese people made them more simple and symbolic. Each symbol stands for a word or idea.

Her first major point compares the unfamiliar Japanese writing to the familiar English alphabet.

The two types of Japanese characters, *hiragana* and *katakana*, are similar to the English alphabet, so I will call them the Japanese alphabet. The symbols themselves do not have meaning; instead, they only stand for combinations of sounds, much like the letters "m" and "a" stand for the sound "ma." When we put the characters together, they form a word. They are like a puzzle; there are only single pieces before we put them together.

Here she shows how the two types of Japanese symbols contrast to the English alphabet.

Now, I will explain the difference between *hiragana* and *katakana*. Both of these alphabets stand for the same sounds, but the usages are different. *Hiragana* is used for real Japanese words that are not represented by Chinese characters. *Katakana* is used for words from foreign countries. For example, when we imported Buddhism from China, all of the books and Buddhist scriptures were translated using *katakana*. Today, we use it for a lot of foreign words that we have brought directly into our language—words like basketball, school, coffee, TV, and names of people, places, and brands. We pronounce them with almost the same sounds that you use in English. Thus, they are English, but also Japanese.

Ariko now moves to writing that is very different.

Finally, Chinese characters, or *kanji*, are the most interesting. We use over 2,000 Chinese characters in our writing. However, there are two or more ways to pronounce each character, and each pronunciation results in a different word with a different meaning. Their number is almost the same as the number of stars.

She uses her handout to get her audience members actively involved.

Each *kangi* character looks very interesting. They are both artistic and functional. Originally Chinese characters pictured objects. Please turn over your handout and look at the top row of figures. You can see that many *kanji* characters are symbols of objects. Look at how the drawing of an eye changed to form the *kanji* character meaning "eye." Trace over the dotted lines to make your own character for "eye." Please move to the next line. A picture of a person was drawn in a simplified way to form the character on the right that means person. In much the same way, the sketch of a river becomes the character that means "river". The character representing the word for "mouth" is similar. Finally, you can see in the last row how the character that depicts a tree evolved from a line drawing of a tree. Let's practice by tracing the rest of the symbols. It is a great help to memorize all of the Chinese characters.

These five symbols are very simple. More complicated Chinese characters can be made by combining symbols.

Her conclusion contains a brief review.

I hope you enjoyed the process of making *kanji* characters and gained some knowledge of Japanese and Chinese characters that are used in my language. Briefly, there are three kinds of characters that we use in writing Japanese: *Kanji*, the Chinese characters, are the basic ones; *hiragana* is used for real Japanese words; and *katakana* for words taken from foreign languages.

Ariko's ending relates to the introduction.

See if you can find Japanese characters in things around you in your daily life—you may even recognize one that you learned today!

Questions and Exercises

1. Observe public speakers—for example, professors in other courses—who use visuals in their presentations. What kind(s) of visual displays are most common? Which do you see used least? Evaluate the speakers' use of the visuals; that is, do they use them well, or should they read this chapter? Explain.

2. Which means of displaying visuals will you probably use for your classroom speeches? Which would you not consider? In your future employment, what equipment do you see yourself using the most? The least? Why?

3. Think about the speeches you have heard during the last week. What kind of visual support, if any, did the speakers use? Are there instances where the use of visuals would have made it easier for you to listen and understand the material?

4. What kind of visual might work most appropriately for a speech on:
   - The circulatory system
   - The physical effects of smoking on the lungs
   - The fabled "silk" trading route
   - Ozone depletion
   - Changes in interest rates

Key Terms

overhead projector
transparency
handouts
posterboard
objects
models
tables
lists
charts
line graphs
bar graphs
pie graphs
picture graphs or pictographs

Notes

1. Ong, W. (1982). *Orality and literacy: The technologizing of the word.* London: Methuen.
2. Jeremiah 13.

3. Fernando, A. (1992). Multimedia in the classroom: A project at St. John's. Academic computing and networking news. St. John's University. p. 9.

4. Ibid.

5. See Martel, M. (1984). *Before you say a word: The executive guide to effective communication.* Englewood Cliffs, NJ: Prentice-Hall.

6. This information came from an advertisement from the 3M Company.

7. Shannon, L. R. (1992, January 14). Help in making a point. *The New York Times*, p. C6.

8. Ibid.

9. This information appeared in a handout distributed by the 3M Company.

10. Iso, A. (1990). Japanese characters. Student speech, Oregon State University, Corvallis, Oregon.

Language

- Explain how words are linked to cultural memories
- Distinguish between the denotative and connotative meanings of words
- Define dialects and jargon, and explain when they are appropriate in public speaking
- Tell how the ability to name or label groups and issues is linked to power
- Give examples of epithets and euphemisms and ageist and sexist language
- List six guidelines for effective language in public speaking
- Understand how alliteration, rhyme, repetition, personification, hyperbole, metaphor, and simile can make a speech more interesting
- Give guidelines for listening and speaking when there are language differences

Note

This chapter focuses on language—the principles for usage that are found in the canon of style. It discusses linguistic changes, sociocultural variations, and language usage in public speaking. It concludes with tips for speaking to a linguistically diverse audience by using an interpreter to translate a public speech. Throughout, it develops the cultural theme of the text.

The language a public speaker uses conveys much more than information on the topic of the speech; it can also provide listeners with clues for discerning the speaker's occupation, region of origin, age, educational level, income level, gender, and ethnicity. For example, the following quotations were derived from a range of individuals: a professor, a person from the Middle Ages, a nonnative speaker of English, and a New Yorker. Read them and match the individuals to their quotations.

I got a brothuh who's goin' into thoid grade. The kid's got no hang-ups whatsoeveuh.

Theatetus and the Eleatic stranger discover in the Sophist that defining accurately the "type" sophist is not easy. The difficulty of their task stems from the fact that the difference between the sophist and the philosopher are so minute that it is easy to mistake the one for the other.[1]

When passenger of foot heave in sight, tootle the horn. Trumpet him melodiously at first, but if he still obstacles your passage then tootle him with vigor.[2]

Whan that my fourthe housbond was on bere [funeral bier], I weep algate, and made sory chere, as wyves moten, for it is usage, and with my coverchief covered my visage.[3]

You probably had little difficulty distinguishing (in this order) the New Yorker, the professor, the nonnative speaker of English, and the woman from the Middle Ages. The fact that you could successfully match up the pairs demonstrates that the words and the grammatical choices people make provide evidence of their social and personal identities such as their region of origin, educational level, gender, and age. The quotation from medieval English additionally demonstrates that language changes over time.

Your language choices similarly reveal information about your personality. You have developed a distinct "voice"—your way of using words and phrasing your ideas that expresses your unique view of the world and distinguishes your speaking style from that of your friends. In public speaking, similarly, you are developing a unique way of communicating your ideas before a group of people within the norms and constraints of the culture. Consequently, your public voice differs from that of other speakers within your classroom.

In the study of rhetoric, the language you choose to frame your ideas falls within the canon of style, which is the focus of this chapter. First, the chapter will look at some aspects of language itself and examine how the linguistic code both reveals and expresses cultural assumptions. Next, it will provide tips for effective language choices in U.S. classrooms. Finally, it will discuss ways of speaking in linguistically diverse settings.

Figure 11.1

Language and Culture

Cross Reference

This section elaborates on the theme of the book—the relationship between culture and public speaking.

Languages are verbal codes composed of a system of symbols that a community of language speakers uses to communicate with one another. Symbols are signs that represent or stand for objects and concepts the community shares socially. However, for these signs to be meaningful, the persons who are communicating must understand them similarly. To illustrate, we sometimes use symbols in the form of simple drawings to convey ideas, such as those depicted in Figure 11.1.

If you are familiar with these symbols, you understand that they mean: (a) recycle, (b) no smoking, (c) a curve in the road, (d) New Mexico. Some, such as the highway sign, are well known to everyone who drives because prospective drivers must learn what it stands for in order to pass the licensing examination. Others, such as the "zia," or sun symbol, used to represent the state of New Mexico, are less widely known. Obviously, a person who is unfamiliar with one or more of these signs will not understand their meanings.

Although we are able to represent some of our ideas by pictograms and drawings, most of our communication is far too complex for such signs. Consequently, each society has developed a linguistic system made up of symbols in the form of words. In order to communicate your ideas to others, you must put them into words that your audience will understand.

Words and Meaning

In *New Words and a Changing American Culture*, Raymond Gozzi[4] explains that words are the names we give to our "cultural memories." They serve as "markers of cultural attention" or encoded memories. Put simply, one or more members of a culture take note of a phenomenon, formulate a concept or abstraction related to it, and codify—or encode—the idea into a word. The process looks something like this.

For Further Reading

R. Gozzi. (1990). *New words and a changing American culture*. Columbia, SC: University of South Carolina Press.

Long ago humans:

1. *Noted a phenomenon—some creatures could fly.*

2. *Formed a concept—all the observed creatures had two legs, two wings, a beak, and feathers.*

3. *Created a label—"bird" (English), "oiseau" (French), "pájaro" or "ave" (Spanish).*

According to this theory, language indicates what the members of a society find significant, and the labels or words they create carve out their interpretations of the world, forming the social realities in which they live, think, and act. For instance, think of the words you know for different kinds of snow. There's *snow*, of course, maybe *blizzard*, *downy flakes*, and *sleet*, but can you think of more words to represent snow? This task would be easier if you were an Eskimo, for Eskimos have numerous names for different kinds of snow. Does that mean that they perceive varieties of snow that you do not? Maybe. It almost certainly means that knowing the differences between various kinds of snow is far more significant within that culture than it is in ours.

Teaching Idea

Discuss with students words they know from the "youth culture" or from another group they belong to that have been created to denote ideas or memories shared by members of their group. For example, some fraternity students in the West refer to "Shasta" —not as a mountain or lake in California, but as a series of fraternity events that take place over the Memorial Day weekend.

It is fairly easy to see how humans create words when you think of objects such as birds, snow, buildings, or chairs. However, many of our words label less tangible clusters of experiences, actions, feelings, and ideas rather than objects. To understand this better, think of the meanings (if any) you attach to the word *Woodstock*. In the 1950s, if people knew the word at all, it was as the name of a little town in upstate New York. However, as a result of an extended rock concert that took place on a farm outside the town in 1969, combined with recordings, films, books, interviews, articles, and so on surrounding those events, the word *Woodstock* came to stand for a way of living, thinking, and acting characteristic of a group in the "Woodstock generation."

Languages also change in ways that reflect cultural transformations. For instance, more than 10,000 words have been added to English since 1961.[5] They include *gridlock*, *yuppie*, *microchip*, *junk food*, and *the mall*. In addition, English has adopted words from other languages including *glastnost* from the Russians, *kamikaze* from the Japanese, *zeitgeist* from the Germans, and *ambiance* from the French. Finally, meanings change over time. Read a Shakespearean play and you will be struck by the differences between the English of Shakespeare's time and the English of today.

Speech Assignment

There is an assignment and a sample speech of definition in the Student Resource Workbook.

Denotative Meaning   Words *denote* or "point" to something that members of a culture consider worthy of notice and subsequently label; thus, the *denotative meaning* is what the word names or identifies. Here are several categories of items and examples of words that denote or stand for objects or ideas within each.[6]

- *Real objects* dogs, trees, grass, the sun
- *Imaginary things* unicorns, martians, elves, Superman
- *Qualities of objects* hardness, goodness, tall, narrow
- *Feelings* love, hatred, envy, joy, peace
- *States of being* happiness, depression, contentment, gratitude
- *Abstractions* personality, quarks, conscience, wealth, success
- *Actions* jogging, pointing, smiling, studying

When you look up words in the dictionary, you will find their denotative meanings. For example, if you look up "report card," you will see that this label denotes "a report on a student that is periodically submitted by a school to the student's parents or guardian."[7]

Teaching Idea

Have students consult a dictionary and bring to class other words that have only one meaning and those that are ambiguous. Example: "lifelike" has one meaning; "like" has more than ten.

Some words, however, stand for more than one idea; consequently, their meaning is *ambiguous*. For instance, the word *pot* has at least five meanings: (1) a rounded container used chiefly for domestic purposes; (2) a sum of money, as in the total amount of bets at stake at one time (the jackpot); (3) ruin or deterioration, as in "her business went to pot"; (4) slang for marijuana; (5) a shot in which a billiard ball is pocketed.[8] Because the word is ambiguous, the context in which it appears determines its meaning.

As you plan the language for your own speech, make sure that you use the correct word in the correct context to denote your intended meaning. This may mean that you use a dictionary or a thesaurus during your preparation to look up the precise words you need to convey your thoughts. Increasing the number of words in your vocabulary, and distinguishing among shades of meaning between words is a good idea, for the more words you know, the more power you will have to communicate your thoughts clearly.

Teaching Idea

Using exercise 1, have students bring ads to class and discuss the connotations of words used for brand names. (Alternatively, it could be a journal entry.)

Connotative Meaning   Although words *denote* objects and concepts, they also carry emotional overtones or *connotations*. That is, words not only stand for ideas, they also represent related feelings and associations that cluster around a concept. Thus, though "report card" denotes a periodical report of a student's progress, it has different connotations for different individuals, depending on their experiences. Many people have positive feelings toward these reports because in the past they resulted in rewards from adults and increasing self-confidence. Others dreaded report cards because they had negative effects.

Teaching Idea

Show an excerpt from a political speech. Identify and discuss connotative words found in the speech. Predict how a political opponent might choose different words.

Carefully choosing connotative words is effective in creating emotional responses within your listeners, for some words evoke strong feelings. Watch for connotative language as you conduct research. For example, you may find that a U.S. military leader refers to an opponent as a *warlord* rather than as an *influential leader*. Political leaders label their opponents *obstructionists* who *attack* and *destroy* legislation, while they, of course, *stand up* for the *rights* of *ordinary people*. By using carefully chosen words, these speakers hope to create images and perceptions that produce the "spin" or interpretation they want their listeners to have. As you select the wording for your own speech, be aware of the connotative meanings of the words you choose.

Dialect

A dialect is a variant form of a language.[9] There are many dialects of English. One is British English. Others include American English, Black English, ESL (English as a Second Language) English, international English, and a variety of other regional and ethnic group variants of the language. The dialect most commonly used in societal institutions is known as Standard English. It is the language of print—and the dialect most widely used in public speaking settings in the United States.

You may speak another dialect as well as Standard English. Although a non-standard dialect functions well in many settings, speakers are often bidialectical, using one dialect around families and friends and the other in public settings. This is called *code switching*. Pauline Jefferson, for instance, uses Standard English when she transacts business with customers in her bank and when she makes public presentations for her co-workers. However, when she speaks before a small female audience in her local church, she switches codes, alternating between Standard English and Black English.

In summary, languages are systems of symbols—words that denote or stand for ideas and evoke feelings or connotative meanings that differ from person to person. Languages have variant forms, or dialects, that are appropriate in some settings but do not communicate as effectively in most public speaking situations.

Teaching Idea

Have interested students do research and report to the class on Black English, ESL English, international English, and so on.

For Further Reading

W. Labov. (1972). *Sociolinguistic patterns.* Philadelphia: University of Pennsylvania Press; and S. N. Weber. (1994). The need to be: The sociocultural significance of black language. In L. A. Samovar and R. E. Porter (Eds.). *Intercultural communication: A reader,* 7th ed. (pp. 221–226). Belmont, CA: Wadsworth.

KEY CONCEPT   ## Language and Culture

Words and meaning   Humans label their cultural memories and the realities that are significant to members of the group.

Denotative meaning   This is what the word names or identifies.

Connotative meaning   The emotional overtones, feelings, and associations that are attached to the word are its connotations.

Dialect   Dialects are variants of a language. In most public speaking settings in the United States, speakers use the dialect termed Standard English.

Effects of Language Choices

For Further Reading

See M. Vanderford. (1989). Vilification and social monuments: A case study of pro-life and pro-choice rhetoric. *Quarterly Journal of Speech*, 75, 166–182. Vanderford shows how language is used to shape perceptions. In this case, both sides in the abortion debate vilify and demean one another.

As you might imagine, there is power in the ability to name, and there are social and political implications inherent in the terms we choose to label groups and issues. For instance, what differences do you perceive when you hear each of these terms?

- A typist vs. an administrative assistant
- Handicapped vs. physically challenged
- New taxes vs. investments in America, revenue enhancement

You can see that the language you choose to express your idea shapes your listeners' perceptions and influences their interpretations. In debates over verbal labels such questions as these arise: Who has the right to name movements and groups? What terminology should frame debates over issues? Whose language is acceptable? In what situations is this language acceptable?

Naming

Because the language you select for your speech has the power to influence perceptions, let's look at the way a single term used during the national health care debates in the early 1990s framed the issue. Some policymakers lumped together physicians, nurses, physical therapists, and home care companions into a single category termed "health care providers." By categorizing physicians, who have medical school degrees, with home care companions, who may or may not have a high school education, the policymakers minimized the distinctions in education and skills traditionally made among medical personnel. One physician theorized that it is easier to regulate "providers" than it is to regulate "doctors."[10]

There are also implications in choosing labels for groups. Take the term *Hispanic*. Some who are labeled Hispanic prefer to call themselves "Latino" and "Latina" or "Chicano" and "Chicana," saying that "Hispanic" is a name the Census Bureau made up, one that recalls the days of Spanish conquest. Others say that "Latino" is an even older term, going back in time to the Roman conquest of Spain. Most people in this category prefer to call themselves Puerto Ricans, Colombians, Mexicans, Cubans, or simply Americans.[11]

Teaching Idea

Many campuses are dealing with issues of "hate speech." In journal entries or class discussion, have students explore the ethics of using epithets. What, if anything, should be done about speech that demeans individuals or groups?

Epithets

Epithets are words or phrases used to describe some quality of a person or group; they often have negative connotations. For example, during the 1988 presidential campaign, George Bush called his opponent Michael Dukakis "a card-carrying member of the ACLU," knowing that the ACLU (American Civil Liberties Union) was considered a very liberal organization and that many voters viewed it negatively.

Some epithets have such powerful negative connotations that it is difficult even to write them. Words such as *nerd*, *pig* (for police officers), *anti-choice*, *queer*, and *nigger* are epithets that people in these groups did not choose as names for themselves. You can see how they function to frame perceptions about the group. For example, calling antiabortion advocates "anti-choice" creates a negative image, whereas the group's self-chosen title, "pro-life," has positive connotations.

Teaching Idea

Exercise 3 asks students to discuss related issues.

Members of labeled groups often attempt to lessen the negative power of the epithet by accepting and using the term themselves. For instance, police officers take the letters of the word *pig* and reinterpret them to form the slogan P*ride*, I*ntegrity*, G*uts*. Similarly, some homosexuals take the epithet "queer" and transform it for use in slogans such as "We're queer and we're here" or in labels such as Queer Nation. One who did so explained, "We have to take the power out of these words."[12]

Euphemisms

Euphemisms are words or phrases that substitute an agreeable or inoffensive term for a more direct one that might offend, embarrass, or suggest something unpleasant. We regularly use euphemisms for things we hesitate to speak of such as bodily functions, religion, and death. Consequently, instead of saying someone "died," we select euphemisms such as "she passed away." Euphemisms also mask unpleasant situations, such as corporate layoffs. It sounds better for a company to "downsize" than to "fire" workers. Looters are humorously termed "nontraditional shoppers," and drug addicts become "chemically inconvenienced."[13]

Speakers often use euphemisms in an attempt to substitute innocuous terms for actions, ideas, and policies that listeners might find objectionable. For example, government officials call new taxes "revenue enhancements" or "investments in America" in an attempt to soften the reality of planned tax increases. Similarly, military officers use the term "collateral damage" rather than "bombing of civilians" to describe the results of a military action.

Demeaning Language

As we have seen, language can be used to create negative impressions. It can also be used in sexist, racist, ageist, and other ways that demean people or groups. The following two examples show how the words you choose can influence your audience's ideas about specific groups.

Ageist Language[14]   The U.S. culture places a great deal of value on youth, and older people are not given the same respect they are in other societies. This can be seen in the language used to portray older people. Here are a few common examples.

In cultures where elderly citizens are highly respected, ageist language is not an issue. However, in the United States, where youth is valued, ageist language can serve to demean older people by subtly influencing listeners to perceive them in a negative manner.

For Further Reading

V. S. Friemuth and K. Jamieson. (1979). *Communicating with the elderly: Shattering stereotypes.* Urbana, IL: Eric Clearinghouse on Reading and Communication Skills.

1. *Stereotypes* Common misconceptions are that older people are closed minded, less capable mentally, unhealthy, physically unattractive, lonely, and poor. Language choices can perpetuate these stereotypes. For instance, how do the following phrases influence your thinking: "set in her ways," "losing his marbles," "ready for a nursing home," and "well-preserved"?

2. *Labels* Often you hear labels with negative connotations applied to elderly people. A few examples are "old duffer," "little old lady" (in tennis shoes), "granny," "old biddy," "old hag," "dirty old man." What kind of mental image do you form as you read through this list?

3. *Dismissive language* Language can be applied to elderly people in ways that discount the importance of their ideas, as these examples show: "too old," "senile," "no longer in the thick of things," "over the hill."

4. *Language that values youth* Such phrases as "feel younger" or "look ten years younger" subtly reinforce the notion that it is better to be younger.

For Further Reading

S. Mura and B. Waggens-pack. (1983). Linguistic sexism: A rhetorical per-spective. In J. L. Golden, G. F. Berquist, & W. F. Coleman. *The rhetoric of western thought*, 3rd ed. (pp. 251–260). Dubuque: Kendall/Hunt.

Teaching Idea

If you want to explore gender, language, and cul-ture in more depth, dupli-cate and hand out Activity 10.1, Japanese Women's Speech, in the Instructor's Manual.

For Further Reading

Writer Ursula Le Guin delivered a commence-ment address at Mills College in "women's lan-guage." See U. K. Le Guin. (1989). A left-hand-ed commencement address. In U. K. Le Guin. *Dancing at the edge of the world: Thoughts on words, women, places* (pp. 115–117). New York: Grove Press.

Sexist Language   In a similar way, language can subtly influence the way we view women and men, and in the last few decades, there has been an emphasis on removing sexist terms from English. In fact, most instructors insist that their students eliminate sexist speech. Here are a few of the areas in which linguistic sexism traditionally occurred.[15]

1. *Generic "he" or "man"*   In traditional English grammar, the pronoun "he" designated a person of either sex, as this illustration from a 1938 speech text shows.

    When one has settled upon a subject and has some notion of what he wishes to do with it, his immediate concern is with the materials, the stuff out of which his speech is to be woven. He must have ideas and data with which to hold attention and to make and impress his point.[16]

    Such language arguably excludes females by making them invisible. The use of the suffix "man" is similar. For this reason, replace such words as "chairman," "spokesman," "caveman," "mailman," and "policeman" with gender-inclusive labels such as "chairperson," "spokesperson," "cave dweller," "mail carrier," and "police officer."

2. *Nonparallel language*   Nonparallel means that the two sexes are not treated equally in language, and these vocabulary differences reflect underlying cul-tural assumptions. There are several types of nonparallel language. One occurs when a suffix is added to a male term used to designate a female, as in "actor-actress," and "steward-stewardess." Another comes from marking job titles, as in a "male nurse" and a "female judge." (Would you ever say a "female nurse" or a "male judge"?) Another is in terms of address; a woman may be known as "Mrs. Roberto Sanchez," but no man is known as "Mr. Jane Andrews." Similarly, couples may be perceived as "man and wife," but never as "woman and husband."

In summary, terminology is not neutral. The words you use to frame your discussion have both positive and negative connotations. Consequently, you must take into account the cultural concerns surrounding terminology as you plan the language for your speech, especially as you speak on controversial topics.

KEY CONCEPT **Effects of Language Choices**

Naming   The names and labels we apply to groups and issues have the power to shape listeners' perceptions.

Epithets   These are negative terms used to label a person or group.

Euphemisms   These words state something unpleasant in a more neutral way.

Demeaning language Language can be used in ways that put groups of people down.

> *Ageist language* This language stereotypes and minimizes older people.
>
> *Sexist language* This language excludes women or makes men and women nonparallel.

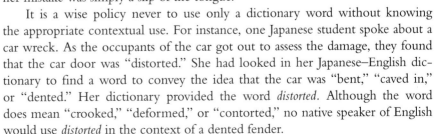

Language in Public Speaking

Theme
Emphasize that these guidelines for language usage reflect cultural norms in the context of public speaking. Other languages or nonstandard dialects are not "bad" or "inferior."

There are several principles in the canon of style that will help you use language more effectively. As you select the wording for your speeches, choose language that is accurate, appropriate, concise, clear, concrete, and interesting.

Be Accurate

There are two major areas in which you need to speak accurately. First, be correct in your vocabulary or word choices; second, use standard grammar in your speeches.

Vocabulary It is common for speakers to use a word that sounds a lot like the one they want but has an entirely different meaning—sometimes causing the audience to laugh. This is called a *malaprop*. The word comes from the name of a fictional character created by R. B. Sheridan. In his comedy *The Rivals*, Mrs. Malaprop consistently used similar-sounding but incorrect words, leading her listeners to chuckle in amusement. Children often use malaprops. For example, a little boy who was discussing eating habits with his mother asked, "If you're a *vegetarian*, why don't you fix our cat?" He obviously confused the word with *veterinarian*.

One government cabinet officer, speaking before a group of physicians, used the wrong word, much to her audience's amusement. She stated that alcohol caused *psoriasis* [sir EYE uh sis] of the liver. As she continued with her talk, she realized that her listeners were chuckling in a place that she had not intended to be humorous. When she realized her mistake, she laughed, too, and quickly acknowledged that she, of course, meant *cirrhosis* [sir OH sis] of the liver. She obviously knew the difference between psoriasis (a skin disease) and cirrhosis; her mistake was simply a slip of the tongue.

It is a wise policy never to use only a dictionary word without knowing the appropriate contextual use. For instance, one Japanese student spoke about a car wreck. As the occupants of the car got out to assess the damage, they found that the car door was "distorted." She had looked in her Japanese–English dictionary to find a word to convey the idea that the car was "bent," "caved in," or "dented." Her dictionary provided the word *distorted*. Although the word does mean "crooked," "deformed," or "contorted," no native speaker of English would use *distorted* in the context of a dented fender.

Grammar   Not only do speakers choose incorrect words, they also choose grammatical forms that are inappropriate for public settings. When it is important to use Standard English grammar, as called for in most public presentations, good speakers choose standard forms. Here are a few very common errors overheard in student speeches.

Nonstandard	Standard
He/she/it done	He/she/it did
They was	They were
He/she/it don't	He/she/it doesn't
Me and him	He and I
Me and my friend	My friend and I

Be Appropriate

In preparing a speech, match the language to the topic, the audience, the situation, and yourself as an individual. Certain forms of language are appropriate for situations and speakers that are inappropriate for others, and the language you choose for public settings should generally be more formal, containing less slang. African Americans in certain settings speak in Black English. It is expected, and it is appropriate in those settings. However, it is not appropriate for someone of Euro-American heritage or for an Asian American to use Black English in a speech, even in a setting where an African-American speaker would do so.

Good speakers adapt their language, meaning that they choose different ways of expressing their ideas depending on the audience and the situation. The language used in a lecture differs from the language used in a eulogy delivered at a funeral. Moreover, the language used with a group of homeless people gathered in a park differs in word choice and level or formality from that used to address members of an alumni association at a formal banquet—even when the topic is the same.

Be Concise

Teaching Idea

Have students, individually or in pairs, rewrite a wordy portion of a student speech using the sample found in the Student Resource Workbook, or make a transparency and use this as a whole group activity.

In U.S. culture, good speakers eliminate any words considered unnecessary for communicating meaning. Using unnecessary words is called *verbiage*, and when you speak in U.S. institutions, eliminate verbiage whenever you can. A caller on a radio talk show failed to do this, and he said, "*What they did is* they *took the issue and* distorted it, *and how they did it is they did it* by . . . ." He would have been more concise had he said, "They distorted the issue by . . . ."

Often students fail to eliminate extra language, and they pad their speeches with too many words. This example from a student speech on the value of learning a second language shows both how he actually gave the speech and how he could have given it.

As he gave it:

I became interested in this topic upon the constant hounding of *my father* urging me *to take a foreign language, preferably Japanese,* the reason being is because *my major is business and the Japanese are dominating the international business scene.*

As he might have given it:

I became interested in this topic because my father constantly hounded me to take a foreign language—preferably Japanese. He reasoned that my major is business, and the Japanese are dominating the international business scene.

One very common form of verbiage is to begin a sentence with "What." Other cluttering phrases are "you want to" and "you need to," as these examples show.

> Avoid: *What you want to do next is you want to* take this corner and fold it toward this point.
> Avoid: Next, *you want to* take this corner and fold it toward this point.
> Use: Next, take this corner and fold it toward the point.
>
> Avoid: *What you do is you* go to the placement center on campus.
> Avoid: *You need to* go to the placement center on campus.
> Use: Go to the placement center on campus.

Again, it should be noted that brevity or conciseness is a trait valued in speeches within U.S. culture. In contrast to these norms, many cultures value flowery words and language, and what we consider to be verbiage other groups evaluate as good verbal skills.

For Further Reading

J. W. Anderson. (1991). A comparison of Arab and American conceptions of "effective persuasion." In L. A. Samovar and R. E. Porter (Eds). *Intercultural communication: A reader,* 7th ed. (pp. 96–106). Belmont, CA: Wadsworth.

Teaching Idea

Use information that students discover in exercise 2 as the basis for a classroom discussion.

Be Clear

The purpose of public speaking is to clarify ideas, rather than to make them more difficult to understand. For this reason, it is important to make sure that your ideas are understandable. One of the best ways to make ideas clear is to avoid jargon.

Jargon Jargon is a specialized, technical vocabulary and style that serves special groups, interests, and activities. For example, football has its own jargon with specialized meanings for *drive* and *down* and *safety*. When you are speaking in a group where everyone knows the meaning of the specialized vocabulary, it is appropriate to use jargon. However, if you are attempting to communicate with nonspecialists, you need to define and clarify technical terms.

As you research your topic, you will probably find a number of technical words in your sources. However, avoid using terms that you do not understand,

Use of jargon—a set of technical, in-group vocabulary words— is appropriate when everyone is familiar with the terminology. However, undefined jargon in a speech to a lay audience is generally more confusing than enlightening.

or define any jargon you use. One student failed to do this in his discussion of the transmission of the HIV virus that is linked to AIDS.

> *We've all been taught that AIDS is* perinatal *and that it is transmitted through sexual contact.*

In the question-and-answer period that followed the speech, a member of the audience asked what *perinatal* meant. The speaker did not know; he said that the word came from an article he read. No one else in the room knew what it meant either. Because of this, they did not understand this part of the speech. The word means "associated with the birth process, the period immediately before, during, or just after the time of birth." If the speaker had taken the time to look up the word, he could have said instead:

> *We've been taught that AIDS is transmitted from mother to child perinatally; that is, during the birth process, and that it is transmitted through sexual activity.*

This would have been more effective, for the brief definition provides listeners with an understanding of the word's meaning. Defining clarifies, rather than obscures, his ideas.

Be Concrete

Another important aspect of style, one that can help your listeners form precise understandings, is to choose concrete words, that is, specific rather than abstract words. We usually think of words as moving along a scale of abstraction such as this:

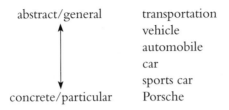

abstract/general   transportation
    vehicle
    automobile
    car
    sports car
concrete/particular   Porsche

Consequently, if you say, "She drives a Porsche," your ideas are much more concrete than if you say, "She has a sports car." But "She has a sports car" is more concrete than "She has her own transportation." The more distinct and specific the words you choose, the more vivid will be the images your listeners have and the more precise will be your meanings.

This excerpt from a speech on electronic drums was exceptional for its use of concrete language.

Cross Reference

This speech is found in its entirety at the end of the chapter.

> *Picture your stereotypical rock drummer: shaggy, smells, looks, and sometimes acts like a lower primate, body type—lean and wiry, definitely the fast twitch kind of muscles, and they aren't in the head. And it always seems that they're the first in the band to OD. On The Muppets TV show, the drummer's name is "Animal," and they kept him chained to his set of drums.*

As you can see, the concrete images help the listeners form a specific picture of the sights, movements—even the smells of drummers. This is an example of language that appeals to listeners' senses.

Vague words are those with indefinite boundaries. Put simply, they are words that do not precisely define a concept. For example, what is a hill? When does it become a mountain? Who is old? A child thinks a nineteen-year-old is old. A nineteen-year-old thinks a forty-five-year-old is; a forty-five-year-old thinks that old is seventy, and a seventy-year-old thinks old is about eighty-five. What is large? Small? Compared to what? A giant pizza is not on the same scale as a giant building.

As you plan your speeches, define what you mean by vague words by choosing specific details to define them. Thus, if you are speaking of a "small" inheritance, give a dollar figure. Otherwise, one listener may think of a small inheritance as $2,000, whereas another thinks $20,000 is small.

Be Interesting

Teaching Idea

For an example of vivid, interesting language, show a videotape of Martin Luther King's speech, "I Have a Dream." Guide students' listening by first listing some of the metaphors and recurring "wave" patterns that Dr. King uses. See Chapter 9. Dr. King himself thought of this speech as his "Bank of Justice" speech. *Or do exercise 5, which uses the sample student speech found at the end of the chapter.*

A major purpose of your speaking is to help listeners see, feel, and remember your speech. Choosing colorful, vivid language is a good way to keep listener attention and interest. Vivid words and images help your listeners form the necessary inner dialogue to form mental images that go with the words and ideas you present. There are a number of ways to make the language of your speech more memorable: alliteration, rhyme, repetition, personification, hyperbole, metaphors, and similes.

Alliteration   Alliteration is the use of words that have recurring initial sounds. For instance, one conference took as its theme, "*Choose change* or *chase* it." The keynote speaker, then, used this alliterative phrase as the topic of her speech. In another example, one student used alliteration in a speech about seatbelts.

> *Don't let fate forecast your future. Buckle up.*

One way to help listeners remember the main ideas in a topical message is to alliterate the main points. The president of a university gave an alliterative three-point speech to a new group of trustees at a welcoming luncheon.

> *Trustees bring three things to an institution:*
> *Wealth.*
> *Wisdom.*
> *Work.*

Rhyme   As you know, rhymes are words that end in the same sounds. Speakers effectively rhyme single words, phrases, or lines. For an example of a speech that is rhymed throughout, listen to a recording made by a rap artist. Though it is possible to rhyme an entire speech, most speakers use rhymes in more limited ways. This excerpt from the drum speech shows how the speaker rhymed three words within one sentence.

> *So, I want to examine this new world of the push-button beat and pose the question to you: "What or who would you rather have in your band, a mean and clean drum machine or a stereotypical rock drummer?"*

Speakers also use rhymes effectively for wording the main points of their speeches. When such a rhyme is available, this stylistic device often enables listeners to remember the major points easily, as this outline indicates.

> *We are faced with two choices:*
> *Retreat.*
> *Compete.*

Repetition   Technically, there are two ways to use repetition. One is to repeat the same word or phrase at the beginning of clauses or sentences. For example, Ronald Reagan's tribute to the Challenger crew of seven astronauts who lost their lives when their spacecraft exploded included these repetitive clauses: "we will cherish each of their stories, *stories of* triumph and bravery, *stories of* true American heroes."[17] Another type of repetition restates the same phrase at the end of a phrase or sentence. Lincoln's famous phrase "government of *the people*, by *the people*, for *the people*" is an example. The following example comes from a speech by a Native-American speaker.[18]

> *This idea is not original with me. It was taught to us by a great leader of the Lakota people—my people—Chief Sitting Bull.* He taught us that *Indian children could succeed in modern society and yet retain the values of their culture,* values such as *respect for the earth, for wildlife, for rivers and streams, for plants and trees; and* values such as *caring for each other and for family and community.* He taught us that *we must leave behind more hope than we found.*

Personification   Personification means giving human characteristics to non-human entities. These entities include animals, countries, natural objects and processes, and social processes. In his radio address acknowledging his defeat at the polls, President George Bush likened the nation to a person in this way:[19]

> *Ours is a nation that has shed the blood of war and cried the tears of depression.*

The Indian Chief Seattle similarly used personification in an 1853 speech before the governor of the Washington Territory.[20]

> *Yonder sky that has wept tears of compassion upon my people for centuries untold, and which to us appears changeless and eternal, may change.*

For Further Reading
Hyperbole is valued in some speech communities. See P. A. Sullivan. (1993). Signification and African-American rhetoric: A case study of Jesse Jackson's "Common ground and common sense" speech. *Communication Quarterly,* 41 (1), 1–15.

Hyperbole   Hyperbole is the use of exaggeration for effect. For example, Donna Shalala, Secretary of Health and Human Services in the Clinton administration, commonly speaks in hyperbole, "If we don't do something about health care, there will be *no more* jobs." Or "If we don't do something about AIDS, there will be *no more* people."[21] Dr. Shalala uses these exaggerations to indicate that the problems are serious and deserve government attention.

Use of hyperbole is effective in some contexts, but there are several criticisms of excessive use of this stylistic form. Some exaggerations border on the ridiculous, and people feel the speaker is overreacting or lying. For instance, some of Dr. Shalala's critics criticized her use of hyperbole. *No* jobs? Really? *No* more people? At all?

One student used hyperbole ineffectively in this way.

Imagine a world where you have no *trees, total* pollution, *and a landfill in* every *neighborhood. This is where we are heading because of our abuse of the land and lack of concern for ways to replenish the earth and her resources. There is a way where each person . . . could help,* maybe even solve the problem. *It's called recycling.*

His point that recycling will contribute to the preservation of natural resources is a good one. However, the use of *no* trees, *total* pollution, and *every* neighborhood overstates the case; furthermore, though recycling may help, it will not *solve the problem* of environmental pollution in itself. Thus, his overexaggeration led some listeners to think he was not exercising good reasoning. Since this was the introduction to his speech, they discounted his ideas from the very beginning.

Cross Reference

Chapter 8 discusses comparisons and contrast as a form of support. Chapter 15 discusses reasoning by analogy.

Metaphor   The use of metaphor is discussed extensively in other places throughout this text (see Chapters 8 and 15). Metaphors are implied comparisons in which one thing is spoken of as being something else; the words *like* and *as* are not used. In a speech given at Kansas State University on the anniversary of women's suffrage, newscaster Bernard Shaw used a metaphor comparing democracy to food preparation.[22]

Democracy is not a smooth sauce. . . . Democracy is the lone dish in constant need of seasoning, stirring, tasting. Democracy is never . . . never done.

One danger in using metaphors is the possibility of beginning with one comparison and ending with another. This is called a *mixed metaphor*. By way of illustration, one panelist on the "MacNeil-Lehrer News Hour" was guilty of using a mixed metaphor as he discussed the U.S. policy in Somalia.[23]

We must solve the root problem, or the line will be drawn in the sand, and we'll be back in the soup again.

As you can see, he combined three images. "Root" is a metaphorical reference that compares a problem to a plant. The "line drawn in the sand" and the "soup" are comparisons to two totally different things—an uncrossable boundary and a food. By going in three directions with his analogy, he ended up leaving listeners with no clear image regarding the problem.

Simile   Similes are short comparisons that are like metaphors in that they compare two items that are unlike in most ways but that are alike in one essential detail. However, they differ from metaphors in that they explicitly state the connection, and they contain the words *like* or *as*. The Native-American leader Chief Seattle used vivid similes, as this excerpt from his speech indicates.[24]

Teaching Idea

Exercise 4 asks students to identify cultural metaphors in Indian oratory.

Iraqi President Saddam Hussein used hyperbole to describe the Gulf War as "The Mother of All Wars." This struck many Americans as absurd, and became the basis for a number of jokes. While hyperbole is common in many cultures, take care when using it with Euro-American audiences, who may consider you to be overreacting to a situation.

[The white] people are many. They are like the grass that covers vast prairies. My people are few. They resemble the scattering trees of a storm-swept plain. . . . There was a time when our people covered the land as the waves of a wind-ruffled sea cover its shell paved floor, but that time long since passed away with the greatness of tribes that are now but a mournful memory.

When you read through speeches, you will see some metaphors and similes emerge and reemerge. Some arise from our experiences of being human. For instance, all human groups experience day and night, sickness and health, seasonal

For Further Reading

M. Osborne. (1977). The
evolution of the archetypal
sea in rhetoric and poetic.
*Quarterly Journal of Speech,
63*, 347–363.

changes, and family relationships. Professor Michael Osborne[25] calls these archetypal symbols because all humankind understands them. Other comparisons relate to cultural modes of transportation (the ship of state), sports (the game of life), and the like, and as the culture changes, new metaphors linked to electronic technology are emerging (experience static, plug in).

KEY CONCEPT   # Language in Public Speaking

Be accurate Use both correct vocabulary and grammar.

Be appropriate Match language to the topic, audience, occasion, and yourself.

Be concise Eliminate unnecessary words, called verbiage.

Be clear Translate jargon and define words that are vague.

Be concrete Use specific and particular words rather than abstract or general vocabulary choices.

Be interesting Choose colorful, vivid language.

Alliteration These words have the same initial sound.

Rhyme Rhymed words end with the same sounds.

Repetition Use a word or phrase more than once.

Personification This gives human characteristics to nonliving or nonhuman entities.

Hyperbole Hyperbole is exaggeration for effect.

Metaphor In metaphor, one thing is spoken of as being something else.

Simile These short comparisons of two things that are alike in one essential detail use the words *like* or *as*.

Language and Pluralistic Audiences

Cross Reference

Chapter 6 has a section on
language differences.

In classrooms across the country, students from different speech backgrounds give speeches in English.[26] It is important to remember that the major goal of the speech is communication of ideas, not perfection of language skills. Therefore, as you listen to a speaker who is not fluent in the language, seek to understand what is being said by concentrating on the ideas of the message rather than on the specific words of the speaker. This may require a special kind of patience as well as the ability to take the perspective of the communicator. *Perspective taking* means that you can put yourself in the other person's shoes. That is, you try to imagine what it would be like to give a speech in a foreign language to a group

For Further Reading

S. Thiederman. (1991). *Profiting in American multicultural marketplaces: How to do business across cultural lines.* New York: Lexington Books.

Cross Reference

See Chapter 1. This supports a recurring theme of dialogical listening.

of native speakers of that language. Keep in mind that nonfluency is not linked to intelligence or lack of education; it is linked to experiences with the second language.

These guidelines can help you be a better listener under these circumstances.

1. Approach the speech with a positive attitude, and expect to understand.
2. Listen all the way through. Make special efforts to keep your mind from wandering in the middle of the speech. It may help to take notes.
3. Practice *respons*-ibility in co-creating meaning. Plan to give appropriate nonverbal feedback to demonstrate your interest, patience, and support for the speaker.
4. Control your negative emotional responses. Let's face it, it is difficult to deal with linguistic barriers, and people often get frustrated or bored when there are language differences.
5. Do not laugh, even if the speakers do, at their language skills. Often they laugh nervously to relieve tension.

Speaking Through an Interpreter

Teaching Idea

In a classroom with a great deal of linguistic diversity, it can be effective to have two students who speak a second language prepare a speech together. Then, one delivers it in his or her native language while the other interprets. Or, have a speech translated into sign language.

Although using an interpreter may seem remote from the classroom world of speaking, there may be times in the future when you will have to communicate through someone who translates your words into another language, including sign language. If you have occasion to use an interpreter, here are a few words of advice.

1. Keep your language simple. Do not use overly technical words or uncommon vocabulary.
2. In advance of your speech, provide your interpreter with an outline of your talk so that she or he may check the meaning of any unfamiliar words. The interpreter may also use it during the speech as a guide to what you will say next.
3. Speak in short units. Do not pause after entire paragraphs; rather, say one or two sentences, then allow the interpreter to change your words into the other language.
4. Consider looking at the interpreter as he or she speaks or signs. This will signal her that you are ready for the translation; it also signals the audience to look at the interpreter rather than at you.
5. Because it takes two to three times longer to speak through an interpreter, shorten your speech accordingly.

Teaching Idea

Exercise 6 is appropriate here. Use it for a class discussion or a journal entry.

Remember that using interpreters is not easy, but without their presence, you would not be able to communicate your ideas effectively. Consequently, work on maintaining a positive attitude throughout the speaking event.

 **KEY CONCEPT**

Language and Pluralistic Audiences

Listen for the major ideas of the speech. Take the perspective of a speaker who is giving a speech in a second language.

Speaking through an interpreter Provide a copy or an outline of the speech in advance. Speak in short units, then pause for interpretation. Plan a shorter speech.

Summary

Language is a tool that humans use to communicate with one another and build complex societies. We use words as names for our cultural memories—meaning that we name those things we notice and need to know in order to survive. As a result, we label events, people, and things in a way that indicates what we find important. Languages are dynamic, with words being added, borrowed, and discontinued in response to social changes. A dialect is a variant of a language, and jargon is a technical vocabulary common to members of an occupation that can be used to confuse outsiders.

Words denote or stand for objects, actions, and ideas; however—and probably more important—they have connotative meanings that consist of the feelings and associations that the word implies. Because of this, there is power in words, and the ways groups are labeled and issues are linguistically framed can have the power to shape perceptions. Epithets are words that generally carry negative connotations, whereas euphemisms are terms that put negative things in a more positive light. In recent years, people have become concerned about the power of words—especially those used in ways that hurt others—and have worked to eliminate sexist, ageist, racist, and other demeaning speech from acceptable vocabulary.

Your speech effectiveness will largely depend on how well you are able to put your ideas into words. Thus, there are several guidelines for using language effectively in public speaking. First, be accurate in both your vocabulary and grammar. Further, use language that is appropriate to the audience, the occasion, and yourself. Eliminate extra words and phrases that make your speech less concise. Define jargon in an effort to be clear. Select concrete words that will allow your listeners to form more precise meanings. Finally, choose words that are interesting, and consider using alliteration, rhyme, repetition, personification, hyperbole, metaphors, and similes that draw from shared cultural references.

Finally, it is possible that you will be in a public speaking situation where you either speak in a second language—necessitating the use of an interpreter—or, more probably, you will listen to a speaker who has the accent of another language. Remember in these situations that it is most important to communicate ideas rather than have linguistic precision. When you listen to a speaker from another linguistic background, take the responsibility of listening with an open mind in a supportive manner.

Student Speech

Who/What Would You Want in Your Band?
Or, "Why Did I Spend 25 Years Playing Drums?"

Bob Pettit, Oregon State University

Bob, a rock drummer who returned to college to get an engineering degree, first gave this speech in the summer of 1990. Later, it was recorded on videotape and shown in beginning public speech classes. Every audience who has heard it agrees that Bob's vivid and colorful use of language makes the speech interesting throughout.

At the outset, Bob gains attention by playing off the word *extinct.* He skillfully and vividly moves from one part of the introduction to the next—establishing at the outset the jargon style he will employ throughout the speech.

According to a record producer in the cartoon strip Doonesbury, "Drummers are extinct." Now, by drummers here, I'm not talking some type of weird dinosaur or puff-chested bird, but rather drummers as we've all come to know and love them, a la Ringo and Bongo, the dudes that beat the skins and drive the tunes with the bad beat. And what's making them go extinct is computers. Nowadays, the drum machine is the heppest of session cats. Computerized drums are getting all the good gigs. And if you've got ears, you've heard the new sound. It is everywhere—on radio, TV, blasting from big portables. You can't escape it, even if you'd like to. The beat is intense and relentless, inhuman. A lover like it would drive you insane. And it makes a drummer like me wonder why I've bothered to spend the last twentysome years playing drums. Fact is, twenty years ago 100 percent of the drums heard on record were real drums played by real drummers. Nowadays, as an article in *Rolling Stone* magazine points out, "On any recent record, there's a good chance that . . . the drums aren't real." So, I want to examine this new world of the push-button beat and pose the question to you: "What or who would you rather have in your band, a mean and clean drum machine, or a stereotypical rock drummer?"

Bob does not state his first main point immediately. He approaches it indirectly by describing a drummer's life. Notice how his use of jargon enhances his credibility.

In the old days a musician "paid his dues" in the school of hard knocks. Being hungry was where it was at. You got lean and mean, and you had to want it bad. "Wood shedding," "working on your chops," and "playing your axe" were the only ways out of the rut, or should I say "groove"? For me the groove got so deep it started to look more like a rectangular hole six feet in the ground. Now, I had my successes, but the good times were countered by the bad times, and I finally reached the point where I realized both me and my dog were getting skinny. They say starvation is a sure sign you're in the wrong business, but not in music. There, it's just some kind of musical purgatory one must pay to get a soulful sound. But, wait a minute, computers don't eat, and computers don't starve. Then, how come they sound so good?

Well, some people don't think they do. An editorial in *High Fidelity* magazine calls on the industry to, "throw away those machines." And *Rolling Stone* claims computers will never take the place of the quote, "crazed inspiration" and the "spontaneous performance" of a "bare chested drummer pounding out a beat." It seems drummers are still in demand in spite of themselves.

Bob uses a number of humorous images here.

Picture your stereotypical rock drummer: shaggy, smells, looks, and sometimes acts like a lower primate, body type—lean and wiry, definitely the fast twitch kind of muscles, and they aren't in the head. And it always seems that they're the first in the band to OD. On The Muppets TV show, the drummer's name was "Animal," and they kept him chained to his set of drums. I suppose they threw him bones and scraps from the butcher shop every few days or so. (I worked with a female vocalist who thought that was exactly what should have been done with me, but that is another story, and beside the point.)

Finally, he states his first major point, which leads immediately to his second.

The point is, that in spite of a reputation for difficulty, real drummers are still in demand. As the columnist for *High Fidelity* put it, he ". . . longs for the hollow crack of a snare drum."

On the other hand, the computer does have a lot of things going for it. For one thing, it always shows up, it never acts like a prima donna, and it doesn't get drunk on stage. *And* it has Perfect Time. That means it *never* slows down or speeds up. *Rolling Stone* reports that one programmer "added an imperfection to humanize" a drum part. The record producer noticed immediately and made him take it out. He said, "If I'd wanted a timing error, I'd hire a drummer!" Ouch!!

He intentionally uses a nonstandard grammatical form that helps create his persona.

So, there is no doubt computers "do got the beat," and though they may not always get respect, they are being taken seriously. *Rolling Stone* admits they have "taken over Top Forty" and *High Fidelity* describes them as having "come of age." And *Down Beat* magazine, that old standard of the jazz world, calls them "electronically sophisticated . . . musically adaptable" and having "great digitally stored drum sounds."

There is one thing both sides agree on. The electronic drums save time and money. In the recording studio, the machine gets it right the first time, every time, and you don't have to send it a check afterwards.

He is both informative and entertaining.

An example of the impact of drum machines can be seen in what happened to the band Nu Shooze. They got their start playing nightclubs in Portland, Oregon. In those days, they used regular drums. But when it came time to make a record album, they used computerized drums and fired their drummer, who then got a job washing dishes on the graveyard shift at Ho Fung's Bar & Grill. Just kidding. . . . Actually, their drummer incorporated the computer's sound into his own beat, and that, according to *Down Beat,* is the trend of the future; real drummers playing real drums and using real computers. It's a combination that's making people get up and dance—all around the world. The fans know what makes them shake their booties round. And they're buying the records by the millions.

So, to wrap it up, progress has finally caught up with the ancient and primal art of drumming. Ready or not, the electronic drum has arrived. And while the traditionalists may grumble, the new technology is being embraced by progressive performers and fans alike. So, we are back to the question of what would *you* prefer in your band, a lean and clean drum machine, or your stereotypical drummer?

Well, what do you think? I think the future holds promise for everything authentic, whether it's the sound of skin-on-skin jungle drums, or those crazy bongo machines.

Questions and Exercises

1. Look up ads in newspapers or magazines. Make a list of some of the words that are used to sell the products, and jot down some connotations of each term. For example, why are the words *obsession* and *eternity* used to name perfumes? Why are cars Cougars or Firebirds? What associations do the merchandisers want consumers to make?

2. Interview a member of a specific occupation (for example, carpenters, waiters, foresters, pharmacists, truckers, bankers), and make a list of jargon terms associated with the job. Discuss your list with a classmate. How many terms do you know? Which terms are unfamiliar?

3. Select a group that has been put down by language usage. This may include women, specific ethnic groups, religious groups, or groups with nondominant lifestyles. Discuss some of the terms that outsiders have used to label these group members. Then if you know them, discuss the labels the group places on itself. Talk about how a speaker should use language sensitively in respect to this specific group.

4. Find a speech by a Native American or speaker from another culture. W. C. Vanderwerth's book *Indian Oratory* (University of Oklahoma Press, 1971) is a good source for historical Native-American oratory. Try to locate the metaphors and similes in it. Note the differences, if any, between the metaphors of that culture and your own.

5. Study Bob Pettit's speech "Who/What Would You Want in Your Band? Or, 'Why Did I Spend 25 Years Playing Drums?'" at the end of this chapter. Note the vivid use of language in the speech.

6. When (if ever) might you use an interpreter in the future? When might you listen to a speech delivered with the assistance of an interpreter? (Consider speeches you might watch on television.) When (if ever) might you speak in a second language? When might you listen to a speaker who is presenting a speech in a second language?

Key Terms

"voice"
languages
words
denotative meanings
ambiguous words
connotative meanings
dialect
Standard English
jargon

naming
epithets
euphemism
ageist language
sexist language
malaprop
verbiage
concrete words
vague words
alliteration
rhyme
repetition
personification
hyperbole
metaphor
simile
archetypal symbols
interpreters

Notes

1. Poulakos, J. (1990, Spring). Hegel's reception of the sophists. *Western Journal of Speech Communication, 54,* 160–171.
2. Kocabiyik, F. (1989, April 6). Teeth extracted by Methodists. *Dalhousie Gazette,* p. 9.
3. This speech is from Chaucer, G. The wife of Bath. In A. K. Hieatt & C. Hieatt (Eds.), *Canterbury Tales* (p. 208). New York: Bantam.
4. Gozzi, R. (1990). *New words and a changing American culture.* Columbia, SC: University of South Carolina Press.
5. Ibid.
6. Sherwood, J. D. (1960). *Discourse of reason: A brief handbook of semantics and logic.* New York: Harper & Row.
7. *Webster's seventh new collegiate dictionary.* (p. 728). (1967). Springfield, MA: G. & C. Merriam Co.
8. Ibid.
9. Trudgill, P. (1983). *Sociolinguistics: An introduction to language and society.* New York: Penguin. See also Labov, W. (1972). *Sociolinguistic patterns.* Philadelphia: University of Pennsylvania Press.
10. Safire, W. (1993, April 11). Health care provider, heal thyself. *The New York Times Magazine,* p. 12.
11. Information on the Hispanic–Latino naming debate can be found in Gonzalez, D. (1992, November 15). What's the problem with "Hispanic"? Just ask a "Latino." *The New York Times,* sec. 4. p. 4, and de la Garza, R., et. al. (1992). *Latino voices: Mexican, Puerto Rican and Cuban perspectives on American politics.* Boulder, CO: Westview Press.
12. J. Ray & C. Badle, hosts of a "queer talk" call-in radio show made this statement on February 3, 1993. WABC, New York.
13. Beard, H., & Cerf, C. (1992, July 14). P.C. on the campaign trail. *The New York Times,* p. A25, and Kakutani, M. (1993, January 31). The word police. *The New York Times,* Sec. 9, pp. 1, 9. G. K. Chesterton is responsible for "social subtraction."
14. Friemuth, V. S., & Jamieson, K. (1979). *Communicating with the elderly: Shattering stereotypes.* Urbana, IL: Eric Clearinghouse on Reading and Communication Skills.
15. Mura, S., & Waggenspack, B. (1983). Linguistic sexism: A rhetorical perspective. In J. L. Golden, G. F. Berquist, & W. F. Coleman. *The rhetoric of western thought,* 3rd ed. (pp. 251–260). Dubuque: Kendall-Hunt.
16. Winans, J. A. (1938). *Speechmaking.* New York: D. Appleton-Century Co.
17. Reagan, R. (1986, January 31). Memorial service for the crew of the space shuttle *Challenger.* Houston, Texas.
18. Archambault, D. (1992, May 1). Columbus plus 500 years: Whither the American Indian? *Vital Speeches of the Day, 58,* 491–493.
19. Bush, G. (1992, November 8). Transcript of President Bush's radio address on his defeat at the polls. *The New York Times,* p. A26.
20. Seattle. (1853, 1971). The Indian's night promises to be dark. From *Indian oratory: Famous speeches by noted Indian chieftains* (pp. 118–122), by W. C. Vanderwerth. Copyright 1971 by the University of Oklahoma Press.
21. Secretary Shalala made these remarks on MacNeil-Lehrer News Hour. (February 25, 1993). New York: WNET.

22. Shaw, B. (1993, February 1). An attitude about women: Democracy is not a smooth sauce. *Vital Speeches of the Day, 59*, 245–247.

23. The panelist appeared on MacNeil-Lehrer News Hour. (1993, June 7). WLIW. Garden City, New York.

24. Seattle. (1853, 1971). The Indian's night promises to be dark. From *Indian oratory: Famous speeches by noted Indian chieftains* (pp. 118–122), by W. C. Vanderwerth. Copyright 1971 by the University of Oklahoma Press.

25. Michael Osborne has written extensively on metaphor and archetypal symbols. See (1967). Archetypal metaphor in rhetoric: The light-dark family. *Quarterly Journal of Speech, 53*, 115–126,

and (1977). The evolution of the archetypal sea in rhetoric and poetic. *Quarterly Journal of Speech, 63*, 347–363.

26. Many of these suggestions come from four sources: Thiederman, S. (1991). *Profiting in American multicultural marketplaces: How to do business across cultural lines.* New York: Lexington Books; (1991). *Bridging cultural barriers for corporate success: How to manage the multicultural workforce.* New York: Lexington Books; Lustig, M. W., & Koester, J. (1993). *Intercultural competence: Interpersonal communication across cultures.* New York: HarperCollins College Publishers; Simons, G. F., Vazquez, C., & Harris, P. R. *Transcultural leadership: Empowering the diverse workforce.* Houston: Gulf Publishing Company.

Delivery

12

At the end of this chapter, you should be able to

- Describe how personal appearance, clothing, and accessories can affect public speaking
- List three functions of gestures, and explain how each can be used in public speaking
- Understand how eye contact makes a difference in your delivery
- Describe elements of your voice that influence your message
- List four methods of delivery
- Understand how you can use time to make your presentations more effective
- Discuss ways to use technology effectively in speech delivery

Note

In Chapter 1, communica-
tion theorist Helmut
Geissner notes that com-
munication must be *embodied* or delivered by a
speaker. This chapter fo-
cuses on the canon of de-
livery by emphasizing nonverbal communication
systems that include per-
sonal appearance, gestures,
eye contact, use of the
voice, and use of time.

Cross Reference

Most students have more
anxiety about delivery than
any other aspect of speechmaking. Understanding
and using nonverbal ele-
ments effectively in de-
livering the speech
will increase students'
competence.

For Further Reading

E. Goffman. (1959). *The
presentation of self in everyday
life.* Garden City, NY:
Doubleday Anchor Books.

After Bill Clinton gave his 1993 inaugural address, a group of professional speech writers[1] graded the new president's performance. William Safire, who wrote speeches for Richard Nixon, graded it a B for content and a B+ for delivery. Commentator Elizabeth Drew gave it a B+, saying that giving a short speech was no small achievement for Mr. Clinton, who "blew other speeches" in the past because of length. Peggy Noonan, a chief writer for Ronald Reagan and George Bush, argued that people will remember the overall image President Clinton presented more than the words of the address. His "telegenic quality" and the way he "acted his speech" portrayed Mr. Clinton as cool and in control, seemingly "at ease" as president. As you can see, all three commentators remarked not only on the actual words of the speech but also on his skillful delivery.

Delivery—the way you perform your speech—creates anxiety for beginning speakers. When you stand in front of a group, you are the object of listener attention, and audience members are forming impressions of you. In addition, listeners infer meaning, not only from your words and ideas but also from the nonverbal messages you send. As a result, the way you use your voice, your gestures and mannerisms, even your clothing contribute to your entire message.

Remember from Chapter 4 that competence involves the motivation as well as the knowledge and the skills you need to communicate in a personally satisfying and socially appropriate way. Most people are motivated to leave a positive impression and to avoid leaving negative images of themselves as they deliver their speeches. However, beginning speakers often feel less confident that they have the knowledge and skills to do so. If you are in this category, you need to understand and competently manage your nonverbal messages as well as your verbal ones.

The concept of *impression management* is derived from Erving Goffman's influential book, *The Presentation of Self in Everyday Life.*[2] Goffman compares an individual's self-presentation to a dramatic stage performance in which speakers attempt to create and maintain impressions within their listeners as if they were on a stage, using a combination of props and personal mannerisms to accomplish this. Peggy Noonan's evaluation of President Clinton's inaugural address reflected stage terminology when she spoke of him "acting" his speech.

In the last three decades, numerous scholars have undertaken a great deal of research into nonverbal communication.[3] This chapter presents some of their findings in the categories of nonverbal communication that affect public speaking in the United States. It begins with the speaker's personal appearance, movements, voice variation, and uses of time that enhance or detract from the verbal message. The chapter looks at four major types of delivery. It then concludes with a discussion of technology that aids delivery.

Personal Appearance

Teaching Idea

Play a video or several clips of student speeches with the sound turned off. If possible, have one student reading, another using nervous gestures. Have the class look only at the nonverbal aspects of delivery. Discuss how dress, eye contact, gestures, and so on create an impression of the speaker. Then discuss elements of delivery that lead to effectiveness. Throughout the chapter, refer to this video.

Listeners form impressions of you based on the way you look. Some of the elements of your personal appearance are relatively permanent; however, many more are changeable, and as you learn to use your appearance to create a positive impression, your delivery will be more effective. Three important areas include your physical appearance, your clothing, and your accessories.

Physical Appearance

The way you look—the body that is yours—has several relatively permanent features that disclose information about you. As you take the platform to speak, listeners can observe your physical features and infer your sex, general age range, racial background, height, weight, and body type. Sometimes audiences respond to personal appearance in a stereotypical manner. As a result, they may discount messages given by speakers who are very much younger than themselves. Other audiences similarly pay less attention to the speeches of women or of people from other cultural groups.

Many people have one or more physical features or conditions that make them reluctant to speak publicly. These include crooked teeth, visible birthmarks, above-average or below-average weight or height, poor eyesight, or the use of canes or wheelchairs. Because U.S. society is saturated with images of physically perfect bodies, any perceived difference often causes beginning speakers to feel anxious—as if they are in the limelight and everyone is scrutinizing them. Although it is true that people do see your features, it is generally not true that they spend the entire speech focusing on them. If you worry about your appearance, one of your best strategies is to have an interesting topic and a good opening statement that draws people's attention to your subject rather than to your looks.

Regardless of your looks, you can pay special attention to grooming. In U.S. culture, neatness and cleanliness are sometimes as significant as natural beauty; in fact, a common proverb, "Cleanliness is next to godliness," exemplifies this. Further, as we will see, social attractiveness is enhanced by other nonverbal variables such as smiling and gesturing appropriately. Moreover, physical characteristics are not the only thing your listeners see. The clothing and accessories you choose are part of your total presentation of yourself.

Clothing

The way you dress is important in creating an impression—either positive or negative. Author John Molloy[4] made a great deal of money telling people that what they wore made a difference in the way other people perceived them. This principle applies to public speaking contexts where listeners use your clothing and accessories to make judgments about you.[5]

How you look and dress makes a big difference in how your audience responds to you. Evaluate ways that differences in this speaker's grooming, clothing, and accessories might affect the impressions he makes on his listeners.

Before you speak, find out the norms for the occasion. For instance, in the future, if you give a presentation at an organization that is unfamiliar to you, find out if members generally dress in tailored or informal fashions. In your classroom, select clothing that is appropriate to the class—and perhaps slightly more formal than normal. Instead of a sweatshirt with writing on it, many students substitute plain pullover sweaters on speech day. Instead of a favorite baseball cap turned backward, they speak with a bare head. Avoid clothing that distracts from the speech. Clothing that is too tight or that shows a bare midriff or bare legs is less appropriate than more conservative wear.

Teaching Idea

Exercise 2 discusses the notion of putting on a front—intentionally or unintentionally. Have students discuss Saddam Hussein, then think of other speakers who put on a front. Discuss the ethics of a speaker who intentionally calculates his or her use of nonverbal elements in order to manipulate appearances. When might a calculated "front" be wrong? Morally neutral? Good?

Accessories

Accessories are the objects you carry or add to your clothing that contribute to the overall impression you create. They include items such as jewelry, corsages or boutonnieres, glasses, briefcases, notebooks or folders. Imagine the different impressions an audience gets from a speaker who carries a leather briefcase in which her notes are kept and a speaker who carries a pile of bulging manila folders from which she takes a sheaf of notes. The basic rule applying to accessories is that they be simple and appropriate so that they do not detract from your speech.

See Box 12.1 for a look at the ethical dimensions of personal appearance.

BOX 12.1

Ethical Considerations[6]

As with every aspect of speechmaking, there is an ethical dimension involved in impression management because impressions can be manipulated. Speakers who present verbal and nonverbal messages that they themselves believe are said to be *sincere*. In contrast, speakers can make strategic choices to control nonverbal messages with the intention of creating false or misleading impressions. They themselves do not believe the messages they send, and when they attempt to create a false image, they are said to be *cynical*.

You can probably think of many public personalities who try to appear genuinely interested in people when they only want the audience's time, money, or votes. Lawyers now advise their clients very carefully on dress and grooming; they bring in coaches to guide them in selecting clothing, mannerisms, and nonverbal techniques that will create an impression of innocence in jury members. This may be appropriate if the client is indeed innocent; however, if the client is guilty, the false impression is misleading.

KEY CONCEPT ## Personal Appearance

Physical appearance Physical appearance is the way your body looks, including hair, weight, sex, height. Regardless of your actual features, good grooming is a must.

Clothing Clothing should be appropriate and not draw undue attention that detracts from the speech itself.

Accessories Accessories include such things as jewelry, glasses, and briefcases; they should be simple and appropriate.

Personal Mannerisms

Teaching Idea

Show a video, "Communication: The Nonverbal Agenda." If your campus media library does not have this video, you can order it through CRM/McGraw Hill, 2233 Faraday Avenue, Carlsbad, CA 92008.

Your manner—or the way you speak, move, and look at the audience—is an area of nonverbal communication over which you have a great deal of control. Your personal mannerisms work in unison with your appearance to create an overall impression. Mannerisms that we discuss in this section include gestures and eye contact.

Gestures

The study of body movements or gestures is a field of research popularized in Julius Fast's best-selling book *Body Language*.[7] Bodily movements range from large motions, such as posture, walking, and gesturing, to very small motions, such as raising one eyebrow. Two scholars who extensively studied body language were Paul Ekman and W. V. Friesen.[8] They devised a widely used system to classify the functions of gestures, which include emblems, illustrators, and adaptors.

Teaching Idea

Have students demonstrate a variety of emblems. Then have them share what they know about different meanings of emblems in different cultures. Discuss problems that might result from cultural differences in meaning.

Emblems are gestures that stand for words or ideas. You occasionally use them in public speaking, as when you hold up a hand to cut off applause. Your forefinger to your lips in a "sh-h-h-h" gesture functions in the same way. Emblems vary from culture to culture. For instance, Ethiopians put one forefinger to their lips when silencing a child, but they use four fingers when they are communicating with adults. The sign that stands for "A-OK" in this country refers to money in Japan.[9] It is an obscene gesture in some Latin American countries. Imagine Richard Nixon's blunder when he exited a plane in Latin America and responded to a reporter's question, "How was the trip?" by signaling "A-OK."

In addition to emblems that stand for words, some gestures simply illustrate or add emphasis to your words, and most experienced public speakers use them in their speaking. These *illustrators* function in a variety of ways. Probably the most common are those you use to accent words or phrases such as, "Boot camp discipline for juvenile offenders appeals to the public's desire to *do* [hand and arm extended outward] something about crime." In addition, you can illustrate spatial relationships, as when you say, "It is about *this* [extend your hands to show the distance] wide." Or you can actually point to objects, saying, "Look at *this* [point to the area on the map] part of the ocean."

Teaching Idea

Demonstrate some of these distracting adaptors during your discussion of adaptors. That is, tap your pencil against a desk, pull on your ear, ruffle your hair, fold your arms, jingle your keys, and so on.

An entire group of actions, called *adaptors*, satisfy your physical or psychological needs—such as the need to release stress or to protect yourself against potential danger. There are three kinds of adaptors. *Self-adaptors* are those in which you touch yourself. If you fidget with your hair, lick your lips, scratch your face, or rub your hands together during your speeches, you are adapting to stress by using a self-adaptor. You use *object adaptors* when you play with your keys or jingle change in your pocket, pull at necklaces or earrings, twist a ring, tap your pencils or note cards. Finally, *alter-adaptors* are gestures you use in relation to the audience. For instance, if you fold your arms across your chest during intense questioning, you may be subconsciously protecting yourself against the perceived psychological threat of the questioner. Since adaptors indicate anxiety or other stresses, especially when they are seen as nervous mannerisms, strive to eliminate them.

Eye Contact

One of the most important aspects of delivery is looking at the audience—making eye contact with your listeners. In U.S. culture, looking at someone is important in communicating trustworthiness and honesty. The cultural phrase "Look me in the eye and say that" is partly premised on the notion that someone will not tell a lie if he or she is looking directly at you. Eye contact is also a

Although cultures differ in the amount of eye contact that is appropriate, in the United States it is important to engage your audience directly. Think of how you would respond if this speaker gave his entire speech looking in the direction shown in each picture.

Teaching Idea

It is often difficult for students to make eye contact with the entire class. Some instructors have every student wordlessly stand at the front of the class and look at the audience straight ahead of them, then to the right and to the left.

way of communicating that you are friendly with another person. In interpersonal relationships, for instance, one person who avoids the other's gaze signals that he or she is not interested in developing a relationship.

In contrast, Japanese communicators do not use as much direct eye contact as do U.S. communicators. It is not unusual to see downcast or closed eyes at a meeting or a conference; within Japanese culture, this demonstrates attentiveness and agreement rather than rejection, indifference, or disagreement. Nigerians as well as Puerto Ricans consider it disrespectful to make prolonged eye contact with superiors.[10]

Because eye contact is associated with honesty and friendliness in this culture, it is important to look at your audience during your classroom speeches. This is one of the hardest things for many beginning speakers to do. They often want to look at their notes. If they raise their eyes, they look at the desk tops in the front row, at the back wall, or out the window. All these glances may communicate that they are nervous and uncomfortable. To avoid this, look around the room in at least three general directions: at the listeners directly in front of you, those to the left, and those to the right. In most rooms, because of peripheral vision, you can still keep most listeners within your vision as you change the direction of your gaze.

Finally, look at various people within the room—not just at one or two. Some speakers make more eye contact with audience members they see as more powerful. As a result, many students make more eye contact with the instructor than with students. Other speakers look at men more than at women. To illustrate, as part of a job application process, one would-be professor addressed a group of faculty members. During his speech, he made noticeably more eye contact with the males on the faculty than with the female professors—largely ignoring the female department chair during his presentation. Needless to say, he was not hired.

KEY CONCEPT **Personal Mannerisms**

Gestures Gestures are communicative bodily movements.

Emblems stand for words or ideas.

Illustrators add emphasis to words or illustrate spatial relationships.

Adaptors satisfy physical or psychological needs such as stress release; they indicate nervousness.

Eye contact In U.S. culture, eye contact signals trustworthiness and willingness to engage in a relationship.

Your Voice

Teaching Idea

Use examples from popular culture such as television and movies. Have students think of voices that reveal both positive and negative characteristics, for example, the character Fran Fein on the sitcom "The Nanny," Al Bundy's voice on "Married . . . with Children," Urkel on "Family Matters." Contrast them with Tom Brokaw, Connie Chung, Lauren Bacall (or another woman with a husky voice).

When close friends call on the telephone, you recognize their voices instantly because of distinctive vocal features. Even without seeing a speaker—as happens when you hear someone on the radio—you can distinguish voices of young speakers from those of elderly speakers, males from females, southerners from New Yorkers, native speakers of English from those for whom English is a second language. Moreover, by using vocalic indicators, you can often detect moods such as boredom, hostility, or enthusiasm.

As you know, a great deal of meaning lies, not only in words, but in your tone of voice, rising or falling inflection, and stressed syllables. For instance, in a recent movie, a major character is accused of shooting a clerk in a convenience store. When the sheriff asks, "Why did you shoot the clerk?" the suspect responds, "I *shot* the clerk??" (pause) "*I* shot the clerk??!!" At his trial, the sheriff testifies that the accused confessed twice, clearly saying, "I shot the clerk." The sheriff's inflection and stress pattern indicate a declarative statement, but the suspect's rising voice inflection and the words he stresses indicate that he is asking a question. In this instance, as in many others, the vocal cues as well as the literal words carry meaning.

Knowing about several important aspects of vocal behaviors will help you be a better public speaker: pronunciation, vocal cues, and pausing.

Pronunciation

As Chapter 6 indicated, pronunciation, the actual way you say words, has several aspects. One is the *articulation* of individual sounds such as "*th*is" instead of "*d*is" or "*bir*d" instead of "*bee*rd." The second is the *stress* you place on the syllables— "poe-LEESE" (police) instead of "POE-leese" or "AT-mos-phere" instead of

Teaching Idea

If many of your students mispronounce words, there is a transparency, "Problem Words," in the Instructor's Manual you can use.

"at-MOS-phere." Sometimes speakers reverse sounds—saying "aks" instead of "ask." Others change both articulation and stress. For example, they pronounce "comparable" as "come-PARE-uh-bul" rather than the standard pronunciation of "COM-purr-uh-bul," and "potpourri" becomes "pot-PORE-ee" instead of the accepted pronunciation of "poe-per-EE." When you are in doubt about the pronunciation of a word, consult a dictionary. You will find that some words such as "status" have two acceptable pronunciations—"STAY-tus" and "STATT-us." When the dictionary provides two variations, the first is considered preferable.

Differences in pronunciation often indicate social status. This is the premise for the movie *My Fair Lady*. Eliza Doolittle *says* the same words as the professor, but her pronunciation marks her as an uneducated member of the lower class. Professor Higgins takes her on as a project. His intention is to change her pronunciation (and some other nonverbal variables, such as dress and grooming) and to pass her off as a higher-class woman in order to improve her job prospects. In the turning point of the film, Eliza's "The RINE in SPINE falls MINELY in the PLINE" is transformed to match the professor's more standard pronunciation, "The rain in Spain falls mainly in the plain." She ends up at a society ball where she passes for a Hungarian princess.

Cross Reference

Chapters 4, 11, and 12 all deal with language, accents, and communicative competence.

In addition to social status, pronunciation can indicate regional origin or ethnicity. There are regional variations in the *extent* to which sounds are held. Southern speakers often extend sounds, resulting in the "southern drawl." Bostonians are famous for adding an "r" at the end of a word such as *Cuba*. Consequently, President John Kennedy, a native of Boston, worried about U.S. relations with "Cuber." In addition, speakers from different regions sometimes articulate sounds differently. Many people from Brooklyn say "oi" instead of "er," with the result that "thoity" means "thirty." Ethnic dialects such as Black English also have distinct articulation and stress patterns.

Many students in pluralistic classrooms are not native speakers of English. They speak with accents that reflect the articulation and stress patterns of their first language. This is often a source of anxiety to them as they consider standing in front of a classroom speaking in their second (or third) language to native speakers of English. However, in a multicultural world, with more voices speaking in public, there are bound to be accents, and as the world continues to shrink as a result of increased travel and immigration, there will be even more in the future. Unfortunately, people judge one another on the basis of regional and ethnic dialects and accents. (See the letter in Box 12.2 that argues for acceptance of a variety of accents.)

Vocal Cues

Teaching Idea

Activity 11.1 in the Instructor's Manual is an exercise for vocal variety.

Around 330 B.C., Aristotle wrote and lectured on the importance of delivery in creating the right impressions on listeners. The three important components of voice discussed in this excerpt from his text *Rhetoric* continue to be included in discussions of public speaking to this day.

BOX 12.2

Immigrants, Don't Be in Such a Hurry to Shed Your Accents[11]

This letter to the editor appeared in *The New York Times,* March 21, 1993.

To the Editor:

You report that immigrants in New York City are turning to speech classes to reduce the sting of discrimination against them based on accent. . . . I'd like to tell all my fellow immigrants taking accent-reduction classes: As long as you speak fluent and comprehensible English, don't waste your money on artificially removing your accent.

I am fortunate enough to be one of the linguistically gifted. I even acquired an American accent before I left China for the United States five years ago. From the day I set foot on this continent till now, the praise of my English has never ceased. What most people single out is that I have no, or very little accent.

However, I know I *do* have an accent, which some experts say is Chinese and some say British (I had British teachers for the first three years I studied English.) Whether it's Chinese or British or maybe a combination, I intend to keep it because it belongs to me.

I want to speak and write grammatically flawless English, but I have no desire to equip myself with a perfect American accent. I always feel it is a pity when I hear Asian-looking youngsters speak indigenous English, especially with a typical American teen-ager pattern of speech. I have always wished they had an accent.

America is probably the largest place for accents in English because the entire nation is composed of immigrants from different areas of the world. This country is built on accents. Accent is one of the most conspicuous symbols of what makes America the free and prosperous land its own people are proud of and other people long to live in.

I work in an urban institution where accents are an integral part of my job: students, faculty and staff come from ethnically diverse backgrounds. Hearing accents confirms for me every day that the college is fulfilling its goal to offer education to a multicultural population.

I wonder what accent my fellow immigrants should obtain after getting rid of their own: a New York accent? a Boston accent? Brooklyn? Texas? California? Or go after President Clinton's accent?

Fellow immigrants, don't worry about the way you speak until Peter Jennings eliminates his Canadian accent.

YanHong Krompacky
Assistant Director of Graduate Studies
Jersey City State College

Our next subject will be the style of expression. For it is not enough to know what *we ought to say; we must also say it* as *we ought; much help is thus afforded towards producing the right impression of a speech. . . . It is, essentially, a matter of the right management of the voice to express the various emotions—of speaking loudly, softly, or between the two; of high, low, or intermediate pitch; of the various rhythms that suit various subjects. These are the three things—volume of sound, modulation of pitch, and rhythm—that a speaker bears in mind.*[12]

Teaching Idea

Read the letter in Box 12.2 together, and discuss the value of accents. Link Ms. Krompacky's defense of accents to cultural values as discussed in Chapter 3. What does accented speech say about the core values of the United States? (Hint: opportunity for all, freedom, individuality.)

Modern researchers continue to examine the impressions that listeners receive through vocal variations. Several studies[13] have concluded that people associate personality traits with vocal characteristics. Here are just a few associations that listeners make.

Vocal Cues	Associated Traits
Loud and fast speakers	Self-sufficient, resourceful, dynamic
Loud and slow speakers	Aggressive, competitive, confident
Soft and fast speakers	Enthusiastic, adventuresome, confident, composed under stress
Soft and slow speakers	Competitive, enthusiastic, benevolent

Researchers have also examined the relationship between speakers' voices and their ethos or credibility. Various studies show that faster speaking is linked to traits of competence such as intelligence, objectivity, and knowledgeability. A faster rate is similarly related to perceptions of dominance and dynamism as well as high sociability (for males). Other studies link a moderate rate to perceptions of composure, honesty, people-orientation, and other benevolent traits.

For Further Reading

J. K. Burgoon and T. J. Saine. (1978). *The unspoken dialogue: An introduction to nonverbal communication.* Boston: Houghton Mifflin; G. B. Ray. (1986). Vocally cued personality prototypes: An implicit personality theory approach. *Communication Monographs,* 53(3), 266–276.

Pausing

A final aspect of vocalics is your use of pauses. Pauses can be effective, or they can be embarrassing—both to you and your listeners. Effective pauses are intentional; that is, you purposely pause between major ideas, or you give your audience a few seconds to contemplate a difficult idea. For example, at the end of the body of the speech, you might pause slightly, move one step backward, then say, "In conclusion . . ." Your pause functions to signal a separation in your thoughts. In contrast, ineffective pauses are not intentional; they disrupt your fluency and sometimes signal that you have lost your train of thought. Obviously, you strive to eliminate them, if possible.

Unfilled pauses are silent; *filled* pauses are also called *vocalized* pauses. This means that, instead of silence, you make an "uh" or "um" sound. Beginning public speakers as well as many professionals use vocalized pauses. However, too many "ums" can distract listeners, and it is advisable to eliminate as many of them as you can.

Teaching Idea

Exercise 3 is appropriate here. Have students write their own ads, or use Activity 11.1 in the Instructor's Manual. Have volunteers read one of the ads aloud. Discuss how the speaker uses his or her voice to contribute to the overall message.

Scholars who have studied the question of what makes good delivery have identified two different styles of speaking. The *confident speaking style* has vocal variety, fluency, good use of gestures, and eye contact. The *conversational style* is calmer, slower, softer, and less intense; it also includes good eye contact and use of gestures. Speakers who use this style rate high on trustworthiness, honesty, sociability, likeableness, and professionalism. Listeners associate both styles with persuasiveness in speaking.

The Makeover

In the 1992 election, Democratic candidate Paul Tsongas originally trailed the others. He did not speak well on television. His voice, which was rather high-pitched and nasal, dropped at the end of sentences. Then he agreed to seek guidance from a speech coach, who gave him tips on delivery. He took voice lessons and bought two new suits. He even wore glasses in some televised debates though his eyesight is normal. (His consultants thought they improved his image.) His approval ratings went up for a while although he later dropped out of the race because of lack of funds.[14]

Questions

1. What do you think of Mr. Tsongas's makeover? The glasses? The voice lessons? What difference does it make if a candidate has a "funny" voice? What qualities are im-portant in a president? How does presidential image matter?

2. On MTV's campaign coverage, young people were asked their impression of Mr. Tsongas. One responded, "Uh, uh, old." What difference does age make?

3. President William Taft (1909–1914) weighed around 300 pounds. He later became Chief Justice of the Supreme Court. Could he be elected today? Why or why not? Is this good or bad?

4. Could Abraham Lincoln—with his looks and mannerisms—be elected if he ran for president in a television-dominated society? Why or why not?

5. What do you think about judging people's abilities based on the way they present themselves?

Teaching Idea

Use exercise 4. Arrange to have students videotaped.

As discussed here, there are many ways you can be effective as a speaker. Don't worry if you are not dynamic at this point in your speaking career. Work on creating a style of speaking that is best for you, using personal appearance, personal mannerisms, and your voice to your advantage.

KEY CONCEPT   Your Voice

Case Study

If possible, show Mr. Tsongas speaking—before and after his makeover. For question 5 ask if we take the words of a homeless person seriously. What about an uneducated person whose language is nonstandard?

Pronunciation Pronunciation is the actual way you say words—the articulation, stress, order of sounds, and extent you hold the sounds. Pronunciation is often linked to social status, and people unfortunately judge accents.

Vocal cues Vocal cues include such elements as rate and volume.

Pausing Pausing can be intentional and effective; ineffective pauses disrupt your fluency. Unfilled pauses are silent, whereas vocalized pauses are filled with an "um" sound.

Although cultural groups vary in their expectations regarding the speaker's use of time, in the dominant culture your audience expects you to show up, begin speaking, and stop within appropriate time limits.

Use of Time

For Further Reading

E. T. Hall. (1984). *The dance of life: The other dimension of time.* Garden City, NY: Anchor Press/Doubleday.

Note

Time is important in our culture. People who learn to speak within time limits are generally more effective than those who consistently violate time norms.

Time is a major message system that affects public speaking.[15] In U.S. culture, time is perceived as a line that is cut into segments, each lasting a specific duration, with specific activities assigned to each.

Public speaking occurs within this linear concept of time. All across the country, people gather for speeches at scheduled times, and they expect speakers to limit their remarks to fit into the time frame. The relative formality or informality of the speech setting affects how rigidly time norms are upheld. In more formal, structured events requiring strict scheduling, time matters, and speakers are sometimes cut off if they go overtime. This is especially true in a formal debate, where debaters are allotted a specific amount of time before they must yield the floor to the opposition. Media speeches such as radio and television messages must also fit within precise time limits. You have probably seen a reporter or interviewer cut off speakers, not when they are through, but when their time runs out.

Your public speaking class reflects these cultural concepts of time. Your speeches are scheduled for specific days, and each usually has an assigned time limit—generally with a short built-in plus or minus factor. Your instructor may even make timing a part of your grade. Consequently, if you do not appear on your assigned day ready to speak, or if your speeches run much over the time limit, your grade may be lowered.

 As you consider time norms, remember that there are regional and co-cultural group variations within the United States and that many other cultures in the world are far less concerned that events proceed according to rigid time schedules. In these settings, speakers begin when enough listeners have gathered

Teaching Idea

If you live in a culturally diverse community, have students do an interview, as suggested in exercise 1. They can record the information in a journal entry, or they can report their findings during a class discussion.

Cross Reference

Emphasize the idea of cultural appropriateness. What is appropriate in American classrooms may be inappropriate in Brazil or Jordan.

and when everything is set; they finish when they are through—not when time runs out.

Compare your class to the following classroom in Brazil[16] where an American professor taught psychology. His course was scheduled to run from 10:00 to 12:00. Of course, Professor Levine began close to 10:00. However, students arrived as late as 11:00 without signs of concern or apology. At 12:15, they were still in the classroom, asking questions. Finally, at 12:30, Professor Levine ended the class and left. The students, however, seemed more than willing to stay even longer.

If you are from a culture that has less rigid time expectations, you will have to adjust to U.S. norms when you speak in the classroom and in the institutions of the mainstream culture. One student from Jordan did not understand this, and he was angry when his instructor graded him down for the length of his speech.

KEY CONCEPT   ## Use of Time

In public speaking, time is especially important in two major ways: appearing on schedule and keeping your speech within appropriate limits.

Types of Delivery

Teaching Idea

If you wish to use the lecture format when discussing types of delivery, there is a transparency listing types of delivery in the Instructor's Manual.

Students present their speeches in four different ways. A few forget that they are scheduled to speak, so they just get up and talk. Some memorize their speeches, whereas others read theirs. The final group takes note cards to the podium. They refer to these cards when necessary, but most of the time, they engage their listeners in eye contact. These students demonstrate the four major types of delivery that public speakers have used over the centuries: impromptu, memorized, manuscript, and extemporaneous.

Impromptu

The type of delivery that requires the least amount of preparation and rehearsal is the impromptu style. Impromptu speeches are given spur of the moment, meaning that speakers do not prepare them in advance, though in a sense, their entire life—their knowledge and experience—prepares them for impromptu speaking. Politicians, educators, business leaders, and other public figures are often called on to "say a few words." You might give such a speech someday. For instance, if you are ever called on at a wedding reception to come to the microphone and tell a funny story about the bride and groom, you will not have time to spend weeks in preparation. Instead, you will think quickly, walk to the front, and draw from your long experience with the couple to find material for your speech.

Time in the Classroom

Professor Brain consistently violates time norms. Sometimes she continues to lecture up to six minutes after the class is scheduled to end. At other times, she is late to class, then she shuffles papers and talks to students so that she does not actually start until about twenty minutes after the scheduled beginning. On occasion, she skips class entirely—with no note on the classroom door and no explanation the next day.

Questions

1. Would you stay when she is late? Why or why not? How often would you stay? How long? How would this make you feel?

2. How would you signal Professor Brain that her time is up and she should quit so that you can get to your next class?

3. What if she does not show for class and doesn't leave a message for anyone? What if it were your only class for the day and you had to make a real effort to get there?

4. Would it make a difference if she had a doctor's appointment that she had known about for two weeks? What if she had an emergency flat tire on the way to work? Would it make a difference if it were a sunny day and students saw her out for a drive in the country?

5. Are any of these behaviors grounds for some kind of administrative discipline? If so, what? Why?

6. What kind of end-of-the-course evaluation would you give her?

7. What can you learn from this that applies to your future occupation?

Case Study

Discuss students' emotional responses when professors are late. Are there ethical implications of being on time? That is, does the professor have any responsibility toward the class? Generalize this to other work settings. What should be their attitude toward their own punctuality when others are depending on them?

Most people, students included, shudder at the thought of standing in front of a group and speaking without preparation and rehearsal, especially if their performance will be rewarded or punished in some way—such as by a grade or a job evaluation. However, a few students "wing it," giving an impromptu speech when the professor has assigned a carefully prepared speech. It does not succeed.

Memorized

Memorized speeches used to be very common. In Roman times, for example, orators planned their speeches carefully, then memorized the exact words and phrases of their orations. As a result, they could give the same oration over and over. In many oral cultures also, tribal orators memorize the stories and legends of the tribe. This ensures that the exact stories will continue throughout succeeding generations.

However, you rarely hear memorized speeches in the offices, board rooms, churches, and clubs of contemporary societies. Consequently, it is not advisable to memorize your classroom speech. Regardless of advice to the contrary, some students think that memorizing the speech will help them overcome their fears. One international student wrote:

> *I think if I memorize the entire speech including the pauses, gestures, posture, etc., I will feel more comfortable delivering the speech and I will be less nervous.*

However, the opposite often happens. When they stand before the audience, beginning speakers often forget their memorized words. Some pause (ineffectively), look toward the ceiling, repeat the last phrase in a whisper, repeat the phrase aloud, then look at the instructor, who sometimes has their speech outline. When this happens, they end up quite embarrassed.

Cross Reference

Dialogic public speaking is a theme of this text.

Another drawback to a memorized speech is that it is generally not delivered in a conversational manner. Put simply, the speech sounds memorized, not natural. Rather than focusing on a dialogue with the audience, the speaker appears to be focusing on recalling the words of the speech.

Manuscript

When you write out your speech and read it to the audience, you are using manuscript delivery. On some occasions, manuscript delivery is acceptable. These are often very formal occasions, such as commencement exercises in which the speech will eventually be reprinted or saved in a historical archive. Further, you may use a manuscript if you speak on radio or television when exact timing is essential.

When you use manuscript delivery, type out your entire script in capital letters, using triple spacing on your typewriter or word processor. Then, go over the speech, using a highlighter or underlining the words you wish to accent. Make slashes where you wish to pause. Finally, practice the speech until you can read it in a natural, conversational manner, making as much eye contact with your audience as possible. Conversational delivery is absolutely essential because most people don't like to be read to, especially if the speaker doesn't pause or look up.

Although manuscript delivery is appropriate for some occasions, most people do not speak in such formal settings, nor do they appear on radio or television. Thus, manuscript delivery is not appropriate for most public speaking, including classroom speeches. The final type of delivery, extemporaneous, is the preferred mode for much public discourse. This is the method you will most commonly use in the classroom.

Extemporaneous

In contrast to impromptu speeches, you prepare extemporaneous speeches carefully in advance. However, you do not plan the exact wording of the speech. Instead, you outline your major ideas, and you use note cards with cue words

Note

Mr. Robinson is used as an example because he speaks every week. His preparation shows the value of deciding on a topic, collecting information, then preparing and rehearsing several times for the speech. It also shows the value of knowing the outline but not the exact wording of the speech.

during your delivery. To illustrate how a professional speaker prepares for extemporaneous speaking, reporter Bob Krauss[17] of *The Honolulu Advertiser* interviewed Ted Robinson, a well-known Honolulu clergyman, to discover how he prepares for the forty or more sermons he delivers annually.

> *Robinson confessed that he works all year long on his talks. Every summer he has a one-month study leave. During that time, he spends about two weeks collecting ideas and setting up separate file folders for forty different topics. Then throughout the year, he continues to add ideas to each file. Each week, he follows a similar procedure as he prepares for the following Sunday's speech:*

- *On* Wednesday *he pulls up a folder with the topic for the week, looks at the ideas he has collected, then spends his time narrowing his purpose.*

- *On* Thursday *he types up a tentative outline, admitting, "Often, the hardest part is to start. Sometimes it takes another day to jell."*

- *On* Friday *he enters his empty church, goes to the pulpit and preaches the sermon—twice. As he does, he rewrites, crosses out, changes, and omits ideas on his outline.*

- *On* Saturday *he follows the same procedure—two more times in an empty building. "I have to hear how it sounds. So I have to speak it." Finally, at 9:00 p.m. he sits down with a 5 x 8 file card, outlines the finalized speech on it, then memorizes the outline.*

- *On* Sunday *he reviews his outline and heads off to deliver his talk.*

Likewise, as you prepare to speak extemporaneously, begin the process of researching and organizing the speech well in advance of your speech date. Follow Mr. Robinson's example, and give yourself plenty of time to let the ideas jell. Write out your outline, and put the main ideas onto note cards (see Chapter 7). Then, practice, practice, practice—aloud, to your friends, as you drive, and so on. On the day of the speech, review your outline and your notes; then go to class with the confidence that comes from thorough preparation.

Of the four types of delivery, three—impromptu, manuscript, and extemporaneous—are used regularly in the United States. Each has its strengths and weaknesses. In general, extemporaneous delivery is most commonly used in public presentations, and it is the one you will use in most of your classroom speeches.

KEY CONCEPT   ## Types of Delivery

Impromptu These speeches are given spur of the moment with little advance preparation.

Memorized These speeches are learned by heart.

Manuscript These speeches are read from a script.

Extemporaneous With these speeches, ideas rather than exact words are carefully prepared in advance. Extemporaneous speeches are delivered by using note cards with cue words.

Using Technology in Delivery

Cross Reference

There is material on technology throughout the text.

Although it is unlikely that you will use advanced technical equipment in your classroom, most people who speak regularly in public use some form of technology at one time or another. Consequently, you may find it useful to know how to use some common equipment. We will conclude this chapter with a brief look at tips for using microphones and TelePrompTers in delivering your speech.

Adapting to a Microphone

Since the chances are relatively good that you will someday use a microphone to speak, it is important to know the types of microphones ("mikes") available to you and to understand how to use them well. There are two common types of mikes: fixed and portable.

Fixed microphones are attached to a podium or a stand. Although they project your voice adequately, they limit your movements, forcing you to stay within the pick-up range of the mike. Generally, fixed microphones have a short, flexible "neck" that you can adjust upward or downward or from side to side a few inches.

Portable microphones include hand-held versions (with cords or cordless), small clip mikes that attach to a collar or lapel, and lavaliere mikes that fasten around your neck by a thin cord. These all give you considerably more freedom to move around the room. However, the hand-held mike limits you slightly since you have only one hand free to gesture or handle notes.

No matter which microphone you use, test it before you speak, and ask the sound technician to make any necessary adjustments. Remember that each mike has its own pick-up range—the distance it can be held from your mouth, pick up the sound, and transmit it effectively. This is especially important to consider with a fixed mike. If you find the microphone is not projecting your voice well, move it toward you; do not bend toward it, assuming an unnatural posture. Speak in a conversational voice. Too much volume may distort your words, so step away from the mike if you intend to raise your voice. Finally, be careful not to touch or jar the microphone or mike stand, which can create intrusive and grating sounds.

Using a TelePrompTer

If you ever give a filmed speech, you may have an opportunity to use a TelePrompTer. When you work with a TelePrompTer, you do not have to worry about forgetting your speech, for this screen, located just beneath the

On formal speaking occasions, fixed microphones are common. Sound technicians adjust the mike to pick up each speaker's voice. This podium mike prevents the speaker from walking around as he speaks, but it allows him to gesture with both hands if he desires.

camera lens, projects your script line by line, allowing you to read it while looking directly at the camera. (Reading it is similar to reading the credit lines that unroll on your television screen at the end of a program.) During a rehearsal session, you will work with a technician who controls the speed of the lines so that the text unrolls at your speaking rate. The technician can even circle key words or underline phrases that you want to emphasize. Since this is a special form of manuscript delivery, practice reading so that your delivery sounds conversational.

KEY CONCEPT   ## Using Technology in Delivery

Adapting to a microphone You will probably use both fixed and portable microphones in the future. Test the mike in advance of the speech, and speak in a conversational manner.

Using a TelePrompTer These devices project your script onto a screen that you read during a videotaping session.

Summary

This chapter has discussed the ways that you perform or deliver your speeches. Its intention was to increase your knowledge of nonverbal elements of communication systems so that you can use them effectively to create positive impressions within your listeners. The notion that good speakers manage nonverbal aspects of delivery, affecting listeners' impressions, is at least as old as Aristotle—and he surely did not invent the idea. Modern scholars continue to conduct empirical studies, exploring specific aspects of speaker appearance, speaker mannerisms, and vocal cues that create positive or negative impressions.

You have the ability to make strategic choices in the way you dress, in your grooming, and in the accessories you use to communicate messages of competence. Your mannerisms—gestures, eye contact, and voice—are also important in creating impressions of dynamism, honesty, and other characteristics of ethos. As you make wise choices and learn to use nonverbal communication competently, your competence in public speaking increases correspondingly.

Finally, you may have the opportunity to use forms of technology as you present your speech. Probably the most common aid to delivery is the microphone, and it is important to know the types of mikes and use them effectively. In addition, if you present a videotaped speech, you will often be able to read your manuscript with the aid of a TelePrompTer.

As with all attempts to influence others, the attempt to manage impressions has ethical implications. Speakers who believe in both the verbal and nonverbal messages they are sending are said to be sincere. Those who are trying to create false or misleading impressions are termed cynical.

Questions and Exercises

1. Talk with a person from another cultural group regarding time limits on public speeches within his or her culture. Are they the same? How would you have to adapt if you ever spoke in that culture?

2. The combination of appearance and mannerisms form a "front." Whether intentional or unwitting, the front influences the way observers define and interpret the situation. With this in mind, why do some people appear to be something they are not? For instance, why did the Iraqis appear to be stronger than they were before the Gulf War (1991)? Why do some speakers appear to be competent or trustworthy, and you later discover they do not have these characteristics? What are the ethical implications of fronts? Have you ever tried to put on a front?

3. Demonstrate the type of vocal cues you would use if you were making an ad for:

- A used car dealership
- A perfume
- A vacation to the Caribbean
- A brand of cola

4. If possible, have one of your speeches videotaped, then watch yourself on video. List the gestures you use, noting when you use emblems, illustrators, or adaptors. Plan specific strategies to improve your gestures, eliminating those that create negative impressions and strengthening those that produce favorable impressions.

Watch the tape a second time, if possible. This time, evaluate your eye contact. Throughout your speech, notice the way you use your voice. Check for appropriate rate and volume. Also be alert for pauses, and count the number of "ums," if any. Discuss with a classmate how you can improve these nonverbal aspects of delivery.

If it is impossible to view yourself on video, work with a classmate who will specifically note your gestures, eye contact, and use of your voice; then discuss with that person ways that you can improve in these areas.

Key Terms

impression management
personal appearance
accessories
gestures
emblems
illustrators
adaptors
eye contact
articulation
stress
vocal cues
confident speaking style
conversational speaking style
unfilled pauses
filled (vocalized) pauses
time
impromptu delivery
memorized delivery
manuscript delivery
extemporaneous delivery
TelePrompTer

Notes

1. The panelists appeared on MacNeil-Lehrer News Hour. (1992, January 20). New York: WNET.

2. Goffman, E. (1959). *The presentation of self in everyday life*. Garden City, NY: Doubleday Anchor Books.

3. J. K. Burgoon, D. B. Buller, & W. G. Woodall's encyclopedic work is one of the best sources for a summary of significant research in almost every area of nonverbal communication. See Burgoon, et al. (1989). *Nonverbal communication: The unspoken dialogue*. New York: Harper & Row.

4. Molloy, J. T. (1976). *Dress for success*. New York: Warner Books.

5. Burgoon, et al. (1989). Op. cit.

6. See Goffman. (1959). Op. cit.

7. Fast, J. (1970). *Body language*. New York: Pocket Books.

8. Ekman, P., & Friesen, W. V. (1969). The repertoire of nonverbal behavior: Categories, origins, usage, and coding. *Semiotica, I*, 49–98.

9. Some cross-cultural differences in nonverbal communication can be found in Richmond, V. P., McCroskey, J. C., & Payne, S. K. (1991). *Nonverbal behavior in interpersonal relations* (2nd ed.). Englewood Cliffs, NJ: Prentice-Hall. The Nixon incident is reported in this text and in Burgoon, et al. (1989). Op. cit.

10. Richmond, et al. (1991). Op. cit.

11. Krompacky, Y. H. (1993, March 21). Immigrants, don't be in such a hurry to shed your accents. *The New York Times*, Sec. 4, p. 16. Reprinted by permission.

12. Aristotle. (1954, 1984). *Rhetoric* (Book III, lines 15–35). (Trans. W. R. Roberts). New York: Random House, Inc.

13. This research is summarized and discussed in Burgoon, et al. (1989). Op. cit. See also Ray, G. B. (1986). Vocally cued personality prototypes: An implicit personality theory approach. *Communication Monographs, 53*(3), 266–276.

14. DeWitt, K. (1992, January 29). Trying out a new way to deliver his message. *The New York Times*, p. A14.

15. For an extensive study of time, see Hall, E. T. (1973). *The silent language*. Garden City, NY: Anchor Press/Doubleday; Hall, E. T. (1983). *The dance of life: The other dimension of time*. Garden City, NY: Anchor Press/Doubleday. Also see Jaffe, C. I. (1990, February). "Would somebody please help me with math?" "No, it's time to go to recess." A paper presented to the Western States Communication Association, Phoenix, AZ.

16. The Brazilian case is cited in Burgoon, et al., (1989). Op. cit.

17. Krauss, B. (1993, March 28). Some secrets to a soulful, shining Sunday sermon. *The Honolulu Advertiser*, p. A3. Reprinted by permission of *The Honolulu Advertiser*.

Narrative

13

At the end of this chapter, you should be able to

- Recognize the importance of narrative in public communication
- Describe and give examples of four functions of narrative: to explain, to provide examples, to persuade, and to disclose possibilities
- List components of narratives
- Give guidelines for using language effectively in narratives
- Describe the infinity loop organizational pattern
- Identify the four parts of an exemplum
- Apply three tests for narrative reasoning

Note

Storytelling is important in all types of cultures, including oral, literate, and electronic. Stories can stand alone as speeches in themselves, or they can be part of larger speeches. Because of the importance of stories in every cultural tradition, this entire chapter discusses the functions of narratives and discusses ways to present narratives more effectively.

Teaching Idea

Have students identify times when they have heard a speaker who told only stories—whether a "life" story, myths, or another kind of narrative.

As Chapter 1 pointed out, storytellers in all cultures—oral cultures as well as electronic cultures—pass on their society's narratives, influencing what their listeners believe, what they value, and how they behave. As a result, we live in a "story shaped world."[1] Some cultural narratives are fictional; others recount the deeds of real people and real events. Some stand alone—they *are* the speech; others are portions of larger speeches. The scholar Roland Barthes states the importance of narrative in this way:[2]

> *The narratives of the world are numberless. . . . Narrative is present in every age, in every place, in every society; it begins with the very history of [humankind] and there nowhere is nor has been a people without narrative. All classes, all human groups, have their narratives, enjoyment of which is very often shared by [others] with different, even opposing, cultural backgrounds. . . . Narrative is international, transhistorical, transcultural: it is simply there, like life itself.*

Narratives can be a powerful form of reasoning that ordinary citizens as well as international leaders use effectively. The following list provides examples of governmental leaders as well as ordinary people who give narrative speeches:

- In a historic 1967 speech, the Israeli statesman Abba Eban addressed the United Nations General Assembly in order to present Israel's view of Arab–Israeli tensions that resulted in a six-day war. His entire speech was in the form of a narrative in which he chronicled the history of tension between the two groups.

- Dave Roever, a Vietnam War veteran who lost most of his face and his left arm as a result of a grenade explosion, tells a hushed auditorium full of high school students of the lessons he learned about life throughout his ordeal.

- Diane Wolkstein, New York City's official storyteller, collects global narratives that show how fictional characters from various cultural groups address life's challenges. She can recite more than 2,000 stories from memory, and she has recounted these tales for more than twenty-five years on summer Saturdays in Central Park.

Although these narratives are speeches in themselves, many other speakers use narratives only as part of larger speeches. Shorter narratives are most often found in the form of extended examples or as a series of detailed anecdotes that speakers string together to make their point. This chapter will give principles for using stories in both ways. After an overview of the importance of narrative in every culture, it will look at four functions of narrative: explanatory, exemplary, persuasive, and disclosing of possibilities. A discussion of the important components of stories includes two organizational patterns that are useful in narrative speeches. The chapter concludes by examining the tests for narrative reasoning.

The Importance of Public Narratives

For Further Reading

B. Wicker. (1975). *The story-shaped world: Fiction and metaphysics, some variations on a theme.* Notre Dame, IN: University of Notre Dame Press. A. MacIntyre. (1981). *After virtue: A study in moral reasoning* (2nd ed.). South Bend, IN: Notre Dame Press. W. R. Fisher. (1984). Narration as a human communication paradigm: The case of public moral argument. *Communication Monographs, 51,* 1–22. W. R. Fisher. (1985). The narrative paradigm: An elaboration. *Communication Monographs, 52,* 347–367.

Although the stories we tell in our public speeches sometimes seem insignificant, many scholars agree with Barthes that the telling of narratives is a fundamental characteristic of being human. Both the philosopher Alasdair MacIntyre and the communication scholar Walter Fisher, for example, claim that humans in action and practice are *essentially* storytelling animals.[3] Fisher even refers to humankind as *homo narrans.* This means that in our communication with others, we instinctively tell and retell narratives about people we have encountered and experiences we have faced in the challenges of daily living—and we listen to the stories that others tell publicly. These shared stories help us organize and understand our world and its institutions and feel connections with both our ancestors and our contemporaries.

Every society's narratives form a reservoir where cultural values, attitudes, and expectations are housed, waiting to be passed from generation to generation. As a child, you began the lifelong process of listening—of discovering the stories that surround you, those that explain the activities and institutions of your cultural group. As you learned them, you began to answer the question that Plato asked almost 2,500 years ago, "How should we then live?" According to Alastair MacIntyre, we learn the role of parents, of children, of other characters in the drama of life through hearing about lost children, good but misguided kings, honest carpenters, and prodigal sons who spend their fathers' money on riotous living and end up eating with swine. He concludes, "There is no way to give us an understanding of any society, including our own, except through the stock of stories which constitute its original dramatic resources."[4] Thus, the kinds of stories we choose to tell one another, the content of these stories, the kinds of issues and themes we agree on as worthy of being retold both reflect and shape our culture. See Box 13.1 for some examples of Native-American narrative traditions.

Because human institutions depend on shared narratives, storytellers exist in every occupation. Consequently, throughout your lifetime, you have heard anecdotes told in public by parents, teachers, coaches, club leaders, and police officers. Moreover, religious leaders, scientists, business leaders, and politicians all recount stories. As a part of a storytelling tradition, we all participate as story narrators at some point or another.

As you encounter new experiences and enter unfamiliar places, you instinctively listen for narratives to prepare yourself to meet any challenges that might arise. For example, before you entered college, you may have asked a student you knew to tell you what to expect. If so, your college friend probably explained campus life by telling stories—anecdotes about classes, professors,

Teaching Idea

Ask students what stories they heard before they came to campus, joined a living group, became a member of one of the sports teams, and so on.

BOX 13.1

Native-American Narrative Traditions[5]

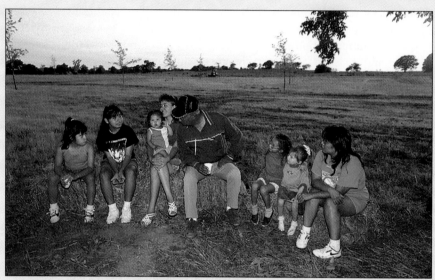

Native American groups have a variety of narrative traditions, but stories are important to all of them. Here, a Cherokee storyteller shares cultural lore with young members of the tribe.

Several native groups of North America differentiate between two types of stories in the following ways:

Eskimos distinguish between *old* stories and *young* stories.

Winnebago natives tell both *waikan* (sacred) and *worak* (narrated) tales.

Pawnees differentiate between *false* stories, which are fiction, nonfiction, or a mixture of both, and *true* stories, which are the old, sacred tales.

Tlingit natives tell *tlagu* stories (stories of long ago) and *ch'kalnik* tales (stories that really happened).

You can see from these labels that cultural groups distinguish between different kinds of stories. Sometimes the ancient stories are called *myths*. Myths serve to communicate the group's answers to the ultimate questions of life; they differ from those stories that aim to entertain or serve less significant functions. For this reason, R. C. Rowland[6] calls myths the most powerful narratives; they are the stories people use to define the good society and to solve problems that are not subject to rational solutions.

registration, and social events. From hearing both positive and negative stories, you began to understand not only what to expect but also what to avoid in the new setting.

 **KEY CONCEPT** ## The Importance of Public Narratives

Narrative is a universal form of public speaking, and a culture's narratives house its store of beliefs, values, attitudes, and expectations.

Narrative Functions

Teaching Idea

The Instructor's Manual has a diagram on a transparency that you can use to present narrative functions.

With wide-eyed wonder, a child listens to the stories of "the birds and the bees" in response to his question, "Mommy, where do babies come from?" This same little boy is told stories of brave and courageous immigrants, characteristics his grandparent-storyteller encourages him to imitate. Several years later, the young man finds himself in an environmental seminar, where vivid examples of abuse of the planet persuade him to become an active recycler. The narratives he hears serve three very specific purposes according to narrative scholar Didier Coste:[7] They explain cultural realities; they provide examples for imitation; and they persuade people to believe or to act. Professor W. G. Kirkwood[8] proposes an additional function: Narratives sometimes function to disclose possibilities. We look at each of these functions in turn.

Explanatory Narratives

Teaching Idea

Exercise 1 is appropriate with this section.

Some stories function to explain what *is* by providing their culture's understandings of natural, social, or ultimate realities. For example, a myth from the Kaluli tribe in Papua New Guinea explains why dogs and cats are enemies—a natural phenomenon. Economists in the United States narrate the recurring cycles of economic recession and recovery—a social phenomenon. Stories that deal with the place of humans in the universe explain ultimate realities.

Cross Reference

Box 13.1 continues the cultural theme of the text. Myths can be a powerful form of reasoning, providing members of a culture with "good reasons" to believe or to behave in culturally desirable ways.

Natural Realities   Euro-American culture turns to scientists to explain the processes of nature. Scientists weave together a number of facts that they discover in empirical observations to form narrative accounts of natural processes. They then share these narratives across cultural borders, forming an international community of scientific storytellers. Scientific narratives can profoundly affect people's perceptions of the world.[9] For example, the Big Bang theory is a story that explains scientists' beliefs about the beginning of the world. When it is combined with evolutionary narratives explaining the development of the species, it influences many people's view of nature and their place in it.

Cross Reference

Chapter 3 also speaks of irreconcilable differences.

Teaching Idea

Exercise 2 is appropriate here, perhaps as a journal entry.

However, not everyone accepts scientific explanations. Many cultural groups modify or reject outright these scientific stories; instead, they tell explanatory narratives of their own—some that are irreconcilable with theories of the Big Bang and evolution. Many continue to believe these stories long after the major institutions of society, such as educational institutions, have adopted the scientific narratives. As we pointed out in Chapter 3, differing belief systems can lead to heated debate—the kind seen in textbook battles and arguments for the inclusion of creationism in schools.

Social Realities In addition to stories that explain physical realities, other narratives explain how the institutions or the structures of the culture came into being. You can find national explanations in history texts. These books provide accounts of the founding of this country, of its wars, of the blameworthy scenes of slavery as well as the praiseworthy scenes of the Constitutional Convention. Naturally, history books from other countries have different explanations of some of the same events.

We often tell narratives on major anniversaries of historical events. In 1992, for instance, many storytellers from around the globe recounted the historical events and the surrounding myths related to Christopher Columbus's voyage 500 years earlier. The perspectives of Italian, Spanish, Native-American, and other narrators differed greatly. We tell other stories annually. On the Fourth of July, for example, we relate the narratives surrounding the writing of the Declaration of Independence.

Frequently, historical facts are obscured by myths, and in this century, a variety of scholars have set out to counter these myths by offering alternative explanations for historical events. For example, feminist historians look at history (or "her-story," if you will) very differently from those they call "malestream" scholars. Another group of historians call for a rewriting of history to include the "Afrocentric" origins of social phenomena.

Ultimate Realities Another group of stories attempt to explain *ultimate* realities—to answer such questions as: Who are we? What is our purpose on earth? What happens after death? How should I live a moral life? They are often told in both philosophical and religious discussions. In addition, stories explain the rituals that give meaning to religious adherents, rituals that are usually based in historical events. Jewish people, for instance, narrate the story of the Maccabees as they light their Hannukah candles. Muslims tell of the Prophet's flight to Medira as they keep the fast of Ramadan. Christians recount the narratives of the death and resurrection of Jesus as they celebrate Easter. In short, religious beliefs and practices are grounded in stories that followers have preserved over generations, stories that give ultimate meaning to the lives of adherents.

Stories serve to explain natural, social, and ultimate realities. The recounting of narratives during the rituals of Hannukah is one way that Jews come to understand their history as a people.

Exemplary Narratives

You have undoubtedly heard many stories that are told for the purpose of providing examples of people who are successful because they live by societal norms and values. In contrast, an abundance of narratives show the negative consequences of enacting behaviors that are not socially approved. Some narratives with a "moral" or point are told nationally and internationally by means of the media; others are told only within family units.

Teaching Idea

Exercise 3 goes with this topic. Students may share positive models as well as "horror stories" that served as negative examples.

Positive Models   Public speakers often choose to narrate the lives of people who model traits and actions that benefit society. These individuals provide inspiring role models for others to emulate. For example, in one State of the Union Address, President Ronald Reagan narrated the story of Clara Hale, also known as "Mother Hale," who opened her home to children whose parents were drug addicts. Eventually, she and her staff at Hale House in Harlem cared for hundreds of drug babies and babies with AIDS. During the address, the president invited Mrs. Hale to stand and receive the applause of the audience. She provided the Congress, as well as the national television audience, with a model of what ordinary people can do when they decide to fight injustices in their worlds.

Cross Reference

Such stories as these often reinforce core cultural beliefs and values. See Chapter 3.

Narratives are valuable because they provide concrete examples of admired traits, such as courage in the face of adversity. In the prime of his baseball career, for instance, pitcher Dave Dravecky lost his pitching arm and shoulder to cancer. Listeners pack auditoriums to hear him narrate the lessons he learned through this ordeal. His story is a model for others to follow as they face their own life challenges.

Other stories are models for actions such as hard work. We hear of people like Yolanda Tavera who grew up as a migrant child following the crops but who now coordinates migrant education for an entire school district. Motivational speakers use examples of entrepreneurs like Bill Gates, who dropped out of Harvard and founded the highly successful Microsoft Corporation. Although the characters in the story change, the plot is similar in all the cases: The characters begin with little except vision and perseverance and end up becoming successful in their fields. They all serve as models for others to follow.

Negative Models   In contrast to stories that model how we should live, other narratives provide a cautionary message, showing us how *not* to behave. They can be about fictional or real characters. For instance, fictional stories, such as the tale of Pinocchio, caution children not to lie. Public speakers also tell true stories of high school dropouts who have a difficult life or of men and women who do not prepare adequately for retirement. Such narratives provide examples for listeners to avoid rather than emulate.

Persuasive Narratives

Speakers often attempt to influence listeners' beliefs, actions, or attitudes through the use of stories. In fact, narrative is such an effective form of reasoning that Aristotle classified it as a type of "deliberative" speaking, the kind of speechmaking that enables people to make wise decisions regarding future courses of action. Persuasive stories function in two ways. Sometimes they provide a rationale *for* a particular course of action, a proof of its *necessity*. At other times, these stories provide good arguments *against* a particular course of action.

Some of the stories are unpleasant to hear, for their telling exposes a societal wrong that needs to be righted. Speakers often use such emotionally involving anecdotes to motivate others to intervene, to make a difference, to improve the lives of the needy. What follows is a persuasive narrative told by Ganga Stone,[10] founder of a volunteer network that cooks and delivers more than 1,200 meals daily to needy people.

Narratives function to provide positive models that serve as examples for others to follow. After he lost his arm and shoulder to cancer, former San Francisco baseball pitcher Dave Dravecky inspired crowds to face personal challenges with courage.

I hugged the heavy bag of donated groceries and began to climb the five long flights of stairs to Richard's studio apartment. I remember feeling a strong sense of satisfaction knowing that I was bringing help to a dying man who was all alone. That satisfied glow disappeared the instant I saw him.

Richard lay propped up in a bed, his swollen features all distorted by AIDS-related disease. He hadn't eaten in two days, so when I approached his bedside he eagerly grabbed the grocery bag. I watched him reach again and again in the bag to find something, anything, that he could eat . . . now. Bread mix, oatmeal, canned beans, a box of macaroni and cheese—there was nothing ready to eat and no way he could get out of bed to cook. He finally gave up.

Then he looked up at me still clutching the empty bag, the useless assortment of ingredients strewn across the bed and floor. For a moment we just stared at one another. Then I made a promise I wasn't sure how I would keep. But I promised to bring him meals for as long as he needed, and I vowed that no one else in the same situation would ever have to face the unthinkable combination of AIDS and starvation. That was nearly seven years and 300,000 meals ago.

Ms. Stone tells this true personal narrative with persuasive intentions. If she can effectively persuade listeners to identify with both Richard and herself—a woman determined to change a negative situation—they will feel her compassion and look for ways they can participate in relieving the suffering of people like Richard. If they become concerned enough, they may tell the story to others, inviting more and more people to become personally involved with such problems.

Not only do persuasive stories change individuals, they also contribute to changes in policies on wider levels. On the campus level, for example, speakers who publicly narrate stories about a series of muggings convince administrators to establish policies that correct the problem. On the national level, widely circulated tales about oil spills led to tighter regulations for oil tankers. International tales of human rights abuses led the United States to send military personnel to Somalia.

Teaching Idea

Exercise 4 deals with testimonials. Some students may have given such a speech in religious settings or in self-help groups.

Many speakers tell stories about their personal experiences; these *life stories* and *testimonials* serve as inspirations to others. For instance, recovering alcoholics narrate their personal stories and encourage one another to change their drinking habits. In organizations such as Amway, distributors gather a group of friends and narrate how they made money through the company. Even television commercials for products from cars to skin care products feature the testimonials of people whose experiences with the product were positive. All these "success stories" function as forms of persuasive reasoning.

The Rhetoric of Possibility

Professor W. G. Kirkwood[11] proposes another function of narrative: to suggest unfamiliar ideals that exceed the beliefs and experiences of the listeners, confronting them with new possibilities, expanding their understandings of themselves and their lives. These narratives show the "may be" or the "could be"; they are the visions, spoken by inspired storytellers, that move others to dream new dreams then work to make them become realities. A famous example of such a vision is Dr. Martin Luther King, Jr.'s, 1963 dream of a nation in which all were judged, "not by the color of their skin, but by the content of their character."[12] In the ensuing decades, many voices have added narratives depicting scenarios in which citizens cooperate to make that vision come true.

KEY CONCEPT   ## Narrative Functions

Explanatory narratives Stories can function to provide explanations of natural, social, and ultimate.

Exemplary narratives Stories often function as positive or negative models for behavior.

Persuasive narratives Stories frequently function to convince or move listeners to act; testimonials are a common form.

The rhetoric of possibility Stories function to disclose, not what is, but what might be.

Guidelines for Narratives

Because you have been hearing and telling narratives all of your life, the patterns common to narratives are probably quite familiar to you. Thoughtfully consider at least four elements as you prepare to use narratives in your speechmaking: purpose, characters, plot, and language.

Purpose

Cross Reference

Speech purposes are discussed throughout the text. See Chapters 2, 3, 14, and 16.

If you give a narrative speech, or if you tell a narrative only as part of a larger speech, still consider the purpose of the narrative carefully. What function will the story perform? Will it be explanatory, exemplary, or persuasive? Will it reveal possibilities that your audience has not yet considered? Remember that, even when a narrative is mainly told for entertainment purposes, it generally conveys a lesson or point.

Characters

Teaching Idea

Ask students to name a favorite childhood story—one with animals, machines, or objects that were given humanlike qualities—that made a point. Often adults such as parents or teachers read such stories. (*Charlotte's Web* is an example.) Discuss the value of such fictional characters in providing explanations, examples, possibilities, and persuasive appeals. How do these fictional characters embody desirable cultural traits?

Obviously, stories have characters, both fictional and actual. Many narratives involve fictional characters such as animals or natural objects that are personified or given human traits—talking trees, for instance. Moreover, some characters are clearly imaginary, and adults use dragons, talking train engines, genies in bottles, and other fanciful characters to convey important cultural values. Aesop's fables, for instance, have communicated Western cultural wisdom for more than 2,000 years. Coyote stories, similarly, communicate the wisdom of various Native-American groups.

However, other stories are about actual people who act, meaning they move, speak, form relationships, and interact with others. These characters are motivated by their distinctive personality traits, ethnic backgrounds, educational experiences, and social backgrounds, and these factors influence the choices they make.

Plot

In stories worth telling, the characters in a narrative face some sort of challenge that tests their assumptions, values, or actions. The way they respond to the challenges and the resulting changes in their lives form the plot or the action of the narrative. In this period of change, natural processes, such as growing up, occur. The characters also meet physical, psychological, and economic challenges; they have accidents; they begin and end relationships; they lose their possessions in a tragic fire. How they deal with the challenges that confront them provides the point of the story. One final look at Ms. Stone's narrative: Richard's challenge was to find something to eat; her challenge was to help him. As a result of her ten-minute experience in a sick man's apartment, Ganga Stone's life changed permanently.

Language

Teaching Idea

Invite a local storyteller to class, or play an audiotape of a narrative speech, or show a videotape of a speaker who tells his or her life story. For example, you can order Dave Roever's life story, titled "Davey: The High School Experience," from Dave Roever Associates, PO Box 136130, Ft. Worth, TX 76136. Video: $19.95; audiotape: $4.95. (817) 238-2000.

Narrative speaking requires careful attention to language.[13] Vivid word choices and details bring the story to life and make your listeners feel as if they are there. Detailed descriptions in stories do more than simply convey information. They help create the scene and provide a sense of authenticity—the names, the places, the times that meet your listeners' psychological preference to set events in space and time. Consider these features of style as you plan the language of your narratives: use of details, constructed dialogue, and listing.

Use of Details   Details are important in several places within a narrative. At the beginning, when you are orienting the audience to the plot of the story, include enough descriptive material so that listeners have a sense of the context for the action. When you describe the key action of the story, important details enable your audience to understand clearly the changes taking place in the characters. Finally, when you move into the climax of the story, a cluster of details contributes to your main point.

Cross Reference

Listening schemas are discussed in Chapter 6.

At the beginning of narratives, opening details function to set the story in a time and a place. For instance, mythical stories often begin with the formulaic phrase "Once upon a time in a faraway land." Listeners who have heard fairy tales immediately pull up their mental "fairy tale" schema and listen to the story through that filter. On the other hand, setting factual narratives in a specific date and time draws listeners into the world of the story. A college student starts her narrative, "When I was a junior in high school, I was enrolled in a very small private school in the mountain country of Montana." Her listeners will evaluate her story using a "personal experiences" schema. Whether the story is fanciful or realistic, details about the story's setting help listeners set themselves psychologically in the story's space.

Although certain details are vital, others may be irrelevant to the story and may actually detract listeners from the main idea. There are several reasons for this. There may be *too many details* for the context. You have probably heard storytellers pile on irrelevant detail after detail until you just want them to get to the point! For instance, just ask a child to tell you about a movie he saw, and you will probably get bogged down in details, maybe even missing the point of the

Kutbidin Atamkulov goes from village to village recounting the epic tale of Manas, the Kirghiz hero. His use of vivid language and concrete details makes the story memorable to both old and new generations of listeners.

story entirely because young storytellers don't always separate *relevant* details from *interesting* ones. Finally, details are sometimes inappropriate because they reveal more than listeners want to know. For instance, narrators sometimes reveal too much intimate information with the result that listeners become embarrassed and miss the point of the story. For these reasons, evaluate the appropriateness of details, then edit out unnecessary or irrelevant material.

Constructed Dialogue   You can add to the story's sense of realism by creating dialogue between major characters. Adding to this the vocal variety that conveys impressions of the personalities and the emotions of the characters further increases not only your involvement but your listeners' involvement in the narrative interactions. For example, you could simply report actions, "He told me to move my car, but I didn't, because I was only going to park for a moment. The next thing I knew, he threatened me." Contrast the different effect it would have on your audience if you created a dialogue, then used different voices, volume, and rate for each character.

> *He rolled down his car window and yelled, "Hey, kid, move your pile of junk!"*
> *I turned down my radio and explained through my open window, "I'll just be here a minute. I'm waiting for my mother."*
> *He jerked open his car door, stomped over to my car, leaned into my window and said slowly through clenched teeth, "I said, (pause) 'Move-your-pile-of-junk, kid!'"*

As you can see, creating a scene with vivid, memorable dialogue is far more likely to involve your listeners in your dilemma, causing them to place themselves in the scene with you. By increasing listeners' emotional involvement in the story, you keep their attention and have greater potential for communicating the point of your speech.

Listing   Providing lists is another way to increase rapport between the speakers and audiences because they introduce specific areas of commonality. For instance, a speaker could say, "I packed my bags and checked twice to see if I had forgotten anything." Or she could add specific details that are familiar to fellow travelers, as this example illustrates.

As I packed for Europe, I was afraid I would forget something vital. I looked through my bag for the seventh time. Toothpaste? Check. Toothbrush? Check. Toilet paper? (I'd been told to bring my own.) Check. Deodorant? Yep. Yet something seemed to be missing—as I was to discover in an isolated village in Germany.

Again, the details contribute to dialogical responses in listeners who are creating mental images for each item in the list. As you can see, the language of narrative does make a difference. Because narrative is one way of appealing to emotions, it is vital that your audience be involved in the story—and word choices that increase audience involvement make your story more powerful and memorable.

Organizational Patterns for Narrative Speeches

Two patterns are common in narrative speeches: the infinity loop and the exemplum. Both stress the importance of identifying a theme that the narrative then supports or illustrates.

Cross Reference

Chapter 9 has other nonlinear, visual patterns. That chapter suggested that the spiral pattern could also be used effectively with narratives.

The Infinity Loop   Cheryl Jorgensen-Earp[14] identified an organizational pattern, illustrated in Figure 13.1, in which a narrative or series of narratives compose the speech. This pattern, the infinity loop pattern, consists of a core theme and narrative loops that develop and support the theme.

If you use this pattern, you may tell a single story that you develop with a degree of complexity; this is especially useful if you tell a personal narrative in which you explain how you met and overcame challenges in your life. At other times, you may find it more helpful to tell two related narratives rather than a single, long story. For instance, in a speech about the benefits of education (the core theme), you could contrast two stories—one person completed her degree and had a successful career; the other did not and was unable to find a fulfilling job. In a third variation, you might develop a main narrative with one or more subnarratives, as shown in this outline for a speech about raising a hearing-impaired child.

Figure 13.1 *The infinity loop pattern.*

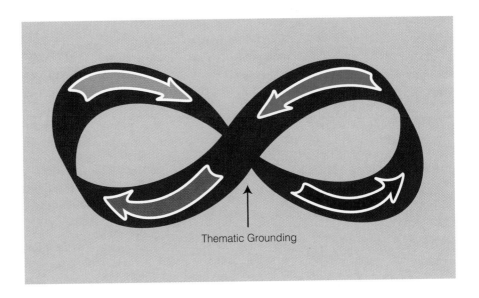

Thematic Grounding

Teaching Idea

The infinity loop pattern is on a tansparency in the Instructor's Manual.

Stated theme: Raising a hearing-impaired child is both rewarding and frustrating.

Narrative—the family's reaction on learning their child could not hear.

Subnarrative relating to health care professionals.

Return to narrative—the child's preschool years.

Subnarrative of child care issues.

Return to narrative—the child's schooling.

Insights into American Sign Language.

Return to narrative—the hearing-impaired teen.

Restatement of theme: Raising a hearing-impaired child is both rewarding and frustrating.

Teaching Idea

Using exercise 5, direct students to Farah Walters' narrative in the Appendix. Diagram her speech on the board or on a transparency. The Instructor's Manual provides guidance for constructing an infinity loop outline.

Begin the infinity loop pattern at the middle point by either stating or implying a theme, or you may do a standard introduction. Some narratives begin with a formulaic statement that indicates to the audience that a story is coming. Examples are "My grandmother used to tell the story of a woman who . . . " or "In the final days of World War II . . . " or "I once knew a man who . . . ." Then develop one loop of the narrative and return to the theme; move on to another loop and return to the theme. If you are telling only one long story, you might not restate the theme until the end of the story. However, you should make a mental check during the story to make sure the theme of the speech is revealed in the narrative.

In summary, an infinity loop pattern is often used to organize a narrative speech. The loops are the narrative and subnarratives within the speech. The center point to which they return is the thematic grounding. If you give the same speech repeatedly, your central narrative may remain the same, but you can develop different subnarratives, depending on the needs of your particular audience.

Speech Assignment

An accompanying assignment and grade sheet are found in the Student Resource Workbook. See the teaching notes in the Instructor's Manual.

The Exemplum   A common narrative pattern, used by speech teachers for hundreds of years, is the exemplum.[15] It has five elements. When you use this pattern, include all five elements; without them, it is just another narrative. The five parts of the exemplum follow one another in this order.

1.   State a quotation or proverb.

2.   Identify and explain the author or source of the proverb or the quotation.

3.   Rephrase the proverb in your own words.

4.   Tell a story that illustrates the quotation or proverb.

5.   Apply the quotation or proverb to the audience.

Cross Reference

These speeches are given to reinforce cultural beliefs and values, as discussed in Chapter 3.

Select a narrative from your personal experiences, from historical events, or from episodes in the life of someone else. It should represent, illustrate, or explain something important to you, perhaps a turning point in your life. Identify a lesson or point to your story, then find a quotation that supports the main lesson of the narrative. You may use a commonly quoted saying, such as "Silence is golden." You may also go to books of quotations for ideas.

For example, Paul Lee used his personal experience of immigrating to America to reinforce the importance of all citizens working to create a better society. Here is a summary of the major points of his classroom speech.

1.   Quotation: "Ask not what your country can do for you; ask rather what you can do for your country."

2.   Source: President John Kennedy, the thirty-fifth President of the United States, said this in his inaugural address.

3.   Paraphrase: "In other words, instead of taking for granted the things our country has to offer us, we should actively seek opportunities to work to improve our country."

4.   Personal narrative: Immigrating to the United States from Hong Kong posed many challenges and hardships as the family learned a new language and customs.

     The Lee family took the oath of citizenship—with all the rights and privileges that brought—before a presiding judge who welcomed the new citizens with Kennedy's challenging words.

5. Application: Everyone—both native born and immigrants—should reflect on the privilege of being in the United States; each listener should think of some way to make the country better for all.

In short, an exemplum builds around a quotation that is developed through a narrative. This pattern is often used in speeches that reinforce cultural values.

KEY CONCEPT   Guidelines for Narratives

Purpose Stories inform, persuade, and entertain as they provide explanations and examples.

Characters This element of narratives includes fictional and actual characters, personified natural objects, and fanciful creatures.

Plot Plot makes the story worth telling by showing how the characters met challenges and overcame them.

Language Details in strategic places, constructed dialogue, and listing are ways to make the narrative come alive for listeners.

Organizational patterns Two common organizational patterns are used for narrative speeches.

The infinity loop Speakers develop a core theme by telling a narrative or narratives that illustrate it.

The exemplum This is a narrative pattern in which a speaker states a quotation, gives its source, restates it, uses a narrative that illustrates it, and relates the theme to the audience.

Narrative Reasoning

So far we've seen that all peoples, historically and globally, have made sense of their worlds by telling and listening to stories. Narrative reasoning is especially common for women and speakers from ethnic groups such as African Americans, Native Americans, Asian Americans, and Americans of Hispanic origin. For example, Professor Patricia Williams[16] uses family narratives as case studies for the law students in her "Women and Property" course at the University of Wisconsin. As she tells of her great-great grandmother who was sold when she was eleven years old to a white man who later fathered her child, Williams's students learn to reason about the law from a perspective that may be new to them.

Teaching Idea

Discuss the third test by referring to a current "scandal" that is brewing around some well-known figure. (Examples: 1994 scandals included Tonya Harding's role in injuring fellow-skater Nancy Kerrigan and a thirteen-year-old boy's accusations against singer Michael Jackson.) Why do we tell such stories? What good can come from this? What possible harm could there be? To the participants? To society as a whole?

A narrative does not have to be literally true in order to function as a good reason or a proof. However, since narrative reasoning is so pervasive, we need to assess stories to see if they are logical. But how do we judge narratives? According to theorists, we use narrative logic to determine which stories to endorse or accept as the basis for our decisions and actions. There are three major ways to test narrative reasoning.[17]

1. Is the story coherent or understandable? That is, does it hang together in a logical way? Do the events follow one another in a predictable sequence? Do characters act in ways that are probable, given their personalities and cultural backgrounds?

2. Is the story a true or faithful representation of what you know about the world and the way it works? If it is a myth, folktale, or hypothetical story, does it contain important truths that demonstrate appropriate ways to live?

3. Does the story deserve to be told? Is it a good story that conveys an important or worthwhile message? Will it result in positive, ethical outcomes for individuals and for society as a whole?

The following example of narrative reasoning comes from a speech by Chief Joseph of the Nez Percé Indian tribe. On January 14, 1879, he spoke before a large gathering of cabinet officers, congressional representatives, diplomats, and other officials, offering his story as a good reason for Congress to act in behalf of his people.

My name is In-mut-too-yah-lat-lat (Thunder traveling over the Mountains). I am chief of the Wal-lam-wat-kin band of Chute-pa-lu, or Nez Percé (nose-pierced) Indians. I was born in eastern Oregon, thirty-eight winters ago. My father was chief before me.

We did not know there were other people besides the Indian until about one hundred winters ago, when some men with white faces came to our country. . . . These men were Frenchmen, and they called our people "Nez Percé," because they wore rings in their noses for ornaments. Although very few of our people wear them now, we are still called by that name. . . . Our people were divided in opinion about these men. Some thought they taught more bad than good. . . .

The first white men of your people who came to our country were named Lewis and Clark. They also brought many things that our people had never seen. They talked straight, and our people gave them a great feast, as a proof that their hearts were friendly. These men were very kind. They made presents to our chiefs and our people made presents to them. We had a great many horses, of which we gave them what they needed, and they gave us guns and tobacco in return. All the Nez Percé made friends with Lewis and Clark, and agreed to let them pass through their country, and never to make war on white men. This promise the Nez Percé have never broken. No white man can accuse them of bad faith, and speak with a straight tongue. It has always been the pride of the Nez Percé that they were the friends of the white men. . . .

[Chief Joseph continued the speech, detailing the Nez Percé perspective of the relations between the Indians and the whites. He ended with a plea for equal justice under law.][18]

The chief's narrative passes the tests for narrative reasoning and provides a good reason to accept his claims. The events in his account follow one another in a predictable sequence. The actions of both the Indians and the white-faced men are also understandable, given their personal and cultural characteristics. We know that Lewis and Clark did travel through Nez Percé country. Other details in the story are verifiable in other historical documents such as diaries, letters, and treaties. Chief Joseph's motives are positive. He asks for justice and fairness, for equal treatment under law—a constitutional right.

KEY CONCEPT   ## Narrative Reasoning

Ask yourself if the story is coherent or internally consistent, if it represents reality, and if it deserves to be told.

Summary

In every society, narrative is present as a form of reasoning. Narratives both reflect and shape cultural beliefs and values. Three types of narratives are found in all cultures: explanatory, exemplary, and persuasive. Explanatory narratives provide answers for why and how things are the way they are. Exemplary narratives are stories with a moral or point that listeners should—or should not—imitate. Persuasive narratives provide a reason to do something, or a reason *not* to pursue the action. In addition, narrative helps us see possibilities that we had not imagined before.

Four elements should be developed in a narrative—the purpose, characters, plot, and language. Vivid language is especially important because it brings the characters to life and makes the action in the plot compelling, causing listeners to identify with them throughout the story. The infinity loop pattern and the exemplum are two ways to organize a narrative speech.

There are three ways to test narrative reasoning. The stories should be coherent or understandable. They should tell important truths about life. Finally, we test the merit of stories to see if they *should* be told—evaluating each story by considering its effect on society and its effect on individuals.

Questions and Exercises

1. How do you use narratives to explain the world of nature? The social world? The ultimate meanings in life?

2. Do your stories ever clash with the narratives of others? If so, what do you do about these differences?

3. Share with a group of classmates a few examples of exemplary narratives you heard while you were growing up. In what ways did they influence your behaviors?

4. In what settings have you heard testimonials? Have you ever given one? If so, describe the occasion. Where might you give one in the future?

5. Many speeches are given in the form of a narrative, or an extended narrative takes up a significant part of the speech. The excerpt from Farah Walters' speech in the Appendix is an example. Read through it to see how she uses her life experiences to make her point. As you read, identify the infinity loop pattern. What purpose does Ms. Walter have in telling her story?

Key Terms

homo narrans
myths
explanatory narratives
exemplary narratives
persuasive narratives
the rhetoric of possibility
testimonials
constructed dialogue
the infinity loop pattern
exemplum
narrative reasoning

Notes

1. Wicker, B. (1975). *The story-shaped world: Fiction and metaphysics, some variations on a theme.* Notre Dame, IN: University of Notre Dame Press.

2. Barthes is quoted in Polkinghorne, D. E. (1988). *Narrative knowing and the human sciences* (p. 14). Albany: SUNY Press.

3. Much of the material in this chapter comes from four sources: MacIntyre, A. (1981). *After virtue: A study in moral reasoning* (2nd ed.). South Bend, IN: Notre Dame Press; Fisher, W. R. (1984). Narration as a human communication paradigm: The case of public moral argument. *Communication Monographs, 51,* 1–22. He further develops his ideas in (1985). The narrative paradigm: An elaboration. *Communication Monographs, 52,* 347–367. For a thorough discussion of narrative in conversations, see also Tannen, D. (1989). *Talking voices: Repetition, dialogue, and imagery in conversational discourse.* Cambridge: Cambridge University Press.

4. MacIntyre. (1981). Op. cit., p. 216.

5. Bierhorst, J. (1985). *The mythology of North America.* New York: William Morrow.

6. Rowland, R. C. (1990). On mythic criticism. *Communication Studies, 41*(2), 101–116. See also the works of Joseph Campbell. For instance, (1970). Mythological themes in creative literature and art. In J. C. Campbell (Ed.). *Myths, dreams, and religion,* (pp. 138–175). New York: E. P. Dutton. For an examination of how myth functions as a proof in speeches, see Solomon, M. (1979). The "positive woman's" journey: A mythic analysis of the rhetoric of stop ERA. *Quarterly Journal of Speech, 65,* 262–274.

7. Coste, D. (1989). *Narrative as communication.* Minneapolis: University of Minnesota Press.

8. Kirkwood, W. G. (1992). Narrative and the rhetoric of possibility. *Communication Monographs, 59,* 30–47.

9. Spangler, D., & Thompson, W. I. (1992). *Reimagination of the world: A critique of the new age, science, and popular culture.* New York: Bear & Company.

10. Stone, G. (n.d.). Promotional letter.

11. Kirkwood. (1992). Op. cit.

12. King, M. L., Jr. (1963). I have a dream. Copyright, Martin Luther King, Jr.

13. Tannen. (1989). Op. cit.

14. Jorgensen-Earp, C. (1993, September 28). Telephone interview. Also (n.d.). "Making other arrangements:" Alternative patterns of disposition. Unpublished paper.

15. McNally, J. R. (1969). Opening assignments: A symposium. *The Speech Teacher, 18*, 18–20.

16. Goldberg, S. B. (1992, July 17). The law, a new theory holds, has a white voice. *The New York Times*, p. A23.

17. Fisher. (1984, 1985). Op. cit.

18. Chief Joseph. An Indian's view of Indian affairs. From *Indian oratory: Famous speeches by noted Indian chieftains* (pp. 259–284), by W. C. Vanderwerth. Copyright 1971 by the University of Oklahoma Press.

Informative
Speaking

- Describe the global importance of information
- Select topics on a variety of levels ranging from personal to international
- List possible topics in seven informative categories
- Use four guidelines to make your informative speeches more effective

Note

The sharing of information is important in U.S. institutions and in international settings, for arguably, knowledge is power. That is, those who are "in the know" have more control of their personal lives and more of a say in what goes on in their communities. This chapter presents speech outlines in a variety of topic categories for informative speeches.

Dr. Sandra Garcia, an AIDS specialist from the University of San Francisco Medical School Hospital, gave a two-day series of informative lectures explaining various aspects of the disease to an audience assembled by the California Judicial Education and Research Group. After her presentations, one judge commented, "She was outstanding. There are so many physicians who are excellent but who can't talk." When Dr. Garcia became a physician, she probably did not expect to make many public speeches. However, she is one of many professional people who find that their jobs require them to provide information to the public on a regular basis. Professionals are not the only ones who regularly give informative speeches. This list suggests a few ways that ordinary people speak to inform.

- A member of the student government who reports the results of committee findings about bringing a well-known entertainer to campus

- Police officers who provide school children with information on safety and on crime prevention

- An experienced mother who teaches other mothers how to care for young children

- Accountants who explain the annual audit to a client company's board of directors

This chapter first examines the global importance of information. It then turns to the purposes of informative speaking. This is followed by skeletal outlines of speeches in several informative topic categories. Finally, the chapter concludes with guidelines for creating effective informative messages.

Information in Our Lives

Theme

This section links to the recurring theme of living in an electronic culture—an idea developed in Chapters 1, 7, and 10.

Our age has been called the Information Age. This means, among other things, that a greater number of people in our country and around the globe know more about issues, people, places, theories, objects, and processes than any other humans throughout history have known. Moreover, it means that entire industries exist to disseminate information through print and electronic channels. And these channels are spreading throughout the globe as advancements in data bank storage and cable linkages connect televisions, telephones, and computers to form "electronic superhighways"[1] of information. It further means that there is an "information explosion," with the available amount of factual data increasing hourly.

Because of these factors, we receive fragments of disconnected information that often seem irrelevant to the rest of our lives. For instance, in one five-minute newscast, we can learn about a train derailment in France, a fire in

Tennessee, and a coup in a Central American country—all pieces of information that are quite remote from the daily experiences of most Americans. This barrage of facts can result in "information overload" for many people; that is, people know a great deal about many things, but these fragmented facts are not integrated with one another, and the sheer number of them is almost overwhelming.

For these reasons, it is important for speakers to draw connections between disparate facts and ideas and to help their listeners integrate new information with what they already believe, value, and act on. When they do this successfully, informative public speakers function in two major ways: (1) they help their listeners make sense of the world, and (2) they provide the basic information that audience members can use as a basis for wise decisions and actions.[2] For example, a speaker who provides information on unsafe food gathers and presents facts, examples, comparisons and contrasts, statistics, and testimony to help listeners understand that some of the nation's food supply can pose health risks. Audience members can then make decisions to avoid such risks by altering the way they purchase food.

The Right to Information

Teaching Idea
Lead the class in a discussion of the implications of having some people or groups with lots of information and others with very little. Examples: What if some societies have information on making sophisticated weaponry and others do not? What if some people have information that would benefit them economically and others do not? What if some groups have information about their cultural history and others do not?

Although information overload is possible, we need to increase our knowledge, at least in some areas, for the right kind of knowledge is power. That is, having the right kind of information empowers us with the facts we need to make reasoned decisions and act appropriately within our cultures. Having access to information is so important that the ability to both give and receive information is considered by many to be a global human right that deserves to be protected by international law. Indeed, Article 19 of the Universal Declaration of Human Rights (1948) states:

> *Everyone has the right to freedom of opinion and expression; this right includes freedom to hold opinions without interference and to seek and impart information and ideas through any media and regardless of frontiers.*[3]

Article 19 recognizes the potential dangers of an information imbalance where some people or groups know a great deal and others know very little. Those who are kept in ignorance, with vital facts concealed from them, may lack fundamental understandings of the world. For this reason, Radio Free Europe broadcast messages to people in Communist-controlled countries during the Cold War, providing listeners behind the Iron Curtain with information that their governments withheld from them. Similarly, throughout the world, public health educators give people information that may save their lives. One example is women in Central Africa and Southeast Asia who empower one another with facts that explain how individuals can protect themselves against sexually transmitted diseases.

Informative Purposes

Teaching Idea

Return to the list of topics you made in Chapter 2. With which topics might they produce knowledge? reinforce knowledge? clarify understanding? Teaching note 14.1 in the Instructor's Manual provides supplementary material. *Exercises 1, 2, and 3 are appropriate here.*

The general goal of informative speaking is to add to listeners' knowledge and, thus, their understanding of a subject. As you have seen throughout this text, it is important to assess what your audience already knows and believes about your subject. Some audiences know nothing about the topic; they have never even heard of it. If your listeners fall into this category, you will speak to produce knowledge. Others have limited knowledge, and knowing additional details and facts will increase their level of understanding. Another category of listeners once studied a subject, but they have forgotten some or most of what they learned. These people need to review information and refresh their memories. With these types of audiences, your narrowed purpose is to reinforce knowledge. Still other audiences have misconceptions and misunderstandings that an informative speaker can clear up. Here, your purpose will be to clarify and to counter misunderstandings.

KEY CONCEPT   **Information in Our Lives**

The right to information According to Article 19 of the Universal Declaration of Human Rights (1948), it is important for everyone to receive and to give information, for the right kind of knowledge empowers people.

Informative purposes You can speak to produce or to reinforce knowledge, to clarify misunderstandings, or to counter misconceptions.

Categories of Informative Topics

Cross Reference

Chapters 2, 5, and 9 emphasize relating material to the audience.

As we have seen, information is important because knowledge is linked to power. Not only do we need to be empowered in our personal lives, we need to understand our local communities as well as the larger world. For this reason, as you select your topic, consider subjects on a variety of levels.

As the inverted pyramid in Figure 14.1 illustrates, people tend to be most interested in topics that are close to them in location, time, and relevance to their daily lives. Consequently, it is probably easiest to maintain your listeners' interest and motivation when you speak about subjects that affect them personally. As you move from personal topics to campus, local, and regional subjects, your subject becomes more remote from the daily concerns of most students—and national and global topics may seem worlds away from their experiences. However, what happens around the globe and in society as a whole often has real significance for your audience's future, and your challenge is to help them see how the topic relates to their perceived interests and needs.

Figure 14.1
People usually find themselves and their immediate environments most interesting.

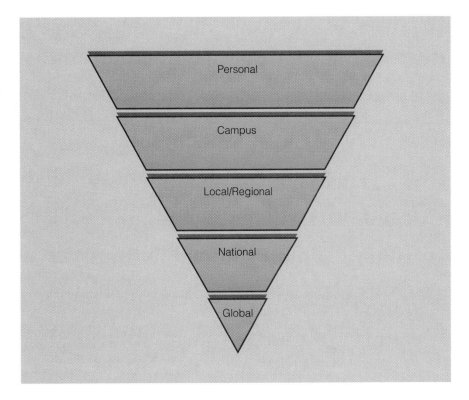

Teaching Idea

Provide or elicit plenty of examples throughout this chapter. Include international and ethnic topics as well as personal ones.

In this section, we look at skeletal outlines of speeches in some of the most common informative categories: people, places, objects, events, processes, concepts, and issues. The general purpose in each of these outlines is to inform.

People

Who are the people who have shaped our world? What did they accomplish? How did they live? When you speak to answer such questions, you provide biographical sketches of influential historical or contemporary characters. Subjects of biographies are philosophers, military men and women, artists, writers, and others who have had or currently have an impact on the societies throughout the world. In contrast to tributes that reinforce cultural beliefs and values through the praise of an individual's achievements, the primary intention of biographical speeches is to increase listeners' knowledge of the facts pertaining to the subject's life. For this reason, you might describe villains as well as heroes since biographical subjects may have had positive as well as negative influences.

Generally, either a chronological or a topical organizational pattern best fits a biographical speech. This example is organized topically with two points: (1) Confucius's life and (2) his influence. Notice that the speaker develops the first point—Confucius's life—in a chronological order.

Specific purpose: To inform my audience of the life and ideas of the Chinese philosopher whose teachings influence more than a billion people globally.

Central idea: Confucius, who lived in China about 2,500 years ago, developed a life-affirming philosophy that has influenced many Asian cultures.

I. Confucius's life
   A. Birth and youth
   B. Early career
   C. Period as a wandering scholar
   D. Later years
II. Confucius's influence
   A. His teaching method
   B. Concepts of "li" and "ren"
   C. Five relationships

Students have successfully given biographical speeches on the lives of Anastasia, Golda Meir, Hitler, Dwight Eisenhower, Phyllis Schafly, and other well-known people.

In addition to individuals, you may select a topic that informs your audience about groups of people such as skinheads, the Mafia, Aborigines, Motown musicians, and others. Here is an outline of a student speech on the Amish that is organized topically.

Specific purpose: To inform my audience about Amish people by describing their beliefs and explaining challenges facing their group.

Central idea: The Amish are a religious group with written and unwritten rules for living that are being challenged by education and tourism.

I. The Amish people
   A. Number and location
   B. Historical information
II. Amish beliefs
   A. Written ordinances—Dortrecht Confession of Faith (1632)
   B. Unwritten rules of local congregations—Ordnung
III. Challenges to Amish culture
   A. Education and teacher certification
   B. Tourism attention

Cross Reference

Remind students of the dialogical aspects of speechmaking. They can focus on answering audience questions about the topic.

As you develop the points in your speech, keep in mind your audience's questions, "Why should I listen to a speech about this person or group?" "What impact has this subject had on society?" "How does knowing about this individual or group tie into my concerns?" When you answer these questions successfully, your listeners will understand how campus, local, national, or international persons or groups affect their culture or their personal lives.

Places

Many people like to travel, and they enjoy having information about different countries or other geographic locations such as national parks or tourist attractions. People also need useful information about places such as universities or about buildings such as museums and libraries. Such information is so important that organizations often hire professionals to inform audiences about places; they include college recruiters, travel agents, and tour guides.

When you describe a place, it is important to pay careful attention to vivid, descriptive language that helps your listeners form detailed images of the place. It is also common to supplement speeches about places with visual aids, including maps, drawings, slides, brochures, or enlarged photographs.

Spatial or topical organizational patterns generally work well for speeches that describe places. By way of illustration, here are the main points of a speech about Thailand given by a Thai student.

> Specific purpose: To inform my audience about the beauty of Thailand and the many tourist attractions in it.
> Central idea: Thailand is a beautiful country with many scenic attractions that complement the human-made wonders to be found there.
>
> I. Geographic features
>   A. Inland areas
>   B. Famous beaches
> II. Tourist attractions
>   A. Cities
>   B. Temples and shrines

Students have successfully described places such as the campus library, local museums, Disneyland, the Mississippi River delta, the Grand Canyon, the Holocaust Museum in Washington, D.C., Indonesia, Italy, and Singapore.

Objects

Often speakers describe and explain objects, including natural objects, such as stars and glaciers, as well as those made by humans, such as monuments and memorials. These objects can be very large; for instance, the planet Jupiter is a large natural object that makes a good speech topic. In contrast, objects can be microscopic. Scientists, for example, describe and explain the composition and the actions of atoms and molecules. Subjects can be inanimate (computers) or animate (panda bears). When you explain objects, provide information about the origin of the object, its composition or how it is made, how it works, and how it is used, and so on.

The most common organizational pattern for speeches about objects is topical. Here is an example of a topical pattern used in a student speech about chopsticks.

> Specific purpose: To inform my audience about the history and usage of chopsticks.
>
> Central idea: Learning the history and usage of chopsticks will make them easier and more fun to use.

I. History
  A. Origin of the term
  B. Differences among Chinese, Korean, and Japanese chopsticks
  C. Chopsticks used for cooking
II. Disposable chopsticks
  A. Negative environmental impact
  B. Ways to decrease the negative impact
III. Usage
  A. How to
  B. Associated etiquette

Cross Reference

Refer to Figure 14.1. Chapter 2 also discusses topic levels.

Think back on the topic levels ranging from personal to international. On the personal level, students have described bodily features such as skin or fingernails. They have talked about campus objects such as a historical tree or a memorial plaque. They've described cultural artifacts such as the Golden Gate Bridge, CD players, and guitars. International topics have included the Taj Mahal, the Great Pyramids, and the Great Wall of China.

Events

In addition to people, places, and objects, speakers often describe events or occurrences. These range from personal events such as birthday customs, to community events like festivals or celebrations, to national and international historical events such as the Russian launch of *Sputnik* or the bombing of Hiroshima.

Both chronological and topical organizational patterns are common in speeches about events. The former works well for step-by-step events, such as the launch of *Sputnik* or the steps involved in planning a wedding. The topical pattern is also useful to describe happenings that consist of several different components. Here is an example of a topical outline for a speech describing a sporting event.

> Specific purpose: To inform my audience of the different events that occur in a rodeo.
>
> Central idea: Rodeos are athletic contests with people and animals competing in a variety of events.

I. Bull riding
II. Barrel racing
III. Bronco busting
IV. Calf roping

When you choose to describe events or occurrences, it is important to provide details and use vivid language so that your listeners can place themselves at the event; that is, speak so that they participate vicariously.

Processes

How does a telephone work? How do Koreans greet one another? How is a levee constructed? To answer these questions, speakers regularly inform their audiences of the stages, ordered sequences, or procedures that describe or explain processes. These can be naturally occurring processes as well as those that exist in cultural realms. Speakers, thus, explain how things are done (bungee jumping, juggling), how they work (elevators, cuckoo clocks), or how they are made (origami, gourmet ice cream). Think for a minute, then add to the following list of topics that you might use for a speech about a process:

Teaching Idea
Use this list as the basis for a class discussion. Include international topics where appropriate.

- *Natural processes* volcanoes, the birth process, diseases
- *Social processes* religious rituals, courtship, mob actions, the grief cycle
- *Political processes* the way a bill is made into law, the process of running for state office
- *Economic processes* recessions, market fluctuations, selecting a mutual fund
- *Art processes* how to take perfect photographs, Native-American blanket making

Because most processes proceed in ordered stages or steps, these speeches are usually organized chronologically, as this outline demonstrates. This speaker was born in the Philippines; she was adopted by an American family when she was sixteen years old.[4]

Specific purpose: To inform my audience about the process of adopting a child from another country.
Central idea: The four parts of the adoption process are application, selection of child, child arrival, and postplacement.

I. Application—both the family and a social worker evaluate the adoptive home.
II. Selection of child—the agency provides pictures and histories of available children.

III. Child arrival—the child arrives with an "Orphan Visa."
IV. Postplacement—for up to a year the family and a social worker evaluate the placement, after which time the adoption is finalized.

Some procedures, however, do not depend on ordered sequences. For instance, some how-to subjects consist of a number of subtopics that can be explained in any order. (See Box 14.1, on p. 326, for an example of a series of how-to seminars that are in this category.) When this is so, use a topical pattern, as this example illustrates.

Specific purpose: To inform my audience of money-saving tips they can use in four sections of the supermarket.
Central idea: There are several tips for saving money in the dairy, grocery, vegetable, and meat departments of a supermarket.

I. Tips for saving money in the dairy department
II. How to save on canned goods
III. Making it through the vegetable department safely
IV. Saving on meats

Sometimes you will actually want your listeners to *do* the process for themselves, either during the speech or after they go home. When this is your purpose, you often demonstrate the process and have your listeners actually make a product as you speak. However, if the task takes too long to accomplish in the time allotted, a better strategy is to demonstrate the process and provide handouts with step-by-step instructions for audience members to try at home. During the speech outlined here, each audience member actually created a cartoon by selecting one feature from each row found on the visual aid in Figure 14.2.

Teaching Idea

Figure 14.2 is a transparency in the Instructor's Manual. Have your class draw a cartoon as you uncover each row of features.

Specific purpose: To inform my audience about specific cartoon features they can easily draw to create a cartoon character almost instantly.
Central idea: By drawing in simple cartoon shapes for eyes, noses, mouths, hair, and facial outlines, almost anyone can easily draw a cartoon.

I. First, select the eyes.
II. Then, draw a nose.
III. Choose a mouth.
IV. Add hair.
V. Outline your character's face.

You can see that process speeches often require the use of visual support—especially speeches that demonstrate how something is done. In addition, if you want your listeners to create the product as you speak, you must make sure each listener has the supplies he or she needs for the finished product.

Figure 14.2

For his speech on drawing cartoons, one speaker put these cartoon features on a transparency. He uncovered each row as he talked about those features.

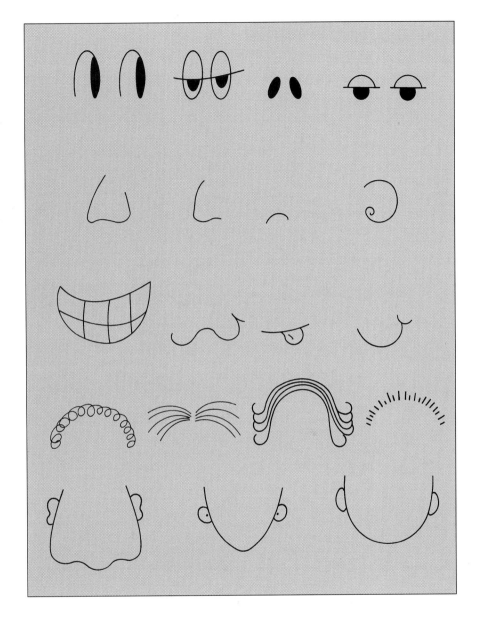

BOX 14.1

Japanese Seminars on Fathering

Some how-to speeches occur in a series of lectures or seminar presentations that take place over a period of time. For example, the Sunstar Corporation in Takatsuki, Japan,[5] hired Mieko Hosomi, a newspaper editor, to present a series of lectures informing a group of about forty company executives—not on the art of making better shampoos and other toiletries, but on the art of being better fathers. When a recession in Japan led to a five-day, rather than a six-day work week, many companies began to hire speakers like Mrs. Hosomi to help men, who know how to be workaholics, learn how to be fathers as well.

One Japanese corporation sponsored a series of lectures that informed men about effective parenting skills.

Teaching Idea

Ask students to identify situations when they have heard a series of informative lectures or when they have gone to an all-day workshop on a specific topic. Ask them to envision how such speaking might occur in their future employment. That is, when might their employers offer seminars or workshops? When might they attend a work-related conference?

Concepts

What does intelligence mean? Why do serial killers behave as they do? What is sexual harassment? These questions relate to concepts or abstractions—the principles, theories, and ideas we form mentally to explain both natural and social realities. Although we see people act in ways we classify as intelligent behavior or as sexual harassment, we can neither see nor touch intelligence or harassment. And though we cannot know for certain what causes some people to kill a sequence of victims, we formulate theories or explanations for the unusual behaviors of serial killers.

Since concepts are sometimes difficult to define and explain, your major challenge with such a topic is to make the complex ideas and theories understandable and relevant to the lives of your listeners. Here are some guidelines to follow for speeches about concepts.

1. Simplify complex ideas by breaking them down into their components. For example, subdivide intelligence into categories that include social intelligence, spatial intelligence, and musical intelligence.[6]

Cross Reference

Use of jargon is covered in Chapter 11. Analogies can be found in Chapters 8, 11, and 15. Examples are discussed in Chapter 8.

2. Carefully define your terminology, avoiding the use of technical jargon. Exactly what falls into the category of spatial intelligence? Use examples that clarify this component of intelligence. Show the items from the tests that measure spatial intelligence.

3. Clarify confusing details by using analogies, both figurative and literal, to compare the concept to something that listeners already understand. In this case, you might compare musical intelligence to simply playing an instrument.

4. Use detailed examples of concrete situations that illustrate the actions of people who test high in various kinds of intelligence.

Topical organizational patterns are often used to explain concepts, as this example demonstrates.

Specific purpose: To inform my audience of core values of many groups in sub-Saharan Africa.
Central idea: Four major value clusters are characteristic of many cultural groups in sub-Saharan Africa.

 I. Spiritual force
 II. Ancestralism and cyclism
 III. Communalism
 IV. Rationality

Here are a few topics that students have explained in informative speeches: black holes, time, Afrocentrism, personality theories, Islamic notions of justice, success, False Memory Syndrome (thinking you remember something happening—often as a result of psychological therapy—when the event did not occur).

Cross Reference

Many issues are controversial, and Chapter 3 discussed differences in beliefs.

We sometimes clash over theories, concepts, and ideas because definitions and explanations differ among people and groups. For instance, exactly what does sexual harassment mean? People's ideas differ. What caused the dinosaurs to become extinct? Theories vary. What constitutes a date rape? Few people give the same answer. What is truth? There is no consensus. The purpose of informative speaking is not to argue for one definition or another, but to clarify the concept, sometimes by comparing and contrasting differing definitions and theories regarding it.

Issues

Newspapers and magazines are good sources for a list of current issues that we discuss within our communities and our society as a whole. These include concerns over teens and guns, adoption laws, trade imbalances, famines in other nations, or local and campus problems—all complex and controversial issues. Generally, issues are related to policies that are put forth as solutions to problems and answer the question "What should we do about such and such an issue?" Here are a few examples of controversial issues.

- What should be our policies regarding illegal immigration?
- Who should decide if or when to terminate life support systems?
- What should happen to child molesters who serve their time and then reenter society?
- When, if ever, should children be allowed to divorce their parents?

Speech Assignment

An informative current issue speech is one in which students investigate an issue and present factual information relating to it. Guidelines for such a speech can be found in the Student Resource Workbook.

Informative speeches on issues are similar to investigative reports, where reporters research the facts surrounding an issue, then present these factual findings. When you choose to speak on an issue, your major purpose is to enlighten listeners so that they understand the issue in greater depth. Your report provides a factual foundation for individual listeners to use in formulating their own conclusions. Thus, reports are not intended to provide persuasive arguments advocating one position or another. However, you may follow up your report by giving a persuasive speech.

Informative speeches about issues are common assignments in public speaking classrooms. If you give one, look for the answers to such questions as: What exactly is the problem or issue? What are the current beliefs or theories commonly held about the issue? What is the extent of the problem (how many people does it affect)? How did this situation develop? What solutions are proposed? What are the arguments on both sides of the issue? Generally, pro–con, cause–effect, problem–solution, and topical patterns work well for speeches about issues.

The following outline for a speech on euthanasia defines some basic terminology related to this controversy. It provides listeners with a foundation that frames the entire discussion. It is organized topically.

Specific purpose: To inform my audience of four types of euthanasia.
Central idea: Euthanasia is a complex issue with four distinct factors relating to choice and means that result in four types of euthanasia.

  I. Controversies over euthanasia involve the element of choice.
     A. In voluntary euthanasia, the patient asks to die.
     B. In involuntary euthanasia, the patient does not request death.

II. Euthanasia involves two means.
    A. In active euthanasia, an outside cause is introduced to induce death.
    B. In passive euthanasia, no direct cause is administered, but no life-support machines or life-sustaining measures are taken.
III. This leads to four types of euthanasia.
    A. In active/voluntary euthanasia, the patient chooses to die, and uses an outside cause to induce death.
    B. In active/involuntary euthanasia, the patient does not personally choose to die, but someone else introduces an outside cause to induce death.
    C. In passive/voluntary euthanasia, the patient voluntarily chooses not to have life-support machines or life-sustaining measures.
    D. In passive/involuntary euthanasia, the patient makes no choice and no life-support or life-sustaining measures are administered.

Here is an example of an outline for a speech that reports the issue of using Native-American symbols in sports. The speaker used a pro–con pattern.

Specific purpose: To inform my audience about the supporters' and opponents' views regarding Native-American symbols that are used as mascots and nicknames for schools.

Central idea: There are several arguments both for and against using Native-American nicknames as mascots and nicknames for schools.

I. There are many arguments against the use of Native-American symbols as nicknames.
    A. Use of the symbols is an offensive gesture toward the native people.
    B. Using Native-American symbols perpetuates racist stereotypes.
    C. Non-Indians do not have the right to use sacred Indian symbols.
II. A large group of people support the continuance of such nicknames.
    A. The Indian mascot is chosen because it represents school values.
    B. Many people simply do not want to change.
    C. Use of such nicknames gives schools an opportunity to educate students on the Indian heritage represented in their name.

For informative speeches about issues, you may select personal issues such as eating disorders, campus and local controversies that vary from place to place, and national and global issues, as seen in the preceding examples. Many global issues, such as the decision the United States makes to support or not support a country in a war, will have long-term effects. Other issues are less significant, but they are related to larger controversies. For example, the issue of whether or not Miss America contestants should have plastic surgery is associated with issues of women's rights and stereotypes of female beauty.

Often informative speakers discuss both sides of controversial issues such as the use of Native American mascots for sports teams.

Categories of Informative Topics

People Provide information about living or dead subjects, heroes or villains who have shaped the world.

Places Describe countries, buildings, and natural wonders.

Objects Explain things that are natural or those made by humans.

Events Describe occurrences including personal events as well as international events.

Processes Explain natural or social processes or procedures, including how-to speeches.

Concepts Explain complex ideas and abstractions such as the concept of intelligence.

Issues Report on the facts surrounding a current issue—often one that is controversial.

Guidelines for Informative Speaking

Teaching Idea

The Instructor's Manual contains a transparency with these guidelines. Although the list appears in full sentences, the transparency follows the 6 x 6 rule (introduced in Chapter 10): No more than six lines and six words per line.

Because the purpose of informative speaking is to increase each listener's knowledge and deepen his or her understanding, the material presented in these speeches must be comprehensible. In addition, as we saw earlier in the chapter, it is important to enable listeners to make connections between your facts and their interests. Here are some keys to remember in informational speaking.

Teaching Idea

Exercise 5 works here. Partners or groups of three work together to fill in the table. Have a representative share their answers with the class as a whole.

1. *Relate your material to your audience* Help your listeners understand why knowing about your subject matters to their lives. As we have seen, the topic itself can make a difference in audience motivations. Your challenge is to help listeners integrate what they learn from your speech with their experiences, goals, beliefs, and actions. The following excerpt is from a speech intending to clear up misconceptions about sharks. Although concerns about sharks are quite distant from the lives of most students, this speaker ties into listeners' daily experiences by showing how humans regularly use products made from sharks.[7]

   A substance derived from shark livers is known as squalene. Because it has a low congealing point, Japanese airmen used it to lubricate their aircraft in WWII. Today, squalene is used as a base in burn ointments and cosmetics, such as lipstick. Can you imagine a woman kissing her boyfriend or husband through a film of shark liver oil?

   In the United States, shark skin is tanned to produce leather that is stronger than cowhide. This leather is used to make high-quality shoes and items such as bullet-proof briefcases. Shark corneas have proven to be successful substitutes for human corneas, and scientists are now experimenting with the use of shark cartilage to shrink cancerous tumors.

2. *Choose vocabulary carefully* You may have heard lectures on technical information in which professors used jargon and other words that you did not know; if so, it was difficult to understand the topic clearly. Since a major purpose of informative speaking is to clarify ideas, eliminate as much jargon as possible. Define your terms, and explain them in everyday images, as this speaker did.

*Like other fish, sharks are vertebrates, which means they have backbones. Their skele-
ton, however, is made up of cartilage, a strong, very tough material that holds its
shape. Take a moment to feel the bone in your nose. Start at its bridge and work
your way down to the tip. Along the way, you can feel where the bone leaves off and
the cartilage begins. Both are tough, but you will find that you can wiggle the cartilage when you try.*

3. *Strive to be interesting* One of the most common complaints about informative presentations is that they are boring.[8] In your preparation, occasionally
try to distance yourself from the speech and hear it as if it were delivered by
another person. Think of ways to enliven the factual material. Provide
detailed descriptions that engage the audience in the dialogical process since
they use your descriptions to form mental images. The following excerpt
from the shark speech demonstrates how the speech is more interesting
because the speaker chose concrete language and vivid descriptions:

*Many surfers and boaters have complained of shark attacks, but scientists who study
the animals argue that most shark attacks occur out of mistaken identity. The sharks
see long, oval-shaped objects that look similar to a fish or seal from the vantage point
of the shark in the water below. It is no wonder that they sometimes bite large chunks
out of surfboards.*

*Most often, however, a shark attack results from the animal being provoked and
forced to defend its territory. It may be merely trying to drive off a human intruder,
much as it would another animal that ventured into its space. While some animals
can use claws to scratch or hoofs to trample, a shark's only defensive weapon is
its teeth.*

4. *Compare the known to the unknown* Use what is familiar to introduce less
familiar ideas. That is, begin with the knowledge your listeners already have;
then, build on this foundation and show similarities and differences between
what they already know and your topic. This is just one way to help listeners integrate new information with their previous knowledge and experience. This final excerpt from the shark speech demonstrates how the
speaker helped his listeners understand a number by relating it to more
familiar statistics.

*It is true that sharks kill people globally at an annual rate of about fifty per year.
However, in Florida alone, lightning kills about 300 people annually and automo-
biles kill 2,000 annually. In Brazil, fatal snakebites claim over fifty lives yearly, and
in Australia, more people are killed as a result of automobile accidents every month
than have died in 100 years from attacks by sharks.*

Teaching Idea

*Use exercise 4 to summarize
the guidelines.*

If you follow these guidelines, you will increase your listeners' motivation
and interest in your topic. As a result, you will avoid some of the pitfalls that
result in boring speeches.

Guidelines for Informative Speaking

Relate your material to your audience Link your topic to their lives in as many ways as you can.

Choose vocabulary carefully Avoid jargon and technical language that might be confusing.

Strive to be interesting Provide vivid details and descriptions.

Compare the known to the unknown Relate what is already familiar to your audience to the aspects of your topic that are unfamiliar to them.

Summary

We are in an Information Age where having the ability to give and receive information is empowering; those who lack information do not have the basic knowledge they need to perform competently in complex societies.

Because of this, informative speeches are given by a variety of people in a variety of settings. These speakers set goals of producing knowledge in listeners who do not know about a subject. In addition, they attempt to provide a deeper understanding of the topic for those whose knowledge is superficial. A second goal attempts to reinforce and maintain information that people are in danger of forgetting. Finally, informative speakers sometimes attempt to clear up misconceptions their listeners may have about a specific subject.

There are several categories for informative speaking. These include people, places, objects, concepts, events, and processes. In addition, speakers commonly report the results of their investigative inquiries into important issues. Throughout your topic selection, consider the importance of providing information on personal, campus, local, national, and international topics.

Finally, remember the keys to informative speaking. Relate the topic to the listeners. Make vocabulary choices that clarify your ideas. Think of creative ways of presenting the information. Throughout the speech, tie abstract concepts to concrete experiences that are familiar to your listeners.

Student Speech

Amphibian Population Decline

Tiffany A. Meyer, Oregon State University

Tiffany Meyer gave this speech competitively when she was a member of the speech team at Oregon State University. It is an example of an informative speech that uses a visual aid.

Tiffany gains attention with a story that she will use as an analogy throughout the speech.

In the early 1900s, coal miner William Suttfield was sent down into a mine shaft carrying a caged canary. His daily task was to sit with the bird for a few hours, and then walk back up to the other workers waiting above. At that point all eyes would be on the canary. The workers believed that the health of the bird indicated the chemical toxicity of the mine, a factor that decided for them whether or not it was safe to work that day.

She introduces her topic—declining frog population.

Today, the caged canary is no longer used by coal miners, but the analogy may still be appropriate for our current environmental situation. As strange as it may sound, toads and frogs are dying by the thousands, and many researchers believe that we should look to the frog, just as the coal miner looked to the canary, for signs of trouble concerning the health of the natural environment. Amphibian population decline may be a warning, telling us that we have harmed our environment far more than we ever thought possible. In a society that portrays a frog as nothing much more than a cute and fuzzy Muppet® or a logo for a Mexican bar, it may be hard to take such a claim seriously. Yet both researchers and factual information have placed the frog at the center of environmental debate.

She previews the three points she will develop.

In order to understand the important link between the deaths of amphibians and the canary–coal-mine theory, I will begin by discussing the characteristics of frogs that make them such an important part of the natural environment. Second, I will talk about why frog population declines have researchers so worried. Finally, I will discuss the implications of these declines, from environmental to personal. But first, let's begin by talking about amphibians in general, and what it is that could be making them croak.

Her first main point provides background information.

According to *International Wildlife*'s November/December 1990 issue, amphibians are among the oldest creatures on earth, first appearing over 350 million years ago. Toads and frogs, the oldest of today's amphibians, first appeared as long as 150 million years ago, says the same source. This means that they have survived the Permo-triassic crisis (or as it is more commonly known, the dinosaur die-off), the breakup of the single land mass Pangaea into what we now know as the seven continents, the ice age, glacial periods, the age of mammals, and other global changes and natural disasters. At the first World Congress of Herpetology, Dr. David Wake, ecologist at the University of California, Berkeley, stated that because amphibians have been the most adaptable creature in times of natural change, "if they are checking out now . . . it is significant."

Current research discussed at the National Research Council Workshop, dedicated to the amphibian population decline issue, claimed that there is a general decline of amphibians worldwide, and as many as one-third of all amphibians may have disappeared since 1970. Interestingly, studies have shown that the characteristics of frogs that have enabled them to adapt for so long in the past may be the same characteristics that are making them die so rapidly today. In other words, perhaps Kermit was right when he said it ain't easy being green.

Tiffany includes a humorous reference to Kermit the frog that balances the technical information in the speech.

It seems that toads and frogs may have come across something to which they can no longer adapt—the human element. Every trait distinctively froggy—their skin, their homes, and their food—seems to be linked in some way to their deaths. For example, toads and frogs live their early lives in the water as tadpoles, and their adult frog-lives on land. Now while this life history allows them to cope with seasonal drought, it also exposes them to changes in both their land- and water-based habitats. These changes range from damming a river to dredging a marshland to seemingly simple changes like pollution. As Robert Kaplan of Reed College in Oregon put it in the November/December 1990 issue of *International Wildlife*, "They have a chance, maybe, of getting nailed in either place." This dual-habitat makes them affected by any manipulation of either environment, by land-use practices such as agriculture and land development, and by the introduction of a species to the water environment, like stocking a lake with fish.

Second, toads and frogs have permeable skin, a trait that allows them to absorb oxygen from water in addition to their regular breathing. A frog's skin is much more sensitive to its chemical environment than we realize. Problems like air and water pollution, acid rain, or very small increases in ultraviolet radiation due to decreases in the ozone layer could directly affect amphibians much more potently than they affect us.

A final interesting trait of amphibians is what they choose to eat. Because they feed on insects, the world's most abundant food source, we might think that they rarely ever have a chance of going hungry. Yet, like the other two mentioned traits, its food source also exposes the frog to human contaminants such as pesticides.

Because of their history of adaptability and their biological makeup, toads and frogs have retained a very central and important position on the food chain. They are not only a major predator of insects, but also a major prey of nearly every other vertebrate found in their surrounding habitat. The April 1991 issue of *Science* says that amphibians are among the most abundant creatures by weight in a typical forest. Their food chain position plus their high quantity make them not so cute and slimy anymore, but a lot more important in every aspect of the ecosystem they occupy.

So far I've painted a picture of the frog in terms of its ecological importance and its possibly self-destructive characteristics in its changing world; as we move on to discuss where and why the declines are taking place we can begin to fully understand the importance of these declines. Not only is an age-old friend of the earth dying off, but the death of this friend can be our canary, saying this earth is just too toxic to live on anymore.

In an effort to understand where and why amphibian declines are taking place, early in 1990 forty scientists met in Irvine, California, at the first conference dedicated to amphibian population declines. Marsha Barinaga reported in the March 2, 1990 issue of *Science* magazine "The workshop focuses on two key questions: Are the declines taking place? (And) Do they have a single, global cause, such as greenhouse effect or decrease in the ozone layer?" Despite the concerns for human-made effects of the safety of amphibians' habitat, Kathryn

Throughout the speech, she cites her sources of information.

With this transition statement, Tiffany moves on to her other points.

Phillips of *International Wildlife* stated that "perhaps the most confounding cases discussed were those occurring in wildlife preserves and national parks, free of farms, logging, hunters, and industry.* Most people consider these parks to be the sacred ground for all of our endangered species. And as you walk down a wooded trail toward a beautiful fish-filled lake, things often do look perfect. [Display Figure 14.3]

She continues to use credible sources.

But many people don't realize that that large lake or river isn't necessarily the star attraction for all amphibians within that forest. According to Deanna Olson, Research Fisheries Biologist for the U.S. Forest Service Pacific Northwest Research Station, many different species of amphibians may be dependent on the connecting waterways. You can understand what the effects would be if you were to run a road right down the middle of this forest, build trails and campgrounds, or introduce "stock" fish predators that are prized by anglers into the waterways. [Display Figure 14.4]

Here Tiffany provides a specific example.

The system becomes fragmented and inhospitable to toads and frogs. It's not pristine at all. The Gastric Brooding Frog, a native of the rain-forested mountain ranges of Australia, is a perfect example of these mysterious national park population declines. When Dr. Michael Tyler, a leading expert on the species from the University of Adelaide in Australia, first discovered it in 1974, he found the forest to be practically overrun by the frog. In fact, as he put it, "An agile collector could have picked up a hundred of them in a single night." Tyler was attracted to frogs because of their very unique form of reproduction. The female actually swallows her fertilized eggs until they develop and hatch. At that point, she regurgitates the little tadpoles into a nearby pond. As fascinating as this was to Tyler because of the possible medical ramifications, when he returned to study the frog in 1980—only six years after their discovery—he found their population to be practically nonexistent. Since 1980, Tyler admits to having explored every possible reason for this species decline, but he cannot come up with a sensible answer. As he put it in the November/December 1990 issue of *International Wildlife*, "It's just a silent forest."

Her third point—implications of this decline—is still being debated by scientists.

Tyler isn't alone in his confusion. While many scientists pinpoint disturbances such as deforestation or acid rain as the probable cause of a species' decline, in other cases, they don't know what to blame. In a global effort to come up with answers, in 1990 herpetologists from all over the world created an information source aptly named "The Froglog." The International Coordinator, Dr. James Vial in Corvallis, Oregon, claims that the Froglog has helped give the subject of amphibian population decline the credibility it deserves. However, until 12–15-year-long studies are completed, none of the scientists can expect to take any kind of procedural action. These long-term studies are the only way of separating normal population fluctuations from dangerous declines.

---

* *International Wildlife*, Nov–Dec 1990.

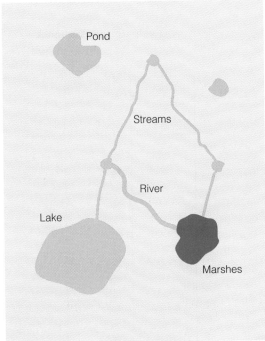

Figure 14.3   *A pristine environment.*

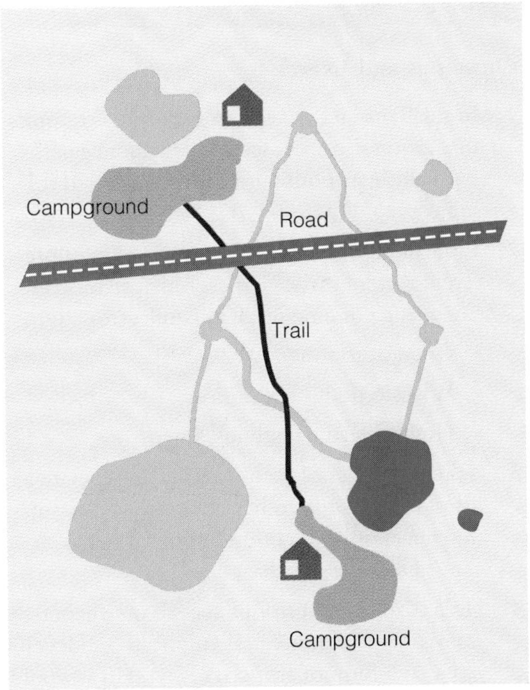

Figure 14.4   *A recreational campground.*

Campground

<table>
<tr><td>Tiffany quotes an expert who presents a different interpretation of the decline.</td></tr>
</table>

Tiffany quotes an expert who presents a different interpretation of the decline.

Until then, arguments made by scientists like Dr. James McMahon of Utah State University will still hold merit. As he states in the March 2, 1990, edition of *Science*, "Toads and frogs are dying, but so is everything else. Whether there is one nefarious, unknown factor isn't so clear; it just looks like a lot of individual cases."

Well, individual cases or not, most herpetologists believe that more research needs to be conducted because of the possible dangers involved if the canary–coal-mine theory is true.

Her conclusion begins with a summary, then returns to the opening example to provide closure and an impact ending.

Today we have taken a second glance at toads and frogs in an effort to understand them as an important link toward calculating the harms we have inflicted on the environment. We first examined the characteristics unique to amphibians; second we explored why frog declines have researchers so worried, and finally we discussed the implications of these declines, especially in terms of a warning system for all of us. In the early 1900s, it was very easy for coal miners to tell if a mine was dangerous; they simply looked to the canary. Today, we may be overlooking a real but very simple symptom of amphibian population decline. Too often these simple symptoms are the ones we can't afford to overlook.

Questions and Exercises

1. In small groups, generate a list of speech topics that group members have heard about but know little or nothing specific relating to the subject.

2. In small groups, think of creative ways of presenting an informative speech that reinforces knowledge on one of these familiar topics:
   - Good nutrition
   - What to do in case of fire
   - How to read a textbook

3. With a number of your classmates, generate a list of topics for speeches designed to clear up misconceptions or counter myths (such as those about killer bees or sharks).

4. Here is an excerpt from a speech on silicon retinas, which biomedical engineers are developing as a form of artificial vision. How would you critique this speech? Using principles from this chapter, jot down some advice for this speaker.

   The silicon retina consists of photoreceptors that mimic the cone cells of the individual's natural retina. Primarily, the photosensor is assigned the task of translating the photons that are reflected from the viewed object into an electrical signal that is processed by the retina chip or circuit.

   The horizontal cells of the natural eye are replaced by resistors, junctions between adjacent retinal cells, and capacitors which hold the electrical signals. Like its natural counterpart, the horizontal cell computes a light intensity value to be interpreted by the bipolar cells.

5. The following table lists a number of topics that might be used in informative speeches. How would you interest a student audience in each of these topics? Work with a classmate to fill in the table.

Evaluate the Audience's

	Need to know?	Interests?	Attitudes? (+ or −) Values?
Stalin			
Tips for a successful interview			
Broadway musicals			
Your campus library reference room			
Chinese medieval armor			

Key Terms

information explosion
information overload

Notes

1. Elmer-Dewitt, P. (1993, April 12). Electronic superhighways. *Time*, pp. 50–55.
2. See Fancher, M. R. (1993, August 8). Will journalism travel on the information highway? *The Seattle Times*, p. A2.
3. Article 19 is quoted in Harms, L. W., & Richstad, R. J. (1978). The right to communicate: Status of the concept. In F. L. Casmir (Ed.), *Intercultural and international communication* (p. 220). Washington, DC: University Press of America, Inc.

4. Cribbins, M. (1990). International Adoption. Student Speech. Oregon State University, Corvallis, OR.

5. This information is reported in Sanger, D. E. (1993, November 12). In Japan's astounding future: Life with father. *The New York Times*, p. A4.

6. Gardner, H. (1993). *Multiple intelligences: The theory in practice*. New York: Basic Books.

7. Abt, J. (1991, December 4). Sharks. Student speech, St. John's University, Jamaica, New York.

8. Goodall, H. L., & Waaigen, C. L. (1986). *The persuasive presentation: A practical guide to professional communication in organizations*. New York: Harper & Row.

Reasoning

15

At the end of this chapter, you should be able to

- Distinguish between claims of fact, value, and policy
- Explain how a warrant connects evidence with a claim
- Know the importance of using qualifiers and recognizing possible rebuttals in stating claims
- Define logos, pathos, and ethos
- Explain these types of reasoning, and identify tests for each: analogy (metaphor and parallel case), inductive, deductive, and causal
- Understand how appeals to emotions and needs are aspects of pathos
- Identify ways that ethos or speaker credibility functions as a reason to believe
- Explain how reasoning strategies vary across cultural groups

Note
This chapter presents information from the canon of invention. It discusses the way we make sense of our world and come to reasoned decisions about claims of fact, value, and policy. It covers three areas of reasoning: rational appeals (logos), appeals to emotions and needs (pathos), and appeals that arise from the speaker's credibility (ethos).

Cross Reference
"Good reasons" vary across cultural groups—a theme of this text.

On October 17, 1992, a sixteen-year-old Japanese exchange student dressed up as a character from the movie *Saturday Night Fever* and left his host home to attend his first Halloween party in America. Unfortunately, Yoshihiro Hattori rang the doorbell of the wrong house. Bonnie Peairs (pronounced PEERS), finding a strangely dressed Asian teen at her doorstep, called her husband, who reached for his gun. By this time, Yoshihiro had moved to the carport. When Rodney Peairs yelled "Freeze," the teen, whose English was limited, continued to advance, holding what turned out to be a camera. Seconds later, he lay dead of a gunshot wound to the chest.

In May of the following year, a jury acquitted Mr. Peairs of manslaughter. Hattori's parents, who flew from Japan to attend the trial, listened in disbelief as the jury concluded Peairs acted in "a reasonable manner." Afterward, Mr. Hattori called the verdict "incredible, unbelievable."[1] The Japanese press responded similarly, "We don't understand."[2] Masako Notoji, a Tokyo University associate professor, expressed the shock that many Japanese people felt—shock that an entire jury could conclude that shooting someone before even talking to him was reasonable. She explained, "We are more civilized. We rely on words."[3]

The key word in this illustration is *reasonable*. The same evidence that convinced an American jury that Peairs's actions were reasonable failed to convince Japanese onlookers whose cultural perspectives led them to a different conclusion entirely. What seemed rational or within reason to jurors was nonsensical to the grieving parents.

Throughout your lifetime, you have reasoned your way through everyday matters, making sense of your world and making decisions that affect your life. Based on the observations that you made in the course of ordinary living, reading, studying, watching TV, and so on, you have formed a number of conclusions that seem sensible to you. However, you have probably found that others have reached different conclusions, and you may feel compelled to speak publicly to explain your ideas. You present your conclusions as claims; then you construct reasons for others to accept your ideas.

This chapter presents the three types of reasoning common in the Western tradition. Aristotle explained them in his book *Rhetoric*.[4]

> *Of the modes of persuasion furnished by the spoken word there are three kinds. The first kind depends on the* personal character *of the speaker; the second on putting the* audience *into a certain frame of mind; the third on the proof, or apparent proof, provided by the* words of the speech *itself.*

We commonly call these appeals *ethos* (the proofs associated with the speaker's credibility), *pathos* (the appeals to audience emotions), and *logos* (the reasoning found in the words of the speech itself). We begin with an overview of reasoning. Then we will discuss the rational proofs of logos and the emotional proofs of pathos. We have already looked at ethos in the chapter on speaker–audience interactions, so we will only revisit it briefly here.

The Process of Reasoning

In order to have others accept your ideas, you make a claim and support it with evidence that others will use to warrant or justify your conclusions. Chapter 8 already considered several types of evidence. To review, you assemble facts, examples, testimony, quantification, and comparisons and contrasts in support of your points. In this section, we present three types of claims, then we investigate the concepts of warrants, qualifiers, and conditions for rebuttal that allow us to fine-tune our claims.[5]

Claims

A claim is an assertion that is open to challenge—that is, it is a conclusion or generalization that is not necessarily accepted by everyone, a statement that requires evidence or backing.[6] We commonly make three types of claims: of fact, value, or policy. They answer questions such as:

- Is it true? (fact)
- Is it ethical or good? (value)
- What should we do about it? (policy)

Claims of Fact   Is there life on other planets? Is smoking marijuana linked to health problems? Will metal detectors in schools cut the incidence of violent crime in the school? All these questions deal with facts—what exists or does not exist, what will or what will not happen. We assess claims of fact as true or false, correct or incorrect, probable or improbable. Consequently, there are three categories of factual claims that form the basis for argument: debatable points, cause–effect relationships, and predictions.

1. *Argue a debatable point* Debatable points cannot be proved by conventional means such as observation or scientific inquiry. At other times, the evidence to support the claim is inconclusive. Here are some controversial claims of fact:
   - Angels exist.
   - Lee Harvey Oswald, acting alone, killed President John F. Kennedy.
   - The ozone layer is not in danger.

2. *Attempt to prove a cause–effect relationship* Often two things follow one another with a degree of regularity. The question then arises: Are they linked in such a way that one causes or leads to the other in a greater-than-chance occurrence? Statisticians are quick to point out that just because A is associated with B, that does not necessarily imply that A causes B. Debatable cause–effect questions are:

Cross Reference

It is important to stress that facts, examples, testimony, and comparison/contrast are necessary for supporting claims.

Teaching Idea

Have students think of examples—or find examples in newspaper or magazine editorials, printed speeches (from *Vital Speeches of the Day*, and so on)—of the various types of claims.

- Divorce has harmful effects on children.
- Comets killed the dinosaurs.
- Exposure to electromagnetic fields, found in microwaves, hairdryers, and the like, increases the incidence of leukemia.

3. *Make a prediction* Finally, we cannot know future events for certain; we can only make predictions. There are probabilities—but not guarantees—that they will, in fact, occur. Because of this, when you foresee the implications of an event or a policy, you are projecting into the future and guessing what will happen. You might hear such predictions as these:

- If guns are outlawed, only outlaws will have guns.
- This deficit reduction bill will create 10,000,000 new jobs.
- Allowing more immigrants to enter the United States will make it a stronger nation.

Claims of Value   In claims of value, you attempt to have your listeners evaluate your proposition, judging it as right or wrong, good or bad, beautiful or ugly, and so on. You try to either reinforce your audience's current evaluations or convince them to accept your judgments, as these claims illustrate:

- It is *wrong* to burn the flag.
- It is *not fair* to use standardized test scores as a major means of screening college applicants.
- Horse racing is an *inhumane* sport.

Cross Reference

The idea of irreconcilable beliefs is a recurring theme of the text, found in Chapters 3 and 14.

Because claims are, by definition, disputable, people disagree over value issues. Such conflicts might be easier to resolve if opposing groups could agree on criteria for judging an act as right or wrong, fair or unfair, humane or inhumane. However, people commonly set up different standards for judgment. Witness society's continuing debates over capital punishment, physician-assisted suicide, and so on.

Claims of Policy   We make decisions regarding our behaviors both as individuals and as members of groups—decisions about *whether* or *not* we should act and about *how* we should proceed. Policy claims are often characterized by the word *should*. There are basically three types of policy claims:

1. *Current policies should change* When you appeal for change, you argue against the *status quo*, which means "the existing state of affairs." Here are some examples:

- Year-round schooling should be required in all school districts.
- The United States should change its tax system to a flat rate income tax.
- Marijuana should be legalized for medical purposes.

Cross Reference

Chapter 16 will discuss speeches with the purpose "to actuate."

2. *Current behaviors should change* When your purpose is to influence people's behavior, your major speech intention is *to actuate*. Here are claims that aim to change behaviors:

- Every student should learn to do computer-aided research.
- You should sign up as a volunteer for either the Boys Club or the Girls Club.
- Americans should save more money by building diversified investment portfolios.

3. *A current policy (or action) should not change* At times, you argue that present policies or actions should be maintained. In these cases, you are arguing *for* the status quo. As long as something is working satisfactorily, there is often little reason for change; as the saying goes, "If it ain't broke, don't fix it." Here are some claims that advocate the status quo.

- Boxing should not be abolished.
- The current speed limit should remain in effect.
- The administration should not increase tuition.

Briefly, thus, there are three major types of claims: fact, value, and policy. Because a claim is something that your listeners might dispute, you must provide enough supporting material for audience members to see reasons for accepting your claim.

Warrants

For Further Reading

S. Toulmin. (1958). *The uses of argument.* Cambridge: Cambridge University Press. See also J. L. Golden, G. F. Berquist, and W. E. Coleman (Eds.). (1983). *The rhetoric of western thought,* 3rd ed. (pp. 372–401). Dubuque, IA: Kendall/Hunt.

The justification or reasoning that both you and your listeners use to connect your evidence with your claim is called a warrant. Think of a legal setting. When police officers want to arrest a suspect, they must produce enough evidence to warrant or to justify the arrest. The key is the logical connection between the evidence and the conclusion. Consider this scenario. Fingerprints on the gun match the murder suspect's prints. Logical conclusion: The suspect held the gun *because* no one else could have caused that set of prints.

Here is an example of reasoning used by Leonid Fridman,[7] founder of Harvard University's Society of Nerds and Geeks. His basic claim is that America needs its nerds. Throughout his discussion, Fridman makes a number of other claims. One is a value claim: "There is something wrong with a society's value system that has only derogatory terms for intellectually curious and academically serious members." Another is factual: "Anti-intellectualism is higher in the U.S. than in most other countries." Still another is a policy claim, calling for a change in behavior: "We should stop making fun of nerds."

Leonid Fridman, founder of Harvard University's Society of Nerds and Geeks, argues that nerds are not fully appreciated in U.S. society. His challenge is to present enough evidence to warrant or justify that claim.

Examine one of his arguments for yourself. Look, first, at a basic claim of fact and the support he offers for it.

He Observed This Evidence ⟶ He Made This Claim

Nerds are called "geeks," a term that means "a street performer who bites the head off a live chicken."

In grade school, classmates torment bright kids with thick glasses.

Parents are ashamed of sons who read Weber instead of playing baseball and of daughters who study math rather than going dancing.

Young males are left out of social activities if they read or build model airplanes rather than play football or get wasted at parties.

Nerds are not adequately appreciated by society.

Cross Reference

Chapter 8 discusses types of evidence and tests for each.

If you were in his audience, you would begin to evaluate whether or not his argument is reasonable. Are his examples *true*—are parents really ashamed of smart children? How many parents? Are his examples *representative*—that is, do typical children make fun of kids with glasses? What about his definition—are nerds really called "geeks"? Is this definition of geeks widely accepted? Does he present a *sufficient* amount of evidence to warrant his conclusions? You might evaluate Fridman's argument and conclude, "I agree that he presents enough evidence to show that our society makes fun of its 'brains,' and his claim that nerds are unappreciated is warranted." However, you might argue with some of his evidence and reason that he does not adequately prove his claim. Therefore, you reject his assertion.

There are two additional elements of reasoning that you can employ when necessary in order to make your ideas seem more reasonable to your listeners. These are qualifiers and the rebuttal.

Qualifiers

It is important not to assert that your claim applies in all circumstances, and it is wise to eliminate words like "always" or "never" from your claims. Recognizing this, you often include *qualifiers*, words and phrases that limit or narrow the scope of your claim. A few qualifiers are "in most cases," "in males between the ages of seven and nine," "among voters with a college degree," or "usually."

Rebuttal

Since claims are disputable, people who argue for them understand that some listeners will probably disagree with or rebut their claims. It is as if "listening speakers" try to hear the arguments that audience members will raise, and they prepare to counter these arguments directly. This part of the model is called *rebuttal*. It might help you to think of rebuttals as the arguments your audience might raise that begin with the phrase, "*But* what about . . . ?"

If you learn to recognize the type of claim you are making, qualify it, provide evidence necessary to warrant it, then deal with possible attempts to rebut it, you will be more effective in presenting your ideas to others and having them recognize your views as reasonable. With this overview, we now turn to the various types of reasoning we use to warrant or justify our conclusions.

KEY CONCEPT   **The Process of Reasoning**

Claims Claims are assertions that are not accepted by everyone and thus are open to challenge.

Claims of fact Argue a debatable point, attempt to prove a cause–effect relationship or make a prediction.

Claims of value Argue that something is good or bad, right or wrong, moral or immoral, ugly or beautiful.

Claims of policy Argue either for or against a change in policy or action.

Warrants Warrants are the justification or reasoning—the logical connections—that links the evidence with the claim.

Qualifiers These words and phrases limit or narrow the scope of your claim.

Rebuttal Here you recognize and counter arguments that might be raised against the claim.

Types of Reasoning

Case Study

Students often hear conclusions such as these if they keep up with the news. For example, news about the Chinese athletes appeared during the Olympics. Sportscasters and coaches hinted that these athletes had used steroids. Do the case study as a class in order to understand how they arrived at this conclusion.

The three principal forms of proofs that Aristotle called logos, pathos, and ethos roughly translate as rational proofs, emotional proofs, and credibility. The three are not mutually exclusive; that is, they work together to form a totality of "good reasons" that listeners use to reach conclusions of their own. Thus, emotion can be reasonable; reason can have emotional underpinnings; and it is both reasonable and emotionally satisfying to believe a credible speaker.

Although all three types of proofs help us make sense of our world and come to reasoned decisions, there are times, places, and situations where certain kinds of reasoning work better than others. By way of illustration, you can see that a speaker explaining an economic recession uses different kinds of reasoning or proofs than one who attempts to explain the accidental death of a young child.

As emphasized throughout this text, the types of reasoning presented here are those patterns common in U.S. cultural institutions. Thus, knowing them and knowing how to use them effectively will empower you both as a speaker and as a critical listener within this culture. However, as Box 15.1 demonstrates, there are other reasonable ways to present and evaluate information.

Logos or Rational Proofs

Teaching Idea

If you present this information in a lecture format, use the transparency master in the Instructor's Manual. Write additional information in washable ink as you lecture.

So far we have analyzed the rational processes that connect the evidence to the claim. This process is part of what Aristotle called *logos*. His text explains:[8]

> *. . . persuasion is effected through the speech itself when we have proved a truth or an apparent truth by means of the persuasive arguments suitable to the case in question.*

Logos, thus, deals with the verbal arguments that speakers make relating to the subject. There are many types of arguments that speakers use to establish the reasonableness of their position. In Chapter 13, we examined narrative reasoning. Here we look at analogy and inductive, deductive, and causal reasoning.

Are Chinese Female Swimmers on Steroids?

Chinese female swimmer.

Read the following argument, and answer the questions that follow.

- Chinese female swimmers have voices in the low range, compared to other women.
- They are comparatively large.
- They are heavily muscled.
- Their country has been advised by coaches from the former East Germany, which was found to provide steroids to its women swimmers for many years.
- Scientists admit that steroids can be administered in training so that they will leave no traces during the competition.
- George Steinbrenner of the Yankees baseball team said that it is impossible to build such a strong team in just two years without some other explanation.
- The Chinese women swimmers used steroids in their training programs.

Questions

1. What is the claim?
2. Is the claim one of fact, value, or policy?
3. What is the evidence?
4. What possible rebuttal might an objector make? [Hint: *But* what about the population of China?]
5. Do you believe there is *enough* evidence to warrant the claim?
6. What qualifier would you add to the claim?

BOX 15.1

The Influence of Culture on Reasoning

Cultural influences affect every aspect of our reasoning strategies, as these comparisons demonstrate.[9] After you read through this material, return to the story of Yoshihiro Hattori at the beginning of this chapter. What do you think caused the Louisiana jury to arrive at different conclusions from those of the Japanese public?

1. *What is even considered to be an issue for discussion varies from culture to culture.* Because of their society's way of life, some cultural groups, for instance, would not debate such issues as gay rights, day care, or euthanasia.

2. *Cultures vary in the way they conceptualize issues.* Although people in mainstream U.S. culture think of issues as problems and solutions to be defined, proposed, tested, and eliminated or enacted, some cultural groups see problems as evidence of a bad relationship with the deity or deities or as evidence of people out of harmony with one another. Additionally, some groups see happenings as the result of fate, over which they have little control.

3. *The norms for structuring and framing a discussion vary.* In U.S. institutions, people tend to look at causes and effects or pro and con arguments, as they make claims and counterclaims. Other cultural groups ground their discussions in the historical perspectives of the various participants. Still others

rely on narrative structures to frame many of their speeches.

In the United States, people often debate an issue so that one side wins and another loses. Other cultures approach an issue as an opportunity for a community of equals to cooperate in reaching consensus.

In U.S. institutions, the tendency is to spell out conclusions explicitly and concretely. Cultures with contrasting norms tolerate more ambiguity in their conclusions; speakers often use more subtle means of influence such as metaphors and indirect suggestions.

4. *What is considered rational or irrational varies cross-culturally; thus, what counts as evidence and what constitutes a good reason vary across cultural groups.* Although U.S. culture relies heavily on facts, statistics, and studies by experts, other cultural groups find good reasons in traditional sayings, authoritative texts, and the words of the elders who are considered wise because of their experiences. Still others rely on narratives and analogies to provide good reasons.

The bias in the mainstream culture is toward linear, analytical models of reasoning. Other cultural groups reason more holistically through drama, intuition, and emotional expressiveness.

Cross Reference

Box 15.1 develops the cultural theme of the text.

Reasoning by Analogy We saw in Chapter 8 that you can use comparison and contrast as forms of evidence to support your claims. To review, when you use analogies, you compare one item that is less familiar or unknown to something concrete that the audience already knows. Just as you use both figurative and literal comparisons, you can reason figuratively by metaphor or literally by parallel case reasoning. Both are effective in public speeches.

Cross Reference

Compare to the tests for using comparisons and contrasts as evidence. See Chapter 8.

Reasoning by Metaphor When you reason by metaphor, you *figuratively* compare two things that are generally different but share a recognizable similarity. This form of reasoning is fundamentally dialogical, for it requires the active participation of listeners who must see a sensible connection between the two things you compare. Public speakers frequently use metaphors in their public reasoning. Jesse Jackson referred to his supporters as the "Rainbow Coalition" and his vision for society as a "patchwork quilt." Through these images, listeners form mental images of things that are made up of many colors, shapes, or textures.

Many scholars argue that along with narrative, reasoning by analogy is a fundamental form of reasoning, practiced by all people globally. According to the scholar Brian Wicker,[10] metaphor is an older, more poetic way of seeing the world, related to the modes of thinking of poets and storytellers, a continuation of our oral heritage. The African-American scholar Asa Hilliard agrees that use of analogy is a basic form of reasoning in Africa and in African-American speakers—one that some scholars overlook. He supports his claim in this way.[11]

Cross Reference

Chapter 1, on oral traditions.

> *Early use was made of proverbs, song, and stories. Direct or symbolic lessons were taught through these. . . . Parenthetically, it is interesting that racist psychologists claim that Black people are not capable of "Level II Thinking," the kind of abstract thinking which is reflected in proverbs and analogies. To the contrary, this is our strong suit. . . . Psychologists . . . miss the extensive use of proverbs and analogies among us.*

For Further Reading

A. Hilliard. (1986). Pedagogy in ancient Kemet. In M. Karenga and J. Carruthers (Eds.). *Kemet and the African world view* (p. 257). London: University of Sankore Press.

We do not generally consider reasoning by metaphor to be a "hard" proof; rather, analogies suggest associations that vary from individual to individual, depending on each one's personal experiences. Metaphors are effective in arousing listener emotions, especially when they elicit positive images. Jesse Jackson's "rainbow" leads some to think of a pot of gold—good fortune. His "patchwork quilt" evokes images of home, of warmth, of love and security—unless, of course, the quilt is fraying.

The major test for reasoning by analogy is that listeners must make the mental association and agree that the comparison does, in fact, illuminate, clarify, and illustrate the concept.

For Further Reading

D. A. Lieberman. (1991). Ethnocognitivism and problem solving. In L. A. Samovar and R. E. Porter (Eds.). *Intercultural communication: A reader*, 7th ed. (pp. 229–233). Belmont, CA: Wadsworth.

Parallel Case Reasoning Whereas metaphor shows likenesses between two *different* things, reasoning by parallel case or *literal analogy* finds likenesses between two *similar* things. We use this type of reasoning to formulate policies by asking what another person or group decided to do when faced with a problem similar to our own, as this 1993 example shows.

> *During the debate over health care reform in the United States, policy makers turned to other countries and to states within the U.S. to see how they kept health care costs under control. What did Canada do? How did Oregonians and Hawaiians control their health care costs? What policies had Germany formulated?*
>
> *Out of this search, individuals and groups lined up behind various plans. Some argued loudly for the Canadian system; others supported the Oregon or the Hawaiian plan. Still others worked out plans using elements of the German model.*

Not only do we use an actual case to formulate policies, we also make predictions about the future, based on the past. Thus, we predict that what happened in a known case will happen in a similar case that we project.

Both speakers and listeners must employ tests such as the following for reasoning by analogy—especially when literal analogy or parallel case reasoning is offered as a proof.

Teaching Idea

Discuss the reasoning in the health care debate using the tests for parallel case reasoning.

1. Are the cases alike? Or are you "comparing apples to oranges"?
2. Are they alike in essential details?

Inductive Reasoning When you reason inductively, you begin with specific instances and formulate a reasonable generalization or conclusion from them. Think of induction as reasoning from the *particular* to the *general*, like this:

Particular instances of temporary employment:

- *The state of Maine uses "temps" as bailiffs and financial investigators.*
- *IBM traded 10 percent of its work force for "peripheral" employees—temps.*
- *Some doctors, X-ray technicians, engineers, and executives work in temporary positions.*
- *The Secretary of Labor said 90 percent of the jobs created in February, 1993, were involuntary part time.*

Generalization:

America has entered an era that will rely heavily on temporary workers, or "temps."[12]

For Further Reading

M. Griffiths and M. Whitford (Eds.). (1988). *Feminist perspectives in philosophy* (pp. 131–151). Bloomington: Indiana University Press.
C. McMillan. (1982). *Women, reason, and nature: Some philosophical problems with feminism.* Princeton: Princeton University Press.
See additional references at the end of the chapter.

Although both men and women reason inductively, a number of feminist philosophers[13] see inductive reasoning as a *major* way that women come to know about the world and draw conclusions about it. For instance, Morwenna Griffiths and Margaret Whitford[14] explain that women often begin by describing particular cases grounded in the experiences of real people—the rape victim, the

Figure 15.1

You observe a number of spaniels and inductively reason that they make good pets. Using that premise you deduce that Curly—the dog you want to buy—will be a good pet.

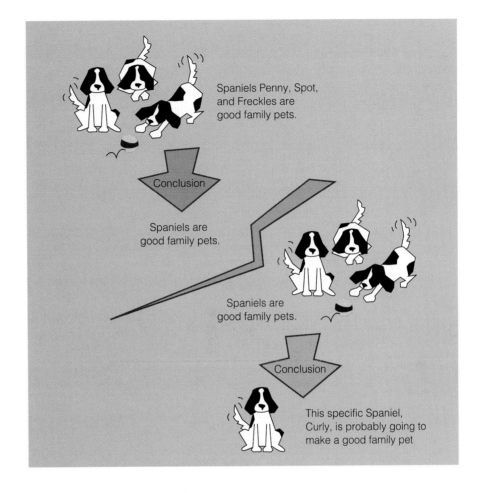

Spaniels Penny, Spot, and Freckles are good family pets.

Conclusion

Spaniels are good family pets.

Spaniels are good family pets.

Conclusion

This specific Spaniel, Curly, is probably going to make a good family pet

Theme

This section develops the book's theme of diversity.

family that lost its life savings by investing in speculative stocks, the student athlete whose partial scholarship is cut off when her sport is eliminated. Then, as in all inductive reasoning, they draw conclusions from these specific examples. The major point feminist philosophers make is that women's ways of knowing and reasoning are grounded in personal experiences that arise out of their relationship with others.

Scholars[15] who examine the reasoning patterns and the rhetoric of ethnic groups similarly argue that many ethnic groups reason inductively. Patricia Sullivan, for instance, explains that African-American speakers tie knowledge to human experiences, human actions, and the human life world.[16]

Knowledge does not exist for its own sake, or in the abstract, but exists as grounded in human experience. What is relevant is relevant because it makes a difference in people's lives.

Since you can be sure that your conclusions are valid only when you are able to observe 100 percent of a population, it is ideal to look at every case before you form a conclusion. However, you can rarely observe every member of a specific group. That is, you cannot speak to every temporary worker in the United States. For this reason, you must select a sample that is typical of the rest of the members of the group, formulate conclusions from the characteristics in the sample, then generalize your findings to the larger population.

There are three major tests for inductive reasoning; all are linked to the tests you used to evaluate examples (see Chapter 8).

1. Are enough cases represented to justify the conclusion? Or are you forming a conclusion based on only a few cases?

2. Are the cases typical; that is, do they represent the average members of the population to which the generalizations are applied? Or are they extreme cases that may show what *could* happen but not what *usually* happens?

3. Are the examples from the time under discussion, or are they out of date?

Deductive Reasoning   Inductive reasoning moves from specific examples or particulars to conclusions or generalizations, but deductive reasoning does the opposite. It begins with a generalization or principle, called the premise, and moves logically to an application in a specific case. If you study logic, you will see a model of the deductive reasoning process shown in a syllogism such as this:

(Major premise)	All U.S. senators are at least thirty years old.
(Minor premise)	She is a senator.
(Conclusion)	Therefore, she has lived at least thirty years.

When you are sure of the major premise, you can assert the conclusion with confidence. Because it is a constitutional rule that members of the U.S. senate cannot be younger than 30, you can be sure that a particular individual who was elected or appointed to the office has met the age requirement.

Teaching Idea

Use Figure 15.1 to illustrate the relationship between inductive and deductive reasoning.

However, many of the generalizations that we use as premises are less certain. They are inductively derived in the first place as a result of observation of particulars. Whereas some, such as "All men are mortal," are 100 percent certain, others, such as "Teen marriages lead to problems," are not true in all cases. For this reason, it is wise to qualify both your premises and your conclusions like this:

A high percentage of teen marriages end in failure.
Tiffany and Ryan married while still in their teens.
Their marriage *has a high probability* of ending in failure.

When you reason deductively, you rarely provide the entire syllogism in your arguments; you leave your listeners to fill in the unstated premises. This is called an *enthymeme*. For example, you might say, "She is at least thirty years old, for she is a senator" or "Teen newlyweds Tiffany and Ryan may find that their marriage will end in failure." Aristotle[17] understood the dialogical nature of deductive reasoning when he identified the *enthymeme* as an important component of deductive reasoning. Your listeners must form conclusions based on their knowledge of what you do *not* say. For instance, if you say, "Oksana Baiul was the top winner in Olympic skating," listeners (if they know anything at all about the Olympic games) understand, without it being said, that she won a gold medal because it is common knowledge that a gold medal is awarded to the top competitor in each event. The complete syllogism in this case is:

Top winners in Olympic skating receive a gold medal.
Oksana Baiul was the top winner in Olympic skating.
Therefore, she won a gold medal.

There are two major tests for deductive reasoning.

1. In order for the conclusion to be valid, the premises must be true or highly probable.
2. In order to be reasonable, the conclusion must follow from the premise.

Causal Reasoning   A speaker made this assertion recently: "There were nine million immigrants last year, and there were nine million Americans out of work." These two facts can be verified by counting both immigrants and people without jobs. However, if the speaker links them, stating that one results in or leads to the other, he is then using cause–effect reasoning, and his statement sounds like this: "There were nine million Americans out of work *because* there were nine million immigrants." In the first statement, the two conditions exist together in time—perhaps by chance; in the second statement, the second condition results from the first—and would cease to exist without it.

Because the belief in causation is a core Euro-American belief, this type of reasoning is very common. However, in order to be a *cause*, one factor must precede another, and it must be linked to it in such a way that the second factor follows as a matter of rule. Thus, it is evident that the lack of oxygen to the brain *causes* death—this link is observed time after time. But other causal links are not as well proven, sometimes because many other factors may be linked to the effects. Consequently, the causes of unemployment are more complex than the influx of immigrants. The key to causal reasoning is to produce enough reasons to warrant the link or connection between the two factors.

As with all the other types of reasoning, you ask a series of questions in order to assess if the reasoning is valid.

1. Is there a real connection? Does one follow *as a result of* the first, or do the two events simply exist together in time?

2. Is this the only cause? The most important cause? Or are other variables a factor?

3. Is the cause strong enough for the effect?

Teaching Idea

Activity 15.1 in the Instructor's Manual provides additional examples of reasoning for students to evaluate. *Or analyze reasoning from letters to the editor that students bring in. See exercise 1.*

In summary, in your speeches, you use a variety of reasons to warrant your claims. Sometimes you use both figurative and literal analogies to enable listeners to connect what they already know to what is less familiar. At other times, you reason inductively by beginning with experiences and specific instances; then you formulate generalizations. Or you use generalizations as the premises for deductive reasoning. Finally, you establish causal links that establish relationships between two conditions that exist together in time. All these types of reasoning fall under the category of logos, or rational proofs.

KEY CONCEPT   **Logos or Rational Proofs**

Type of Reasoning	Definition	Tests
Analogy		
Metaphor	Comparison to unlike things.	Does it clarify the concept?
Parallel case	Comparison to similar things.	Are the cases alike? Are they alike in essential details?
Inductive	Using particulars to form generalizations.	Are there enough cases? Are they typical? Are they up-to-date?
Deductive	Applying a generalization to a particular case.	Is the premise true? Does the conclusion follow from it?
Causal	Linking two events so that one leads to another.	Is the connection real? Is it the only cause? Is the case strong enough?

Pathos

Contrast these two situations: In the first, you are listening to a speaker who has all of her facts and figures straight, and she provides evidence that passes all the tests: her examples are representative; her statistics are from reputable sources; the experts she cites are knowledgeable in their fields, but you still are not persuaded to act because you feel there is no good reason for you to do so. In other words, you are not motivated—you are neither interested nor concerned about the topic.

In the second situation, you are hearing a speaker who similarly provides excellent evidence and reasoning that is sound. However, he is showing why you need to believe and act on the issue by tying it into your core beliefs and values, providing a connection between the topic and your personal goals, and touching your emotions. As a result of his speech, you are beginning to care about the topic and want to believe and act as he proposes.

The second speaker realizes what good speakers have always known—motivation is an internal, individualistic or subjective factor that results when listeners understand how topics affect their lives in a personal way. Consequently, we not only make sense of issues by logically considering evidence and evaluating reasoning, we also consider them sensible for emotional and psychological reasons. And in the end, our subjective reasons may be as powerful an influence as our logical ones.

In this section, we focus on two major types of emotional appeals: appeals to emotions and appeals to needs. But emotional appeals are not so simple that we can fit them neatly into two boxes, one labeled "emotions" and one labeled "needs." Remember as you read that emotions are intricate sets of feelings that emerge in part from our core beliefs, values, and attitudes. They are interwoven or mixed, and they vary in us from time to time.

Appeals to Emotions   Emotions, according to Aristotle, are all the feelings that change people in ways that affect their judgments. We often think of two general categories of emotions, though these categories overlap: positive emotions are those we want to be part of our lives, and negative emotions are those we want to avoid or prevent. Political campaign ads provide an illustration of both kinds of emotions, as you can see in Box 15.2.

Desirable or positive emotions make us feel pleasure. Psychologists who study motivations say that we "approach" rather than "avoid" them. Most people find emotions such as love, peace, pride, approval, hope, generosity, courage, and loyalty to be desirable. Additionally, we have positive emotions about our core beliefs and values such as freedom and individualism. By appealing to these positive feelings, you can often motivate your listeners to accept and act on your claims.

One of the best ways to appeal to emotions is to use narratives and examples, as this excerpt from a student speech demonstrates. The student speaker, originally from the Philippines, was adopted into an American home when she was a teenager.[18]

You might be thinking that adopting an international child is a lot of work. Well, it is, but I believe it is worth it. My parents say that bringing me into their family is one of the most gratifying things they have ever done. And their generosity has obviously

BOX 15.2

Use of Emotional Appeals in Political Campaign Ads

One of the most memorable campaign ads came from the 1964 race pitting Democrat Lyndon Johnson against Republican Barry Goldwater. Goldwater was known as a "hawk" who believed in a strong military. During the 1960s, the Cold War was in full swing, and millions of Americans feared the final countdown that would unleash a nuclear attack. Johnson's ad showed a young girl pulling the petals off a daisy, while an off-screen narrator was counting down—"10, 9, 8, 7, 6 . . . ." Although the ad did not explicitly say Mr. Goldwater would activate the countdown that would begin a nuclear war, the appeal to fear was so great— and many said overdone—that the ad ran only once before it was pulled. George Bush's famous Willie Horton ad similarly played on voters' fears of crime—with racial overtones. The ad showed an African-American male who brutally attacked an innocent woman while on release under a program instituted in his opponent's state.

In contrast to these appeals to fear, President Ronald Reagan was famous for the ad campaign "It's morning in America," which showed beautiful scenes of families and homes. President Clinton's campaign, similarly, appealed to hope. In fact, he was born in Hope, Arkansas, and presented himself as "The Man from Hope."

Teaching Idea

Using Box 15.2 have students discuss other political ads they have seen and identify emotional appeals that are used in them.

benefited me. If it were not for my parents, I would not be able to continue my college education. I wouldn't have any parents or sisters to call my own. As far as I know, I would probably still be in an orphanage because I wouldn't have a place to go.

Her personal story emphasizes generosity and hope as well as the underlying values of self-sacrifice for the good of others, education, family, and belonging. It provides a powerful argument for international adoption.

In contrast to desirable emotions, there are a number of strong emotions that we view negatively, avoiding them whenever possible. Among these are guilt or shame, hatred, insecurity, anger, fear, and anxiety. Appeals to negative emotions can be forceful—sometimes with disastrous consequences. Consider the rhetoric of white supremacists and other hate groups who appeal to their listeners' weaknesses, angers, fears, and insecurities.

Teaching Idea

Discuss speech topics in which appeals to negative emotions might be appropriate. Examples: practice safer sex, quit smoking, don't drink and drive, buy a car alarm system.

Negative emotions, such as fear, are resources that you can use to motivate your listeners to act in ways that can help them avoid some real dangers, and you may regularly appeal to audience fears in such cases. Take, for example, a hypothetical speech about wearing seatbelts. Most listeners know that they *should* wear seatbelts; however, they still do not buckle up consistently. Thus, they need to fear the possible consequences so much that they snap on their belts every time they get into a car. If you use fear as a motivator, your appeal will probably be more persuasive than if you dispassionately present facts about seatbelts. For this reason, a vivid example of a person killed when he "just this once" neglected to use his seatbelt is a proof that fatal accidents can happen at any time.

One way to arouse listener emotion is to use analogies. Here is an example of the way one student used this style of reasoning to arouse his listeners' emotions, in this case anger. His speech explored the use of Native-American symbols as sports mascots. During his talk, he wanted his listeners to care about the topic and to identify with the Native Americans' perspective. To arouse anger in his audience at a Catholic university, he used the following analogy:[19]

> *Opponents feel that non-Indian people do not have the right to use sacred Indian symbols. Phil St. John, a Sioux Indian and founder of the Concerned American Indian Parents group, said the behaviors of Indian mascots at sporting events were comparable to a Native American tearing apart a rosary in front of a Catholic church. Can you imagine someone dressing up as the Pope and swinging a cross wildly in the air at one of our football games? This is how some Native Americans feel when their sacred symbols are used in sports.*

However, it is easy to overdo negative appeals and turn off your listeners. For instance, speakers who use excessive appeals to guilt or fear in speeches related to their causes sometimes turn their audiences away from, rather than toward, their beliefs, as the following case illustrates. Writing in *The New York Times*, history professor Theodore Roszak explains his reaction to a speech by a famous environmental activist.[20]

> *[The activist's] presentation is meant to instill unease. In my case, she is succeeding, though not in the way she intends. She is making me worry . . . for the fate of this movement on which so much depends. As much as I want to endorse what I hear, [her] effort to shock and shame just isn't taking. . . . I find myself going numb.*

Roszak concludes that the environmental movement needs to evaluate the psychological impact of such appeals to fear and guilt. Rather than make people feel guilty about living, the movement needs a "politics of vision" that connects environmental goals to positive emotions—to what is "generous, joyous, freely given, and noble" in people.

Appeals to Needs Not only do you appeal to emotions, you can also appeal to your listeners' needs and wants. Of course, these are not separate from emotions, for we tend to feel powerful emotions directed toward the things we need and desire.

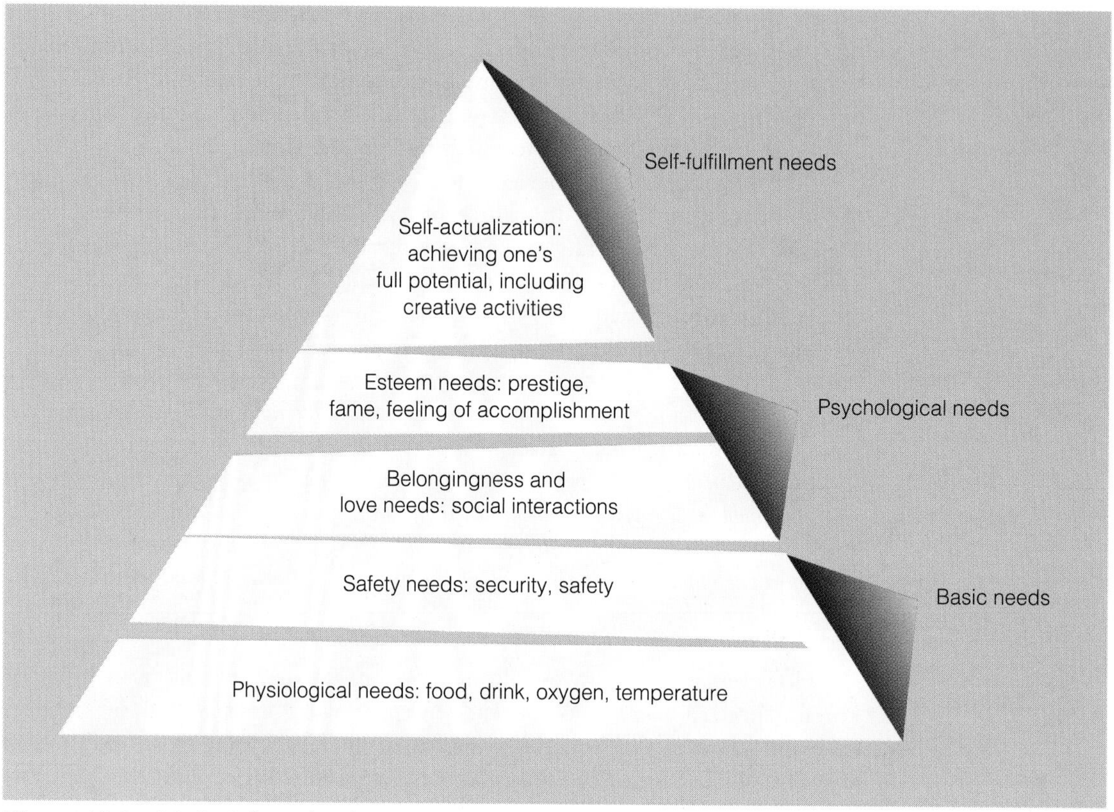

Figure 15.2   *Maslow's hierarchy of needs.*

In recent decades, many scholars have attempted to classify human needs. One of the most widely cited systems of classifying needs is the work of Abraham Maslow.[21] Maslow theorized that our needs are ranked into five levels, each building on the others (see Figure 15.2). The basic needs are essential for our physical survival; everyone must have them met. Although succeeding levels are important, they become less and less vital for survival. The result is that not everyone fulfills his or her needs in the final level. Briefly, the five levels and how they relate to public speaking are as follows:[22]

Teaching Idea

Elicit possible topics that relate to each of the needs in the list. Or use the list of topics generated in Chapter 2, and identify needs that each topic represents.

1. *Basic needs* It has been said that we can live forty days without food, four days without water, and four minutes without air. Thus, food, water, and air are basic survival needs. Shelter, sex, rest, and stress release are others.

    Topics that appeal to basic needs include air pollution, bottled water, the homeless in America, sex education, and food irradiation.

2. *Security needs* Once we have the basics, we need to feel secure and safe with them. This level includes the need for self-preservation; it also includes the

need for secure employment as a means of obtaining the other needs. In addition, we need to feel we are able to take control of our circumstances.

In a speech, you may show your audience how to gain peace of mind through such security measures as retirement funds, insurance policies, national defense, and self-defense. Demonstrate how your subject will make your listeners' jobs more secure, their homes more safe and comfortable, their health better.

3. *Needs to love and belong* This category includes our needs for love and affection that can be met through meaningful, stable relationships with others, including friends, families, and social groups on whom we can depend.

You can address these needs by showing how your topic helps your listeners be better friends, creates a stronger community, or builds ties between people.

4. *Esteem needs* We need approval and recognition from others. We need to see ourselves as competent, respected individuals who can be proud of what we do. This category includes self-respect and reputation.

Throughout your speeches, demonstrate that you respect your listeners, and mention their accomplishments when appropriate. Find ways to make them feel competent to carry out your proposals. Let them know that their ideas, opinions, and concerns are important.

5. *Self-actualization needs* In the final level, we seek to reach our highest potential through personal growth, doing good deeds, creating unique works, and overcoming challenges.

Challenge your listeners to look beyond themselves and reach out to others. Encourage them to dream big dreams and accomplish unique things. The Army's slogan, "Be all that you can be," is an example of an appeal to self-actualization.

For Further Reading
A. H. Maslow. (1954, 1987). *Motivation and personality,* 3rd ed. San Francisco: Harper & Row. V. Packard. (1957, 1970). *The hidden persuaders.* New York: Pocket Books.

In addition, Vance Packard[23] lists several "compelling needs" that advertisers often use in persuasive appeals. Many of them overlap with Maslow's list, but two are unique enough to deserve mention.

1. *Need for roots* We need to have a sense of connection with our past, a feeling for our historical heritage. We want to know where we came from, both biologically—as Alex Haley's search for his roots demonstrated in Chapter 1—and philosophically, meaning our place in the greater scheme of life.

To meet this need, help your listeners psychologically place themselves in time as part of a group who follow in a long train of admirable individuals. At a sports banquet, for instance, refer to former "greats" on earlier teams; in patriotic settings, speak of national heroes. Include references to countries of origin when appropriate.

2.   *Need for immortality* Not only is the past important, but we also need a sense of connection to the future. Questions such as these express this need: What will happen to me? What will happen after I die? Will I be remembered?

Show listeners how their actions today will perpetuate their influence in the future. For instance, if they recycle now, subsequent generations can thank them for a clean environment.

Teaching Idea

Use the supplementary material on motivation in the Instructor's Manual as the basis for a lecture.

Think back to the speech on international adoption for a moment. The speaker appeals to the emotion of generosity—and all the feelings associated with it. In addition, she appeals to Maslow's level 1 need for shelter, the level 3 need for belonging, and the level 5 need for self-actualization by showing how her parents unselfishly gave of their resources so that she could benefit.

Cultural Considerations A common stereotype of women is that they reason with their hearts rather than their heads, an overgeneralization that may have some basis in fact. Scholars who study women's patterns of thinking stress the importance of emotion in the reasoning process. Allison Jaggar,[24] for example, believes that emotions are essential to knowing. Although they are obviously different from "dispassionate investigation," they complement logic, and they are intertwined with rational proofs. These scholars insist that feelings are not inferior to reason; furthermore, they are not something that women must overcome in order to reason clearly. Instead, emotions can be a source of knowledge in themselves, and "truth" or "knowledge" without them is distorted.[25]

Teaching Idea

Discuss examples of reasoning that use emotional appeals—effectively and ineffectively. Sources: student speeches, *Vital Speeches of the Day*, letters to the editor (see Yan-Hong Krompacky's letter in Chapter 12), advertisements.

Tests for Emotional Appeals Although emotions are essential, they are not always trustworthy, and it is appropriate to subject them to criticism and appraisal. This means that you can examine emotions to see if they are reasonable. Let's say you are using fear as a motivator in a speech. Is the fear justified, or are you making your listeners unduly fearful? Are you creating or playing on irrational fears in your listeners?

When you are an audience member, ask questions such as these: Why do I feel guilty? Is my guilt reasonable? Is the speaker using my guilt feelings to manipulate me into donating to his or her cause? Although the speaker is causing me to feel angry, is anger my primary emotion? Could it be that I am really fearful instead? That is, are the speaker's ideas challenging my cherished beliefs and creating fear that I am masking with anger toward him or her?

Cross Reference

Ethics is a theme of this text.

Further, is emotion being used ethically? Generally, it is considered unethical to appeal to emotions in an attempt to bypass logical reasoning. For example, does an appeal to national pride create an argument for going to war in such a way that it obscures a more rational argument against military involvement? Does a speaker use fear to motivate listeners to act for his own profit rather than for the audience's good?

KEY CONCEPT   **Pathos**

Appeals to emotions Appeal to both positive and negative emotions.

Appeals to needs Maslow's five levels include basic needs, safety needs, needs for love and belonging, esteem needs, and self-actualization needs. Vance Packard adds needs for roots and needs for immortality that connect us with the past and the future.

Cultural considerations Women stress the importance of emotions in reasoning. Emotions can be a source of knowledge in themselves; they are not a subjective factor to be overcome.

Tests for emotional appeals Critically evaluate emotional appeals to determine if they are reasonable or irrational. Speakers should not use emotions unethically to bypass logical reasoning.

Ethos

Cross Reference

Chapter 5 discusses ethos in the context of the dialogical interactions that occur between speakers and audiences.

As we discussed in Chapter 5, one type of proof—or reason to believe—comes from qualities of the speakers themselves. A brief review of that chapter reveals that we evaluate speakers on their:

- Good sense—their intelligence, sound reasoning, and composure
- Good character—their integrity, honesty, and trustworthiness
- Goodwill or friendliness of disposition—their friendliness, respect, and dialogical attitude
- Dynamism—their forcefulness and enthusiasm

Aristotle believed that your character—a proof he called *ethos*—was the most effective means of persuasion you possess. Here is how he explains ethos:[26]

> *Persuasion is achieved by the speaker's personal character [ethos] when the speech is so spoken as to make us think him [or her] credible. We believe good [people] more fully and more readily than others: this is true generally whatever the question is, and absolutely true where exact certainty is impossible and opinions are divided.*

Listeners' inner dialogue—or reasoning—might look something like this as they consider whether or not to believe a speaker's claims.

> *This person knows what she is talking about—she is demonstrating that she has done her homework on the subject. In addition, she seems to have a good intention toward me; I trust her. Thus, I believe it when she tells me that . . . .*

Dr. C. Everett Koop, former surgeon general, demonstrates ethos—the proof that comes from the character of the speaker. Known for his professional credentials, his personal integrity, and his reputation as a straight shooter, Dr. Koop is an effective persuasive speaker.

In contrast, audiences frequently use a speaker's ethos as a reason not to believe what he or she is asserting to be true. Their reasoning may run something like this.

That guy had no clue of what he was talking about. I had the feeling he wasn't being entirely up front with us. He seemed so arrogant—like he really didn't care about us—he just wanted us to sign up for his pet project. I don't trust him. Therefore, I don't really believe his information about . . . .

Your listeners want to see you as someone who is concerned about them, someone who speaks to them in their "own language." Kenneth Burke,[27] one of

For Further Reading

K. Burke. (1950). *A rhetoric of motives.* New York: Prentice-Hall. See also M. H. Nichols. (1952). Kenneth Burke and the "New Rhetoric." *Quarterly Journal of Speech, 38,* 133–144.

the twentieth century's most astute rhetoricians, stressed the importance of "identification" with an audience. According to Burke, we are separated from one another by a variety of "divisions," but identification is a potential unifying force that has the power to bring diverse people together.

But how do you identify with your audience? One way to do this is to find areas of *common ground*—to link yourself with your listeners by emphasizing ways you are similar to them. This is fairly easy when members of your audience are very much like you. When you share many common beliefs and have similar values, attitudes, and behaviors, it is not difficult to find areas of commonality to draw on for your speech. However, identification becomes more difficult when you speak to a diverse group. Then, you must consider closely the areas you do share. However, the same principle applies: Find areas of common ground, and build on them. For instance, even in the most diverse of speaker–audience relationships, all humans share the needs for survival and safety.

The following example demonstrates how Susan Au Allen, president of the U.S. Pan Asian American Chamber of Commerce, emphasized common ground with her largely African-American audience.[28]

> *So I salute you, a cherished ally. The United States Pan Asian American Chamber of Commerce represents a diverse group of Asian Americans. We are Japanese, Filipinos, Chinese, Asian Indians, Koreans, Vietnamese, Laos, Thais, Cambodians, Hmongs, Pakistanis, and Indonesians. Each has a distinct beautiful ethnic cultural heritage, but our goals are the same as yours. We want to remove racial barriers, we want equal opportunity for our members, and we want to create greater horizons for those who follow.*

Although most speakers rely on commonalities with their audiences, some use their differences to make them more credible. The topic of the speech is generally the key. For example, Gary Caliender suffered a stroke when he was seventeen years old; consequently, when he spoke about strokes and stroke victims, his words were much more persuasive because of his disability. When Ariko Iso (whose speech is found at the end of Chapter 10) spoke on Japanese writing, she was more credible because she was from Japan.

Here is the way Native-American David Archambault[29] opened his speech to an audience of Rotary Club members; he used the differences between them to his advantage.

> *Thank you and good afternoon. Hau Kola. That is how we Lakota say "Greeting, Friends." I am happy to be here today to represent Native American people. I am a Ikoeya Wicaska—an ordinary man. We think of an ordinary man as not superior to anyone else or for that matter to anything else. We—all people and all things—are related to each other.*

BOX 15.3

International Reasoning Styles

Reasoning styles vary cross-culturally.[30] Although negotiators across the globe learn to "think like Americans," ordinary Americans do not generally attempt to understand the thought patterns of other groups. The result is that, if you are typical, you probably do not know how to interpret the reasoning of an international figure like Saddam Hussein, and as you might imagine, these differences can impede international communication.

French Reasoning

Ethos is a powerful proof to the French because of the value they place on educated persons. In addition, the French tend to reason deductively. At the outset of the reasoning process, they establish and prioritize the principles or generalizations on which the rest of their reasoning will be based. Once they have decided on these generalizations, they do not then search for new evidence or facts. Because of this, French negotiators often appear to be inflexible to others from cultures that are willing to look at new information at each stage of the policy discussion. Therefore, negotiators who are successful in the French culture introduce their evidence early.

Mexican Reasoning

Mexican negotiators tend to be less impressed with expert opinions, statistics, and inductive reasoning than are U.S. negotiators. Like the French, they reason more deductively. They begin with the general aspects of the problem; then they define the issues, categorize them, and decide on the main principle that applies to the problem. Once that is decided, they follow logical principles to their conclusions.

Asian Reasoning

Although there is not one Asian rhetoric, public speakers from countries such as Japan, China, Korea, and India tend to quote from the ancient

Teaching Idea

As a culminating activity for this chapter, evaluate the student speech in exercise 3, printed at the end of the chapter.

Not only do your listeners come to trust you because they perceive that you identify with them, they also trust you because you link yourself with knowledgeable sources throughout your speech. That is, you cite the results of studies, quote the testimony of well-established authorities, and otherwise reveal the sources of your information. As we have seen throughout the text, you also become more credible when you use sound reasoning, approach your audience with a dialogical attitude, and deliver your speech with enthusiasm.

Finally, simply because other cultures do not name these proofs in the way that Aristotle described them does not mean that they do not exist in some form within the culture. Across the globe, public speakers appeal to their listeners' authorities and sacred texts such as the Vedas, Sutras, Koran, and writings of Confucius. They discount contemporary quotations because they have not stood the test of time. Consequently, logic and reasoning based on empirical data is not enough to refute the ancient books. The ethos of the speaker is important, and good character and trustworthiness are more valuable than the expertise that comes from technical training. As a result, older, experienced speakers' ideas are more easily accepted. Finally, Asian theorists state that developing the proper sentiments in the audience is the major purpose of communication. Love, pity, and peace are the greatest of the sentiments, and great communicators create all three in their audiences.[31]

Arab Reasoning

Arabs tend to ground their arguments in their core values of hospitality, generosity, courage, honor, and self-respect. They value storytellers who are the group's historians and moralists.

Before an issue can be understood properly, it must be grounded in historical perspectives. Arab speakers rely on the rhythm and sounds of words to heighten audience emotions during the speech. Overstating the case indicates sincerity, not distortion within the culture. In contrast, a soft tone indicates that the speaker is weak or lying.[32]

Additionally, within Arab cultures, there is a tradition of verbal dueling, or trading insults, that Arab groups have historically substituted for war. These speakers rhyme their insults in an ancient language. Although Saddam Hussein did not claim to be a master of this type of speaking, some of his rhetoric during the period before the Gulf War was highly insulting toward President Bush, and the United States almost certainly misunderstood some of the functions of Arab rhetoric.[33]

Teaching Idea

Exercise 2 relates to Arab reasoning.

rationality, their emotional responses, and their assessment of speakers as trustworthy. However, as you might suspect, different cultural groups emphasize different reasoning strategies, and the standards for assessing these appeals vary cross-culturally. (See Box 15.3 for a description of several international reasoning styles.)

 **KEY CONCEPT**   # Ethos

We evaluate speakers on their good sense, good character, goodwill, and dynamism. Kenneth Burke stressed the importance of identification with an audience—to find points of common ground—in an attempt to bring diverse people together and overcome a variety of divisions among them.

Summary

You draw on a variety of reasoning strategies as you make simple daily decisions or as you argue about complex national policy questions. In the reasoning process, claims of fact, value, and policy are based on various kinds of evidence, with a connecting link or warrant that justifies them. Listeners must weigh the evidence to see if it is sufficient and trustworthy enough to lead to the conclusion. Lest you overstate your claim, it is important to limit its scope by using qualifiers.

There are generally three kinds of proofs, which Aristotle clearly presented thousands of years ago. The first is called *logos* or rational proofs. This is the reasoning formed by the words of the speech itself. People reason with one another through analogies, both figurative and literal. Figurative analogies or metaphors find a likeness between two otherwise different things. Literal analogies or parallel cases attempt to find likenesses between two things that are similar. Inductive reasoning moves from particular cases or examples to generalizations or conclusions. Deductive reasoning moves from generalizations to applications in particular cases. Finally, causal reasoning links things that exist in time in such a way that the second is a result of the first. All these methods require the application of specific tests; otherwise, they may lead to faulty conclusions.

Pathos is the use of emotional proofs, and these can be compelling when you appeal to your listeners' basic emotions—both positive and negative—and to their needs. The chapter presented seven basic needs: survival, security, belonging and love, esteem, self-actualization, connection with the past, and connection with the future.

Finally, *ethos* is the proof that comes from the credibility of the speaker. Although Chapter 5 discussed this in greater detail, the concept of identification as a force to overcome division was presented here. One of the most common forms of identification is finding areas of common ground with your listeners. However, sometimes speaker–audience differences make the speaker more credible.

Throughout the chapter, we saw that reasoning is linked to cultural ways of knowing, thinking, and relating interpersonally. The case illustrating the Japanese reaction to American legal reasoning demonstrates that cultures vary in what they see as good reasons. In addition, some scholars argue that many women and members of ethnic groups tend to emphasize different forms of reason over others. Their good reasons are frequently grounded in concrete experiences; consequently, they commonly reason inductively. In addition, many people value emotion in reasoning; however, they caution that emotional appeals must be evaluated so that they complement rather than replace logic.

Questions and Exercises

1. Find a letter to the editor in your local newspaper written by a citizen about a controversial topic. Identify the type of reasoning the writer uses. Evaluate the arguments he or she presents.

2. Review the information on Arab reasoning, then read the Saudi ambassador's speech found in the Appendix, noticing how the ambassador presents his case.

3. Read the student speech that follows. It was given in a typical college classroom. It is presented here because it contains both good and faulty reasoning.

Evaluate the speaker's reasoning using the questions interspersed throughout the speech as guidelines.

Although the speaker listed nine sources in her bibliography, she cites none in her speech. Identify areas where you would like to know the source of her information.

How would you assess the speaker's credibility? Where (if at all) does she identify with her listeners? How might you respond if you were an animal rights activist in her audience?

Student Speech

The Benefits of Hunting[34]

Central Idea

Hunting, if correctly done, is natural and actually helps maintain the population of deer and other hunted animals.

Introduction

Animals, I'm sure, have a place in everyone's heart. No one would like to see animals live pitiful lives and die by the hundreds from overpopulation and starvation. Well, this has happened before, and it could very well happen again if hunting is once again abolished by people who are uneducated about its true benefits.

If the welfare of animals means anything to you, it is essential that you listen closely to the biological facts that support hunting as being beneficial to wildlife, for, in order to conserve wildlife, we must preserve hunting.

In the next few minutes, I will tell you about the damages resulting when people's right to hunt in certain areas is taken away. I will inform you of the uneducated ideas of animal activists and, finally, explain the differences between hunters and poachers.

  a. *What about the use of the words "I'm sure," "everyone," and "no one"? What effect does the use of the word* uneducated *have?*

  b. *What claim is the speaker making?*

So many people are unaware of the damage that occurs to the wildlife when hunting is taken away from a particular area. The best example of this happened in the state of Massachusetts. There, an animal rights group rallied and petitioned against deer hunting. Their efforts led to the banning of hunting in Massachusetts. During the period in which deer hunting was allowed, the deer population was around 100,000. Within the first year after the law was enacted, the population soared to 150,000.

Sound's good . . . ? Well, it wasn't! The overabundance of deer created a famine. Deer began to eat forest trees, gardens, and roots. They ate down to the foliage, leaving the plants unable to grow back the next year. Three years after the law went into effect, the deer population went from 150,000 to only 9,000. It took the state 10 years to return the deer population to normal. Eventually, the hunting ban was reversed, and the deer population has remained at its carrying capacity. I think it is hunting that plays a major role in keeping species from overpopulation.

   c. What kind of reasoning is the speaker using? Does it pass the tests? Do you think her conclusion is obvious? Why or why not?

   d. She says in her introduction that she will present biological facts about hunting. Does she do so to your satisfaction?

People often argue that animals were fine before man invented guns. Before the white men came over here with guns, there weren't sprawling cities like Los Angeles and Portland to take up most of the animals' habitat. In those days, there was far more land for the animals to live on. Today, modernization has pushed the animals into a smaller wildlife area, leaving them less food and less room for breeding. Therefore, it is easier for the animals to overpopulate. Hunting has played a major role in keeping the animal population at a normal number. If hunting is taken away, the animals are sure to overpopulate.

It has been proven that humankind, even in its earliest form, has always hunted animals. Here in North America, before white people and guns came over, Indians hunted animals on a consistent basis. They killed hundreds of buffalo by herding them over cliffs every year. They caught school after school of salmon that migrated up the rivers. These hunts have always played a major role in population management, whether or not you choose to label it as a law of nature.

   e. What argument does the speaker attempt to rebut? Does she do so to your satisfaction?

However, people argue that Indians needed to hunt animals to live; whereas, today's North Americans don't need to kill animals to survive. So what if we can survive on fruit and vegetables? Humans are born omnivorous, meaning it is natural for us to eat both meat and plants. What is inhumane about eating an animal for food? Weren't we designed to do so?

   f. Here is the second argument she attempts to counter or rebut. How well does she do it? Explain your answer.

People also argue that the laws of nature will take care of animals. Hunting has always been a major part of the laws of nature. Without mountain lions there to kill rabbits, the rabbit population would be a long gone species because of overpopulation. Humans as well as mountain lions are animals. Our predation is as important to other animals, such as deer, as the mountain lion's predation is to rabbits.

> *g. What is the third argument the speaker attempts to refute? What kind of reasoning does she use?*
>
> *h. Which of the three arguments do you think she did the best job of refuting? Which argument did she refute the least adequately?*

Animal activists harass hunters all the time. These people have false perceptions of what hunting really is, and who hunters really are. At a rally against deer hunting, a woman speaker argued that, "Hunters are barbarians who are in it for the kill. Hunters would use machine guns if they could. Plus, the deer are so cute." I think that argument is pathetic and holds absolutely no validity.

Another instance of hunter harassment occurred at Yellowstone National Park. An animal activist was not satisfied with only verbal harassment, so he struck the hunter on the head twice. Are animal activists really the peaceful and humane people they claim to be? And they still believe that hunters are bloodthirsty, crazy, and inhumane!!

> *i. Do these two examples pass the tests for their use? Are they typical? How does the speaker generalize from them? How might she make her point instead?*

Many of these misperceptions about hunters come from the association of hunters with poachers. Hunters are not poachers!!

Poachers are people who kill animals when they want, regardless of laws and regulations that were set to protect the animals. These are the kind of people who hunt elephants for their ivory tusks, or kill crocodiles for their skins. Poachers kill deer in areas that are off-limits, during off-limited hunting seasons. These people are criminals who are extremely harmful to wildlife.

Hunters would turn in a poacher in an instant if they caught one. Poachers give hunting a bad image in the eyes of the public. It's too bad that the animal activists don't go after the poachers who are extremely harmful to animals, and stop pointing a finger at hunters who follow the laws and regulations.

> *j. Why does the speaker contrast hunters to poachers? In what ways is this an effective argument?*

If hunting is banned, just imagine a drive through the mountains on a road covered with emaciated skeletons of cadaverous deer who died of starvation. No longer can you take a picture of Bambi, your favorite deer that you saw every year at Yellowstone National Park. For Bambi and his family were overpopulated, and they slowly wilted away until their final day. Too bad there weren't a few healthy bucks taken by hunting that year to keep Bambi and family at a cozy carrying capacity where there was plenty of delicious food for all of them.

   k. *Here, the speaker uses a great deal of pathos. Identify emotional language and images. Is this effective? Why or why not?*

The argument that animal activists use against hunting is fabricated mainly from emotions. If they are personally against killing an animal, I can respect that. But they have no place trying to ban hunting. It is proven by biological facts that hunting is necessary for wildlife management. It provides millions of dollars that fund the construction of programs that help wildlife. It keeps species from over-populating and starving to death. In order for wildlife to flourish at an optimum population number, hunting must continue to be a major part of wildlife management.

   l. *What does she put in her summary that does not appear anywhere else in her speech? If she had provided some evidence for that point, would her speech be stronger?*

Key Terms

claims of fact
claims of value
claims of policy
status quo
warrant
qualifier
rebuttal
logos
pathos
ethos
reasoning by analogy
metaphor (figurative analogy)
parallel case reasoning (literal analogy)
causal reasoning
inductive reasoning
deductive reasoning
enthymeme
needs
Maslow's Hierarchy of Needs
identification
common ground

Notes

1. Hattori is quoted in Acquittal in doorstep killing of Japanese student (1993, May 24). *The New York Times*, pp. A1, 11.

2. Japanese press reaction is printed in the editorial, Gun crazy (1993, May 25). *The New York Times*, p. A22.

3. Ms. Notoji is quoted in Sanger, D. E. (1993, May 25). After gunman's acquittal, Japan struggles to understand America. *The New York Times*, pp. A1, 17.

4. Aristotle. (1954, 1984). Op. cit., 1356.

5. See Toulmin, S. (1958). *The uses of argument*. Cambridge: Cambridge University Press.

6. Mullins, D. (1993). Lecture. St. John's University, Jamaica, New York.

7. Fridman, L. (1990). America needs its nerds. Various speeches.

8. Aristotle. (1954, 1984). Op. cit., 356, 20.

9. Many sources explain differences in cultural reasoning styles. See, for example, Fisher, G. (1991). International negotiation. In L. A. Samovar & R. E. Porter (Eds.). *Intercultural communication: A reader,* 6th ed. (pp. 193–200). Belmont, CA: Wadsworth. See also Lieberman, D. A. (1991). Ethnocognitivism and problem solving. In Samovar & Porter, op. cit., 229–233.

10. Wicker, B. (1975). *The story shaped world: Fiction and metaphysics, some variations on a theme.* South Bend, IN: University of Notre Dame Press.

11. Hilliard, A. (1986). Pedagogy in ancient Kemet. In M. Karenga & J. Carruthers (Eds.), *Kemet and the African world view* (p. 257). London: University of Sankore Press.

12. This information came from Morrow, L. (1993, March 29). The temping of America, and Castro, J. Disposable workers. *Time*, pp. 40–47.

13. See Jaggar, A. M. (1989). Love and knowledge: Emotion in feminist epistemology. In A. Garry & M. Pearsall (Eds.), *Women, knowledge, and reality: Explorations in feminist philosophy* (pp. 129–155). London: Unwin. McMillan, C. (1982). *Women, reason, and nature: Some philosophical problems with feminism.* Princeton: Princeton University Press. Griffiths, M. (1988). Feminism, feelings, and philosophy. In Griffiths & Whitford (Eds.), *Feminist perspectives in philosophy* (pp. 131–151). Bloomington: Indiana University Press.

14. Griffiths, M., & Whitford, M. (Eds.). (1988). Ibid.

15. For information on ethnic reasoning, see Cortese, A. (1990). *Ethnic ethics: The restructuring of moral theory.* Albany: SUNY Press.

16. Sullivan, P. A. (1993). Signification and African-American rhetoric: A case study of Jesse Jackson's "Common ground and common sense" speech. *Communication Quarterly, 41*(1), 1–15.

17. Aristotle. (1954, 1984). Op. cit., 1357, 17.

18. Cribbins, M. (1990). International adoption. Student speech. Oregon State University.

19. Suzuki, M. (1992, April 3). Native American symbols in sports. Student Speech. St. John's University, Jamaica, New York.

20. Roszak, T. (1992, June 9). Green guilt and ecological overload. *The New York Times,* p. A23.

21. Maslow, A. H. (1954, 1987). *Motivation and personality,* 3rd Ed. San Francisco: Harper & Row.

22. Some of the material in this section is from Packard, V. (1957, 1970). *The hidden persuaders.* New York: Pocket Books.

23. Ibid.

24. Jaggar, A. M. (1989). Op. cit.

25. Griffiths, M. (1988). Op. cit.

26. Aristotle. (1954, 1984). Op. cit., 1356, 4ff.

27. For a classic essay that explains Burke's complex ideas, see Nichols, M. H. (1952). Kenneth Burke and the "New Rhetoric." *Quarterly Journal of Speech, 38,* 133–144. Or read the work of Burke himself, especially (1950). *A rhetoric of motives.* New York: Prentice-Hall.

28. Allen, S. A. (1993, February 15). To be successful you have to deal with reality: An opportunity for minority businesses. *Vital Speeches of the Day, 59,* 271–273.

29. Archambault, D. (1992, May 1). Columbus plus 500 years: Whither the American Indian? *Vital Speeches of the Day, 63,* no. 15, 491–493.

30. Fisher, G. (1991). International negotiation. In L. A. Samovar & R. E. Porter (Eds.), *Intercultural communication: A reader,* 6th Ed. (pp. 193–206). Belmont, CA: Wadsworth.

31. K. S. Sitaram is a scholar from India. With R. T. Cogdell, he wrote, (1976). *Foundations of intercultural communication.* Columbus: Charles E. Merrill.

32. Anderson, J. W. (1991). A comparison of Arab and American conceptions of "effective persuasion." In L. A. Samovar & R. E. Porter, op. cit., 96–106.

33. Ya'ari, E., & Friedman, I. (1991, February). Curses in verses: Unusual fighting words. *The Atlantic Monthly,* pp. 22–26.

34. This student speech was given on March 6, 1992, at Oregon State University.

Persuasive Speaking

16

At the end of this chapter, you should be able to

- Find a subject for a persuasive speech
- Select a fact, value, or policy claim for your speech
- Narrow the focus of your speech in light of your listeners' beliefs, attitudes, and actions
- Identify organizational patterns for your speeches, including problem–solution, direct method, comparative advantages, criteria–satisfaction, the negative method, and Monroe's Motivated Sequence

Note

Because of our cultural commitment to persuasion as a means of influencing one another's beliefs and actions, we are surrounded by persuasive messages of all kinds. This chapter discusses persuasive topics and narrowed purposes; then it provides organizational patterns that are effective in persuasive speeches.

Cross Reference

See Chapter 3. Chapter 17 also emphasizes the importance of public speaking on ceremonial and ritual occasions.

If you watch C-SPAN on cable TV, you see persuasive speakers in action every day. Televised coverage of the House of Representatives, for instance, shows the "gentlewoman from Hawaii" and the "gentleman from New York" who argue *against* a proposed amendment on the floor of the House. The "gentleman from Indiana" rebuts their arguments by urging his fellow representatives to vote *for* the proposed amendment. You don't have to watch live coverage of real events, however, to realize the importance of argumentation and debate in American society. Tune into fictionalized courtroom dramas, and you will see both defense and prosecution lawyers address the jury. Turn on a talk show and listen to representatives of various viewpoints argue for their beliefs and lifestyles.

Persuasion is vital in a democracy that values citizen participation and freedom of speech. Indeed, as we pointed out in Chapter 1, Aristotle designated three arenas in which rhetoric or the art of persuasion functioned in a healthy democratic society: law courts, governing assemblies, and ceremonial and ritual occasions where the culture's core beliefs and values are reinforced. However, the role of persuasion varies across cultures, as the material in Box 16.1 illustrates.

This chapter focuses specifically on purposes and types of persuasive speaking. In it, you will find information on selecting a topic, using what your listeners know and how they behave to narrow your speaking purpose, and selecting strategies and organizational patterns that will be effective in conveying your ideas and arguing for your positions.

Selecting Persuasive Topics

Student Assignment

The Student Resource Workbook has an assignment for a persuasive speech.

Selecting a topic for a persuasive speech can be a daunting project for a beginning speaker. Even those who have some idea of the subject they want to discuss are frequently unsure of how to focus clearly on one major idea for the speech. In this section, we look at strategies you can use to find a subject. Then, we look at ways to select a claim and formulate the tentative central idea for your speech.

Finding the Subject

Teaching Idea

Students are generally most persuasive when they care enough about a topic to try to convince others to believe or act in specific ways. *Have students do exercise 1. Or refer again to the list the class generated in Chapter 2, and have students apply the questions in this section to the topics on the list.*

It is important to find a *need* that can be addressed by public speaking—one that can be modified as a result of speechmaking. These needs can range from personal to campus issues, from national to international concerns. Additionally, it is important to select a topic that matters to you—especially in the area of persuasion, for it is difficult to persuade others if you yourself are neutral about a subject. These two guidelines lead to a series of questions you can ask yourself as you search for an appropriate topic.[1]

BOX 16.1

Persuasion in Other Cultures

Not every culture places the same value on persuasion as a means of publicly discussing issues and formulating reasoned conclusions. These examples, from historical and contemporary cultures, illustrate this.

1. *Rome* Rome had a long history as a republic in which representatives of the people used persuasive arguments in public debates that resulted in decisions that affected the community. Although Romans influenced public speaking in the West for thousands of years, by the first century A.D. emperors, such as Nero and Caligula, were dictators. This means that they made decisions and pronouncements that were binding, whether or not the senators approved; dissenters often met with torture or death. Although the Senate continued to exist in form, Caligula mocked its power when he declared his horse to be a senator!

2. *The Soviet Union* Throughout most of this century, the Communist party ruled the former Soviet Union. Party leaders made decisions and spoke for the people; they strongly discouraged ordinary citizens from dissenting from the "party line," often by use of coercive force. This resulted in many dissenters finding themselves in Siberian work camps.

3. *China* China and other Asian countries generally do not have a tradition of open public debate or dialogue over controversial issues. Traditionally, the Chinese people considered such debate futile and inconclusive. That is, they did not believe that open debate results in reasonable people arriving at better conclusions than those reached by individuals alone. This resulted in a culture that did not develop lists of rules for public speaking or explicit standards for determining which arguments were better than others.[2]

4. *International Negotiation* Although many countries in the world are not democracies, more and more groups are realizing the benefits of persuasive speaking—at least in their dealings with representatives of the West. Because of trade negotiations, the existence of the United Nations, peace talks, and other opportunities for global exchanges, many countries with different standards for public discourse are becoming more bicultural in their international dealings, adopting some of the strategies of Western rhetoric. An additional influence is the fact that many world leaders have received an American university education.

   For example, Takakazu Kuriyama, the Japanese Ambassador to the United States, adopts a direct style when he meets with members of Congress and representatives of the U.S. media. This direct approach is part of Japanese efforts to communicate their nation's views to the United States. The ambassador was educated at Amherst College in Massachusetts and Wisconsin's Lawrence University.[3]

Strong Beliefs   What do I believe in strongly? What ideas and issues would I argue for? What ideas and issues would I argue against? Students have selected topics such as:

Theme

Choosing an international topic relates to the cultural theme of the book.

- Censorship, criminals who profit as a result of committing crimes (for example, through selling books and movie rights), sanctions against countries that violate human rights agreements

Strong Feelings   What do I feel strongly about? What makes me angry? What are my pet peeves? What arouses my pity? What makes me sad? What do I fear? The following examples demonstrate the variety of topics that students choose:

- Abused children, drivers with bad records, high insurance rates, people who are always late, white supremacists

Teaching Idea

Using Box 16.1 discuss societies in which people debate ideas and those in which debate and dissent are not encouraged. For example, refer to the Chinese student democracy movement that resulted in the Tiananmen Square massacre (April 1989).

Betterment of Society   What changes would I like to see in society and the world? What current problems or conditions could improve if enough people begin to believe that there is a problem, that there are solutions, and that they can be part of the solution? Students have chosen topics such as:

- Urban renewal, litter, volunteerism, latchkey children, affordable housing, literacy, international child sponsorship programs

Personal Fulfillment   What can make life more meaningful for myself and others? What activities will expand our horizons? What improves our health? What leads to more fulfilling personal relationships? A few examples of subjects that students have chosen are

- The power of forgiveness, the joys of bungee jumping, tolerance, learning a second language, managing conflict, vacationing in South America

Teaching Idea

Divide students into groups of three, and assign them a controversial topic. Have them come up with a claim of fact, value, and policy for their topic. Examples: legalized gambling, abortion, physician-assisted suicide, condom distribution in the schools, gun control. *Exercise 2 goes here.*

Making Persuasive Claims

Selecting your subject is only the first step. After that, ask yourself what claim you want to defend. Do you want to argue the facts of the case? Do you want to defend a value question? Or should a policy be formulated to solve a problem related to the topic? As you decide on your major claim, you are tentatively formulating the central idea of your speech.

Let's say you decide to speak about ocean pollution—specifically, dumping garbage in the ocean. The following chart identifies possible claims that you might defend:

	Claim	Tentative Central Idea
Fact	Argue a debatable point.	Dumping garbage in our oceans is not excessive.

Claim	Tentative Central Idea
Attempt to prove a cause–effect relationship.	Dumping waste products in the ocean poses health risks to seaboard residents.
Make a prediction.	If we do not take seriously the issue of dumping garbage in the ocean, our beaches will become too contaminated to use.
Value Argue something is right or wrong, good or bad, beautiful or ugly.	It is wrong to dump garbage in the ocean.
Policy Propose a policy change.	We should enact laws to end dumping of garbage in ocean waters.
Propose a behavioral change.	Write your congressional representative and voice your concerns about the disposal of garbage in oceans.
Argue against a policy change.	There is no good reason to stop disposing of garbage in oceans.

In summary, select the subject of your speech from topics and issues that concern you—from the personal level to the international level. Then, tentatively formulate the central idea of your speech by deciding if you want to argue a factual claim, a value claim, or a claim of policy.

KEY CONCEPT   ## Selecting Persuasive Topics

Finding the subject Examine your strong beliefs and strong feelings or think of ways to enrich society or bring personal fulfillment to your listeners.

Making persuasive claims Decide on a claim of fact, value, or policy.

Persuasive Purposes

Although the general purpose of your speech is to persuade, you narrow your focus and form specific intentions related to what your listeners already know and do, how they feel, and what they consider important. Because all these factors are interrelated, keep in mind that one speech may, in reality, have multiple

Teaching Idea

Throughout this section, have students identify possible topics in each category. Provide examples of such topics from past student speeches.

purposes that exist on a number of levels. For instance, while you are trying to convince your listeners about hazards of dumping garbage in the ocean—focusing on their beliefs—you may also be reinforcing their health-related values and the negative attitudes they currently hold toward pollution.

Beliefs and Actions

What we think is true affects how we act. Our beliefs and actions, in turn, are influenced by our values and attitudes. To illustrate, people who take vitamins regularly *believe* that the vitamins actually have beneficial effects on their health; in addition, they feel it is *good*, even *moral*, to take care of their health. They also have positive *attitudes* toward good nutrition. This combination of beliefs, values, and attitudes leads them to *act* by not only purchasing but also swallowing the vitamins.

Table 16.1 shows some possible combinations of belief and action that you should consider as you narrow the focus of your speaking intention.

Teaching Idea

Use exercise 3 as you teach this section.

Unconvinced   In the first quadrant, audience members are unconvinced for a variety of reasons, all of which result in inaction. Some lack information about your subject. Others are informed, but they have come to different conclusions than you have. Still others have misconceptions about your subject. With all these listeners, you must produce enough evidence to *convince* them of the truth of your factual claims before you call for action. The following general strategies are useful when your listeners are unconvinced:

Cross Reference

You can see throughout this section how reasoning through ethos, pathos, and logos, explained in Chapter 15, are interrelated in persuasive speeches.

- Begin with logical appeals. Build your factual case carefully, using evidence that passes the test for credible supporting material.
- Prove your competence by being knowledgeable about the facts. Further, show that you have respect for their intelligence and for their divergent beliefs.
- Use comparatively fewer emotional appeals.

Unmotivated or Unfocused   Sometimes your audiences are already convinced, often because they know a lot about your subject. However, they do not act on their beliefs. Your purpose, then, is to *actuate* or move them to behave in ways that are consistent with their beliefs. Attitudes of listeners within this category vary. Unmotivated listeners are inactive due to apathy; unfocused listeners are convinced they should act; they simply do not know how. These varying attitudes lead to two different persuasive strategies.

- When your audience is unmotivated, give them good reasons to act. Use emotional appeals to show that behaving as you propose will fulfill their needs and satisfy them emotionally.

TABLE 16.1 Beliefs and Actions

	Don't Believe	Believe
Don't Act	unconvinced	unmotivated, unfocused
Act	inconsistent	consistent

- When they lack focus, provide a detailed plan that spells out specific steps they can take to implement your proposals.

- In both instances, establish goodwill so that they can see you have their best interests in mind as you appeal for action.

For Further Reading

Leon Festinger. (1957). *A theory of cognitive dissonance.* New York: Row, Peterson; and R. Brown. (1965). *Social psychology.* New York: Free Press.

Teaching Idea

If you would like to introduce your students to more theories on persuasion, there is additional information in the Instructor's Manual, Teaching Note 16.1.

Inconsistent   When people act in ways that differ from their beliefs, they experience what various theorists call *inconsistency* or *dissonance*. One influential theory of persuasion, called "dissonance theory,"[4] argues that humans, like other living organisms, seek balance or equilibrium. When challenged with inconsistency, they feel psychological discomfort, and they strive to return to a place of psychological balance. Inconsistency between belief and action is one of the best motivators for change.

Sometimes people question or change their beliefs but continue to behave as if they were still convinced. For example, consumers lose faith in products that they still purchase; students continue to major in subjects that they know are not right for them; people persist in binge drinking—they once thought it was harmless; now they think it is dangerous. With inconsistent audiences, you either strengthen or reinforce wavering beliefs, or you persuade listeners to modify their actions to match their changed beliefs.

This list summarizes a few of the specific strategies that you can use when your listeners' actions are inconsistent with their beliefs.

- Support faltering beliefs by concentrating on logical appeals, using as much persuasive evidence as you can muster. Include emotional appeals as well, giving reasons for listeners to *want* to strengthen their wavering beliefs.

- When you want behaviors to change, appeal to emotions such as honesty and sincerity. Use narratives or testimonials that exemplify how you or someone else made changes when faced with a similar situation.

Consistent   People often act in ways that are consistent with their beliefs. They generally need encouragement to "keep on keeping on." Audiences whose actions are consistent with their beliefs are commonly found in places like service

Inconsistency between belief and action is one of the best motivators for change. For example, many people know that smoking is bad for them, but they still smoke. Highlighting this dissonance is a good way to persuade them to make at least an effort to kick the habit.

clubs, religious organizations, and political rallies. Here, your narrowed purpose is to reinforce both their beliefs and actions by following this set of guidelines.

- Help listeners maintain a positive attitude about their accomplishments. Use examples and testimony that illustrate how their efforts are making a difference in the world.
- Relate yourself personally to their fundamental beliefs and values.

Throughout this section, we have explored the ways that audience beliefs and actions influence both your persuasive purposes and the methods you use to present your ideas. Although you continue to employ logic, emotion, and personal credibility in every speech, each type of audience requires somewhat different emphases and strategies.

The Simon Wiesenthal Center of Los Angeles sponsored a conference for teenage skinheads. Conference organizers hoped that some of the teens might change their attitudes toward Jews and the Holocaust when they heard speakers such as Renee Firestone describe her experiences in the Auschwitz concentration camp.

Attitudes

Cross Reference

Chapter 3.

Attitudes are our likes and dislikes, our tendencies to have positive or negative feelings both about subjects and about speakers. Researchers measure attitudes along a range from highly negative—hostile, in fact—to highly positive. Attitudes can also be neutral, meaning the audience probably hasn't thought enough about the subject to have formed an opinion. The following are typical scales that you might use to measure audience attitudes:

Cross Reference

Students may have seen attitude scales if they constructed an audience questionnaire in Chapter 5. (The guidelines are in the Student Resource Workbook.)

Spanking, used moderately, can be an effective method of disciplining children.

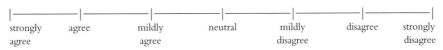

| strongly agree | agree | mildly agree | neutral | mildly disagree | disagree | strongly disagree |

Ronald Reagan should have his own commemorative stamp.

| strongly agree | agree | mildly agree | neutral | mildly disagree | disagree | strongly disagree |

Audience attitude is a major factor in determining both the focus of your speech and the strategies you will use to present your arguments. It is usually easy to speak when the audience is positive and shares your attitude. Then, your

An audience that is hostile to the speaker personally is one of the most difficult to address. President Clinton faced catcalls and negative placards during his 1993 speech at the Vietnam Memorial. He attempted to counter this hostility by emphasizing common ground with his listeners.

major purpose is to *reinforce* or strengthen their opinion. Neutral audiences have not yet formulated an opinion on a topic. Sometimes they lack enough information about the subject. At other times, they are neutral out of apathy; they simply do not care about the topic, often because they fail to see how it touches their lives directly. Here, your purpose is to *initiate* an attitude in your listeners. When listeners are negative about a subject on which you hold a positive view, your speaking strategies change. If they are mildly or moderately negative, your overall strategy is to lessen the negative and enable listeners to see your subject more positively. If their feeling is strongly the opposite of yours, you are dealing with a hostile audience. Set modest goals, and aim for small attitude changes. Perhaps the most distressing speaking situation arises when you face an audience that is hostile toward you personally. For example, President Clinton, who resisted the draft, stood before a noisy, booing audience when he spoke at the Vietnam War Memorial on Memorial Day, 1993. Then, you attempt to emphasize common ground between yourself and your listeners.

The following guidelines will help you plan your speech more effectively:

- When listeners are positive, strengthen their emotional ties to the topic by using examples, connotative words, and appeals to needs and values that

Teaching Idea

Exercise 5 directs students to Mr. Clinton's Vietnam War Memorial speech in the Appendix.

Cross Reference

Refer to identification and common ground, discussed in Chapter 15.

evoke emotional responses. Establish common ground throughout your speech.

- With uninformed audiences, present factual information early in the speech so that they have a basis to form an evaluation. Then, use emotional appeals to create either a positive or negative attitude toward the topic.

- With apathetic audiences, use emotional appeals. Link the topic to listeners in as many ways as you can. Appeal to values such as fairness or justice.

- When the audience is mildly negative, approach listeners directly. Make a clear case with objective data; present the positive facets of your subject; and link it to personal and community values your audience accepts. This way, even if they disagree with you, they will at least understand the rationale for your position.

- With negative audiences in general, approach your subject indirectly by establishing common ground on which you can all agree. For instance, begin with a statement with which everyone agrees and explain why there is agreement. Then make a statement that most would accept and explain why this is so. Move gradually to the point on which they think they disagree. By this time, they have already seen that they agree with you on many points, and as a result, they may be less negative toward your proposal.

Teaching Idea

Ask students to identify other areas in which our national attitudes have changed or areas in which their personal attitudes have changed. How did public speaking contribute to those changes?

Generally, attitudes change incrementally. This means that listeners do not move rapidly from one extreme to another; rather, they change gradually over time. Each new encounter with the subject is only one small step that produces a slight attitude shift. Eventually, over a period, the small shifts add up to a measurable attitude change. Many people in the United States, for instance, once had a neutral attitude toward congressional term limitations. However, over a period of months and years, after many speeches and much media coverage, many citizens began to view limitation of congressional terms positively.

Values

Almost every topic touches on values indirectly because the speaker at least considers the subject important enough to discuss. However, some speakers directly address value questions. Their claims include such evaluative words as right or wrong, beautiful or ugly, moral or immoral, important or insignificant. Many speakers, especially on ceremonial occasions, intend to *reinforce* or strengthen existing values. Others hope to *initiate* or *produce* an evaluation within neutral listeners; still others want audience members to change their evaluations.

For Further Reading

V. Jensen. (1985). Teaching ethics in speech communication. *Communication Quarterly*, pp. 324–330.

As with attitudes, it is helpful to think of value judgments as existing across a range. Vernon Jensen,[5] longtime professor at the University of Minnesota, offered this scale as a way to visualize the gradations of opinion regarding ethical questions. He called it the Ethical Quality Scale (or EQS). Although the scale deals with ethical or moral judgments, it could easily be adapted to judgments related to beauty, fairness, and other value issues.

| highly | ethical | somewhat | morally | somewhat | unethical | highly |
| ethical | | ethical | neutral | unethical | | unethical |

For example, the following is a value claim: Keeping the minimum wage at its present level is wrong. In order for your listeners to make an evaluation, you must establish the criteria or standards on which to judge a policy. Answer questions such as these: How do we make and apply moral judgments in the economic realm? What criteria do we use? Where do these criteria come from? Why should we accept these sources? If your listeners agree with your criteria, it is easier for them to accept your evaluation. However, you can see that value questions are often conflict-laden, for the standards used to make many value judgments are not universally accepted.

Cross Reference

This echoes the theme of irreconcilable differences, developed in Chapter 3.

Since each individual's personal beliefs and experiences affect his or her value judgments, within a single audience, these judgments may vary so widely that some listeners view a topic as unethical, whereas others view it as ethical. Since values are the assumptions we hold of what is good, value questions often generate strong emotional responses that are difficult to change. Thus, it is nearly impossible for one speech to move listeners from viewing a topic as highly unethical to the point where they evaluate it as highly ethical.

The following specific strategies can be effective in arguing value claims:

- Establish the criteria you have used to make your evaluation.

- Appeal to the audience's emotions. Use examples to help listeners identify with the issue. Appeal also to related values such as fairness, generosity, kindness, and freedom.

Cross Reference

Chapter 8 discusses authoritative sources in more detail.

- Appeals to authority can be persuasive *if* the audience accepts the source as authoritative. Some audiences are moved by appeals to cultural and religious traditions. Others accept evidence from philosophers, poets, scientists, and other people whom the culture considers wise.

Teaching Idea

Assign exercise 4. Have students watch a televised speech and answer the questions in the exercise. This could be a journal assignment or material for a class discussion.

Although we have discussed beliefs and actions, attitudes, and values as separate, the truth is that they cannot be separated from one another. Keep in mind the interrelated aspect of these cultural factors as you analyze your audience, select the specific purpose for your speech, and choose supporting material that will be persuasive.

CASE STUDY 16.1

Adapting a Topic to Different Audiences

Analyze the following public speaking situation: An anthropology major is going to present a speech on government funding for archaeological digs. Her claim is that the study of archaeology is important enough to receive government funding because knowing about other human cultures helps us better understand our own.

Divide into three groups within the classroom. Each group will discuss how the speaker should prepare for one of the following audiences:

1. A group of anthropology majors who agree with her and are highly positive toward her topic.

2. An audience that knows nothing about anthropology but is concerned about how their tax money is spent.

3. Listeners who feel that archaeology is a waste of time.

Questions

1. How will the speaker analyze the particular audience?

2. What purpose should she select for that group?

3. What specific strategies will she use to make her points?

4. What kind of reasoning and evidence should she use?

5. What should she emphasize and why?

KEY CONCEPT   Persuasive Purposes

Beliefs and actions What we believe affects how we act. Listeners are often unconvinced, unmotivated, or unfocused—and therefore inactive. Others are inconsistent when their actions do not match their beliefs. Still others consistently act on their beliefs. All these audiences require different speaking purposes and strategies.

Attitudes Listeners can have a positive, neutral, or negative attitude toward you and your topic. Generally, you attempt to strengthen positive attitudes and minimize negative ones.

Values When making value claims, establish criteria for the value judgment, link listeners with the topic emotionally, and appeal to authority when it is appropriate.

Persuasive Organizational Patterns

Teaching Idea

Provide examples from old student speeches that demonstrate the organizational patterns presented in this chapter. Ask students to identify the speaker's purpose. Is the speaker trying to convince? To reinforce beliefs, actions, or attitudes? To actuate listeners? Does the speech seem appropriate to the audience's beliefs, actions, attitudes, and values? (Example: A speech to convince people of the importance of seatbelts is probably not appropriate because most people are already convinced that they are important.)

After you have analyzed your audience, by considering their positions regarding your issue, you then begin to look at the organizational pattern that will best communicate your ideas and elicit the kind of response you desire in your listeners. There are many organizational strategies you can use. In this section, we discuss common patterns used in persuasive public speaking.

Problem–Solution Pattern

You have already seen the problem–solution pattern in Chapter 9. It is commonly used in both informative and persuasive speaking. When you use it for an informative speech, the purpose of your discourse is to increase the audience's *understanding* of the issue and the proposed solution or solutions. When you use it as a persuasive pattern, however, your purpose is generally to *convince* or to *advocate* the implementation of a specific policy. When the intent is to convince listeners that there is indeed a problem, the outline looks like this.

Specific purpose: To persuade my audience that there are too many air disasters, but the problem can be solved by concentrating efforts in three areas.

Central idea: Global air traffic has too many disasters and near disasters that could be minimized by working to eliminate the sources of the problems.

I. There are too many air disasters and near disasters around the globe.
  A. The problem of near-misses and crashes is serious.
    1. It is extensive (statistics).
    2. This has negative implications for travelers.
  B. There are several causes of this problem.
    1. There are communication problems between crews and air traffic controllers.
    2. Weather is a consideration.
    3. Mechanical and maintenance failures cause disasters.
II. The problem can be minimized.
  A. Airplanes should be more carefully inspected and maintained.
  B. Both crew members and air traffic controllers should continue to receive on-the-job training both in communication and in understanding the effects of weather.
  C. Engineers and researchers should continue to develop state-of-the-art equipment to prevent some of these disasters.

At other times, you aim less at convincing your audiences that there is, indeed, a problem. You, instead, argue for a particular solution. You do this by comparing several possible solutions then advocating or arguing that one is best. This adds a third point to the outline.

I. Problem and need
II. Possible solutions
III. One best solution

This is how a more complete outline looks.

Specific purpose: To persuade my audience that incineration is the best solution to the problem of medical waste.
Central idea: Of the three methods of medical waste disposal—steam sterilization, ocean dumping, and incineration—incineration is the best.

I. More and more medical waste is being generated, creating a need for a safe method of disposal.
   A. There are several waste products from medical procedures.
   B. The problem is extensive (statistics).
   C. Some of the waste products pose risks.
II. There are three ways to dispose of medical waste.
   A. One is the steam sterilization process.
   B. The second is ocean dumping.
   C. The third is incineration.
III. Incineration is the best solution.
   A. It completely destroys the product.
   B. Fire purifies.

Direct Method Pattern

In the direct method, sometimes called the statement of reasons method, you make a claim then directly state your reasons to support it. Each point, thus, provides an additional rationale to agree with your views. It is a good pattern to use when listeners are apathetic or neutral, mildly favoring, or mildly opposing the claim. Often it is used when the major persuasive purpose is to convince, though it can also be used to organize a speech to actuate (or motivate the audience to *do* something).

This first outline is from a speech to actuate. You can see that each main point gives listeners an additional reason to act. The speaker, additionally, moves to a climax by beginning with the least important reason and ending with the most important.

Specific purpose: To persuade my listeners to drive 55 miles per hour.
Central idea: If everyone drove 55 miles per hour, we would save fuel, money, and lives.

Everyone should drive 55 miles per hour.
  I. It will save fuel.
  II. It will save money.
  III. It will save lives.

The intention of the following speech was to convince listeners that a particular policy should be enacted. The major points are factual claims of prediction that provide reasons to agree with the major claim.

Specific purpose: To persuade my listeners to believe that all primary and secondary students should wear uniforms to school.
Central idea: All students should wear school uniforms to eliminate social distinctions, save money, and prevent crime.

All precollege students, even those in public schools, should wear uniforms.
  I. This will eliminate social distinctions between rich and poor.
  II. It will save money.
  III. It will prevent clothing-related crime.

As you can see, this pattern is a variant of the topical organizational pattern. It is very easy to use, both in speeches intended to convince and those intended to motivate listeners to act.

Comparative Advantages Pattern

A comparative advantages pattern shows that one proposal is superior to competing proposals by comparing its advantages to those of the competition. It is often used successfully to argue policy questions, as it was in 1993 and 1994 when the nation debated health care reform. Proponents of managed care argued that their solution was better than other proposed solutions; in contrast, proponents of the direct payer system argued that their system provided more advantages and that it should be adopted.

Study the following outline from a speech to convince an audience of the superiority of osteopathic doctors:

Specific purpose: To persuade my audience that a Doctor of Osteopathic Medicine (D.O.) is superior to a chiropractor for many reasons.
Central idea: D.O.s are better than chiropractors because of their training and their ability to do surgery.

Doctors of Osteopathic Medicine (D.O.s) are superior to chiropractors.

A. They can do everything chiropractors do, and more.
B. Their training is superior because it includes courses comparable to those in medical schools.
C. Many D.O.s perform surgeries in hospitals with which they are affiliated.

The comparative advantages method is also used when the speaker wants listeners to act. For instance, a representative of a small private college compares the advantages her institution has over larger state schools. She is hoping to recruit students. This type of organizational pattern is also used in advertisements, sales speeches, and campaign speeches as these outlines demonstrate:

Specific purpose: To persuade my audience to purchase a [certain kind of car].

Central idea: Buy [this automobile] because of its repair record, resale value, and fuel economy—better than its competitors'.

Buy [a certain make of automobile].

    I. It has a better repair record than its competitors.
   II. It has a higher resale value than comparable cars.
 III. It is more economical than its major competitors.

Specific purpose: To persuade my audience to vote for [candidate].

Central idea: [Candidate] is superior because of his equitable tax plan, his voting record, and his ethics proposals.

Vote for [candidate].

    I. His tax plan is more equitable than that of his opponent.
   II. His voting record is more in tune with the beliefs and attitudes of his constituents than is his opponent's.
 III. His ethics plan is more concrete than that of his opponent.

Cross Reference

Both Chapters 8 and 15 discuss comparisons.

It is easy to see that this pattern is related to reasoning by comparison and contrast, for in the speech, you continually compare and contrast your proposal or product to other proposals and products the audience already knows.

Criteria–Satisfaction Pattern

Criteria are standards that form a basis for judgments, and the criteria–satisfaction pattern first sets forth the standards to judge a proposal; then it shows how the solution, candidate, or product you propose meets or exceeds these standards. Because it describes the standards for evaluation at the outset, it is useful in speeches that argue value claims.

Take, for example, the problem of sending a good senator to Washington. The criteria section of the speech answers the question, "What qualities does a good senator have?" or "What are the necessary ingredients for a lawmaker?" The speaker might assert that a good senator should support tax reform, be a person of strong principles, and have leadership qualities that get things done.

The second part of the speech—the satisfaction section—shows how the proposed candidate satisfies all the criteria. In this case, the candidate has a workable tax reform plan, his character has been demonstrated in a number of difficult decisions, and he has been instrumental in making many changes on the local level.

> Specific purpose: To persuade my audience that community service meets all the criteria for a good punishment for nonviolent criminals.
> Central idea: Community service is a punishment that fits the crime, reduces recidivism, and is cost-effective.
>
> What does a good punishment for nonviolent felons look like?
>
> I. The punishment fits the crime.
> II. It reduces recidivism.
> III. It is cost-effective.
>
> Community service is the best punishment for nonviolent crimes.
>
> I. The punishment can be tailored to fit the crime.
> II. It keeps felons out of prison where they can be influenced by career criminals.
> III. It is far less costly to administer than incarceration.

Cross Reference

In the following chapter, the problem-solving method also stresses the value of setting criteria and choosing solutions that meet those standards.

You may find the criteria–satisfaction pattern to be especially useful when your issue is controversial. This is so because at the outset you establish common ground with your listeners by setting up criteria on which you all agree. As in the direct methods pattern, consider building to a climax by developing the most persuasive criteria last.

Negative Method Pattern

When you use the negative method, you concentrate on the shortcomings of every other proposal; then you show why your proposal is the one logical solution remaining. That is, you point out the negative aspects in competing proposals; then, after you have destroyed or undermined everyone else's plan, you propose your own. This pattern is often used to argue a policy claim.

> Specific purpose: To persuade my audience that global legalization of drugs is the only way to control the supply and demand of illicit drugs.
> Central idea: Because of the failures of drug enforcement agencies and education, we need to regulate drugs through legalization.
>
> We need a solution to the problem of drugs around the world.
>
> I. More drug enforcement agencies are not the answer.
> II. Better education is not the answer.
> III. Global legalization of drugs is the only way we will regulate supply and demand.

As you can see, you have many persuasive speech patterns from which to choose. As you plan the strategies that will persuade your audience to accept your proposals as reasonable, use the pattern that is most appropriate to both your material and your audience. These patterns, obviously, are not exhaustive, but they are among the most common patterns that you will hear as you listen to public speeches, advertisements, and other persuasive messages.

Finally, we now turn to one of the most widely used patterns, Monroe's Motivated Sequence.

Monroe's Motivated Sequence

Teaching Idea

If you would like to present this material in a lecture, the Instructor's Manual has a transparency outlining this pattern.

For Further Reading

Alan H. Monroe. (1962). Principles and types of speech, 5th Ed. Chicago: Scott, Foresman, and Co.

Alan Monroe, a professor at Purdue University for many years, developed and refined a pattern that is commonly used in persuasive speaking, especially in speeches with the purpose of actuating behavior. As you will see, it is a modified form of a problem–solution speech.

In order to move people to act, it is necessary to motivate them to do what they know they should do. Because of this, it is important to provide emotional reasons as well as logical ones. Monroe's pattern includes the word *motivated* because it has several built-in steps to increase motivational appeals. (Note that this pattern is not a "formula" in the sense that you have to include each element that Professor Monroe describes. Rather, Monroe suggests various ways that you can develop each point in the speech.) Here are the five easily remembered steps in the sequence as explained by Professor Monroe himself.[6]

Attention Step   At the outset of the speech, as in any speech, you must gain the audience's attention and draw it to the speech topic.

Need Step   This step is similar to the problem part of a problem–solution speech. Dr. Monroe suggests four elements in establishing the need.

1. *Statement* Tell the nature of the problem.
2. *Illustration* Give a relevant detailed example (or examples).
3. *Ramifications* Provide additional support such as statistics or testimony that show the extent of the problem.
4. *Pointing* Show the direct relationship between the audience and the problem. What are the personal implications for each listener?

Satisfaction Step   After you have demonstrated the problem, how extensive it is, and how it will affect the audience, propose a solution that will satisfy the need you have created. This step can have as many as five parts.

1. *Statement* Briefly state the attitude, belief, or action you want the audience to adopt.

2. *Explanation* Make your proposal understandable; visual aids may help at this point.

3. *Theoretical demonstration* Show the logical connection between the need and your solution.

4. *Practicality* Use facts, figures, and testimony to show that the proposal has worked effectively or that the belief has been proved correct.

5. *Meeting objections* Here you show that your proposal can overcome any potential objections that listeners might have.

Visualization Step   This step is unique from the patterns we have seen so far. In it, you ask the audience to imagine what will happen if they enact the proposal or if they fail to do so.

1. *Positive* Describe future conditions when the plan is put into action. Put the audience into a realistic scenario, enjoying what your solution has provided. In this section, you commonly appeal to pathos—safety needs, pride, pleasure, and other emotions.

2. *Negative* Have the listeners imagine themselves in an unpleasant situation because they did *not* put the solution into effect.

3. *Contrast* Compare the negative results of not enacting the plan with the positive results the plan will produce.

Action Step   In the final step, call for the listeners to act in a specific way.

1. Call for an overt action, attitude, or belief.

2. State your personal intention to act.

3. End with impact.

This outline shows how one student speaker used Monroe's Motivated Sequence to prepare his speech on tinnitus.[7]

Specific purpose: To persuade my listeners to take proper care of their hearing.

Central idea: The ear is an often-ignored part of the body that does not get the attention it requires; although we often damage our ears, there are a number of things we can do to preserve our hearing.

  I. *Attention Step*
    How many of you like your music loud? [Take a whistle out and blow it loudly.] Would you like to have something like that in your head 24 hours a day, 7 days a week, 365 days a year until you die? Keep the music loud, and one day you may get your own buzzing and whistling called tinnitus.

Monroe's Motivated Sequence is a useful pattern for speeches that attempt to change people's behaviors. One speaker urged his listeners to turn down the volume on their music.

Today, I will explain the condition called tinnitus; then I will give tips from medical experts on what we can do to prevent it happening to us.

II. *Need Step*

A. Tinnitus is caused when the tiny hairs in the ears are irreversibly damaged, causing a permanent ringing.

  1. Tinnitus is generally caused by advancing age and loud noise.
  2. Scientists measure sound intensity in decibels with each doubling of energy adding 10 decibels; exposure to higher decibel levels places young people at risk.
  3. Rock concerts and extensive use of Walkmen result in more diagnoses of tinnitus among young people.

B. Pete Townshend, of The Who, suffers from a severe case of tinnitus; as a musician, I realized that what happened to him was starting to happen to me.

C. The Department of Otolaryngology at the University of California Medical School estimates 30 to 50 percent of the people in America have tinnitus at some time.

  1. Most people never report it, but the low end of the estimate is 72 million people, mostly elderly.
  2. The others are people like you and me—young, urban commuters who listen to music daily do not think about our ears until the damage is done.

D. Although the problem is serious, there are several things you should do to make your chances of getting tinnitus slim.

III. *Satisfaction Step*
   A. First, don't expose your ears to loud music. This is the main killer of young people's hearing.
      1. Turn down the volume dial to 4 or less.
      2. Never wear headsets.
      3. Speak up for your silence.
   B. You can see that less noise results in less work for your ears.
   C. I know that many of you think this is impractical; however, you don't have to stop playing music entirely, just take precautions.
IV. *Visualization Step*
   A. Just imagine yourself forty years from now; if you have taken this advice, your hearing is good.
   B. But imagine, if you have not, that you hear a permanent ringing sound at all times; I'm sure you'd want to avoid this if you could.
V. *Action Step*
   A. In order to protect my hearing, I have turned down the volume on my music.
   B. When you leave this classroom and reach for the dial on your favorite music station, I urge you to do the same.
   C. Remember, once the damage is done, that's it. Your ears will not repair themselves; even completely losing your hearing cannot stop the buzzing and whistling of tinnitus.

As you can see, this pattern is very good for a sales speech. It is also effective in policy speeches and other claims that include a "should" or an "ought."

 **KEY CONCEPT**

Persuasive Organizational Patterns

Problem–solution pattern In this pattern, you explain a problematic situation and offer a policy that will correct it.

Direct method pattern This is called the statement of reasons method. You directly state reasons to support a claim.

Comparative advantages pattern You show the advantages of one proposal by comparing it to another.

Criteria–satisfaction pattern Using this pattern, you set up the standards or criteria in the first section; then you demonstrate that the proposal meets the standards or fulfills the criteria in the second section.

Negative method pattern This pattern shows the shortcomings of every other proposal before presenting the proposal being advocated.

Monroe's Motivated Sequence This pattern has five steps: attention (focus on the topic), need (state the problem), satisfaction (propose the solution), visualization (predict the future), action (call for response).

Summary

The best subjects for persuasive speeches come from the things that matter most to you personally. For this reason, you ask questions such as, What do I believe strongly? What arouses strong feelings within me? What would I like to see changed? What enriches my life? The answers to these questions generally provide topics that you are willing to defend, for it is hard to persuade others if you yourself are not interested in the subject. Choosing a subject is only the first part of topic selection. You then tentatively formulate the central idea of the speech by deciding whether you will argue a claim of fact, value, or policy.

We consistently argue for our ideas in an attempt to influence one another's beliefs, actions, values, and attitudes, and we strategically organize our speeches and adapt our ideas to different types of audiences. However, assumptions and actions are always interwoven. The result is that, while you are motivating listeners to act, you are also trying to reinforce their positive attitudes and beliefs. All the while, you rely on underlying values to support your calls to action.

There are a number of patterns from which to choose as you organize the major points of your speech. They include the problem–solution pattern and its variant in the Monroe's Motivated Sequence—both of which define a problem and identify a solution. The direct method, also called the statement of reasons pattern, directly lists reasons to support the claim. The criteria–satisfaction pattern is good for value speeches because you first set up criteria or standards for judgment, then show how your proposal meets these standards. The comparative advantages method shows the advantage of your proposal over similar proposals; the negative method, in contrast, shows the disadvantages of every proposal but your own.

Student Speech

Unnecessary Institutionalization of Teens

Kimber Weaver

Kimber Weaver presented this speech in a typical public speaking classroom. Because the subject is relatively unfamiliar to her audience, the major purpose of her speech is to convince her listeners that there is a problem, and that something should be done about it. She uses a problem/solution organizational pattern.

Kimber gains attention with a concrete example.

Thirteen-year-old Cynthia Parker was an overly hyperactive child. Her physician prescribed a mild medication to help her pay attention in school. When this was ineffective, her parents could not keep up with her, and in 1985 she was admitted to a private psychiatric hospital.

She has to convince her listeners that Cynthia is typical. In addition, she links the topic to her specific audience.

We might feel sympathetic to Cynthia's worn-out parents, but is this reason enough to turn her over to strangers who fill her full of drugs and think she's crazy? Unfortunately, according to May 1990 *Ladies' Home Journal*, Cynthia's case is not unique. Private institutions are becoming a fad among frustrated parents who can afford them. Between 1971 (about the time many of us were born) and 1985, admissions jumped from 7,000 to 99,000 patients. That is more than 9 times the number of undergraduates here at Oregon State University.

She makes a value claim as well as a factual claim here.

Sadly, many of these patients are fairly normal teens whose major offenses are talking back, messy rooms, or less-than-straight A grade point averages. This is not right. Private institutions are hurting many American youth.

Kimber links herself to the topic.

This topic intrigued me because I am interested in psychiatry and the service it provides to society, and I have read many articles and seen shows on the injustices suffered by teens in mental wards.

She previews her two major points.

Today, I will explain several aspects of this problem and explain some solutions that have been proposed.

Here is the first main point—the problem.

Many factors contribute to the problem of teens being institutionalized in such alarming numbers.

Her first main subpoint examines causes of the problem.

They start with publicity from the hospitals themselves. Many of these hospitals engage in intensive campaigns using newspapers, radio, TV, magazines, even billboards. For example, one ad shows a boy dressed in a leather jacket, wearing handcuffs, with the caption, "Don't wait until you get a call from the police to get help for your teenager."

This type of ad combined with severe drug and suicide problems among youth make parents even more suspicious of their child's actions. According to Dr. Paul Fink, past president of the American Psychiatric Association, "Bad conduct is not a reason to put someone in the hospital. Eighty to ninety percent of what they are calling conduct disorder could be treated outside."

Another cause is stated by Dr. Thomas S. Szasz in Bruce Ennis' book *Prisoners of Psychiatry*, "Many psychiatrists are now ready to classify anyone and everyone as mentally sick and anything and everything as psychiatric treatment."

Another part of the problem is actual treatments.

The problem is not simply that a large number of teens are being treated, it is also in the kind of treatment they receive. Many hospitals use a rewards/punishment system to control patients. For example, if the patient follows trivial rules, she gets a good meal or gets to wear street clothes instead of pajamas. Once, when Cynthia was "uncontrollable," attendants rolled her in a gym mat and tied it up. "I got rope marks all the way down my body," Cynthia remembers.

Ira Schwartz, Director of the University of Michigan Center for the Study of Youth Policy, says, "These techniques are demeaning and dehumanizing. They adversely affect self-esteem and make kids bitter and angry."

In addition, drugs are also used routinely. For example, Cynthia had a "conduct disorder"; she testifies, "They put me on drugs right away. They told me I was depressed and suicidal. That really threw me."

According to Maryland psychiatrist Peter Breggin, who is quoted in a *Mother Jones* article in July/August 1989, "We have the power, with electroshock and neuroleptic drugs like thorazine, to take away people's minds. The frightening thing is that we use it."

These facts raise some troubling questions: What gives these psychiatrists the power to manipulate minds, and what motivates their desire?

She further examines reasons for the problem.

Sadly enough, the law gives psychiatrists the power to institutionalize teens. Laws allow mental health experts to define normal and abnormal behavior. Laws allow them to decide treatment for various behavioral problems.

And the law prevents teens from having a say in whether they belong in an institution, how they should be treated, or when they should be released. A 1979 Supreme Court decision ruled it constitutional to deny minors the right to have a review of their admission in court, as long as the psychiatrist at the institution believes the child should be hospitalized.

Many contend that doctors diagnose out of greed. They argue that the cost of treatment in private hospitals may reach $27,000 per month, and it benefits a hospital financially when all the beds are full. Cynthia is a good example of how money may make a difference. After three months, Cynthia was released, even though she still exhibited strong mood swings and suicidal fantasies. Her doctors claimed she was doing better. However, a few days later, she tried to cut her wrists. Coincidentally, this "improvement" occurred only after her father informed the hospital that his insurance was running out.

Kimber provides a transition statement between the two major parts of the speech—the problem and the solution.

Since this is a speech to convince her audience that there is a problem, Kimber spends most of her time developing the first point. In the second section— "solution"—she merely sketches some of the solutions that have been proposed.

As you can see, institutionalization of teens is a serious problem; something needs to be done. No one should be treated this way. Several solutions to this problem have been proposed. They include publicity, better law enforcement, more power to patient advocates, and more outpatient care.

We need more publicity to let the public know what goes on in mental wards. Many are unaware that there is a problem in such institutions. Knowing the experiences of Cynthia and others like her may make parents think before they admit their child to an institution.

Legislation needs to be written to regulate the behaviors of physicians. As we saw earlier, many psychiatrists have abused their authority, and strong legislative guidelines are needed to protect the rights of institutionalized teens. We can support lawmakers' efforts to provide this legislation.

More patient advocates would make this process more efficient. Patient advocates are outsiders to the hospital who come in and watch over the ward procedures. They could be very useful in helping those who are falsely diagnosed, that is, if the law gives them more power to evaluate psychiatrists' decisions and make suggestions to override them, when appropriate.

Finally, we need more outpatient care. In the *Mother Jones* article, Sally Zinman, ex-patient, says, "We need to help people before they get caught up in the mental-health care system." With multiple problems facing us today, we need more places where adults and teens can go to have someone help them work through problems, not create more.

Even we can help by being aware and by helping friends and family members go through hard times. People need to believe that mental hospitals are not the answer in many cases.

In conclusion, unnecessary institutionalization of teens is a growing problem in our nation. We have examined the problem and some proposed solutions. You and I can have a part in those solutions by being aware of the problem and supporting stronger legislation to control what goes on in mental hospitals.

As for Cynthia, I guess you could say she is lucky; she made it out of the system, but her experiences there will always haunt her.

Her conclusion briefly summarizes the major points of her speech, then ends memorably with a reference to Cynthia— whose story has developed throughout the speech.

Questions and Exercises

1. Identify possible topics that you might use for a persuasive speech by finishing each of these sentence starters:

    - I have strong beliefs about
    - I feel strongly about
    - I believe society could be better if
    - Life could be better or more meaningful if we would

2. Select a controversial topic such as abortion, euthanasia, capital punishment, or welfare. Work with a classmate (or classmates) to write out a factual claim, a claim of value, and a policy claim relating to the topic.

3. Considering the relationships between beliefs and actions, identify topics that might fall into each category. For instance, for the "unfocused" category, people often believe that they should learn to study more effectively, but they don't know how to proceed. For the "unconvinced" category, people don't know enough about oat bran, so they don't eat it regularly.

4. Listen to at least one persuasive speech on television, taking notes on the speaker's arguments. (C-SPAN or the "MacNeil-Lehrer News Hour" on Public Broadcasting are good sources for such speeches.) What kinds of claims does the speaker make? How does he or she support the claims? Who are the intended audiences? How effectively does the speaker adapt to the audience's beliefs, actions, attitudes, and values?

5. Read the excerpts from President Clinton's speech at the Vietnam War Memorial in 1993 (found in the Appendix). Evaluate Mr. Clinton's effectiveness in the speech, which was delivered to an audience that contained many hostile listeners.

Key Terms

to convince
to actuate
to produce or initiate
to reinforce
dissonance
dissonance theory
apathy
direct method
statement of reasons pattern
comparative advantages pattern
criteria–satisfaction pattern
negative method
Monroe's Motivated Sequence

Notes

1. Mullins, D. (1993). Guest lecture. St. John's University, Jamaica, New York.
2. Becker, C. B. (1991). Reasons for the lack of argumentation and debate in the Far East. In L. A. Samovar & R. E. Porter (Eds.), *Intercultural communication: A reader* (pp. 234–243). Belmont, CA: Wadsworth.

3. An article on the Japanese ambassador's speaking style is found in Ota, A. K. (1993, July 11). Japan's ambassador to U.S. sets welcome new tone. *Seattle Times*, p. A12.

4. Festinger, L. (1957). *A theory of cognitive dissonance*. New York: Row, Peterson. See also Brown, R. (1965). *Social psychology*. New York: Free Press.

5. Jensen, V. (1985). Teaching ethics in speech communication. *Communication Quarterly*, 324–330. Used by permission.

6. Monroe, A. H. (1962). *Principles and types of speech,* 5th Ed. Chicago: Scott, Foresman, & Co. Reprinted by permission of HarperCollins Publishers.

7. Barbo, P. (1993). Tinnitus. Student speech. St. John's University, Jamaica, New York.

Public Speaking in Organizations

At the end of this chapter, you should be able to

- Explain what is meant by organizational culture and how this affects public speaking within the organization
- Identify two types of audiences that representatives of an organization might address
- Explain how various types of special occasion speaking function as integrative messages
- Describe seven kinds of special occasion speeches
- List five steps in a problem-solving method
- Tell three common formats for group reporting

Note

This chapter discusses the cultural features of organizations and shows how special occasion public speaking functions to integrate the members of the group. It concludes with information on small group problem solving. (The term *organization* is defined broadly to include voluntary associations as well as professional and business organizations.)

After you finish your degree, many of the public speaking opportunities available to you will be in organizations. That is, you will probably address audiences at work, and you may have opportunities to represent your employer to groups outside your organization. Furthermore, you may speak before the clubs and volunteer organizations you join for social, educational, political, or religious purposes.

To be effective, you will adapt your presentation specifically to match the distinct cultural characteristics of each organization you address. For instance, consider the adaptations each of these speakers makes when speaking to these different organizations.

Police officer Fei Fei Li speaks about the horse patrol unit:
- *To her fellow officers.*
- *To a group of Eagle Scouts in the community.*
- *To parents attending a PTA meeting.*

Education professor Carlos Ovando speaks at a teacher inservice meeting:
- *For incoming graduate assistants at his university.*
- *In the Indianapolis Public Schools.*
- *At a small, private, expensive prep school in Massachusetts.*

Health teacher Jill Layport speaks on the topic of bulimia:
- *To the faculty and staff of her high school.*
- *To members of a sorority on a neighboring college campus.*
- *To an organization made up of pre-med students.*

Since the major theme of this text is the effect of public speaking on culture and the effect of culture on public speaking, this chapter will look at public speaking within organizations from a cultural perspective. It will briefly look at ways that an organization's culture influences the public speaking that goes on within it. Then it will examine specific speech patterns that are common in organizational speaking. Finally, because speakers in organizations often report on work done in small groups, the chapter concludes by examining group problem solving within organizations.

Organizations as Cultures[1]

It is important to understand what is meant by organizational culture in order to recognize the influence of a group's culture on both the speaking and listening practices that are characteristic of the group. After a discussion of several aspects of an organization's culture, we consider two types of audiences.

Organizational Culture

 As we discussed in Chapter 3, culture includes both the visible, stated aspects of a group's way of life as well as the more embedded beliefs and assumptions that guide group members. When this concept is applied to organizations, the organization itself is seen as a small society. This does not mean that it functions independently of the dominant culture. Rather, it means that every organization has a history, a political and economic system as well as art, music, dress, language, and rituals that members of the culture know and newcomers must learn. Consequently, an organization's cultural environment includes:[2]

Theme

Chapter 3 discusses the ways public speaking functions within cultures to reinforce, maintain, and change cultural forms. When people speak in organizations, they adapt their speeches to the specific forms expected within the organizational culture.

- History—the founders, the founding date, the founding mission
- Political system—the way power is distributed, who leads and who follows, and when
- Distribution of wealth—pay equity, merit pay, bonuses, stock options, and dues or collections
- Art and music and dress—group logos, songs, or uniforms
- Language—jargon or special in-group terminology
- Rituals—banquets, picnics, award ceremonies, installations, commencements
- Folklore—the narratives and myths, the heroes and villains, described in the stories that are passed from person to person within the organization[3]

Teaching Idea

Exercise 1 is appropriate here. Students could write their responses in their journals.

These last two aspects of culture are particularly relevant to public speaking within an organization. W. G. Ouchi,[4] author of *Theory Z: How American Business Can Meet the Japanese Challenge,* underlines the fact that an organization's symbols, ceremonies, and myths communicate the beliefs and values of the group. Each organization has a rich inventory of narratives that are told and retold from generation to generation—stories that explain what is valued, believed, and remembered. Knowing these symbols and stories is an important part of understanding the organization; using them in public speaking can act as a powerful form of proof to members of the organization.

Anyone who speaks publicly within any organization must further consider cultural factors that determine which topics are appropriate, how to present messages, how to receive messages, and a host of other communication rules that vary from situation to situation.

Audiences

Because the organization is a culture while it is also part of the larger society, speakers give talks to listeners both within their organizations and to the public at large. These two types of audiences are called internal and external audiences.

Teaching Idea

Have each person identify a career he or she will probably pursue. (If students are undecided, have them identify what they wanted to be when they were ten.) Elicit times when they may speak to an external and an internal audience in the organizations in which they plan to work.

Internal Audiences *Internal* communication occurs between and among members of a business or volunteer organization when they share important information with one another or give ceremonial speeches to mark special occasions. Further, organizations sometimes invite special consultants and speakers to address internal audiences. For instance, an outside consultant may be brought in to speak on stress management or preparation for retirement.

External Audiences *External* communication occurs when representatives of the organization go public with their messages. Such audiences are so important that most large companies hire highly trained public relations officers. External communication includes public sales campaigns for the company's products, goodwill speeches given in community organizations, and "damage control," when the organization is receiving bad publicity.

Note

Scholar James Carey conceives of culture *as* communication. He stresses the importance of rituals in integrating the members of a society. See Chapter 3.

Organizational messages share the three general purposes common to all public speaking: to inform, to persuade, to entertain. An important additional function, called the integrative function,[5] helps bind members of the organization to one another and connects them firmly to their shared goals. It is a type of persuasive purpose that reinforces and maintains the common belief–attitude–value cluster that influences the specific actions of group members. In this chapter, we present a variety of integrative speeches first.

KEY CONCEPT   **Organizations as Cultures**

Organizational culture Organizational culture is the visible and invisible features of an organization that create its members' ways of doing things when they are participating in the organization; it includes rituals and folklore that communicate beliefs and values.

Audiences Organizational speakers address two types of audiences.

> *Internal audiences* These speeches are given to audiences inside the organization.
>
> *External messages* These public relations messages are presented to those outside the organization.

Special Occasion Speaking

Special occasion speaking functions to reinforce and maintain the organization's goals and its shared ideals. It takes place in gatherings that include celebrations, more solemn occasions, and occasions that reaffirm the visions of the organization's founders. Because groups grow and change, members of the group must:

Often speakers represent their organization to an external audience.

- Welcome newcomers and bid farewell to people leaving the organization
- Transfer power from one leader to another
- Affirm the beliefs and values that form the basis for the group's existence
- Recognize meritorious achievement
- Integrate the organization into the community in which it exists

In addition, representatives of the organization give goodwill speeches to external audiences in an effort to integrate the goals of the organization with those of the community in which it exists.

In this section, we look at some common ceremonial presentations that provide these integrative functions: introductions, farewells, announcements, award presentations, acceptance speeches, nominations, and commemorative speeches.

Introductions

When people join an existing organization—whether permanently or briefly—there is a need to integrate them into the group. Current members of the group need information about the newcomers' backgrounds and the characteristics they bring to the organization. Speeches of introduction function to present this important information, enabling new members to enter smoothly into the already existing patterns of the group. *It is essential that your introductory speech be brief.*

1. Provide the newcomer's name and job title.
2. Give a few relevant details about the educational and occupational background as well as the personal characteristics the new person brings to the organization.
3. Close by welcoming the newcomer to the group.

Student Assignment

Throughout the term, give students an opportunity to give these special occasion speeches, as the need arises. For instance, someone may want to make an announcement regarding an upcoming local or campus activity. *Exercise 6 is appropriate here.*

Here is a sample introduction.

> *We are pleased to welcome a new member of our faculty. Pablo Lopez is joining us as a sixth-grade teacher whose specialty is science education.*
>
> *Pablo received both his bachelor's and master's degree from the University of Rochester. As an undergraduate student, he spent a summer at Cornell University, where he was a research assistant, working with astronomy and space science professor Jim Cordes. As part of that program, he spent a week in a computer lab in Puerto Rico writing a computer program to trace pulsars. Before coming here, he taught five years in public schools in Ohio.*
>
> *He comes with the highest recommendations from both his professors and the students with whom he has worked.*
>
> *Pablo, welcome. We know you will continue your tradition of teaching excellence and will be a wonderful addition to our staff.*

Sometimes a guest is invited into the group for only an hour-long presentation or a weekend seminar. Consequently, you must include some information about the occasion that precipitated the invitation as well as about the guest speaker. Here are some elements often included in speeches that introduce guest speakers.

1. Greetings to the group.
2. A statement about the occasion.
3. A welcome.
4. Announcement of the speaker's name and subject.
5. A brief account of the speaker's background, education, training, achievements, personality, or other salient information that relates to the topic or the audience.

After the speech, you often make a few brief remarks that provide closure to that part of the meeting. Briefly thank the speaker, and make a simple, brief remark relating to the central idea of the speech.

Farewells

When people leave an organization, their departure results in a disruption that affects the remaining people to a greater or lesser degree. This is true whether or not they were well liked as individuals. For example, consider the varied emotions that members of an organization feel when a popular professor leaves for a position in another university; a beloved rabbi retires; an unpopular manager is fired; the seniors on the football team graduate. All these departures signal changes in the social patterns of the organization. Because of this, farewell speeches function to ease the inevitable changes both the individuals and the group face.

Special occasion speeches, such as those given at this grand opening, should be brief and inspiring—with emphasis on the shared beliefs and values of the group.

The person who is leaving sometimes gives a farewell speech, while a remaining member of the organization says good-bye for the rest of the group. Both types of speeches call for expressions of emotions, especially appreciation, sadness, hope for the future, and affection for the other members of the group. Generally, speakers balance the sadness inherent in the occasion by remembrances of happy times, often by relating humorous stories.

When you bid a group farewell because you are leaving, include some or all of these elements.

1. Remind the group members of what they have meant to you personally.
2. List some lessons you learned as a member of the group.
3. Tell humorous stories that you will take with you as happy memories.
4. Express both your sadness at leaving and your hopes for the future.
5. Invite people to write or visit you in your new location.

When you bid farewell to a departing member or members of an organization, you speak not only for yourself but also for the group. Remember these elements in your speech.

1. Recognize the tasks the person accomplished that benefited the group.
2. Recognize personal characteristics that made the association enjoyable and will cause the group to remember the person.

3. Use humorous anecdotes.

4. Express your personal sadness and the group's sense of loss.

5. Wish the person well in his or her new location.

6. When appropriate, present a gift as a remembrance.

Announcements

Announcements are brief messages that provide information about upcoming events both within and outside the organization. They generally have a persuasive intention, in that their purpose is to encourage people to attend an event. Thus, it is important to motivate the audience as well as to provide details regarding where, when, and why something will take place, as these guidelines and the sample announcement show.

1. First, draw your listeners' attention to the event.

2. Provide such details as who, what, when, and where the event takes place.

3. Tell both the cost and the benefits of attending.

4. End with a brief summary of important information.

Remember when you were a little kid, and figures from the Peanuts cartoon strip were everywhere? I had a Snoopy T-shirt and couldn't wait for the annual "Great Pumpkin" show on TV. Well, you can return briefly to these beloved characters from childhood if you attend the campus production of "You're a Good Man, Charlie Brown."

This play will be performed on May 8–12 at Mitchell Playhouse here on campus. Evening performances begin at 8:00 p.m. In addition, there will be 3:00 matinee performances on Saturday and Sunday afternoons. Tickets are $5.00—$2.00 with your student body card. You can purchase them in advance at the ticket window in the Memorial Union Building, or you can purchase them at the door at the time of the performance. This is a small price to pay for an evening with such memorable characters as Linus and Lucy.

Remember, "You're a Good Man, Charlie Brown," May 8–12—with both weekend and evening performances. Get your tickets at the ticket office or the play-house. It's worth it just to see Snoopy dance!

Award Presentations

Teaching Idea

Exercise 4 is appropriate here. Awards ceremonies are common on TV. For instance, winning teams are awarded trophies; on the local news, the mayor may announce construction of a new park.

Award ceremonies are rituals that aid the members of a group in articulating their common values. Ordinarily, individuals are recognized for meritorious work or for character traits that embody the ideals of the organization. It is common to present award recipients with a permanent memento of some sort. If you present an award, emphasize the shared beliefs, values, and commitments of the group. In general, awards presentations include similar elements.

In some cultural groups, it is more appropriate to present an award to an entire work group rather than single out an individual for an honor.

1. Name the award, and describe its significance. What personal traits or accomplishments does it honor? In whose name is it made? Why is it given? How often is it awarded? How are the recipients selected?

2. Summarize the reasons the recipient was selected to receive the award.

3. Relate the appropriateness of the award to the traits of the recipient.

4. Express good wishes to the recipient.

  Some cultures emphasize the importance of group performance over individual performance. In these cultures, groups rarely single out one individual to praise over others. (New Zealanders, for instance, have the saying, "The tall poppy gets mown down.") Consequently, the members of these groups tend to feel uncomfortable having their personal characteristics publicly acknowledged. Thus, if you work in an organization made up of people whose values are more collectivist than individualist, you might present the award or honor to entire work groups rather than to an individual.

Acceptance Speeches

When you receive an award, you normally accept it with a *brief* speech in which you express gratitude to those who selected you, thank other people who helped you become eligible for such an honor, and reinforce the cultural values that the award demonstrates, as these guidelines and sample acceptance speech show.

1. Thank those who honored you.

2. Acknowledge others who helped you get it.

3. Personalize what it means to you.

4. Express appreciation for the honor.

Thank you Professor Geffner for those kind words, and thank you committee for selecting me as the Outstanding Speech and Hearing Student this year. As you know, there are many other students who are deserving of honor for their scholarship and their service to the clients in our speech clinic, and I know that each one deserves to receive recognition.

Of course, no student can accomplish anything were it not for the support of a dedicated faculty—and the faculty we have here at St. John's University has been outstanding. I have been impressed, not only with their academic credentials, but also with the personal interest each one takes in the lives of each student who majors in Speech Pathology and Audiology. Thanks also to my parents who supported me both financially and emotionally through these past four years. I appreciate you all.

Next year I will be attending graduate school at Northwestern University. I'm sure that, when I'm homesick for New York, I will remember this honor and be inspired by your confidence in me.

Thank you once again.

Nominations

In democratically controlled groups where voting is a right, you may have the opportunity to nominate a candidate for an elected office. Remember that each speech of nomination is a short persuasive speech that does two things: It introduces your candidate to the group, and it presents brief arguments explaining why he or she should be elected.

The parts of the nomination include:

1. Name the office, and tell its importance to the organization as a whole.
2. List the reasons why the candidate is right for the office.

Because a nomination is a persuasive speech, two organizational patterns discussed in Chapter 16 work especially well—a direct method or statement of reasons pattern and a criteria–satisfaction pattern—as these two brief outlines demonstrate.

Vote for Trung Vo-Vu for the office of treasurer.
  I. He has been the treasurer of three organizations.
  II. He is a business major.
  III. He has worked part-time in a bank, and he understands money management.

A president must have three important traits.
  I. She must have demonstrated leadership ability.
  II. She must be able to represent the organization to outside groups.
  III. She must have the ability to lead people to consensus when opinions differ.

Gisella Cassalino excels in all three areas.

I. She has been vice-president of this organization and currently serves as president of the county's Partners with Disabilities organization.
II. She is a communication major who gives public presentations with ease.
III. She has served on a committee that mediates student grievances.

Commemorative Speeches

On a variety of occasions, members of organizations gather as a community and reinforce and strengthen the values and commitments they share. Put simply, commemorative speeches emphasize the common ideals, common history, and common memories the participants hold.[6] Although the basic purpose of commemorative speeches is to inspire listeners by reinforcing the beliefs and values of the organization, they are often entertaining as well.

Frequently, representatives of outside organizations give these commemorative speeches. In addition to reinforcing the ideals of the group to which they speak, they aim to create goodwill toward the organization they represent. A single large organization may provide speakers for more than 1,000 events annually.

You can hear such speeches all around you. Organizations host breakfast, luncheon, or dinner meetings with an invited speaker. Conventions generally open with a keynote speaker who addresses the theme of the series of meetings. (Professor Stephen Littlejohn's presidential address to the Western States Communication Association, located in the Appendix, is an example of a keynote address.) Educational institutions send their graduates into the world after inspiring commencement addresses.

Although each of these types of speeches is different, they all share some common characteristics, and speakers typically follow these guidelines as they prepare commemorative addresses.

Teaching Idea

Exercise 3 is appropriate here. If you used this speech with Chapter 3, simply have students identify how it follows the guidelines presented here. If you did not use it earlier, use it as a summary for many of the ideas covered in this text.

1. Build the speech around a theme. Find out in advance if one has been selected for the meeting; if so, prepare your remarks around it. If not, select an inspiring theme of your own choosing. Farah Walters, President and Chief Executive Officer, University Hospitals of Cleveland, explains how she selected her theme in this excerpt from a keynote address she gave before an organization called WomenSpace.[7]

   Before preparing these remarks, I asked the leadership of WomenSpace if there was anything special that I should address. I was told that there might be some interest in learning a little more about who I am and how I got to be the head of one of America's largest academic medical centers; and I was asked if I would give my assessment of where women are today in the professional world, and where I think women will be in the years ahead.

   I will touch upon those topics, but in a particular context. And that context is in the title of my talk—"In Celebration of Options." [An excerpt from this address can be found in the Appendix.]

Teaching Idea

Exercise 2 is appropriate here. Show an excerpt—or an entire commencement address. Your school may have videotapes of recent speeches. (Barbara Bush's 1990 address at Wellesley is a good example. Students protested the selection of Mrs. Bush as speaker; they wanted Alice Walker instead. Mrs. Bush was aware of this.) Identify cultural beliefs and values—both of the specific organization the speaker addresses and of the dominant culture.

2. Inspire listeners. Inspiration is often linked to positive emotions and values such as hope, courage, respect, perseverance, and generosity. See how many positive emotions and values you can identify in this excerpt from Barbara Bush's 1990 commencement address at Wellesley College.[8]

   Wellesley, you see, is not just a place, but an idea, an experiment in excellence in which diversity is not just tolerated, but is embraced. . . . "Diversity, like anything worth having, requires effort." Effort to learn about and respect difference, to be compassionate with one another, to cherish our own identity, and to accept unconditionally the same in others. You should all be very proud that this is the Wellesley spirit.

3. Pay special attention to language. To make your speech both inspiring and memorable, select words and phrases that are vivid, moving, and interesting. Begin by describing scenes in detail in order for your hearers to form images in their minds; select words that are rich in connotative meanings. This excerpt from President John Kennedy's inaugural address shows the power of inspiring language.[9]

   And so, my fellow Americans; ask not what your country can do for you—ask what you can do for your country.

   My fellow citizens of the world; ask not what America will do for you, but what together we can do for the freedom of man.

   Finally, whether you are citizens of America or citizens of the world, ask of us here the same high standards of strength and sacrifice which we ask of you. With a good conscience our only sure reward, with history the final judge of our deeds, let us go forth to lead the land we love, asking His blessing and His help, but knowing that here on earth God's work must truly be our own.

4. When it is appropriate, use humor. For certain speeches, such as after-dinner speeches whose major purpose is to entertain, humor is almost essential. This example comes from the beginning of Donald Keough's 1993 commencement address at Emory University.[10]

   Dr. Laney, I wish Mother were here to have heard what you had to say. Thank heavens my wife and children are here. President Laney and faculty and new graduates and nongraduates and those who would be graduates except you still have overdue library books and outstanding library fines; those who parked their cars three years ago and are still searching for them; family, friends, high school teachers who said you'd never amount to a thing—and you wish they were here so they could see you now in these black robes that make you look like Supreme Court justices; relatives who wish you well, parents and spouses who sold the family silver and took out second mortgages to get some of you here, I am honored and proud and delighted to be a part of Emory University's 148th commencement.

5. Be relatively brief. These speaking occasions are generally not times to develop an extensive policy speech or to provide detailed information. Rather, they are times to reinforce important values and themes.

Throughout this section, we have seen that a great deal of organizational public speaking functions to integrate the members of the group with one another and with the community in which they exist. Special occasion speaking occurs in a variety of organizations—from clubs and volunteer associations to business, educational, and religious institutions.

KEY CONCEPT ## Special Occasion Speaking

Introductions These speeches integrate newcomers or visitors into an organization by providing background information about them to the members of the group.

Farewells These speeches are given to ease the parting when a person or persons leave a group. The one who is leaving bids the group farewell; additionally, a representative of the group says good-bye for the group.

Announcements These short speeches enable members of the organization to participate in social or task-related events by providing information about place, cost, time, and so on.

Award presentations These speeches are given in ceremonies that recognize achievements or valued personal characteristics.

Acceptance speeches In these speeches, award recipients express gratitude for an honor, thank people who helped them achieve it, and reaffirm the ideals of the group.

Nominations These short, persuasive speeches introduce a candidate and explain his or her qualifications for an office.

Commemorative speeches These speeches are given at ritual and ceremonial occasions at which participants emphasize the group's history, ideals, and memories. They are often entertaining.

Working in Small Groups Within Organizations

Student Assignment

You may want to have your students do a group report. The Student Resource Workbook has an assignment for a group report.

It is very common for people in organizations to work within small groups and then present their ideas in a public format. This trend has been developing over the last few decades, and it is becoming even more prevalent as members of the U.S. culture begin to emphasize cooperation rather than competition and as businesses and organizations actively seek global connections with people whose cultures are organized around a more communitarian value system. Consequently, it is probable that you will be part of a small group sometime during your working years.[11]

The Problem-Solving Method

Teaching Idea

The problem-solving method is found on a transparency in the Instructor's Manual.

In organizations, locally, nationally, and globally, we work in problem-solving discussion groups to come up with answers to difficult challenges, similar to the ones we have looked at throughout this book—problems such as child care on campus, wheelchair accessibility, global trade imbalances, elder abuse, and safe water.

Members of a group typically follow a five-step reflective-thinking process in Euro-American organizational cultures.[12] Although the five-step process is linear, meaning that you proceed from point to point in one direction, your group may circle back to previous steps and revise its work along the way. If you follow a structured process, rather than a random approach, your group will work more effectively. The following five steps are common.

Note

Teaching Note 1.1 explains that small group problem-solving skills are valued by employers. Because the results of a small group's work are often presented in public reports, panels, or symposia, this material is presented in this chapter. Activity 17.1 in the Instructor's Manual gives ideas for group projects that are suitable to a public speaking class.

1. Define the Problem It is important at the outset to state the problem clearly. If your group fails to do this, its work will be more difficult later, for it is hard to find a solution for something that is vague. Some problems are easy to define; for instance, "Whom shall we hire as the new basketball coach?" is an easy problem for a group to pinpoint when members of the group have in hand the previous coach's letter of resignation. However, many, even most, problems require narrowing the topic in ways similar to what you have done for your speeches throughout the term. Narrow the topic by following these three general suggestions for formulating a question.

1. State the issue as a policy question using the word *should*. For example, "Which athlete should we honor as outstanding gymnast?"

2. Leave the question broad enough to allow for a variety of answers; that is, make it an open, rather than a closed, question. Thus, "Should the student council repair acts of vandalism in the student union building?" which requires a yes or no answer, is less effective for group discussion than the more open question, "How should the student council ensure that campus buildings remain free from vandalism?"

3. State the question as objectively as possible, avoiding use of emotionally charged language. "How can we get rid of this antiquated grading system?" is less effective than "What changes, if any, should be made in the current methods of assigning grades?"

Cross Reference

This point reviews material from both Chapters 7 and 15.

2. Analyze the Problem After you know the problem, begin to collect information about it. This almost always requires the type of research described in Chapter 7. To accomplish the research task, look for the facts—including causes and effects—values, and policies that relate to your topic. Divide the relevant issues among group members and have them consult oral, print, and electronically stored sources for information:

1. What are the *factual issues* involved in the problem? What is the *history* of the problem?

2. What are the *causes* of the problem? Which are primary causes? Which are secondary factors that contribute to it?

3. What *effects* does the problem have on the lives of people or on the environment?

4. What are the *values* that relate to the discussion? Is it wrong or right? In what respects?

5. Are there any *policies* related to this?

At this stage, your group has defined the problem and analyzed related issues. You have also explored facts, possible causes, and resulting effects of the problem; finally, you have analyzed underlying values and historical policies related to the issue. Now you are ready as a group to explore possible solutions.

3. Set Criteria for Deciding on a Solution   Because most solutions must be feasible in terms of time, money, and ease of enactment, your group should set up standards for determining an acceptable solution before you even begin to suggest possible solutions. As part of your consideration, Charles Kepner and Benjamin Tregoe[13] suggest two factors that are vital in the criteria stage: (1) What *must* we do? That is, what is required? (2) What do we *want* to do? That is, what is desired? To illustrate, we *must* solve the problem with less than $10,000; we *want* to solve it with less than $5,000. We *must* have the policy in effect by the beginning of the next school year; we *want* to have it implemented by the end of the spring term. As you might imagine, when you work within a budget and time constraints, some solutions are automatically ruled out as too costly or too time-consuming.

4. List Possible Solutions   During this period, the group's task is to generate as many ideas as possible. Because you are seeking possibilities, it is not important at this stage that every suggestion be feasible. Therefore, the group suspends judgment of individual proposals until a later time.

One of the most common ways for a group to generate ideas is through the process commonly called *brainstorming*, in which group members put a number of ideas on the table for consideration. Again, a mind map, as described in Chapter 2, is a valuable way to record ideas. Here are some tips for a successful brainstorming session.

Cross Reference

Mind maps are also discussed in Chapter 7.

1. Have a recorder write down all the ideas as they are presented; a chalkboard, overhead transparency, or flip chart is helpful for this.

2. Record all the ideas that are proposed without judging any of them.

3. Make sure that each person in the group has an opportunity to contribute at least once.

4. Piggyback off one another's ideas—that is, encourage group members to use one proposal as a jumping-off point for another.

After a successful brainstorming session, in which a number of ideas are generated, you begin the process of evaluating each idea against the proposed criteria. Often the brainstorming session makes you rethink your criteria. Don't hesitate to circle back and make revisions at this time.

5. Select the Best Solution   After these steps, you have a good idea of the problem—its causes, effects, and history. You have decided on what is necessary for a good solution, and you have generated a number of ideas. It now remains to select the best solution and implement it. So you begin to evaluate the suggested solutions against the criteria you have set. You will probably eliminate some easily because they are too expensive, they will take too much time, or they don't fit your criteria for obvious reasons. After you have pared down the number of options, you are ready to analyze and weigh the merits of those that remain in order to find the one that members of the group can agree on.

Presenting the Group's Findings

Cross Reference

Chapter 1 set out the importance of writing in public speaking. Here is another way that speakers must also write. Hagge-Greenberg's table, found in the Instructor's Manual in Chapter 1, reinforces the importance of good written skills.

When working within an organization, the next step is to present your findings to an internal audience who will be involved in its implementation. In almost all cases, you must submit a written report at the time of your verbal presentation. After people within the organization are informed of the group's conclusions, a report may also be presented to external audiences. These reports are presented in several common formats, including a final report, a panel discussion, and a symposium.

A Final Report   When you choose this format, one member of the group acts as the spokesperson for the entire group. The speaker defines the problem and briefly explains background information related to it. Then, he or she summarizes the decision-making process, identifies the criteria decided on for the solution, describes alternative solutions that were considered, and explains and justifies the final choice.

Teaching Idea

Exercise 5 is appropriate here.

A Panel Discussion   In the second format, all the members of the group sit on a panel and discuss the issue in dialogical interactions. During the discussion, a leader or moderator asks a series of questions, and group members provide their insights on each one. They take turns speaking back and forth, and all members contribute from their store of information and opinions.

Afterward, the moderator generally opens the discussion to the audience and encourages listeners to participate in a dialogue with panelists during a question-and-answer period. In this way, both panelists and their audiences cooperate in the co-creation of meaning.

Often people who are knowledgeable about a topic discuss their subject in a panel format. Here, a panel of sports figures discusses drugs and student athletes.

Cross Reference

Geissner established the importance of dialogue in Chapter 1. The text closes with this theme.

A Symposium   In this format, each member of the group selects only one aspect of the problem and prepares and delivers a speech on it. After all the speakers have finished, the moderator usually opens up the floor for a question-and-answer period from the audience.

 **KEY CONCEPT**   # Working in Small Groups Within Organizations

Steps in problem solving   Small group members often follow a five-step linear process to appraise problems and generate solutions for them.

1. *Define the problem*   State the problem clearly in the form of a policy question.

2. *Analyze the problem*   Do research to find facts, values, and policies that relate to the issue.

3. *Set criteria for deciding on a solution*   Ask what is required and what is desired. Consider limitations such as time, money, and ease of enactment.

4. *List possible solutions*   Use the technique of brainstorming to generate possibilities.

5. *Select the best solution*   Weigh the possible solutions against the criteria, and choose the one that will be most effective.

Presenting the group's findings   Reports of the group's findings are presented in several common formats.

A final report   One person acts as spokesperson who reports on the group's work.

A panel discussion All members participate; each is free to contribute to any question.

A symposium Each person prepares and delivers a speech on only one aspect of the subject.

Summary

Organizations have a culture consisting of shared beliefs, values, attitudes, and actions. It is important to produce these resources in new members, to reinforce them in current members, to repair them when they threaten to break down and disrupt the smooth running of the organization, and at times to transform them by making needed changes in some aspect of the culture. To accomplish these ends, public speakers address members of the organization with informative, persuasive, and integrative purposes.

One of the most important functions of public speaking in organizations is that of integration. Special occasion speeches serve to integrate new members with old, bid farewell to departing members, transfer leadership, and find occasions to affirm the group's identity and ideals in award ceremonies and the like. The specific speeches that provide these integrative functions are introductions, farewells, announcements, award presentations, acceptance speeches, nominations, and commemorative speeches.

Finally, a great deal of work within many organizations is accomplished through task groups, which then report to both internal and external audiences. Many decisions in this culture are made through a linear, structured problem-solving method. This involves defining the problem, analyzing the problem, setting criteria for a solution, generating possible solutions, and selecting the best solution. The conclusions of the group are then given to a wider public in a final report, a panel discussion, or a symposium. Generally, a written report accompanies the oral report.

Questions and Exercises

1. Create a hypothetical organization—you can model it loosely on an organization that you already know. Describe the culture that exists within your imaginary group. Especially focus on the language, rituals, and folklore that members use to emphasize their beliefs and values.

2. Watch a video of a commemorative speech such as Barbara Bush's commencement address at Wellesley College. Identify the organizational beliefs and values that the speaker is reinforcing. Look for ways he or she uses the occasion and the setting to develop a particular theme.

3. Read Stephen Littlejohn's speech, "The Quest for Quality in Public Discourse," found in the Appendix. Identify specific instances where Professor Littlejohn meets each of the four guidelines for commemorative speeches.

4. Watch several television news broadcasts or C-SPAN. Look for examples of the kinds of speeches outlined in this chapter—for example, a news clip of the mayor presenting a trophy to a local sports team, a farewell speech given by a retiring dignitary, or a panel of experts discussing a social problem.

5. Attend a panel or symposium presentation that is given on your campus. How do the speakers use their specific areas of expertise to increase the audience's understanding of the topic? In what ways, if any, do audience members participate in the discussion?

6. Prepare and deliver a special occasion speech such as an announcement, introduction, welcome, or award presentation.

Key Terms

organizational culture
internal audiences
external audiences
integrative function
commemorative speeches
panel
symposium

Notes

1. For information on organizational culture, see Pacanowsky, M. E., & O'Donnell-Trujillo, N. (1983). Organizational communication as cultural performance. *Communication Monographs, 50*, 126–147. See also Putnam, L. L., & Pacanowsky, M. E. (Eds.). (1983). *Communication and organization*. Beverly Hills, CA: Sage.

2. H. L. Goodall, Jr., C. L. Waagen, and G. M. Phillips have written extensively on communication within organizations. This chapter draws on their writings. See, for instance, Goodall, H. L., & Waagen, C. L. (1986). *The persuasive presentation: A practical guide to professional communication in organizations*. New York: Harper & Row. In addition, see Goodall, H. L., & Phillips, G. M. (1984). *Making it in any organization*. Englewood Cliffs, NJ: Prentice-Hall.

3. Ernest Bormann discusses the use of *fantasies*, which are creative and imaginative interpretations of the events that take place within the organization. By explaining what they perceive is going on, members of an organization co-create social truths within their organization. See Bormann, E. G. (1983). Fantasy theme analysis and rhetorical theory. In J. L. Golden, G. F. Berquist, & W. E. Coleman (Eds.), *The rhetoric of western thought*, 3rd Ed. (pp. 432–449). Dubuque, IA: Kendall-Hunt. See also Bormann, E. G. (1985). Symbolic convergence theory: A communication formulation. *Journal of Communication, 35*, 128–138.

4. Ouchi, W. G. (1981). *Theory Z: How American business can meet the Japanese challenge*. Reading, MA: Addison-Wesley.

5. Goodall and Phillips (1984). Op. cit.

6. See Brigance, W. N. (1961). *Speech: Its techniques and disciplines in a free society*, 2nd Ed. New York: Appleton-Century-Crofts.

7. Walters, F. (1992, November 15). In celebration of options: Respect each other's differences. *Vital Speeches of the Day*, pp. 265–269.

8. Bush, B. (1990, June 1). Choice and change. Commencement address. Wellesley College, Wellesley, MA.

9. Kennedy, J. F. Inaugural address. In J. Podell & S. Angovin (Eds.), (1988). *Speeches of the American Presidents* (pp. 603–605). New York: H. W. Wilson.

10. Keough, D. R. (1993, May 10). The courage to dream: Seize the day. *Vital Speeches of the Day*, pp. 599–601.

11. For a collection of articles on group dynamics, see Cartwright, D., & Zander, A. (Eds.). (1968). *Group dynamics: Research and theory*, 3rd Ed. New York: Harper & Row.

12. The philosopher and educator John Dewey is credited with identifying the five-step reflective thinking sequence. It has been revised and refined over eight decades.

13. Kepner, C. H., & Tregoe, B. B. (1965). *The rational manager: A systematic approach to problem solving and decision making*. New York: McGraw-Hill.

Appendix

The Quest for Quality in Public Discourse

Stephen Littlejohn, Professor, Humboldt State University

In February 1993, Professor Littlejohn, who was president of the Western States Communication Association, addressed members of the association who had gathered for their annual convention in Albuquerque, New Mexico. Professor Littlejohn deals with some of the same issues raised in Chapter 3. How do we communicate with others who believe and act differently than we do? What can we do as students of speech to improve the quality of public discourse in the culture? Littlejohn concludes that "dialogue" is one possible solution. (His discussion of dialogue and monologue is developed further in Chapter 5 of the text.)

Through no fault of my own, we begin a new tradition for Western this year—a presidential address. While I did not seek this dubious honor, I am pleased, and actually eager, to rise to the occasion. I say "rise" in the bodily sense. We'll have to wait and see whether my performance this afternoon meets the loftier meaning of that common expression.

For the communication researchers in the room, this speech is an example of discourse designed to meet multiple goals. It's a ceremonial occasion for the occasion, it is an opportunity to make a public statement about something I think is important, and on a very personal level, preparing the speech gave me a way to work through some ideas that have been troubling me in recent years.

As many of you have, I've become increasingly concerned about the quality of public discourse in our country. By discourse, I simply mean talk, the kind of talk in which citizens at all levels participate in public settings.

Thorough, balanced, empowered, egalitarian public discussion is the real driving force of democracy. And I am becoming increasingly pessimistic about whether this great bastion of democracy truly fulfills its own ideals. In short, I believe that the quality of public discourse in this nation has become impoverished.

The most common forms of public discourse are simplistic and shallow. Our talk aims to influence and persuade, not to invite dialogue. We blame and demean those who disagree with us; we do not seek to discover why it is that equally intelligent and well-meaning people can come to categorically opposing sides on an issue. For Mary Smith, who marches for life, Betty Jones the pro-choicer is simply and absolutely immoral; and for Betty, poor Mary is stupid and narrow-minded. There is no room for any other judgment.

There is no shortage of public discourse, but there is in my opinion a great shortage of quality discourse. What is needed is the kind of communication in which good questions are more important than persuasive statements and the exercise of power. It is the kind of communication in which dialogue is valued more than monologue. It's the kind of communication in which we are more concerned about discovering the values and ideals that underlie our differences than to shout down opponents in some kind of verbal war. It's the kind of communication in which we even try to find common ground, when on the surface none seems to exist.

In his provocative new book *The Cynical Society*, Jeffrey Goldfarb writes that "serious intellectual reflection continues to exist . . . but it is becoming a specialized market, along with surfing, skiing, and gourmet cooking, consistently not reaching the general public." And he goes on: "Shouting, partisan, talking heads are replacing the pluralistic search for the common good."

My chief research interest in the past several years has been the problem of moral conflict, pitting right against wrong, which is the most profound difficulty of our age. At its best, moral discourse is civil, but shallow. At its worst, moral discourse is frustrated verbal assault that can and often does lead to violence. Some of the ideas we have been working on were published in a recent article in the journal, and much of what I have to say this morning relates to my ongoing struggle with solutions to the public discourse problem in our country.

Like many of you, I suspect, I am a Doonesbury addict. Did you see the strip a few months ago in which Mike and Joanie are trying to live up to the standards of the family values censor? After a round of very sweet marital greetings, Joanie asks what Mike would like to do, and he replies, "Let's go downtown and hurl epithets at people different from us!" Well, I'm afraid that is the quality of much public moral discourse today. The most common forms of moral discourse are mere expressions of exasperation—slogans, signs, chants, songs, bites, and insults. They are literally "hurling epithets at people different from us."

Let me tell you an all-too-familiar story. Perhaps you remember it from the national news. It was also featured in our recent *Western* article, and I'll quote liberally from that source.

In November of 1986, a scheduled visit by recruiters for the Central Intelligence Agency at the University of Massachusetts provoked a torrid sequence of events that disrupted normal university operations. The arrival of the CIA recruiters galvanized a group of liberal students, who succeeded in preventing the CIA from using the university career center for its recruitment.

Meanwhile, certain conservative students organized a counter-demonstration on the grounds that they had been prevented from meeting with the recruiters on campus. This group expressed support for the CIA for its protection of the American way, opposed the liberals for obstructing their freedom of speech, and criticized the administration for being unable to control those students who had prevented the CIA from coming onto campus. This was a mess.

In a confused sequence of angry events, the anti-CIA demonstrators attempted to occupy the main administration building. Finding this building locked they entered an adjacent building. Within minutes, a group of taunting pro-CIA demonstrators formed a ring around the occupied building while another group seized and occupied other university offices.

Although a great deal of communication took place between the various parties in this dispute, the discourse was not sophisticated or eloquent. When talking to their own supporters, advocates on both sides articulated their beliefs and values coherently and with reason. When confronting each other, however, only frustrated passion remained. When one side would yell something like ". . . Commie bastards!" the other would respond in kind: ". . . Fascist!"

This case illustrates philosopher Jeffrey Stout's admonition that "our capacity to live peaceably with each other depends upon our ability to converse intelligibly and reason coherently." "But," Stout continues, "this ability is weakened by the very differences that make it necessary. The more we need it, the weaker it becomes, and we need it very badly indeed."

As a deep analysis, public discourse must look beyond surface disagreement to the experiences and values that lead intelligent people to take conflicting public stands. This is a discourse of tolerance and civility, but it is more: It is a discourse of respect. It is an inquiry that suggests that while we may disagree—we may disagree very much—we aim to understand the basis for one another's belief, and we come to understand why we believe as we do.

A sufficient public discourse involves the deliberation of citizens. I want to emphasize two words here—*citizen* and *deliberation*. I am talking about real people, living their lives, agonizing over the issues that divide them, and participating in government. I am talking about deliberative speech, a dialogue, a give and take, in which citizens slowly and carefully come to public judgment.

In his startling new book *Coming to Public Judgment*, Daniel Yankelovich describes three aspects of real deliberation. The first quality is second thoughts. We come away from deliberation with questions about our own positions on important issues. The second quality is accepting new realities. True deliberation acknowledges the multiple realities that come into conflict in a situation. And the third quality is coming to grips with conflict, not just difference, but the deeply held values of a dispute. It aims to uncover deeply held prejudices, not to eliminate them, but in the words of Gadamer, to establish a "freedom from the tyranny of hidden prejudices." And that's what I mean by deliberation.

Our colleague, Barnett Pearce, now at Loyola University in Chicago, wrote that "in monologue, questions are asked to gain a speaking turn or to make a point; in dialogue, questions are asked to invite an answer. In monologue, one speaks in order to impress or impact on others; in dialogue, one speaks in order to take a turn in an interpersonal process that affects all participants." That's what I mean by deliberation.

Deliberation is choicework. When we truly deliberate, we seek to understand the good reasons for each alternative in a range of choices, to balance the powers and limits of different sides on an issue. Yankelovich describes this as the process of "working through," and I like this phrase because it resonates with our common understanding of what it means to wrestle with a problem. This kind of discourse occurs in what historians Sara Evans and Harry Boyte have come to call "free spaces," which are "the environments in which people are able to learn a new self-respect, a deeper and more assertive group identity, public skills, and values of cooperation and civic virtue." They are places "where ordinary citizens can act with dignity, independence, and vision."

This is what philosopher Richard Rorty refers to as "abnormal discourse." Normal discourse consists of attempts to persuade, frustrated diatribe, threats, and sometimes even violence. Is it possible to transcend these customary responses; to break the pattern; to engage those with whom we disagree on a new level; and to avoid the seemingly unavoidable spiral toward schism, degradation, and violence? Yes, I would answer, if certain forms of *abnormal* public discourse are employed.

The need for a new discourse has not gone unnoticed. Several attempts have been made to experiment with public discourse. There is, for example, the Syracuse Area Middle East Dialogue, a highly successful program bridging the Arab and Jewish communities in the greater Syracuse area. There is the Public Conversations Project in Cambridge which is working on promoting dialogue on a variety of hot social issues, most notably abortion. And there is the Kaleidoscope Project with which I was involved at the University of Massachusetts, designed to bring opponents on intractable issues together in dialogue.

I am most excited right now by the National Issues Forums, a decade-long program sponsored by the Kettering Foundation. I attended an NIF leadership institute last summer, and I think this project has a great deal of potential for improving public discourse in precisely the ways I have suggested.

Each year the NIF chooses three pressing national issues for study, and hundreds of public issues forums and study circles throughout the country are formed to deliberate on these issues. This year the issues are the health care crisis, criminal violence, and the economy.

It is clear to me that the problem of public discourse is a concern that ought to capture the attention and marshal the intelligence of the communication field. Our colleague from Rutgers, Stanley Deetz, has written recently that "there is probably nothing that various groups composing the communication field share more completely than their dedication to the public forum—to create an informed, discerning, articulate public that can negotiate the meaning of events and choose a common future." Deetz, however, is not sanguine about our record in promoting this ideal, and I must say that I share his pessimism.

I do not have time here to develop the several ways in which our field should deal with the problem of public discourse, but surely they include action in research, teaching, and community involvement. We need to require students to do more than learn how to make an argument or build a case. Students must learn to unpack the logics and realities that lead people to build incommensurate cases on opposing sides of an issue. They must learn to think creatively about conflict, and they must learn to come to grips with both the powers and limits of ideas, including their own. As a field, we need to examine more carefully the consequences of inadequate public discourse, to look for examples of successful discourse, and to test new models for improving the ways in which people talk about issues.

Our field is uniquely prepared to explore the quality of public discourse, and I hope you will join me in this endeavor.

The Solitude of Self

Elizabeth Cady Stanton
From an analysis by Cheryl Jorgensen-Earp

A fine example of the repetitive pattern is found in this speech, delivered before the Senate Committee on Woman's Suffrage in 1892. In her introduction, Stanton previews the four general subtopics she will cover. Each subtopic is followed by a number of major points, and each major point is developed by examples. The following is a sample of three of her major points (the "crests" of the wave in the wave pattern) and the examples she uses to tie them together. There is an intense use of repetitive style even in her examples.

Stanton's speech contains a number of major wave crests, rather than a single recurring theme. This demonstrates how variable the wave pattern can be. It may have many major points supported by small waves, a few major points supported by large waves, or a mixture of the two.

Major Point: Seeing then, that life must ever be a march and a battle, that each soldier must be equipped for his own protection, it is the height of cruelty to rob the individual of a single natural right.

> To throw obstacles in the way of a complete education is like putting out the eyes;
>
> To deny the rights of property, like cutting off the hands.
>
> To deny political equality is to rob the ostracized of all self-respect;
>
> > of credit in the market place;
> >
> > of recompense in the world of work;
> >
> > of a voice in those who make and administer the law;
> >
> > a choice in the jury before whom they are tried, and in the judge who decides their punishment.
>
> Shakespeare's play *Titus Andronicus* contains a terrible satire on woman's position in the nineteenth century. Rude men (the

play tells us) seized the king's daughter, cut out her tongue, cut off her hands, and then bade her go call for water and wash her hands.

Major Point: What a picture of woman's position! Robbed of her natural rights, handicapped by law and custom at every turn, yet compelled to fight her own battles, and in the emergencies of life to fall back on herself for protection.

> The girl of sixteen, thrown on the world to support herself;
>
> > to make her own place in society,
> >
> > to resist the temptations that surround her and maintain a spotless integrity.
>
> She does not acquire this power by being trained to trust others and distrust herself. If she wearies of the struggle, finding it hard work to swim upstream, and allows herself to drift with the current,
>
> > she will find plenty of company,
> >
> > but not one to share her misery in the hour of her deepest humiliation.
>
> If she tries to retrieve her position,
>
> > to conceal the past,
> >
> > her life is hedged about with fears
> >
> > lest willing hands should tear the veil from what she fain would hide.
>
> Young and friendless, *she* knows the bitter solitude of self.

Major Point: How the little courtesies of life on the surface of society, deemed so important from man towards woman, fade into utter insignificance in view of the deeper tragedies in which she must play her part alone, where no human aid is possible.

In Celebration of Options: Respect Each Other's Differences

Farah M. Walters

This is an excerpt from a keynote address delivered by Farah Walters, President and Chief Executive Officer, University Hospitals of Cleveland. It was given at a conference sponsored by WomenSpace, a clearinghouse for women's support groups in the Cleveland, Ohio, area on October 8, 1992. It is an example of a narrative speech that uses an infinity loop organizational pattern, discussed in Chapter 13.

. . . I want women to be able to celebrate the options that we have in life and act positively on those options. I firmly believe that in everything we do, we—as women—must both preserve and act upon those options if we are to achieve the goals that we have set for ourselves.

Is it better to light a candle than to curse the darkness? You bet it is! In a minute, I will return to the theme that celebrates options, but first I want to tell you a story. It is not a story about me, but about my daughter, Stephanie.

Two years ago, when she was in ninth grade, Stephanie was on an intra-mural, touch football team. She was one of four girls on the team. And Steph-anie is a pretty good athlete.

Stephanie came home one night, and she was really upset. "You know, Mom," she said, "we've been playing this game for weeks, and the boys never pass the ball to the girls. We complained to the boys, and they didn't listen. We complained to the coach, and he talked to the boys, but they still didn't listen. So today, we were so upset that the four of us sat down in the middle of the field at the start of the game, and we sang: 'I am woman, hear me roar.'"

Out of frustration, they took matters into their own hands. Although it did not enlighten the boys, I need to tell you how proud I was for those four girls who were willing to stand up for themselves—or sit, as in this case—and be heard.

So I want to start my talk with that image—an image of teenage girls sitting in the middle of an athletic field, singing "I am woman, hear me roar."

Learning to Roar

Today, in 1992, I feel that we are all there with those four young women. We are women. Hear us roar. Not just today, but tomorrow and tomorrow and to-morrow. I am saying, "Hear us roar." Not whimper, not complain, not whine. But, hear us roar.

I must be honest with you. When I came to this country from Iran some 28 years ago, I did not know how to roar. I was not a complainer or whiner—and those of you who know me, know that I don't ever, ever whimper!—but I had not yet learned how to roar. Maybe my story, really, is an odyssey—metaphori-cal, at least—of learning how to roar.

Picture this: an 18-year-old from Iran, a freshman at Ohio State Univer-sity—and the one girl in an advanced calculus class with 40 boys, most in their ROTC uniforms.

I had gone to a private girls' school in Teheran, a school where we were expected to do important things with our lives. A school that graduated young women who would go into medicine and engineering and the physical sciences and banking.

It was a school with great academic rigor, so that when I came to this coun-try, I was fully prepared academically to major in physics. However, in no way was I prepared for the blatant sexism that existed.

The boys in that calculus class—as well as the male professor—would constantly make jokes aimed at me, often sexual. My only saving grace was that I barely spoke English, which meant that I mercifully missed out on the worst of it.

I lived in a dorm with 700 women, but only two of us were going to major in physical sciences. Remember, now, that was 1964, and I was 18, and it was considered abnormal for a woman to go into physics.

So I gave up on physics. Why? Not because I couldn't handle the academic rigor, but because I perceived of myself as being odd—a young woman wanting to major in physical science.

I did not know how to roar in those days. I did not know that I had an option to become a woman physicist. I remember thinking, "Gee, maybe I really am strange."

Making Progress

Have times changed? Let me jump ahead 18 years. It is now 1982. I have established myself with a national reputation in nutrition and management. I decide to take an Executive MBA program. Here is what I find.

First, the situation has remarkable similarities. I am one of five women in the program. There are 42 mostly middle-age men in the class. They are mostly middle-age in terms of years on this earth, and middle-age—or is it antediluvian?—in terms of mindset. They are mostly from industries that have not been kind to women. And they are, for the most part, Neanderthal in their thinking vis-à-vis women. Which meant, of course, many jokes directed toward or about women.

What was different, however, was that much had changed in me and in society in the 18 years since I was a freshman.

This time I was old enough to handle it. And this time, I understood that the fault lay not in me—as I had felt, incorrectly, as a freshman at Ohio State—but in these unfortunate men who had missed the message of the most important revolution of the twentieth century: Women not only belonged in "their" Executive MBA program, but by not taking full advantage of what women had to offer, American business was losing out on the greatest resource of all—the power of effectively using great employees, whether they be men or women.

What that experience pointed out to me was threefold. First, I had matured enough not to let the shortcomings of others affect my view of my own worth. Second, women still had to travel along the road of equality—at least in the myopic view of some men in our society. And third, there had been, in fact, a change among men. This time the professors were not a party to sexist activities, nor were many of the younger men in the class. Which meant that change—real change—was taking place.

Bumping the Glass Ceiling

Let me now make one final jump—this time ten years. It is February 1992, and at University Hospitals of Cleveland a national search has begun to find a new CEO [Chief Executive Officer]; in the interim, the board of trustees has appointed me—a woman—to be acting president.

We are talking now about a national search to head one of America's great academic medical centers—a health system that employs almost 8,000 people, has revenues in excess of half a billion dollars, treats more patients than anywhere else in the region, and undertakes more biomedical research than anywhere else in the state of Ohio. . . .

It was a national search that narrowed the field to twelve white males . . . and one lone female. It was a national search that further narrowed the field to four white males . . . and one lone female. In the end, it was a unanimous vote of the search committee—all male with the exception of one—that selected that one female.

You should know that on more than one occasion during that process, I was ready to withdraw my name from consideration. I simply did not believe that I would be selected—not because I didn't think that I was the best qualified for the position, but because I feared that I would bump up against the infamous glass ceiling.

I felt that the same glass ceiling that had prevented other women from rising to the top would prevent me from being selected. The belief that a glass ceiling might be there was enough to make me ask myself if I wanted to be part of the search. Do you hear what I am saying? That the fear alone of the mythical glass ceiling was enough to make me want to withdraw.

Facing All Our Enemies

And I am saying something else. In the end, it may not be the close-minded men of this world who are our biggest enemies, but we ourselves. We must be willing to try, even if we sometimes do not succeed. We must no longer listen to the voices in ourselves that say, "It's not going to happen. Don't go for it. Give up."

Instead, we must listen to the voices that say we can do it. In my case, among those voices I heard most often that encouraged me not to falter were many male voices—the loudest of which was that of my husband, Steve, who has been my greatest friend and supporter.

In fact, among the key reasons I did not withdraw was that some very influential men—that's right, men—at the trustee level, the clinical leadership level, and the senior management level urged me to stay in the search. They didn't ask me to stay in the search because they wanted a female CEO. They felt these were difficult times in health care, and they wanted the best and strongest leadership possible, regardless of gender.

My friends: This is a message of hope I am sharing with you. Look—from 1964 to 1982 to 1992—how much the times did change.

I went from a girl struggling with her identity, to a rising young professional, to my appointment as a CEO who happens to be a woman. This was an incredibly moving experience for me, because if the situation can change this much at the CEO level in my field, it can change anywhere.

As I hope you can tell, I do not view my appointment as "us" versus "them," or a victory of women over men. I view it as a matter of equality in the best sense of the word—where selection is based on quality and not on gender. Period. . . .

A Statement of Concern and Commitment

Prince Bandar bin Sultan, Saudi Arabia's Ambassador to the United States

These comments come from a talk given by the prince at a conference sponsored by the United States Central Command (CENTCOM) on "Challenges to Security in Southwest Asia," on May 20, 1993. It is common for Arab public speakers to emphasize historical information and the Arab core values of hospitality (the general goal of strengthening the group), generosity (helping the less fortunate), courage (bravely sacrificing—even one's life—for the group), honor (bringing pride rather than shame), and self-respect (living according to the ideals of the culture). As you read through this speech, identify the major points the prince makes, and look at what he offers as "good reasons" for his main points. [Note: The bold type appeared in the script.]

To be here is to acknowledge an appreciation and to reaffirm a partnership. After Desert Storm, we have become bonded in a unique way.

You were steadfast; you came in style and did order's work. We, for our part, stood our ground; we did not dodge the crisis, and we fought side by side. We got to know one another a good deal better after the ordeal was behind us, which is something we have always managed to do.

Looking ahead, we are all now really on the forward edge of trying to sort out how the post–Cold War world can maximize international order and successfully work together. **The critical task is how widely separated sectors of the globe and markedly different cultures, religions and political environments can most effectively cooperate and advance shared interests, while remaining respectful of the distinctive conditioning, institutions and values that the various participants are dedicated to safeguarding for themselves, come what may.**

We and the world will almost certainly be caught up in this great cross-cultural challenge for the rest of our lives—and long beyond.

Islam
An overriding practical test of that is how America and the world (as well as those of us who are Muslims) think about Islam and react to it.

The challenges to security in Southwest Asia can hardly be adequately thought through without coming to terms with what is most basic in that sector of the globe—and indeed for nearly a billion people worldwide. Almost one in every five human beings in the world is a Muslim.

The United States prides itself on being open-minded and believing in pluralism. Yet the media and many in your political elite

abound in stereotypes and the most elementary misunderstandings about Islam.

Grand strategies and confidence-building international cooperation can hardly be sorted out and acted on by minds cluttered with rampant misinformation, obvious prejudice at times and chronic one-sidedness.

For the last several years, to cite one example, recurring attempts have been made to replace the old Cold War threat with a so-called Islamic threat. That effort tells a lot about attitudes here. But it tells nothing of practical consequence about Islam.

But the point I want to make can be brought a lot closer to home. Whenever suspects in the deplorable World Trade Center bombing [New York City, February 1993] are mentioned in the media, they are always described as Muslims, Muslims, Muslims.

Yet when news coverage and public discussion turned to Waco, Texas [April 1993], the central figures there were rarely referred to as Christians, even though that was their overriding commitment. The contrast speaks for itself.

Islamic Fundamentalists

Serious public discussion here is out of focus when it adopts the label of "Islamic Fundamentalists" as to various violence-prone groups in the Middle East.

With their blatant extremism, such groups are actually doing violence to basic Islamic teachings—and certainly to its good name. What they are really concerned with is not Islam at all, but economic and other grievances—or much more often, dead-end power.

Keep in perspective that these extremists are a very small fraction of the overall Islamic community and are not at all in the historical or present Muslim mainstream.

The media would provide a much more accurate sense of what is going on if the violent extremists who are seeking political power in their own countries were identified with those particular countries instead of with Islam. They seek to gain respectability with the cloak of Islam, but they are really new, localized, power-bent socialist-nationalists, reborn again.

It is also worth noting that for a great many decades, books and press stories in this country and elsewhere have almost always described Saudi Arabia as "Islamic Fundamentalist."

Yet there could hardly be a greater contrast between the violent extremists recently in the news from various parts of North Africa and elsewhere, on the one hand, and tradition-rooted, Islamic, conservative Saudi Arabia, on the other hand. My friends, you can't have it both ways.

Saudi Arabia

In Saudi Arabia, fidelity to Islam already guides its social and political life. Our *ulama*, our religious scholars, are not disaffected with the state or outcasts to political power. We have never sought to exclude them as their counterparts were excluded in the Shah's Iran. They have extensive access to the print media and the air-waves. They rule on the great issues of the day, on the basis of the mandate of the Sharia law. They were fully consulted when the coalition forces came into our country during the Gulf War. They sanctioned the decision made by King Fahd and our government to invite the coalition forces into our land; they blessed the effort of our Arab, Muslim and Western allies.

Those who second-guessed the decision in our part of the world (and there were many), said that the Western forces had come to stay and colonize the country. They were proven wrong.

We have always sought to serve and lead our people, without running too far ahead of them—and without trying to herd them into some alien future.

The kind of socioeconomic despair that grips extremists in the Sudan, Algeria and other places—the despair of an underclass, the frustrations of the young urban poor, the rejection of excessive Westernism—do not afflict Saudi Arabians. We have long believed in modernization, but not necessarily Westernization.

Bosnia

What greatly concerns the Islamic world now is that a Muslim population in Bosnia—the last remnants of Islam's long presence in southeastern Europe—is under threat of extinction. How can we explain to our people in Saudi Arabia watching Western media reports on Bosnia's slaughter and horror, that the product of a new, democratic and free world ends in ethnic cleansing in Europe?

We have a strong, vested interest in strengthening understanding and the bonds between the Muslim world and the West.

And I must say **we are still hopeful that the U.S. position concerning Bosnia will yet evolve positively, especially compared to the badly flawed European position.**

The choices are clear: either the UN should implement its resolutions or allow the Bosnian Muslims to be armed to defend themselves, as King Fahd and President Clinton have called for.

Relevance to Mideast Peace

We broke with the past and went to the Madrid Peace Conference and into the multilateral talks to resolve the outstanding regional issues between Israelis and Arabs. We are hopeful that a just, comprehensive peace can be achieved based on UN Resolutions 242 and 338 and will result in achieving peace for land, the legitimate rights of the Palestinian people and security for all states in the region.

It would be a setback for all of us to seek to repair the international order in one arena while it comes apart in the Balkans. Politics being what it is, we would have far more political ground at home on behalf of a regional settlement on Israeli–Arab matters if there is to be greater Western concern for Bosnia.

America's Leadership

The sad truth is that we were all caught unaware by the kind of world that emerged from the wreckage of communism. No one had prepared for this world and for the return of so much repressed history.

It is easy to understand how this could have happened: after the sacrifices and anxieties of the Cold War, your great nation understandably yearned for peace and wanted to repair its affairs at home. So did we!

But those of us who have cast their lot with you for so long (and did so even when it was not fashionable in our sector of the world), know that **there is no substitute for American engagement and leadership.**

Bosnia demonstrates the continuous need for American leadership in Europe. And so does the Middle East peace process.

You are also needed to help keep the peace in Asia. Asians want you there as a great seawall against chaos, as a balance and buffer and safety net for security and stability, and as a deterrent to the outlaw North Korea. Without American protection, the prosperity of the Pacific Basin and its dynamic contribution to the international economy would be impossible to think of.

In Africa, you reached out to enforce humanitarian needs; and you delivered. It was America that saved so many Somali lives. And you should be proud of it.

Likewise, you were needed in the waters of the Gulf to help protect critical commerce of all the world, to sustain the precarious balance of power and to keep the flow of oil to the world uninterrupted. Surely, America's stake is in not only what it gets from there but what is essential there for world stability and the well-being of the international economy.

In their exasperated moments, I know the American people wonder why heavy lifting is theirs to do. But it has been so throughout most of this century—and in your interest under a long succession of presidents from diverse backgrounds. It is now your destiny to be the only superpower in the world.

The American people have every right to insist on a fairer system of burden sharing, on cutting out those who take a free ride under the American security umbrella. We are happy to point to Operation Desert Storm as a prototype of this kind of new American engagement. And I would just note we and our brothers in the other Gulf countries honored in full the financial commitments we made to Desert Storm.

Conclusion

Finally, I must confess our region of the world is hard to read. But you can discern a deep disenchantment with the political slogans and ideologies of the fifties and sixties, which led to many disasters that people of the region are still paying for.

The people in that broad sector of the world have a desire to get on with their lives, their hopes and their innate potential, which is great. Whether all this new yearning can withstand the depth of old feuds remains to be seen. But everywhere we must all move ahead—with optimism and together!

Memorial Day Address, 1993

William J. Clinton, President of the United States

President Clinton faced a hostile crowd when he went to the Vietnam War Memorial in May 1993. As he took the podium, a sizable number of Vietnam veterans greeted him with placards along with boos and shouts—which they continued as he spoke. During the presidential campaign, he had been criticized for his draft history and his public protest against the Vietnam War. As you read through the speech, identify all the ways that Mr. Clinton tries to emphasize the common beliefs and values he shares with his listeners.

Thank you, thank you very much. General Powell, General McCaffrey and my good friend Lou Puller, whom I did not know was coming here today, I thank you so much.

To all of you who are shouting, I have heard you. I ask you now to hear me. I have heard you.

Some have suggested that it is wrong for me to be here with you today because I did not agree a quarter of a century ago with the decision made to send the young men and women to battle in Vietnam. Well, so much the better. Here we are celebrating America today. Just as war is freedom's cost, disagreement is freedom's privilege. And we honor it here today.

But I ask all of you to remember the words that have been said here today, and I ask you, at this monument, Can any American be out of place? And can any Commander in Chief be in any other place but here on this day? I think not.

Many volumes have been written about this war and those complicated times, but the message of this memorial is quite simple: These men and women fought for freedom, brought honor to their communities, loved their country and died for it.

They were known to all of us. There's not a person in this crowd today who did not know someone on this wall. Four of my high school classmates are there, four who shared with me the joys and trials of childhood and did not live to see the three score and ten years the Scripture says we are entitled to.

Let us continue to disagree if we must about the war, but let us not let it divide us as a people any longer.

No one has come here today to disagree about the heroism of those whom we honor. But the only way we can really honor their memory is to resolve to live and serve today and tomorrow as best we can and to make America the best that she can be. Surely that is what we owe to all those whose names are etched in this beautiful memorial.

As we all resolve to keep the finest military in the world, let us remember some of the lessons that all agree on. If the day should come when our service men and women must again go into combat, let us all resolve they will go with the training, the equipment, and the support necessary to win, and, most important of all, with a clear mission to win.

Let us do what is necessary to regain control over our destiny as a people here at home, to strengthen our economy and to develop the capacities of all of our people, to rebuild our communities and our families where children are raised and character is developed. Let us keep the American dream alive.

Today let us also renew a pledge to the families whose names are not on this wall because their sons and daughters did not come home. We will do all we can to give you not only the attention you have asked for but the answers you deserve.

Today I have ordered that by Veterans Day we will have declassified all United States Government records related to POWs and MIAs from the Vietnam War—all those records except for a tiny fraction which could still affect our national security or invade the privacy of their families.

As we allow the American public to have access to what our government knows, we will press harder to find out what other governments know. We are pressing the Vietnamese to provide this accounting not only because it is the central outstanding issue in our relationship with Vietnam, but because it is a central commitment made by the American government to our people. And I intend to keep it.

You heard General Powell quoting President Lincoln: "With malice toward none and charity for all, let us bind up the nation's wounds."

Lincoln speaks to us today across the years. Let us resolve to take from this haunting and beautiful memorial a renewed sense of our national unity and purpose, a deepened gratitude for the sacrifice of those whose names we touched and whose memories we revere and a finer dedication to making America a better place for their children and for our children, too.

Thank you all for coming here today. God bless you, and God bless America.

Credits

Text and Figures

Figure 4.2, Communication Anxiety Graph from Brownell, W. W. and Katula, R. A., "The Communication Anxiety Graph: A Classroom Tool for Managing Speech Anxiety," *Communication Quarterly*, 32, p. 243–249. Reprinted by permission of The Eastern Communication Association; **p. 87,** Personal Report of Public Speaking Apprehension from *Communication: Apprehension, Avoidance, and Effectiveness*, 4th Edition, by Richmond, McCroskey. © 1995 by Gorsuch Scarisbrick, Publishers (Scottsdale, AZ). Used with permission; **Figure 5.1,** map from *The Nine Nations of North America*, by Joel Garreau. © 1981 by Joel Garreau. Reprinted by permission of Houghton Mifflin Co. All rights reserved; **p. 265,** speech is reprinted by permission of Robert Pettit; **p. 280,** Y. H. Krompacky, "Immigrants, Don't Be in Such a Hurry to Shed Your Accents," letter to the editor, *The New York Times*, March 21, 1993, Sec. 4, p. 16. Reprinted by permission of the author; **pp. 334–338,** speech is reprinted by permission of Tiffany Meyer; **Figures 14.3 and 14.4,** from Deanna Olson, Research Fisheries Biologist for the U.S. Forest Service, Pacific Northwest Station; **Figure 15.2,** data based on hierarchy of needs from *Motivation and Personality*, 3rd ed., by Abraham H. Maslow. Revised by Roger Frager, James Fadiman, Cynthia McReynolds, and Ruth Cox. Copyright 1954, © 1987 by Harper & Row Publishers, Inc. Copyright © 1970 by Abraham Maslow. Reprinted by permission of HarperCollins Publishers, Inc.; **p. 386,** The Ethical Quality Scale is reprinted by permission of the Eastern Communication Association; **p. 426,** Zediker, K. (1993), "Rediscovering the Tradition: Women's History with a Relational Approach to the Basic Public Speaking Course." Panel discussion at the WSCA, Albuquerque, NM, February 1993. Reprinted by permission of Cheryl Jorgensen-Earp; **p. 431,** "A Statement of Concern and Commitment," by Prince Bandar bin Sultan, *New York Times*, May 30, 1993, Sec. 4, p. 12. Reprinted by permission of the author.

Photographs

Chapter 1 opener, Joel Rogers/Off-Shoot Stock; **p. 5,** Mary Kay Dean/Photo Edit; **p. 6,** Don Smetzer/Tony Stone Worldwide; **p. 9,** Shooting Star; **p. 12,** Bill Bachman/Leo DeWys; **p. 20,** Frank Siteman/Stock, Boston Inc.; **p. 23,** Jeff Dunn/Stock, Boston Inc.; **p. 27,** Daniel Putterman/Stock, Boston Inc.; **p. 33,** Karen Preuss; **p. 37,** Rhoda Sidney/Stock, Boston Inc.; **p. 42,** Barry Iverson/Woodfin Camp & Associates; **p. 45,** Joe Benson/Stock, Boston Inc.; **p. 47,** Alan Weiner/Liaison Intl.; **p. 53,** Ed Kashi; **p. 59 L,** The Stock Market; **p. 59 R,** L. Quinones/Black Star; **p. 61,** Patrick Robert/Sygma; **p. 68,** Paul Howell/Liaison Intl.; **p. 73,** Dennis Brack/Black Star; **p. 75,** Ed Kashi; **p. 78,** Leo DeWys, Inc.; **p. 81,** B. Daemmrich/Stock, Boston Inc.; **p. 82,** B. Daemmrich/Stock, Boston Inc.; **p. 84,** Jack Jaffe; **p. 90,** B. Daemmrich/Stock, Boston Inc.; **p. 94,** courtesy St. John's University; **p. 98,** Carroll Seghers/The Stock Market; **p. 105,** Sandy Clark/The Stock Market; **p. 108,** courtesy of the National Dairy Board; **p. 110,** John C./Liaison Intl.; **p. 116,** Gabe Palmer/The Stock Market; **p. 122,** Wide World Photos; **p. 125 L,** courtesy of St. John's University; **p. 125, Top & Bottom R,** Ed Kashi; **p. 131,** Wide World Photos; **p. 136,** Robert Rathe/Stock, Boston, Inc.; **p. 139,** Jeffery Aronson/Network Aspen; **p. 142,** Karen Preuss; **p. 147,** Charles Gupton/Stock, Boston Inc.; **p. 148,** Jacques Chenet/Liaison Intl.; **p. 160,** Fabricius & Taylor/Liaison Intl.; **p. 164,** Jeff Greenberg/Unicorn; **p. 167,** courtesy of Nick Danzigen/UNICEF; **p. 170,** Wide World Photos; **p. 180,** Steve Underwood; **p. 184 L,** David Austen/Stock, Boston Inc.; **p. 184 C,** Donald Dietz/Stock, Boston Inc.; **p. 184 R,** Photri/The Stock Market; **p. 185,** EOSAT; **p. 197,** Wiley & Wales; **p. 199,** Olivier Laud/Liaison Intl.; **p. 203,** B. Daemmrich/Stock, Boston Inc.; **p. 214,** Ed Kashi; **p. 219,** Tull/Tony Stone Worldwide; **p. 225,** R. Floyd/courtesy of St. John's University; **p. 242,** Joel Simon; **p. 251,** Joel Simon; **p. 256,** Alon Reininger/Woodfin Camp & Associates; **p. 261,** Oliver Rebbott/Woodfin Camp & Associates; **p. 270,** Joel Simon; **p. 274 L–R,** Karen Preuss; **277 L–R,** Karen Preuss; **p. 283,** Elena Dorfman/OffShoot Stock; **p. 289,** courtesy of St. John's University; **p. 292,** Ed Kashi; **p. 296,** Larry Migdale/Stock, Boston Inc.; **p. 299,** Michael Daly/The Stock Market; **p. 301,** Wide World Photos; **p. 305,** Frans Lanting/Minden Pictures; **p. 314,** Joel Simon; **p. 325,** Pite/Liaison Intl.; **p. 330,** Phyllis Picardi/Stock, Boston Inc.; **p. 340,** Dennis Brack/Black Star; **p. 346,** Fred Bodin; **p. 349,** Wide World Photos, **p. 364,** Wally McNamee/Woodfin Camp & Associates; **p. 374,** Ellis Herwig/Stock, Boston Inc.; **p. 382,** Barbra Alper/Stock, Boston Inc.; **p. 383,** courtesy of the Simon Wiesenthal Center; **p. 384,** Brooks Kraft/Sygma; **p. 395,** B. Daemmrich/Stock, Boston Inc.; **p. 402,** Bonnie Kamin; **p. 407,** B. Daemmrich/Stock, Boston, Inc.; **p. 409,** B. Daemmrich/Stock, Boston Inc.; **p. 411,** Paul Lerner/Tony Stone Worldwide; **p. 419,** B. Daemmrich/Stock, Boston Inc.

Index

DISCARDED